PENGUIN BOOKS

OPERA: A PENGUIN ANTHOLOGY

Stephen Brook was born in London and educated at Cambridge. After many years as an editor in Boston, Massachusetts, and London, he became a full-time writer in 1982. His books include *New York Days, New York Nights*, *The Double Eagle*, *The Club: The Jews of Modern Britain* and *L. A. Lore*, and he has edited *The Penguin Book of Infidelities*. He has also written books on wine and contributes articles on wine and travel to many newspapers and periodicals.

OPERA
A PENGUIN ANTHOLOGY

STEPHEN BROOK

PENGUIN BOOKS

Published by the Penguin Group
Penguin Books Ltd, 27 Wrights Lane, London W8 5TZ, England
Penguin Books USA Inc., 375 Hudson Street, New York, New York 10014, USA
Penguin Books Australia Ltd, Ringwood, Victoria, Australia
Penguin Books Canada Ltd, 10 Alcorn Avenue, Toronto, Ontario, Canada M4V 3B2
Penguin Books (NZ) Ltd, 182–190 Wairau Road, Auckland 10, New Zealand

Penguin Books Ltd, Registered Offices: Harmondsworth, Middlesex, England

First published by Viking 1995
Published in Penguin Books 1996
1 3 5 7 9 10 8 6 4 2

Printed in England by Clays Ltd, St Ives plc

Contents

Acknowledgements vii
Permissions viii
Introduction xiii

1. Opera in Italy 1
2: Opera outside Italy 24

SINGERS

3: Eighteenth-century Singers 51
4: Pasta and Malibran 59
5: Early-nineteenth-century Singers 72
6: Late-nineteenth-century Singers 88
7: Three Divas: Patti, Melba, Tetrazzini 105
8: Caruso 120
9: Chaliapin 135
10: A Clutch of Tenors 148
11: Lotte Lehmann 160
12: Maria Callas 171
13: Some Singers of the Twentieth Century 186
14: The Art of Singing 204

COMPOSERS

15: Operatic Composers 231
16: Mozart 248
17: Rossini 256
18: Wagner 264
19: Wagner at Bayreuth 285
20: Verdi 304

21: Puccini 322
22: Richard Strauss 329

ON STAGE

23: Opera Directors 341
24: Auditions 368
25: Rehearsal 374
26: Performances 388
27: Audiences 411
28: Opera and Money 433

ISSUES IN OPERA

29: The Nature of Opera 457
30: Opera and Ideology 470
31: Words v. Music 477
32: Anti-Opera 483
33: Libretti and Translations 488

OPERA IN FICTION

34: Opera in Fiction 497

Index 512

Acknowledgements

My infinitely well-read friends, as I approach them to ask whether they have any suggestions for this book, look at me with some alarm, scratch their heads, think long and hard and come up with nothing. More helpful than most were Stephen Barber, Mary Hoffmann and Nicholas John. Everyone else was utterly useless and thus all omissions and errors in this volume should be blamed on them.

My thanks, as always, to my wife Maria. It was at the Royal Opera House, Covent Garden, ten years ago to the day, that I spotted her and engaged her in conversation, and initiated an operatic anecdote that remains my personal favourite.

September 1994

Permissions

We would like to thank all the authors, publishers and literary representatives who have given permission to reprint copyright extracts included in this anthology.

Adams, Brian: to Random House UK Ltd for *La Stupenda* (Hutchinson, 1981)

Allen, Thomas: to Reed Consumer Books for *Foreign Parts* (Sinclair-Stevenson, 1993)

Amis, Martin: to Random House UK Ltd for *Money* (Cape, 1984)

Auden, W.H.: to Faber & Faber Ltd and Random House Inc. for *The Dyer's Hand and Other Essays*; *Secondary Worlds*; and *Forewords and Afterwords*

Baker, Janet: to Julia MacRae Books for *Full Circle* (1982), copyright © Janet Baker, 1982

Bassett, Richard: to Times Newspapers Limited for 'The man who wanted to be Mr Vienna' (*The Times*, 13 July 1984), copyright © Times Newspapers Limited, 1984

Beecham, Thomas: to Shirley, Lady Beecham, for *A Mingled Chime* (Hutchinson, 1944)

Benson, E.F.: to Longman Group Ltd for *Final Edition* (Longmans Green, 1944)

Bentley, E.C.: to Curtis Brown Group Ltd, London, for *The Dramatic Event* and *What is Theatre?*, copyright © E.C. Bentley

Berg, Alban: to Faber & Faber Ltd for *Letters to His Wife*, trans. Bernard Grun

Berlioz, Hector: to Victor Gollancz Ltd for *Memoirs*, trans. David Cairns (Gollancz, 1969), copyright © 1969 by David Cairns

Boult, Adrian: to Hamish Hamilton Ltd for *My Own Trumpet* (1973), copyright © Sir Adrian Boult, 1973

Bradbury, Malcolm: to Reed Consumer Books for *Why Come to Slaka?* (Martin Secker & Warburg, 1986) and *Rates of Exchange* (Martin Secker & Warburg, 1983)

Britten, Benjamin: to the *Observer* for 'The Composer's Dream' (5 June 1960)

Brook, Stephen: to Richard Scott Simon Ltd for *The Double Eagle* (Hamish Hamilton, 1988), copyright © Stephen Brook

Domingo, Placido: to Weidenfeld & Nicolson Ltd for *My First Forty Years* (1983)

Duey, Philip A.: to Columbia University Press for *Bel Canto in Its Golden Age*, copyright © 1951 by Columbia University Press

Forster, E.M.: to King's College, Cambridge, and The Society of Authors as the literary representatives of the E.M. Forster Estate for *Where Angels Fear to Tread*

Fuchs, Peter Paul (ed. and trans.): to Quartet Books for *The Music Theatre of Walter Felsenstein* (1991)

Gatti-Casazza, Giulio: to The Calder Educational Trust, London, for *Memories of the Opera* (John Calder (Publishers) Ltd, London, 1977)

Gobbi, Tito: to Hamish Hamilton for *Tito Gobbi on His World of Italian Opera* (1984), copyright © Tito Gobbi and Ida Cook, 1984

Goldoni, Carlo: to Alfred A. Knopf, Inc., for *Memoirs*, trans. John Black (Knopf, 1926), copyright 1926 and renewed 1954 by Alfred A. Knopf, Inc.

Hall, Peter: to Reed Consumer Books for *Making an Exhibition of Myself* (Sinclair-Stevenson, 1993)

Hanslick, Edouard: to Henry Pleasants for *Music Criticisms 1846–99*, trans. Henry Pleasants (Pelican, 1951)

Henze, Hans Werner: to Faber & Faber Ltd for *Music and Politics*, trans. Peter Labanyi

Hetherington, John: to Laurence Pollinger Ltd on behalf of the Estate of John Hetherington for *Melba* (Faber, 1967)

Heyworth, Peter: to Cambridge University Press for *Otto Klemperer: His Life and Times*, Vol. 1, 1885–1933 (1983); to Farrer & Co. (Solicitors) for *Conversations with Klemperer*

Hodges, Sheila: to Granada, an imprint of Harper Collins Publishers Ltd for *Lorenzo da Ponte: the Life and Times of Mozart's Librettist*

Jackson, Stanley: to the author for *Caruso* (W.H. Allen, 1972)

Kerman, Joseph: to Alfred A. Knopf, Inc., for *Opera as Drama* (Vintage, 1956), copyright © 1956 by Joseph Kerman

Klein, Herman: to Routledge Publishers for *Great Women Singers of My Time*

Leavis, Q.D.: to Professor Singh for 'The Italian Novel' from *Collected Essays*, Vol. 2 (1985)

Lehmann, Lotte: to Hamish Hamilton Ltd for *Singing with Richard Strauss*, trans. Ernst Pawel (1984), copyright © Lotte Lehmann, 1964, translation copyright © The Macmillan Company and Hamish Hamilton Ltd; to Routledge Publishers for *Wings of Songs*

Scott, Michael: to Sheil Land Associates Ltd for *The Great Caruso* (Hamish Hamilton, 1988)

Shaw, George Bernard: to The Society of Authors on behalf of the Bernard Shaw Estate for *Shaw's Music, Vol. 1: 1876–1890, Vol. 2: 1890–1893, Vol. 3: 1893–1950*, ed. Dan H. Laurence (Bodley Head, 1989)

Sheean, Vincent: to Curtis Brown Ltd for *First and Last Love* (Gollancz, 1957), copyright © 1956 by Vincent Sheean, renewed

Sitwell, Osbert: to David Higham Associates Ltd for *Great Morning!* (Atlantic Monthly Press, 1947)

Slezak, Walter: to Doubleday, a division of Bantam Doubleday Dell Publishing Group, Inc., for *What Time's the Next Swan?* (1962), copyright © 1962 Walter Slezak

Söderström, Elisabeth: to Hamish Hamilton Ltd for *In My Own Key*, trans. Joan Tate (1979), copyright © Elisabeth Söderström, 1978, 1979, translation copyright © Hamish Hamilton Ltd, 1979

Stendhal: to The Calder Educational Trust, London, for *Rome, Naples and Florence*, trans. Richard Coe (John Calder Ltd, 1959)

Stravinsky, Igor: to Faber & Faber Ltd for *Themes and Conclusions*; to Mayer, Brown & Platt (Attorneys) on behalf of the heirs for *Chronicle of My Life* (Gollancz, 1936)

Verdi, Giuseppe: to Richard Scott Simon Ltd for *Letters*, trans. Charles Osborne (Gollancz, 1971), copyright © Charles Osborne, 1971

Wagner, Cosima: to Harcourt Brace & Company for *Cosima Wagner's Diaries, Vol. 1: 1869–1877, Vol. 2: 1878–1883* (HBJ, 1978, 1980), copyright © 1976 by R. Piper & Co. Verlag Munchen, English translation copyright © 1978, 1977 by Geoffrey Skelton and Harcourt Brace & Company; copyright © 1977 by R. Piper & Co. Verlag, English translation copyright © 1980 by Geoffrey Skelton and Harcourt Brace & Co.

Walsh, T.J.: to Gill & Macmillan Ltd for *Monte Carlo Opera 1879–1909* (1975)

Walter, Bruno: to Alfred A. Knopf, Inc., for *Theme and Variations*, trans. James A. Galston, copyright 1946 and renewed 1974 by Alfred A. Knopf, Inc.

Weinstock, Herbert: to Alfred A. Knopf, Inc., for *Bellini* (Knopf, 1971), copyright © 1971 by Herbert Weinstock

Willet, John (ed. and trans.): to Reed Consumer Books for *Brecht on Theatre* (Methuen, 1964)

Worsthorne, S.T.: to Oxford University Press for *Venetian Opera in the Seventeenth Century* (Clarendon Press, 1954)

Every effort has been made to contact copyright holders. The publishers will be glad to rectify, in future editions, any omissions brought to their notice.

Introduction

After many years of being sidelined to the cultural equivalent of the Forbidden City in Peking, to which only the most privileged were given access, opera is now again recognized as a popular art form. Some purists may deplore the vocal exhibitionism of the 'Three Tenors' and the improbable identification of late Puccini with football's World Cup, but the truth is that you are more likely to hear '*Nessun dorma*' whistled in the streets today than at any time since the opera was first performed.

The marginalization of opera is a twentieth-century phenomenon. When, in past centuries, a Genoan or Viennese went to the opera, he or she went more often than not to hear a new opera. Mozart could sprinkle *Don Giovanni* with excerpts from other operas, including his own *Figaro*, because he knew the self referen tial joke would be shared with his audience. Yet not even Mozart, whose genius was swiftly recognized, could be certain of enjoying a secure place in the European repertoire. *Così fan tutte*, for example, was first performed in London in 1811, but a whole century went by before it was revived. Opera, constantly evolving, is always at the mercy of fashion and morals.

The original conditions of operatic production were not very different from the system that still prevails in Hollywood or Bombay. Operatic composition was usually a frantic last-minute collaboration between impresario, composer, and librettist. Most of the results must have been dire, cramming the wastepaper bins of Europe with the scores of failed or negligible operas. It was routine practice for composers such as Handel, Rossini, or Verdi to resurrect potential hit numbers from their previous operas that had failed; self-plagiarism was the order of the day. It was quite rare for an opera to be deemed worthy of revival, and even fewer have secured a berth in what we regard as the modern repertory.

Famous singers wandered across Europe with signature arias, favourite numbers that would be inserted into whatever they were performing, regardless of dramatic incongruity, simply because the audience expected it of them as a familiar and time-tested show-stopper amidst an ocean of musical novelty.

In the search for constant innovation, it is hardly surprising that composers took some short cuts. Just as Hollywood remakes the hits of the past in an attempt to exploit a successful formula, so opera composers exhumed secondhand libretti. Much opera seria was a wearisome reworking of conventional formulae, static tableaux peopled by abandoned lovers, merciful kings, and consoling shepherds. Hardly any of them have stood the test of time.

Although opera was indeed a popular art form in previous centuries, notably in Italy, it was a medium closely associated with the courts of Europe and, as a direct consequence, the high costs of production inevitably restricted its appeal. In Dresden or Vienna, the opera house was a dependency of the court, and audiences were limited either to the guests of the royal household or to those rich enough to acquire boxes. Astronomical sums were spent by royal patrons as one court sought to outshine another, as some of the descriptions in this book will make clear. Although in London or Paris in the nineteenth century the opera may have enjoyed royal patronage, there was no direct link with the court. This was not the case in Germany. Wagner's career was blighted by revolutionary activities that understandably upset the court at Dresden and led to his banishment. Only the subsequent friendship and adulation of Ludwig II of Bavaria allowed him to realize his fantastical dreams of an opera house and festival dedicated exclusively to the performance of his own works.

Although the eccentric Ludwig would sometimes have performances mounted for an audience of one, himself, in all other opera houses there was room for the *hoi polloi*. In the pages that follow there is an account of the young and impoverished Hector Berlioz attending the Paris opera and giving the conductor the benefit of his advice during the performances. Word-of-mouth as well as piano transcriptions helped disseminate the most tuneful operas.

The boxes of La Scala or Her Majesty's Theatre in London may have been crammed with the aristocratic and the rich, but there was no stopping a hit tune such as 'La donna è mobile'.

Many observers commented on the stunning sight that the bemedalled and bejewelled Covent Garden audience, dressed to the nines, presented in Edwardian London. Bernard Shaw routinely derided the stuffiness of an aristocratic audience that regarded the opera as an extension of the drawing-room, although Claude Debussy, while acknowledging the opulence of the Covent Garden audience, praised its attentiveness. Only at the turn of the last century was the supremacy of the audience and its social whims – its right to come and go as it pleased and to distort the shape of an opera by demanding incessant encores – challenged by the musical directors. Mahler in Vienna and Toscanini in Milan imposed discipline not only on the productions but on the behaviour of the audience. After all, before their interventions it was customary for the house lights to remain on during the performance, which must have benefited the socially preoccupied audience more than the dramatic coherence of the performance.

The cooption of the opera house as a setting for social display persists, of course. It wasn't very long ago that Brigid Brophy expressed her admirable longing to turn up at Glyndebourne, that gloriously anachronistic if starchy opera festival, in lederhosen. As a child at Covent Garden, I was refused permission to remove my jacket on a sweltering summer evening. Good form took precedence over comfort and enjoyment. Seated in 1969 in the balcony stalls waiting for a performance of Strauss's difficult Die Frau ohne Schatten to begin, a very grand lady behind me, famous for her collection of Impressionist art, assured her companions that the story didn't matter and there was no point wasting chatter time by reading the synopsis in the programme.

Those stifling days when the opera house was primarily a place to flash your feathers are perhaps not gone for ever, for the duchesses have been replaced by the dispiriting bosses whose companies donate money to the opera house. This bank or that oil company may sponsor a production, but for some reason you rarely see a cashier or oilfield foreman seated in the stalls. I don't think I have ever been to Glyndebourne without hearing the gentle snores of somebody in the audience who would evidently rather be backing a winner at Lingwood or watching 'Celebrity Squares' at home. None the less the audience, in Britain and America, seems increasingly composed of enthusiasts. Though many may regret the appearance of blue jeans in the stalls, opera is recognized again as a source of immense and immediate pleasure that can be enjoyed without the accoutrements of velvet-lined boxes and medal-strewn uniforms. Audiences in their thousands pack Central Park in New York or Hyde Park in London to hear the thrilling tones of a great tenor. Opera recordings can even be enjoyed through earphones while jogging. Up-market advertising executives raid the operatic repertoire to lend cachet to the mass-produced items they seek to promote.

The democratization of opera has not, however, diminished the essential conservatism of the audiences. Opera houses dutifully mount the latest Henze, Barber, or Tippett, but respectful reviews do not often lead to eager audiences. One salutes the handful of opera singers who are prepared to tackle the modern repertoire, but few of them are among the leading singers of the day, many of whom have expressed their dislike of contemporary music.

The audience is the mainstay of opera. Not merely because without an audience there would be no reason to perform, but because audiences are fanatical. Their connoisseurship is genuine and often deep. Italian opera houses vie with one another for the hard ride they give visiting performers; anything slipshod or incompetent will be given the boo and the boot. Some of the anecdotes that follow illustrate the fine art of heckling as practised in Italy. Mediocre performances are indeed excruciating to sit through, and I choose to buy cheap seats in most opera houses so that I can walk out with a clear conscience if the performance is poor.

But when the performance is good or great, the pleasure derived by the opera fan can be grotesquely extreme. Women are known to have endured labour pains and the pangs of birth itself rather than leave a great performance of *Götterdämmerung* before the final curtain. I myself have stood through two performances of *Parsifal* in one week at Covent Garden, as well as two performances of *Tristan und Isolde* in one week so that I could hear Jon Vickers as Tristan – feats that should surely be recognized as an Olympic event almost as arduous as performing in *Parsifal* or *Tristan* twice in one week.

The operatic audience knows its music. The Italians may chatter too much but should the tenor miss a note or dodge a trill, the audience's displeasure will make itself felt, as will their appreciation of exquisite vocalism. Theatre audiences never boo, but opera audiences will, if provoked, express contempt as well as rapture. I myself, the mildest of men, once booed at Covent Garden, and I was not alone, even though the recipient of my wrath was Montserrat Caballé, a very great soprano. But on this occasion she thought she could get through *Aida* without even attempting to act. She was taking the audience for granted, and we weren't having it. We'll forgive a wrong note or a fluffed run, but not musical indolence.

Opera lovers are fanatical because when a performance is great, it's the most exhilarating experience in the world outside the bedroom. As has often been remarked, it combines different media – music, drama, set design – each enthralling in its own way, but sublime when wedded. Music and drama are, of course, the central components and there has been a long-running argument as to which element is supreme. Richard Strauss even wrote an entire opera, *Capriccio*, in which the subject is debated and explored. Of course the two are inseparable, and the fusion (or combat) reaches its apogee in ensembles that allow conflicting emotion to be expressed simultaneously. In the quintet in Act One of *Così fan tutte*, two pairs of lovers take heart-rending leave of each other as the men, allegedly, set off for war. At the same time Don Alfonso, the vengeful cynic who has engineered this bogus situation to prove the fickleness of the female sex, is singing that if this tender farewell goes on much longer he'll burst out laughing. For the audience our immediate identification with the sorrowing lovers and the sublime music Mozart has given them, even though we know the men are not actually going off to war, is sabotaged by Alfonso's reminder that the actual situation is farcical. Only in opera is such conflicting response possible. Towards the end of *Figaro*, if the performance is halfway decent, the emotions of the audience have been raised to such a complex and conflicting height, in which laughter, pain, embarrassment, and longing are all merged, that the boundaries of music and drama dissolve. Moreover, music not only supports the drama and provides a subliminal commentary on the stage action. It can also subvert or warn, using motifs to provide layers of meaning no stage action alone could offer. Subtly used, as by Wagner, this tension between music and drama can confer an almost magical richness and complexity, all the more magical because we know that the two elements are also inextricable.

There are those who mock the artificiality of opera. It's easy to do, and there is no rational defence. If you find the whole thing risible, laugh away – and stay away. Opera lovers know, indeed, that the formal constraints of opera, its supposedly absurd conventions, can heighten rather than diminish its impact. Of course people don't sing their opinions or conversations 'in real life'. That is the whole point of opera. It articulates in glorious music what we 'in real life' can only stutter in semi-articulate prose. A declaration of love, beneath a visiting moon or even on a theatrical stage, is confined by the limited number of words at the disposal of those making it. But the operatic love scene has no such constraints: it confers immortality on an everyday occurrence.

Nor does operatic expressiveness necessarily benefit from naturalism on stage. Operatic convention frees the librettist and composer from the need to appear convincing. Opera embraces melodrama effortlessly. When the liberating trumpet sounds in *Fidelio*, nobody laughs, despite the suspiciously providential timing. Instead, the audience, engrossed in the imminence of Florestan's death, greets the trumpet call with much of the same heartfelt relief as the protagonists on stage. That is why the attempts by late-nineteenth-century Italian composers such as Leoncavallo or Giordano to imbue their operas with the greatest possible degree of naturalism are only intermittently successful. Opera doesn't require grittiness and social realism. The works of formalists such as Gluck, for all the static monumentality of their operas, are often more powerful and profound than those in which characters' hearts are slithering down their sleeves.

It was not too long ago that opera was primarily regarded as a showcase for vocal display. Fortunately, audiences are less willing to tolerate dramatic fatuity on stage merely for the intermittent pleasure of hearing a satisfying warble or a cascading run. Today we expect singers to act as well. Although we tolerate and appreciate great singers, such as Joan Sutherland, who don't know the meaning of the word 'act', we know that such singers are incomplete in their operatic equipment. Operatic genius is dramatic genius and can touch us even when the house is silent. I recall a performance of *Figaro* in which Tito Gobbi as Count Almaviva walked across the stage. The sharp clack of his heels on the parquet expressed chillingly his ferocious anger. Cunning stage direction combined with the timing and stage presence of a great operatic actor did the trick. No one who heard it will ever forget the complete silence that preceded Otto Klemperer's conducting of the *Leonora No. 3* overture in the middle of the final act of *Fidelio* at Covent Garden in 1963.

But such moments are exceptional, and it remains self-evident that one cannot divorce opera from vocalism. For my taste, most audiences place too much value on vocalism for its own sake. The audience of the Metropolitan Opera House, New York, was and perhaps still is notorious for its indifference to dramatic competence and intelligent direction so long as it is fed its quota of corruscating trills and detonating high Cs. The Glyndebourne audience is the opposite, and its musical directors can afford to hire little-known singers because the dramatic values of the production will be impeccably rehearsed and thus richly expressed. (Of course it helps when, as I recall in the 1960s, one of those little-known singers is Luciano Pavarotti, who sang a fine Idamante in *Idomeneo*.)

Vocal glory is, of course, not to be despised. At a London Promenade Concert I once stood about twelve feet away from Birgit Nilsson as she sang Brünnhilde in a concert performance of the last act of *Götterdämmerung*. The Immolation Scene sung at full blast is moving enough in the spaces of the opera house, but from a few paces away that blistering delivery and impeccable accuracy were overwhelming. Moreover, some voices are so beautiful simply as instruments that one never tires of them. Jussi Björling may have had a tendency to sing each aria as though it were interchangeable with every other, but few could resist such stylishness, poise, and gorgeous tone. None the less, operatic performance ought to differ from operatic recital.

Opera appreciation becomes obsessive because no two performances are ever the same. This is true of the theatre as well, but there are more variables in the opera house: the temper of the conductor, the lungs of the tenor, the wakefulness of the lighting director, the sobriety of the orchestra. Callas addicts, of whom I am one, collect numerous recordings of the same opera starring the same prima donna because the nuances give us so much satisfaction. The recording may be an amateur job made illegally by a fan with a tape recorder in his pocket, and surface noise and coughing may make the vocal line scarcely audible – but we don't care. In 1953, we can hear, Callas phrases the line thus, while two years later she changed her mind. Opera bores, of whom American opera queens constitute the most tenacious variety, can keep going for hours about the relative merits of one performance over another. Those who find opera alien cannot understand that true addicts will attend *every* performance of a particularly satisfying production. In the days when it was still possible for mere mortals to obtain tickets for Domingo nights at Covent Garden, I, and many others, would attend all his performances in any one season. Of course! The voice, even the finest tenor voice in the world, has its frailties, and we wanted to be sure of hearing the very best of which Domingo was capable, and the only way to be certain of doing that was to go to the lot.

Opera fans are demanding but tolerant. This book includes an account of a performance of *Tristan und Isolde* in New York when a different tenor sang Tristan in each act. The audience understood why and put up with circumstances that on paper sound utterly preposterous. Indeed, we admire those who overcome obstacles in an art form that is inevitably prone to accident. When in 1969 Josephine Veasey was indisposed and unable to sing the parts of Cassandra and Dido in Berlioz's *Les Troyens*, she was replaced by Miss Janet Baker, who was currently performing the same role with the Scottish Opera, and had graciously agreed to step in at short notice. The management begged the audience to be indulgent, since Miss Baker had been performing the role in English, whereas the Covent Garden cast would be singing in French. In the event, it mattered not one jot. What could have been an evening wrecked by intrinsic absurdity turned out to be an unforgettable occasion: profound musicality and dramatic presence overcame the potential risibility of the dual-language performance.

Most opera fans have personal memories that can furnish an anthology single-handed, but there is more to opera than a sequence of performances. This anthology seeks to expand the boundaries of the conventional collection of opera anecdotes, which tend to use how-the-diva-tripped-over-the-scenery or what-happened-when-the-horse-did-a-whoopsit-on-stage as the prototype. To be sure, the complexities of operatic production, of coordinating stage direction, musical continuity, and the frailties of the human voice, mean that performance is always accident-prone and thus a rich source of guffaw inducing anecdotage.

There are plenty of examples of this in the pages that follow, but I have tried to cast the net more widely. Singers and performances still dominate these pages, but the composer, the impresario, the conductor, the producer, and the audience, who all contribute to the operatic composite, also make substantial appearances in this book. So do some of the controversies about the nature of opera, about the languages in which it should be performed, about the competing roles of words and music. The reader may balk at the historical sections, but opera in previous centuries was so different from our contemporary experience that I believe it is

worth indicating what productions were like in days when the
treasuries of princely states were routinely drained by opera-
besotted rulers, or how, for example, some Italian opera houses
functioned as gaming rooms as well as centres for musical performance. I have also included a few examples of opera in fiction.
Because of the many sections of which the book is comprised,
singers in particular will turn up in different places. An account
of Jenny Lind's early triumphs occurs in 'Late-nineteenth-century
Singers', but the detailed account of her tour of America under
the management of P.T. Barnum is given in 'Opera and Money'.
So the index may prove handy.

I have sought out firsthand accounts whenever possible. They
tend to be lively and entertaining – but they are not necessarily
true or accurate. Singers often detest impresarios, and vice versa.
Their memoirs and diaries become exercises in self-justification.
Accounts of performances are skewed to present the protagonist in
the best possible light, and to rubbish his or her enemies.

For instance, I have quoted liberally from the memoirs of the
Irish tenor Michael Kelly, who left a graphic account of working
with Mozart on his operas. But is it true? Perhaps, but doubts
about Kelly's self-proclaimed importance to Mozart's creative processes and career prospects are deepened on learning that the book
was ghost-written. Mozart's librettist Lorenzo Da Ponte had this
to say about Kelly's book in 1826:

'The jests and the romantic nonsense which you wrote, or *had
written for you*, in your ridiculous book, are so worthless that it is a
waste of time for a man of any sense to give himself the trouble of
denying them; I know that a man of your *mimicking* nature believes
he can say anything and everything, however false, because what
he says will make people laugh: I shall take care, however, to make
it clear to others, and above all to those who do not know you,
even if not to you yourself, that everything you have said about
me in your crazy book contains not one syllable of truth, and that
if it had been the truth you would have been the last to publish
it.'* However, Da Ponte himself was no uninvolved observer. As

* Quoted in Sheila Hodges, *Lorenzo Da Ponte*, Granada, 1985, p. 74.

Sheila Hodges notes in her biography of Da Ponte, 'When he fled from Vienna to England, penniless and without work, Kelly, who then occupied an influential position in the operatic world in London, apparently did nothing to help him.' *

No one would suggest that Melba's ghost-written autobiography *Melodies and Memories* is reliable, even though some of the embroidered or even fictitious anecdotes in which the diva takes a heroic role have become part of her legend. I have usually steered clear of material that I know to be false, though a few anecdotes demanded to be included even though their source was suspect. So the reader is urged not to take as gospel all that follows in the pages ahead.

Many hours have been spent trawling through singers' autobiographies, only to find the session concluded with the ritual flinging of the book against the wall. These documents are usually dull or self serving or both. The French-Canadian soprano Emma Albani wrote *Forty Years of Song* in 1911, a work of unsurpassed tedium, a catalogue of letters received from gracious royalty, generous reviews, mild anecdotes, first-night triumphs, appreciative audiences, adulatory poems, and photos of decorations received from emperors and princes. The singer's gift is vocal, not literary, and it is rare that the outpourings from the diva's pen are illuminating.

There has been no attempt to provide balance. If Geraldine Farrar features on a few pages and Gundula Janowitz on none, it is not because of any personal conviction that one is more worthy of space than the other. It's because Farrar, a brilliant self-publicist, gathered anecdotage around her, while many other fine but more self-effacing singers generated little. Moreover, voices, as opposed to stage antics or intriguing private lives, are difficult to describe. I have deliberately included descriptions of the voices of some great singers of the past – it's interesting, I would argue, to know what a Farinelli or Pasta sounded like to their contemporaries – but a parade of marvelling descriptions of voices would soon become tedious. The same is true of composers. If Purcell and Charpentier and Janáček are absent from the following pages, it is because they

* ibid.

failed to provide or generate written material of sufficient interest, not because I have unaccountably overlooked them.

None the less this anthologist has staggered under the weight of material that did seem worthy of inclusion. If anthologies were allowed to be as long as encyclopedias, I would still have had material to spare. As it is, the stern economies of the publishing trade have been invoked to keep this book to a manageable length. All omissions are therefore the consequence of harsh editorial excision, although, like all anthologists, I must accept the blame when readers, as they always do, find their favourite anecdote unforgivably missing.

1: Opera in Italy

I admit freely that it is good to be roused now and then by the cheering spectacle of a gentleman vigorously chasing a lady round the room in spite of the unoriginality of the motive, or a father towing behind him the mangled remains of his child in a sack: but such excitements are not the necessary Alpha and Omega of every stage work.

Sir Thomas Beecham, *A Mingled Chime*, p. 179

Opera was born in Venice in 1600. Which opera is credited with being 'first' depends largely on definitions, but Peri's Euridice *of 1600 has a strong claim. Monteverdi's* Orfeo *(1607) is the first opera that remains in the modern repertory. By the end of the eighteenth century about two thousand operas had been mounted in Venice's eight opera houses, which had become the focus of the city's social and political life:*

It was the box which had an influence that permeated through the whole organization and captured the public on other grounds than consideration of business. It became simply another room in a rambling mansion, the obvious means of cramming as many people as possible into a confined space, yet preserving the amenities of a civilized social life ... The French ambassador assured a friend that it is necessary for all diplomats to attend the opera regularly because there it was possible to discover secrets which would be concealed from them in the ordinary course of events ... It is remarkable to find that the Doge himself allotted boxes to the heads of foreign missions ... The social convenience of the box encouraged an easy-going approach to the opera. The audience had no need to attend throughout each performance. But the amenities offered drew them to the theatre almost nightly, so that the scores were in the end thoroughly well known, the capabilities of individual singers assessed against the highest standards gained by experience, and an informed taste built up, which alone provides a fertile ground for a flowering of the arts.

S.T. Worsthorne, *Venetian Opera in the Seventeenth Century*, Clarendon Press, 1954, pp. 10–13

A contemporary account of a relatively simple production, of Manelli's Andromeda, *in Venice in the 1630s:*

The curtain disappears. The scene was entirely sea. In the distance was a view of water and rocks so contrived that its naturalness (although feigned) moved the spectators to doubt whether they were in a theatre or on a real seashore. The scene was quite dark except for the light given by a few stars which disappeared one after another, giving place to Aurora who came to make the prologue. She was dressed entirely in cloth of silver with a shining star on her brow, and appeared inside a very beautiful cloud which sometimes grew large and sometimes small, and oh lovely surprise! circled across the sky on the stage. Meantime the scene grew light as day for the prologue, sung divinely by Signora Maddalena Manelli from Rome, after which one heard a very sweet symphony from the most polished instrumentalists ... Then Juno came out on a golden car drawn by her peacocks, blazing in a coat of cloth of gold with a superb variety of jewels on her head or in her crown ...

One saw the scene change from a seascape to a wood so natural that it carried our eyes to the life to real snowy heights, real flowering countryside, a regal spreading wood and unfeigned melting of water ... The scene turned in a moment from the wood to the seascape. Neptune appeared and Mercury came out to meet him in a wonderful machine. Neptune was on a great silver shell drawn by four sea horses and a sky-blue mantel covered him ... To the tune of a sweet melody of instruments Astrea appeared in the sky and Venus in the sea; one in a silver cloud and the other in her shell drawn by swans . . . The scene changed to a woodland, and Andromeda came out with her train. Six of her ladies, for joy at killing a boar, did a light and wonderful ballet with such varied and different weaving of paces that truly one was able to call it a leaping labyrinth . . .

The scene changed to the seashore. In tune to a most sweet harmony of different instruments a very beautiful machine appeared from one side of the scene with Astrea and Venus upon it. It turned to the right and left as these goddesses most pleased. Opposite them Mercury came out and, the sky opening, sat in the middle. This little scene had a most wonderful effect for the quantity of machines and for the successive arrangements of silent characters and movement (on the stage). In a flash the sea scene became a superb palace . . . from which came Ascalà a knight. His clothes exceeded in value and beauty those of all the rest. He was dressed in the Turkish style. This unhappy character, with a thousand charms of heaven, was played by him who took Mercury. Regretfully the palace disappeared and we saw the scene entirely of sea with Andromeda bound to a rock. The sea monster came out. This animal was made with such beautiful cunning that, although not real, he put people in terror. Except for the act of tearing to pieces and devouring he did everything as if alive and breathing. Perseus arrived on Pegasus, and with three blows of a lance and five with a rapier he overthrew the monster and killed it . . . The sky opened and one saw Jove and Juno in glory and other divinities. This great machine descended to the ground to the accompaniment of a concerto of voices and instruments truly from heaven. The two heroes, joined to each other, it conducted to the sky. Hence the royal and ever worthy occasion had an end . . .

Quoted in S.T. Worsthorne, *Venetian Opera in the Seventeenth Century*,
Clarendon Press, 1954, pp. 25–7

Dr Charles Burney, the leading British musical historian of the eighteenth century, gives a critical account of a performance of Domenico Freschi's Berenice *in Padua in 1780:*

There were choruses of one hundred virgins, one hundred soldiers, one hundred horsemen in iron armour, forty cornets of horse, six trumpeters on horseback, six drummers, six ensigns, six sackbuts, six great flutes, six minstrels playing on Turkish instruments, six others on octave flutes, six pages, three sergeants, six cymbalists, twelve huntsmen, twelve grooms, six coachmen for the triumph, six others for the procession, two lions led by two Turks, two elephants by two others, Berenice's triumphal car drawn by four horses, six other cars with prisoners and spoils drawn by twelve horses, six coaches for the procession. Among the scenes and representations in the first act was a vast plain with two triumphal arches; another with pavilions and tents; a square prepared for the entrance of the triumph; and a forest for the chase. Act II, the royal apartments of Berenice's temple of vengeance; a spacious court, with a view of the prison; and a covered way for the coaches to move in procession. Act III, the royal dressing-room, completely furnished; stables with one hundred live horses; portico adorned with tapestry; a delicious palace in perspective. And besides all these attendants and decorations, at the end of the first act, there were representations of every species of chase: as of the wild boar, the stag, deer, and bears; and at the end of the third act, an enormous globe descends from the sky, which opening divides itself into other globes that are suspended in the air, upon one of which is the figure of Time, on a second that of Fame, on others, Honour, Nobility, Virtue, and Glory.

Had the salaries of singers been at this time equal to the present, the support of such expensive and puerile toys would have inclined the managers to inquire not only after the best, but the cheapest vocal performers they could find, as splendid ballets oblige them to do now; and it is certain that, during the last century, the distinct and characteristic charm of an opera was not the Music, but machinery ... Artists of all kinds strained every nerve to display their talents. Machines the most ingenious, flights the most daring, with tempests, thunder, lightning, and all the delusions of the magic wand, were practised to fascinate the eye, while innumerable voices and instruments astonished the air.

But with so many means of surprise, the action always remained cold, and the situations uninteresting; as there was no plot or intrigue but what was easily solved by the assistance of some divinity, the spectator, who knew the poet's power of extricating his heroes and heroines from all kinds of difficulty and danger, reposed such entire confidence in him as to remain tranquil during the most perilous situations. Hence, though the apparatus was great, the effect was small, as the imitations were always clumsy and imperfect . . . upon the whole, it is hardly possible to fatigue an assembly at a greater expense.

Dr Charles Burney, *A General History of Music* (1789), Dover, 1957, II,
pp. 553–5

The eighteenth century was the age of the castrato. The operation had a number of consequences:

When castration occurs before the glandular functioning of the testicles has begun, certain abnormal physical developments result. The body grows somewhat larger than otherwise and the bony structure takes on feminine characteristics. The chest becomes round, measuring approximately the same from front to back and side to side, while the muscles become softer, the skin sallow and flabby, the body hairless, the hair on the head thicker and the face beardless. Moreover, the mammary glands, ordinarily dormant in the male, develop in a marked way which fact accounted much for the castrati being able to assume feminine roles with such success on the stage. But of all the changes resulting from such an operation, that which occurs in the larynx is the most remarkable . . . Due to the delay in ossification of the entire skeleton the larynx remains for a long time cartilaginous and along with this, as in women, there was no growth comparable to the normal male

Adam's apple. This is not to say that there was no mutation
whatever, but rather that it was a very slow and gradual change
that extended throughout most of their life. Moreover this mutation was only a fraction of what would normally have occurred
during the comparatively short period of puberty. As this gradual
change took place the lower range of the boyish voice was
extended, taking on a tenor quality which due to greater physical
strength was capable of far greater volume and brilliance than the
female voice. It was usual for the soprano to change to mezzo and
the mezzo to contralto as they turned into middle and old age.
Their uncommon flexibility was due to continuous and careful
training begun usually at a tender age and extending throughout
this period of very slow mutation. Their phenomenal capacity in
singing long bravura passages and producing their famous *messa di
voce* or 'swell tone' (i.e. crescendo and diminuendo) was due first
to their abnormal chest dimensions which allowed them to inhale a
great amount of air and second to the fact that the larynx was
considerably smaller than normal, thus allowing the voice to be
produced with much less expenditure of breath.

Philip A. Duey, *Bel Canto in Its Golden Age*, Columbia University Press,
1951, pp. 52–3

Castrati became the eighteenth-century equivalent of modern prima donnas:

In terms of salary, status, glamour, the castrati were the true prima
donnas of their time . . . The practice of castrating boys to create
this extraordinary vocal situation dates possibly from the end of
the Roman Empire and was certainly known in Byzantium. In the
sixteenth century, Spanish 'falsettists' – who were either what we
today know as counter-tenors, or true castrati – became popular in
the choirs of the Catholic church, where women were not allowed to
sing. By the end of the sixteenth century Pope Clement VIII had
sanctified the use of castrati in the Sistine Chapel choir, and the rise
of Venetian opera soon gave them an even more spectacular arena.

The exploitation of castration was confined to Italy. The operation itself was strictly illegal, and those who perpetrated it faced death, their accomplices (parents included) excommunication. However, various blind eyes belonging to various interested parties were turned, and while many indulged in nominal moral outrage, many more were happy to accept the sad 'accident' that had befallen the child, and to relish its happy side-effect. It has been estimated that by the mid eighteenth century as many as four thousand boys a year, mostly from poor or peasant backgrounds, were thus assaulted, the parents sometimes receiving a sum from a singing teacher, who in turn would take a percentage in his protégé's career. Of all these, a mere handful would mature to make a decent living as singers. The operation itself was easily performed. The victim was drugged with opium and the vas deferens leading from the testicles to the urethra painlessly severed together with the cord structures . . . To have a fully inhibiting effect this had to happen before puberty: sometimes it was done in infancy . . .

Many castrati spent their lives as church singers, but it was in opera that they became big business. The most famous names had international careers and commanded enormous sums of money. They would travel with their 'suitcase arias' or *aria di baule*, a form of signature tune which they would insert into whatever opera they were appearing in, regardless of dramatic context. Their vanity sometimes went further – Luigi Marchesi, wrote Scudo, liked to 'play the part of someone who could wear a gilded helmet crowned with red or white feathers. He wanted to make his entry descending a hill, from the top of which he could cry, "*Dove son io?*" ("Where am I?") Then he demanded that a trumpet gave forth a blast, after which he could declame "*Odi lo squillo della tromba guerriera*" ("I hear the blast of the war-like trumpet") . . .'

Some of the castrati's effect on eighteenth-century society came from their sexual ambiguity, both on and off stage. Some were homosexual. Obviously they were peculiarly attractive to married women looking for liaisons which could not result in pregnancy. Voyeuristic curiosity provided a further *frisson*; sniggering innuendo must have been another occupational hazard. Forbidden to marry, though still able to perform sexually, they took advantage of a licence sometimes granted to anomalies.

Rupert Christiansen, *Prima Donna*, Bodley Head, 1984, pp. 27–30

Since the operation was illegal, castration had to be explained away as the result of an accident:

More castrations were explained as having been necessitated at an early age by illness or by an unspecified 'need'. A favourite cause was the bite of a wild swan or a wild pig. According to a well-known satire of 1720, the hangers-on of a castrato opera singer would explain away his condition with one or other of these tales, and in 1784 the Franciscan biographer of Farinelli sent round a questionnaire virtually asking to have his subject's voice explained in the same way; the cause he was supplied with was a fall from a horse. By the mid nineteenth century the surviving castrati of the Sistine Chapel had apparently all fallen victim to pigs.

Yet even in a more shamefaced age boys could still allege that they had consented to, even begged for castration. The eleven-year-old Angelo Villa did so in 1783, and – even in a Lombardy where 'enlightened' reform was at its peak – succeeded in having his teacher and adoptive father Pietro Testori let off five years' hard labour; Angelo went on to make a fair career in opera under the name Testori. We need not take the boys' petitions at face value. But they – and their acceptance by rulers – show that for many years castration was almost a routine matter, calling at best for perfunctory concealment.

John Rosselli, *Singers of Italian Opera*, Cambridge University Press,

1992, p. 39

Operatic fashion in eighteenth-century Italy relied on constant novelty:

No opera lived more than a few years; others followed it, as good, but in a different style; and in the immense bustle of new productions and new styles there was very rarely time to revive an old one. An opera was therefore almost invariably new – either newly composed or newly imported – and there was no such thing as a *répertoire*. Every great town had yearly one or two operas composed expressly for it, and one or two imported from elsewhere. When the opera was newly composed it was composed for a given set of singers already engaged; the composer had, as it were, to take their measure, and there was no such thing as writing for an abstract soprano, tenor, or bass, and then trying to fit the part so written (and such a fit must often be bad) on a concrete one; an opera was written for such or such a performer, in order best to display his or her peculiar excellence ... Thus all the most popular serious operas of the eighteenth century were indissolubly connected with some great singer ... To attempt a part written for another was to throw down the glove and pretend to equality with him or her; such audacity was generally severely punished by the audience; and when, for instance, the Italians permitted Pacchierotti, Marchesi, and Rubinelli successively to sing Sarti's *Giulio Sabino*, it was for the pleasure of comparing their three greatest singers, of pitting them against each other, and for the attendant pleasure of street riots and coffee-house fights ...

Each theatre could scarcely prepare more than one opera each season, as the performers and audience both required to be perfectly familiarized with it; the same opera was therefore performed twenty or thirty successive times, and then packed off to another place. Moreover, as the music was all and everything, the music alone was required to be new, while the words were as old as possible; every composer of the eighteenth century had set nearly all Metastasio's plays, and most of them twice, thrice, or even four times. The plays were beautiful, the public knew them by heart; so much the better, it enjoyed them here and there, and gave its main attention to the music.

Vernon Lee, *Studies of the Eighteenth Century in Italy*, Fisher Unwin, 1907, pp. 202–4

Charles Burney visited Milan in July 1770:

The theatre here is very large and splendid: five rows of boxes
on each side, a hundred in each row with a room behind every
one for cards and refreshments. In the fourth gallery was a pharo
table. There was a very large box, bigger than my dining-room
[in London] for the Duke of Modena, who is Governor of Milan,
and the *principessina* his daughter . . . There was an abominable
noise except during two or three arias and a duet, with which
everybody was in raptures. During this last, the applause continued
till the performers returned to repeat it. This is the method of
encoring an air here . . . The band was very numerous and the
orchestra large in proportion to the house, which is much bigger
than the great opera house in Turin. Each box of the three
first rows contains six persons who sit three on each side facing
each other. Higher up they sit three in front and the rest stand
behind. There are very wide galleries that run parallel with all the
boxes, where people after the first act walk about and change
places perpetually.

Charles Burney, *Journal*, Folio Society, 1969, pp. 45–6

Italian opera placed a higher value on the singer than the composer:

Eighteenth- and early-nineteenth-century composition – certainly
in Italy – was a kind of musical journalism, done to order, for a
specific occasion and in a hurry. The prima donna who in 1807
wanted a clause in her contract entitling her to approve the libretto
four months before the start of the season was being optimistic; it
took Bellini's genius – recognized almost at once as something
special – to impose on the opera world his need for time, which
meant that he had to have seven weeks or so to write an opera
from scratch and disliked writing more than one a year . . . In the
early years of the century, when instrumental and choral writing
was simpler, not only Rossini and Donizetti and Pacini but the
academic veteran Zingarelli would normally compose an opera in
anything from two to four weeks . . .

By 1823 operas by and large had more concerted pieces, more scenes with chorus and extras, sometimes more historically conscious sets requiring more elaborate movement; orchestration too, though conservative Italian audiences disapproved, was growing more complex. Theatres which had made it a point of honour to put on two new operas each carnival season, like La Fenice in Venice, were beginning to find such a programme unmanageable. They had to fall back on presenting one opera new to their own town but not expressly composed for it; sometimes, if the first opera of the season was a flop, the impresario might be called upon to rush on to the stage a fall-back work (*opera di ripiego*) while the second main opera contracted for (*opera d'obbligo*) was still being rehearsed, and perhaps written. The notion of repertory opera, with singers coming along to appear at the drop of a hat in a work everyone more or less knew, was not to develop fully until the 1840s . . .

Dress rehearsals sometimes ended at three o'clock in the morning on the day of the performance; singers learnt their parts as these were being written, rehearsed them, and sang performances of the season's first opera, all at once, within a few days of the opening; in a minor theatre they might on occasion virtually learn the work that very day. The result was unpredictable: the company might, like track runners on the last lap, snatch a success through one more burst of nervous energy, or they might sound as tired as they felt and the first night might be a near-failure.

John Rosselli, *The Opera Industry in Italy from Cimarosa to Verdi*,
Cambridge University Press, 1984, pp. 6–9

In the 1820s Lady Blessington visited the opera at Genoa:

Went to the opera, and was disappointed by the *coup-d'oeil* the theatre presented; the want of light throwing a gloom over all but the proscenium, which I must admit gains by the obscurity of the rest of the house. It is impossible to distinguish the faces of any of the ladies in the boxes, so that the handsome and the ugly are

equally unseen; and no *belle* can be here accused of going to the
opera to display her charms: an accusation not unfrequently preferred against beauties in London and Paris, where the theatres are
so brilliantly lighted. The boxes at the opera house here are fitted
up according to the tastes of the owners. They are, for the most
part, simply furnished with plain silk curtains; and it is not
uncommon for ladies to have a card table, and enjoy a quiet game
during the performance, or between the acts ... The performance
was tolerable – that is, it was considered only so here, where the
people are passionately fond, and are critical judges of music; but
I have heard much inferior rapturously applauded at the opera
in London, where the audience is much less fastidious than on the
Continent, and infinitely more liberal in their remuneration
of talent. The king and queen are said to be very partial to music,
and their constant attendance at the opera would go far to confirm
this assertion; were it not that their nightly visits to it may be
accounted for by the proverbial dulness of a courtly circle.

Countess of Blessington, *The Idler in Italy*, Henry Colburn, 1839, II,

pp. 57-9, 63

Hector Berlioz took a dim view of Italian opera in 1832:

On arriving in Milan, out of a sense of duty I made myself go to
hear the latest opera. Donizetti's *L'elisir d'amore* was being given at
the Cannobiana. I found the theatre full of people talking in
normal voices, with their backs to the stage. The singers, un-
deterred, gesticulated and yelled their lungs out in the strictest spirit
of rivalry. At least I presumed they did, from their wide-open
mouths; but the noise of the audience was such that no sound
penetrated except the bass drum. People were gambling, eating
supper in their boxes, etcetera, etcetera. Consequently, perceiving
it was useless to expect to hear anything of the score, which was
then new to me, I left. It appears that the Italians do sometimes
listen. I have been assured by several people that it is so. The fact
remains that music to the Milanese, as to the Neapolitans, the

Romans, the Florentines, and the Genoese, means arias, duets, trios, well sung; anything beyond that provokes only aversion or indifference. It may be that such antipathies are mere prejudice, due above all to the feebleness of their orchestras and choruses, which prevents them from appreciating any great music outside the narrow circuit they have ploughed for so long. It may also be that they are capable to some extent of rising to the challenge of genius, provided the composer is careful not to disturb entrenched habits of mind too rudely. The striking success of *William Tell* in Florence supports this view; even the sublime *Vestale* of Spontini had a series of brilliantly successful performances in Naples twenty-five years ago . . .

Of all the nations of Europe, I am strongly inclined to think them the most impervious to the evocative, poetic side of music, as well as to any conception at all lofty and out of the common run. Music for the Italians is a sensual pleasure and nothing more. For this noble expression of the mind they have hardly more respect than for the art of cooking. They want a score that, like a plate of macaroni, can be assimilated immediately without their having to think about it or even to pay any attention to it.

Hector Berlioz, *Memoirs*, translated by David Cairns, Gollancz, 1969,
pp. 208 9

Seating arrangements in Italian opera houses:

There was no doubt in any leading theatre, whatever its structure of ownership, which were the 'noble' areas. The seating arrangements were hierarchical in the most visible way. The second tier of boxes (out of four, five, or six) was always the most aristocratic: except in commercial ports like Trieste and Leghorn it was largely or wholly occupied by nobles, at least in the fashionable season. The first or the third tier in some theatres enjoyed equal standing with the second . . .

Part of the stalls area at La Scala . . . was filled by the upper servants of the nobility, who were admitted at a special price.

There and in many other theatres liveried servants accompanying their masters had free entry . . .

The most visible distinction, found in Naples and Bologna as well as in Milan and in other garrison towns, was the reservation for military officers of the first row or rows of stalls. This did not just show up the white tunics of Austrian officers in the tense years after the 1848 revolutions. Italian officers – of the papal army – could choose to stand instead of sitting, and so prevent the rest of the audience from seeing the stage . . .

Who else was in the stalls, or in the next-to-last tier of boxes in those theatres provided with a gallery? The answer varied from time to time and from theatre to theatre. It is hazardous to speak of a bourgeois audience everywhere. True, at La Scala by 1821 habitual attenders at the back of the stalls and in the (presumably upper) boxes were described as 'well-bred men and women' . . . who did not dress elegantly, had no carriage, and might arrive dusty or muddy from the Milan streets. These well-bred people were probably lawyers and doctors of the less fashionable kind, civil servants, engineers, pharmacists, the better-off tradesmen and shopkeepers. In university towns like Padua and Bologna the stalls audience included many students; in tourist towns like Venice, Florence, Rome, and Naples, many non-Italians; almost anywhere, a number of out-of-town Italians passing through. On a night of pouring rain in Florence 'foreigners' were almost the only people to turn up.

John Rosselli, *The Opera Industry in Italy from Cimarosa to Verdi*,
Cambridge University Press, 1984, pp. 42–5

The workings of a typical opera house in nineteenth-century Italy, as explained by Stendhal:

This is how the theatre operates in Italy. An entrepreneur – usually the richest inhabitant of a small town who undertakes this task as a labour of love, since it's likely to prove financially ruinous – will agree to run the theatre of the town of which he is the leading

light. He forms a company made up of a prima donna, a tenor, a
basso cantante, a *basso buffo*, a second female singer and a third *buffo*
singer. The impresario then engages a composer, whom he commissions to write a new opera, ensuring that the arias are suitable to
the voices hired to sing them. The impresario then buys a libretto,
which will cost him between 60 and 80 francs; the author is
generally a wretched *abbé*, parasitically attached to some noble
household in the locality ... Then the impresario, who also owns
a fine property, hands over the financial management of the
theatre to an agent, who is usually the same rogue of a lawyer
employed by him in all his affairs. The impresario invariably falls
in love with the prima donna, and the chief talking point in the
town is to guess whether he'll give her his arm in public.

Once organized, the company will give its first performance,
after a whole month of wild intrigues, which provide the locality
with an endless supply of gossip. This *prima recita* is the most
exciting public event in the town, so much so that there's nothing
in Paris itself that can compare with it.

Stendhal, *Life of Rossini*, chapter 6, translated by Stephen Brook

*Censorship in the nineteenth-century Italian opera house did not exercise
vigilance over political matters only:*

Preventive censorship was the norm in Italy. It went on before,
during, and after the period of revolutionary and Napoleonic rule
(but for a very short outburst of free expression in 1796–7), before
and after unification, though the practice of censorship in united
Italy was much more liberal. Studies of the censorship have fastened on its political aspects – the ban on regicide, for instance, that
gave Verdi such trouble over *Rigoletto* and *Un ballo in maschera* ...

Because the opera house was the centre of social life few things
went down so well as local allusions – not, heaven forfend,
allusions to the authorities but to a well-known noble cuckold or
an eccentric literary man. For the same reason there were few
things the paternal authorities of old Italy detested more. Allusions

might cause murmurs, gossip, disorder; they must be stopped. So a comic opera by Pacini making fun of the poet Monti was forbidden after the third performance. La Fenice refused *I due Foscari* as a new opera because the Venetian families of Loredan and Barbarigo might have been upset at seeing their fifteenth-century ancestors in a poor light; it did put on the work after a Rome theatre had taken responsibility for the first performance – a nice distinction . . .

Worse trouble hit the impresario of the Ducale, Parma, just before the opening of the carnival season of 1837. The director-general of police came backstage with the censor and the supervisory board to demand immediate changes in costumes: some for the ballet were 'indecent' and those of the female chorus in *Lucia di Lammermoor* had red and green ribbons on a white background – the tricolour of the Napoleonic Kingdom of Italy, an allusion quite unintended by the designer . . . The man in charge of the costumes had the green ribbons hurriedly taken off, but the impresario was so frightened that he insisted on substituting black ribbons at his own expense; the whole breakneck change cost over 1000 francs.

John Rosselli, *The Opera Industry in Italy from Cimarosa to Verdi*, Cambridge University Press, 1984, pp. 93–4

During the Austrian occupation of Milan, the authorities imposed censorship at La Scala, with bizarre artistic consequences:

With the literature of the English romantic movement almost as well known to the Italians as their own nursery rhymes it probably did not come as a surprise for the patrons of La Scala to see an opera advertised with the name of *Guglielmo Vallace*, with music by Rossini, though they may well have wondered what it was all about. Rossini, as far as they knew, had never written an opera about William Wallace. They were quite right in this, of course; it was not Rossini but the Austrian censorship who picked on the subject for this opera, for it started life in Paris as *William Tell*, and was a theme, in all fairness, hardly likely to appeal to the Austrians since it scarcely presented them in a favourable light. The Swiss of *Tell* were therefore changed into Scots and the Austrians into English. Exactly who or what inspired this particular translation to a period long before the all-important crossbow was invented is not known, but at any rate it seems the music was not altered; which makes me wish more than ever that I could have seen the production. The Tyrolean ballet, for instance, must have been well worth seeing when danced in the kilt . . .

The year 1859 was less than a month old before *Norma* and Verdi's *Simon Boccanegra* had provided opportunities for first rate patriotic demonstrations. In Bellini's opera the audience defiantly took up the war cry of the chorus and shouted '*Guerra! Guerra!*' pointedly at the boxes occupied by the Austrian military governor and his staff (who shouted back 'You shall have it, you dogs!'), while a fortnight later the famous acrostic cry of '*Viva Verdi*' acclaiming *V*ittorio *E*manuele *R*e *D'I*talia, which had started in Naples, was heard for the first time in Milan and quickly spread all over Italy wherever a Verdi opera was performed.

Spike Hughes, *Great Opera Houses*, Weidenfeld & Nicolson, 1956,

pp. 101–2, 107

Some opera companies were composed entirely of children:

'The children's [opera] company is a great hit, the theatre is packed out every night, they're so sweet, poor little things . . .' So a noblewoman reported from Venice in 1842. For some, the singer's life began well before puberty. This was true not just of the children of operatic families, like Adelina Patti, who helped her parents out of a tight corner by singing in concert at the age of seven. From 1783 to 1910 (in South America down to 1920) companies of pre-pubertal Italian children sang complete operas.

One or two seem to have been family groups; most, however, were run by an impresario who recruited the children of needy families, trained them, and toured them. They sang comic operas –

not too difficult for light voices – until in 1903 a teacher-impresario
had his lead singer, Arnaldo Tedeschi (billed as aged six, in reality
nine), sing '*Di quella pira*' from *Il trovatore* between the acts; his
company of forty-eight children later performed *Lucia di Lammermoor* and *Rigoletto*, all singing treble. They earned more than they
could have done in other jobs, though less than minor adult
singers; Arnaldo remembered his teacher-impresario with affection,
so that company at least was not a sweatshop.

If any of these child singers made an adult career in opera we do
not know of it.

John Rosselli, *Singers of Italian Opera*, Cambridge University Press,

1992, p. 151

*Writing on 5 February 1876 to his old friend Opprandino Arrivabene,
Verdi gives a revealing if subjective survey of the state of operatic performance in the 1870s:*

The best thing would be a repertory theatre, but I don't think it
could be achieved. The examples of the Paris Opéra and Germany
have very little value for me, because in all these theatres the
performances are deplorable. At the Opéra, the productions are
splendid, and their costumes, their good taste, are superior to all
other theatres. But the musical side is awful, the singers are always
the most mediocre (except for Fauré a few years ago), the orchestra
and chorus are lazy and lacking in discipline . . .

In Germany, the orchestra and choruses are more attentive and
conscientious. They play accurately and well, although I have seen
some deplorable performances in Berlin. The orchestra is huge,
but sounds merely gross. The chorus is not good, the productions
lacking in character and taste. The singers . . . oh, the singers are
awful, absolutely awful . . .

In Vienna (which is now the leading German-speaking theatre),
things are better in the case of chorus and orchestra (most excellent). I have attended various performances and have found the
majority of them very good, though the productions are mediocre,

and the singers worse than mediocre. But the performance usually costs very little to attend. The public, who are made to sit in the dark during the performance, are either asleep or bored, applaud a little at the end of each act, and go home at the end of the performance neither enthusiastic nor displeased. That may be all very well for those northern natures, but try to put on that kind of performance in one of our theatres, and see what a noise the public will make!

Our audiences are too excitable, and would not be contented with a prima donna who cost only eighteen or twenty thousand florins a year, as in Germany. They want the prima donnas who go to Cairo, St Petersburg, Lisbon, London, etc., for twenty-five or thirty thousand francs a month. But how are we to pay them? Look at this, for example: this year at La Scala they have a company whose betters couldn't be found. A prima donna with a beautiful voice, who sings well, is lively, young, beautiful, and, what's more, is one of us. A tenor who is perhaps the best there is, certainly one of the best. A baritone who has but one rival: Pandolfini. A bass who is unrivalled. And yet the theatre does poor business. Last year, they spoke well enough of [soprano Maddalena] Mariani. This year, they began to say she was a little tired (which, incidentally, is not true), now they say she sings well but does not draw an audience, etc., etc. If she were to come next year, everyone would say, 'Oh, always the same woman . . .'

Giuseppe Verdi, *Letters*, translated by Charles Osborne, Gollancz, 1971, pp. 198–9

It was Toscanini who attempted to restore artistic dignity to La Scala by such measures as enforcing the ban on encores. His campaign soon reached crisis point:

In the Scala season of 1902–3, Toscanini committed an act for which his biographers find it hard to offer an apology. It happened at the final night of the season, during a performance of *The Masked Ball*. The tenor in that performance was Giovanni Zenatello,

a popular star who was later to sing the first Pinkerton at Covent
Garden. In the second act the audience shouted for Zenatello to
sing an encore. Toscanini stood immobile, waiting for the tumult
to die down. It would not die down; indeed, the howls increased
in volume, the cries of *bis* became harsher, and it became clear that
the demonstration was aimed not only for Zenatello but against
Toscanini. In a sudden rage Toscanini turned, flung his baton into
the auditorium, and stomped out ... An assistant conductor
finished the performance. That was the end of Toscanini at La
Scala for three seasons.

Walking out in the middle of a performance is a breach of ob-
ligation so severe that it has almost never occurred. His fury must
have been engendered by a cause deeper than the rowdy demand
for an encore. After all, he had previously yielded to such pressure,
if not with good grace. His nerves must have been rent raw after
a season which included not only the study of new works, the
staging of Berlioz's *Damnation of Faust*, the third act of *Parsifal* (first
Italian performance), but also three performances of the Ninth
Symphony. Verdi's *Luisa Miller* had bored the audience, an opera
by Ponchielli, *I lituani*, was judged deficient, and the one act of
Parsifal was not understood; in short, Toscanini had experienced
disapproval. He was angry not only at the public but at the management of La Scala, which had made facile compromises on bar-
gain nights, not keeping up the standard. He was angry at certain
singers whose vanity chafed under the discipline imposed by him.
He was angry at the claque which haunted the house like a phantom
of the opera. Perhaps most of all he was angry at himself: he had
failed to draw the public – or a large part of it – up to the level
where music meant more to them than sociable entertainment.

George R. Marek, *Toscanini*, Vision Press, 1975, pp. 72–3

*Vincent Sheean found Italian vulgarity at its enjoyable best at the San
Carlo opera house in Naples:*

Funds for elaborate productions and profuse rehearsals were never available there, and as a result the performances sometimes (even with eminent principals singing the chief parts) had a much more provincial quality. We enjoyed them, just the same – and how thoroughly we enjoyed them, sometimes in ways the composer had never intended, was due to their very provinciality. Tenors let their high notes run away with them almost every night, sopranos got so excited they could hardly sing, baritones bellowed like the Minoan bull at high festival. Insufficient rehearsal, and therewith insufficient authority in the conductor's beat, accounted for some of the goings-on, but the audience accounted for the rest. It was one of the noisiest of Italian audiences and it would stop the performance utterly if it did not have its own way. Favoured pieces (usually the worst ones) were therefore repeated whenever the audience showed its determination, which was frequently. Such an air as '*La donna è mobile*', for example, is lyrically and dramatically right, suited to the character and situation, when performed as Verdi wrote it, but the way they liked it in Naples – with prolonged high notes, a cadenza and other ornaments including a piercing *acuto* at the end – it was difficult to endure even the first time. I remember Lauri-Volpi, whose voice was in any case much too big for that house, singing the thing three times over. It was enough to give one a gloomy view of tenors forever after.

Vincent Sheean, *First and Last Love*, Gollancz, 1957, p. 144

Opera was not exempt from the mismanagement and corruption that bedevilled all aspects of Italian life during the latter half of the twentieth century. In early 1994 Patricia Clough afforded us a glimpse of the shenanigans at the Rome opera house:

Whether it was the cost of incontinent camels, ballerinas protesting on stage, tenor José Carreras's eyebrow-raising fee, or the bailiffs' seizure of the 487 seats, rarely has there been a dull moment on the stage at the opera house in Rome – and behind the scenes it was often a farce . . .

What with carpeting the foyer in Persian rugs, doubling the staff, hiring liveried lackeys, parading through the city with elephants and slave girls, and other extravagances, [Gian Paolo] Cresci has, within two years, turned the Opera's L900m (£36,000) surplus into a L60bn deficit. By the summer, it will have no money to pay staff, and next year it may have to close down.

Backed by a unanimous city council vote, Mayor Francesco Rutelli demanded that Mr Cresci resign. The situation is intolerable, he declared . . .

The Rome Opera has been a playground for the old political parties, a rich mine of patronage, influence and nepotism. The people who got top jobs reflected the political make-up of the city council.

It has long been rumoured that to be hired or win a plum part, singers had to be backed by one party or another.

Mr Cresci embodied this system . . . In a carve-up of jobs, the superintendency fell to him, though he admitted he did not know the first thing about opera. [Former prime minister] Fanfani could not see any drawback. 'Cresci is an opera in himself,' he said.

And, in a way, he is. Determined to popularize a lacklustre theatre, he went for mass-appeal productions, showmanship, gimmicks. 'All froth and no substance,' his critics objected – but Mr Cresci was not deterred. To defuse a hostile press, he hired journalists and their relatives on contracts. And he paid well-connected women to cultivate the diplomatic corps and throw after-theatre parties. When the Italian president wanted a special welcome for Argentina's president, Carlos Menem, Mr Cresci engaged Carreras for the night for L130m (some reports say L170m) though the maximum fee allowed is L30m.

The State Audit Office was appalled. Why was an orchestra paid for a Pavarotti concert that never took place? Why are nearly one quarter of tickets given away? Why was a plane hired to bring a tenor from London, carpets rented at L300m a year without tenders, and the new, twenty-five-strong in-house fire brigade given English lessons at L80,000 each an hour? And what about the L14m for hiring six horses and a chariot, and the L35m for a monkey and two camels which, at the sound of fanfares, were unable to contain themselves? . . .

Cresci retorted that the debt was 'a mere trifle . . . no more than the cost of a few tanks'. And with devastating frankness, he added: 'Only an infinitesimal part of it went into bribes' . . .

Union problems were notorious: in *Giselle* once, half the *corps de ballet* occupied the stage in protest at the producer; and in performances of *Carmen* and *Iphigenia in Tauris*, the chorus refused to open their mouths. These issues subsided when Mr Cresci introduced mass promotions and liberal payment of overtime.

Patricia Clough, *Independent on Sunday*, 27 February 1994

2: Opera outside Italy

In this miserable country a man who has seen *Die Walküre* on the stage is a much greater curiosity than one who has explored the Congo.

George Bernard Shaw, article in *The Star*, 14 February 1890

Italy, more than any other country in the world, is opera-crazed. In most other countries, it fits in uneasily, often as a favourite pastime of the rich and the aristocratic, but lacking a firm base in popular culture. Yet although the audience for opera outside Italy was relatively restricted, standards of performance were often superior to those encountered in Rome or Naples.

FRANCE

In 1717 the Duc de Saint-Simon was a confidant of the regent, the Duc d'Orléans, who was governing France during the minority of Louis XV:

He stopped me one afternoon, as I was tidying my papers and preparing to leave after working alone with him, as I usually did two or three times a week. He said he was going to the Opéra, and asked me to accompany him because he had important matters to discuss with me. 'To the Opéra, Monsieur?' I cried. 'What a place to talk business! Talk to me here as long as you please. Or if you wish to go to the Opéra, what could be better? I will come to you tomorrow, or whenever else you choose.' He none the less persisted, saying that we could shut ourselves up in his little private box, where he often went alone, and that we should be even more

comfortable than in his study. I begged him to consider that the
performance would be distracting, and the music too; that everyone
would see him talking and arguing, his mind not on the singers;
that they would draw conclusions from his gestures; that people
coming to pay their court would wonder at finding me shut up
with him alone; that the Opéra was for diversion and entertainment, to allow people to see and be seen; certainly not a proper
place to discuss state affairs and provide a rival spectacle to the one
on the stage. It was all in vain. He merely laughed; took his hat
and cane from a sofa with one hand, and my arm with the other,
and carried me off.

Duc de Saint-Simon, *Historical Memoirs*, translated by Lucy Norton,

Hamish Hamilton, 1972, III, p. 112

Italian opera did not always travel well, especially when routed for France:

When Cardinal Mazarin introduced the Italian opera into France it
was in the monstrous condition inseparable from times of growth
and transition; the dramas were badly constructed, the poetry
languid and quibbling, the music harsh and pedantic; no great
school of singing had as yet arisen, and the chief attraction of the
performance consisted in scenic displays and pantomime wonders,
which were pushed to an incredible point. The French never
dreamed of altering the opera in any of these essential points.
While the Italians gave a new shape to the drama, eliminated all
the extraneous elements of machinery and dancing, and cultivated
singing and vocal composition to the utmost, the French, relying
entirely upon their own powers, never attending to what was
being done in Italy, merely petrified the uncouth and meaningless
forms of the opera of the seventeenth century . . .

French singing was proverbially abominable: the French, as we
learn from Rousseau, knew only one sort of upper voice, the
soprano, raised to the most unearthly pitch; and they replaced the
contralto, so lovingly cultivated by the Italians of the eighteenth
century, by a sort of falsetto tenor, of a most nasal and disgusting

artificial tone. These misplaced voices were further ruined by being produced either purely in the head or in the throat, no such thing as a real chest voice being known in France. They were totally undisciplined in the simplest and most essential qualities: they had no swell, no proper shake, no real agility and neatness of movement – above all, no portamento, that is to say, no art of moving from one note to another without either hopping or dragging, no art of beginning and finishing a phrase; in short, no art of singing. All this was replaced by the most violent vocal contortions, shrieks, howls, gabbles, and squalls; by the most lamentable drawling, and especially by certain movements, called indiscriminately *ports de voix*, which, according to contemporaries, were the sourest and most lugubrious graces conceivable.

Vernon Lee, *Studies of the Eighteenth Century in Italy*, Fisher Unwin,
1907, pp. 112–13, 120–21

The Venetian dramatist Goldoni encounters an opera singer at a dining club in Paris in 1764:

Our new associate did not act that day, but she was desirous of going to the opera; and the society were almost all disposed to accompany her. The only one who displayed no eagerness to go was myself.

'Ah, M. Italian,' said the lady, laughing, 'you are not fond of French music then?' – 'I possess no great knowledge of it,' said I; 'I have never been at the opera; but I hear a deal of singing wherever I go, and all the airs only serve to disgust me.' – 'Let us see,' said she, 'if I can overcome any of your prejudices against our music.' – She immediately began to sing, and I felt myself delighted and enchanted. What a charming voice! It was not powerful, but just, touching, and delightful. I was in ecstasy. 'Come,' said she, 'embrace me, and follow me to the opera.' I embraced her, and went to the opera accordingly.

I was at length present at this entertainment, which several persons could have wished me to see before everything else, and which I should not, perhaps, have seen so soon, if it had not been for this circumstance.

The actress whom we had received into our society took three of our brethren with her into her box, and I seated myself with two others in the amphitheatre. This part, which takes up a part of the theatres in France, is in front of the stage . . .

The action commenced; and, notwithstanding my favourable situation, I could not hear a word. However, I patiently waited for the airs, in the expectation that I should at least be amused with the music. The dancers made their appearance, and I imagined the act finished, but heard not a single air. I spoke of this to my neighbour, who laughed at me, and assured me that we had had six in the different scenes which I had heard.

'What!' said I. 'I am not deaf; the instruments never ceased accompanying the voices, sometimes more loudly and sometimes more slowly than usual, but I took the whole for recitative' . . .

As nothing takes place between the acts of the French opera, they soon began the second act. I heard the same music, and felt the same weariness. I gave up altogether the drama and its accompaniments, and began to examine the entertainment taken as a whole, which I thought surprising. The principal male and female dancers had arrived at an astonishing pitch of perfection, and their suite was very numerous and very elegant. The music of the choruses appeared to me more agreeable than that of the drama . . .

Everything was beautiful, grand, and magnificent, except the music. At the end of the drama there was a sort of *chaconne* sung by an actress who did not appear among the characters of the drama, and seconded by the music of the choruses and by dancing. This agreeable surprise might have enlivened the piece; but it was a hymn rather than an air.

When the curtain fell, I was asked by all my acquaintances how I liked the opera? My answer flew from my lips like lightning: 'It is paradise for the eyes, and hell for the ears.'

Carlo Goldoni, *Memoirs*, translated by John Black, Knopf, 1926, pp. 373-4

In 1802 the English musician George Smart spent an evening at the Opéra in Paris:

This evening was spent at the great French opera house. It is not quite so large as ours, but shows the company better. The dancing and decorations are far better than ours, the choruses go extremely well, but the recitatives and singing are horrid, nothing but ranting, squalling and bawling, only exceeded by the applause of the singing. It is the fashion of the audience to sing with the performer.

Sir George Smart, *Leaves from the Journals of Sir George Smart*,
Longmans, 1907, p. 27

In the nineteenth century the Paris Opéra was grossly mismanaged:

The official Opéra enjoyed several privileges at the expense of the other lyric theatres of Paris and of music in general. Not only had it a liberal subvention from the state, but no ball or concert could be given without the Opéra receiving one fifth of the gross receipts, while the other opera houses had to pay over to it 5 per cent of their takings. In spite of all this, the losses of the institution in the 1820s had been so enormous as to constitute a heavy burden on the civil list – amounting in 1827 to close on a million francs. In 1831 Louis Philippe rid himself of this incubus by turning the Opéra over to one Véron, who undertook to run it for six years, at his own risk of loss or chance of profit, in consideration of a subsidy of 800,000 francs for the first year, 760,000 francs for the second and third, and 710,000 francs for the last three. This Véron was a man of most chequered history. Born in 1798 and trained as a doctor, he had early abandoned medicine for journalism, founding the *Revue de Paris* in 1829. His medical record appears to consist mainly in having published a treatise on the maladies of children and in having made a slight mistake in his practice – summoned to bleed a patient, he had opened an artery instead of a vein – that had resulted in the death of his unfortunate client. He had also put on the market the *pâte pectorale de Regnault*, a specific of such enormous popularity in its own day that it brought its inventor a

fortune. To those who know the mentality of court officials and
politicians where the fine arts are concerned, it is not in the least
surprising that this amateur assassin should have been looked upon
as the ideal man to conduct a national opera house, a job for
which, apparently, any qualifications suffice so long as they do not
include a knowledge of art in general or of music in particular.
Berlioz, who had a wide and mournful experience of these strange
fauna, was often astounded at the comprehensiveness of their
ignorance. He tells of one of the directors of the Paris Opéra who,
when Cherubini – at that time head of the Paris Conservatoire –
called on him without having himself announced, imperiously
demanded of him his name and profession, inquiring if he were
part of the Opéra establishment, and if so, whether he was attached
to the department of the ballet or that of the machines. Of two of
Véron's successors, Duponchel and Roqueplan, Berlioz said they
knew about as much of music as a couple of Chinese – yet 'along
with the completest ignorance, the profoundest barbarism, there
goes the most unbounded confidence in themselves'.

Ernest Newman, *The Life of Richard Wagner*, Knopf, 1933, I, pp. 261–2

Claude Debussy wasn't impressed by the Opéra either:

Everybody knows, at least by reputation, the Paris Opéra. I sadly
have to affirm that it hasn't changed at all. For the sake of the ill-
prepared passer-by, I should say that it still resembles a railway
station, but once inside, it could more easily be mistaken for a
Turkish bath.

There they continue to make a peculiar noise that the paying
clientele like to call 'music' – but you don't have to believe them.

Thanks to special favour and a state subsidy, this theatre can
produce anything at all; it scarcely matters what they perform, as
they have most luxuriously installed boxes with an extra room –
loges à salon – so called because they are especially designed so you
can't hear the music at all: these are the last remaining salons
where you can have a chat . . .

Yet if only the determined apathy of the place could be shaken up thoroughly, one could accomplish some fine things here. After such a long time aren't we due a complete *Ring* by now? For a start, it would have got it out of the way, and the Bayreuth pilgrims wouldn't be able to bore us with their stories any more.

Claude Debussy, article in *La Revue blanche*, 15 May 1901, translated by
Stephen Brook

Parisian standards remained dire, according to most accounts, well into the twentieth century:

The management and the conductors did not expect much of their singers. The public, which had nothing else, was easily satisfied and – as the word goes – 'never knew the difference'. (I think the public always knows the difference, but there are times, and this was one, when it has no choice.) Singers did not trouble to give their utmost care to a performance: success was more easily attained by extracurricular activity, clothes or jewels, Parisian notoriety. Of a certain manager at the Comique it is said that no soprano ever reached the stage for the first time without passing by his bed. Both at the Opéra-Comique and at the Paris Grand Opéra it was customary, as it is today, to permit 'qualified' singers to perform leading parts upon payment of a fee. Only a few years ago the fee at the Paris Grand Opéra for a celebrated American soprano was three hundred dollars a night – that is, from her to them, not from them to her: it is more, much more, than they pay even the best of their own singers.

Vincent Sheean, *First and Last Love*, Gollancz, 1957, p. 70

Spike Hughes was unimpressed after he visited the Opéra-Comique:

No visitor to the Opéra-Comique need fear a boring interval if he chooses to remain in his seat. When he has finished his reading he may sit back and enjoy a show of magic lantern slides thrown on a screen before him and advertising various commodities. This will make particularly the English feel at home who will imagine themselves back in their favourite local suburban or provincial cinema. The showing of the slides, of course, is silent; the Opéra-Comique has not yet installed a Wurlitzer. At any rate, it is doubtful whether a Wurlitzer could be heard over the din of the average interval at this theatre when, far outscreeching the volume of normally conducted French conversation, the auditorium is enlivened by the market-stall cries of a woman who stands in the circle (there are no boxes, of course, except stage boxes) and bawls out her wares . . .

The performance we saw was the 2804th performance at the Opéra-Comique of *Carmen* . . . On the showing of the Opéra-Comique company on the evening we saw *Carmen* it seems that the work is still unfamiliar to them. Staleness, after all, would inevitably be shown in the boredom of the performers. In *Carmen* No. 2804 it was not the performers who were bored.

By some quirk of the copyright laws in France it is forbidden to show the film of *Carmen Jones*. After seeing the Opéra-Comique at work on its own *création*, the greatest of all French operas, one can well understand why, and the French will be wise to keep the quirk in circulation just as long as ever they can.

Spike Hughes, Great Opera Houses, Weidenfeld & Nicolson, 1956,
pp. 312–14

ENGLAND

Eighteenth-century opera in London was treated with no more reverence than it was in its land of origin:

Perhaps the baroque opera house is better compared to a nightclub than to the modern darkened and silent temples of art. In the eighteenth century audiences would come and go throughout the performance, in and out of auditoriums kept fully lit, talking, eating, drinking, conducting amorous intrigue, and generally treating the entertainment with what in some ways was a healthy lack of respect. In such an atmosphere the singers had to work hard to shock the audience into attention . . .

The decorum of opera in this period was a strange mixture of high formality, great casualness, and semi-hysteria. Many early critics found it an idiotic farrago, mainly because of the eternal language problem – the operas being sung either in incomprehensible Italian or nonsensical translation. Financially it depended on capital earned from a sort of seasonal subscription system . . . A box subscriber in 1721 paid twenty guineas to hear fifty performances. Many would attend every night – one must bear in mind the dearth of alternative public diversions – but the engraved ivory or silver ticket was transferable. The pit was more like the orchestra stalls of today than the hard benches of the playhouses, and was filled with young gallants who liked to cruise up and down the aisle known as 'Fop's Alley'. The gallery was usually known as the 'Footmen's Gallery' and was largely populated by that class, waiting on their masters. The amount of seating was variable, the general principle being to cram in as many as would pay. Another oddity was the habit of allowing standing room on the stage. This was frequently condemned as a nuisance but seems to have lasted throughout the eighteenth century.

Rupert Christiansen, *Prima Donna*, Bodley Head, 1984, pp. 20–21

Felix Mendelssohn attended the opera in London in April 1829:

Klingemann took me first of all to an English coffee-house (for here everything is English) where, of course, I read *The Times*. As, like a true Berliner, I looked first for the theatrical news, I saw that *Otello* and the first appearance of Mme Malibran were announced for that very night. In spite of weariness and sea-sickness, I resolved to go. Klingemann lent me the necessary grey stockings, as I could not find mine in the hurry, and yet had to appear in full dress, with a black cravat, like all the rest of the genteel world. Then I went to my lodgings, and from there to the Italian Opera at King's Theatre, where I got a seat in the pit (half a guinea). A

large house, entirely decorated with crimson stuff, six tiers of
boxes, out of which peep the ladies bedecked with great white
feathers, chains and jewels of all kinds; an odour of pomade and
perfume assails one on entering, and gave me a headache; in the pit
all the gentlemen, with fresh-trimmed whiskers; the house
crowded; the orchestra very good ... Donzelli (Otello), full of
bravura and flourishes fraught with meaning, shouts and forces his
voice dreadfully, almost constantly singing a little too high, but
with no end of *haut goût* (for instance, in the last passionate scene
where Malibran screams and raves almost disagreeably, instead of
shouting the recitatives, as he usually does, he drops his voice, so
that the last bars are scarcely audible – and similar things). Mme
Malibran is a young woman, beautiful and splendidly made, be-
wigged, full of fire and power, and at the same time coquettish;
setting off her performance partly with very clever embellishments
of her own invention, partly with imitations of Pasta (it seemed
very strange to see her take the harp and sing the whole scene
exactly like Pasta and finally even in that very rambling passage at
the end which I am sure you, dear father, must remember). She
acts beautifully, her attitudes are good, only it is unfortunate that
she should so often exaggerate and so often border on the ridiculous and disagreeable ... After the second act came a long diver-
tissement with gymnastics and absurdities, just as with us, that
went on till half-past eleven. I was half dead with weariness, but
held out till a quarter to one, when Malibran was dispatched,
gasping and screaming disgustingly. That was enough and I went
home.

Felix Mendelssohn, letter to his father and sister, in *Letters*, Pantheon,
1945, pp. 45–7

*John Ebers, who managed the King's Theatre in London, which Mendelssohn
attended, expounds on the problems created by wilful performers:*

Let a new opera be intended to be brought forward. Signor This
will not sing his part, because it is not prominent enough; so, to

enrich it, a gathering must be made of airs from other operas, no matter whether by the same composer or not, nor whether there be any congruity between the style of the original piece and the adventitious passages introduced. De Begnis, who, from some cause, or no cause, was disliked by the other performers, chose *Il turco in Italia*, for his own and his wife's début. Every obstacle was thrown in the way of its representation; at last, all the best parts of *La Cenerentola* were forced into it, to add importance to the parts of the other performers. Indeed, from the same cause, I never had the full advantage of that valuable performer's services. If the sense of an opera is worth anything, let the effect of this curious process be imagined. Do not let it be supposed that the manager has any power to decide in a case like this. Probably the opera is already advertised for performance, in which case 'I will not play this part' must have its way. The opera being announced must go on, and concessions must be made, as it cannot be represented without the performer in question.

John Ebers, *Seven Years of the King's Theatre*, Philadelphia, 1828,
pp. 82–3

Shaw was highly critical of the condition of Italian opera in London in 1879:

We have at our opera houses a system of gesticulation so unmeaning, so impotent to excite even derisive mirth, that the ghastliest and most ludicrous traditions of the old melodramatic stage would, if revived, be more tolerable to us. Even the few artists who are capable of better things only escape momentarily from the false atmosphere generated by their own thoughtlessness and the ignorance of the public, when the power of the composer dominates artist and audience, and conquers in spite of every disadvantage. Nor do the public seem to be offended by this false conventionalism. Praise which would sound exaggerated if applied to our greatest actors, is lavished in chamber, clique, and column, on the shallowest French charlatanry and the dreariest Italian buffoonery.

Aspirants whose demerits are such as should debar them from
participation in a piece performed by amateurs, are permitted to
appear in the most responsible parts, and often meet with considerable encouragement. And hereby we have arrived at this: that with
musical enthusiasts amongst us sufficiently numerous to crowd
concert rooms where the loftiest abstract music prevails, our opera
houses are abandoned to followers of fashion who feel no higher
interest than a personal favouritism which is never based on
artistic appreciation . . .

The truth is that Italianized opera in England is aristocratic in
the worst sense. It has become effete because it has never appealed
to the people. Its audience has worn evening dress and kept late
hours so long that its vitality has escaped; its power of discerning
between sensational sham and true power has become confused;
and it applauds with palsied hands spiritless desecrations of Mozart,
or dodders feebly over the music of the future, so much louder
and more stimulating than the music of the past. Whatever we may
think of Wagner, we owe him thanks, inasmuch as he has taken
fashionable opera by the throat, and shaken the old paralytic
shrewdly. He has given us works that must be performed, with
words that must be understood.

George Bernard Shaw, in *Saturday Musical Review*, 22 February 1879,
reprinted in *Shaw's Music*, Bodley Head, 1989, I, pp. 192–3

Sir Thomas Beecham gave a dismal picture of the standards of operatic
performance in England at the turn of the century:

[In 1902] I heard of a new opera company which was about to go
on tour in the suburbs, with a cast of artists nearly all well known
to me . . . [I was] offered and had accepted the post of one of the
two conductors of the new company . . .

The tour lasted about two months; we visited such outlying
places as Clapham, Brixton, and Stratford, and I enjoyed myself
hugely, conducting in addition to *Carmen* and *Pagliacci* that trilogy
of popular Saturday-nighters dubbed facetiously 'The English

Ring' – *The Bohemian Girl*, *Maritana*, and *The Lily of Killarney*. But
all the fun and excitement I extracted from the experience (that
inveterate old joker, G.H. Snazelle, who was playing Devilshoof,
succeeded in setting fire to the stage as a farewell gesture on the
last night) could not blind my soberer perceptions to the truth that
if there was one especial way in which opera should not be given,
then here it was in all its rounded perfection. Some of the singers,
of course, were excellent, and I have never heard Marie Duma's
rendering of Leonora in *Il trovatore* bettered anywhere in the world
for tone quality, phrasing, and insight into the true character of
the role. But of attempt, even the slightest, at production there
was none, and both scenery and dresses were atrocious. Some of
the principals brought their own costumes along, but the detached
spectacle of one or two brilliantly clad figures only threw into
more dismal relief the larger mass of squalor in the background.
The chorus, which was composed mainly of veterans of both the
sexes, was accurate but toneless, and the orchestra quite the most
incompetent I have known anywhere. I could not help comparing
the wretched conditions under which great works of art were
being presented to the public with the care, preparation, and even
luxury bestowed upon any of the half-dozen musical comedies or
farces then running in the West End. Sometimes I would feel a
touch of astonishment that we had an audience at all for the
motley kind of entertainment we were offering, and at others an
uncomfortable twinge of conscience, as if I were an accomplice in
some rather discreditable racket, which among a community more
critical and knowledgeable would have provoked an instant breach
of the peace.

Sir Thomas Beecham, *A Mingled Chime*, Hutchinson, 1944, pp. 46–7

*In contrast, Debussy admired what he found at Covent Garden in April
1903, as reported in an article in* Gil Blas:

It's not clear to me exactly what constitutes 'the superiority of the
Anglo-Saxons', but among other things they do have Covent

Garden . . . This theatre enjoys the peculiarity that music is at ease there. One is also less struck by the sumptuous décor than by the perfect acoustics; the orchestra is both large and reliably attentive. What is more, M. André Messager takes care of the artistic side of things with impeccable taste, and nobody seems in the least surprised by this, it seems to me. You can imagine how odd this is, that they imagine a musician can usefully run an opera house! The fact is that such jobs usually go to idiots or pedants . . .

I have recently attended performances of both *Das Rheingold* and *Die Walküre* that were close to perfection. Perhaps one could criticize the scenery and some of the lighting, but I have to pay tribute to the scrupulous artistic care which enveloped the productions . . .

The English listen attentively, as if obsessed. If they are bored, it never shows – though since the hall is plunged into darkness during the performance, it's possible to doze off without anybody noticing. They applaud only at the end of each act, just as Wagnerian tradition demands; and [the conductor] Dr Richter himself seemed pleased, and indifferent to all the ovations. No doubt he was longing for a reviving beer.

> Claude Debussy, article in *Gil Blas*, 30 April 1903, translated by
> Stephen Brook

The Austrian opera administrator Rudolf Bing relished the atmosphere at Glyndebourne in 1935:

There were no unions. Often at dinner something would come up relating to that day's rehearsals, and as the port came round, an old bottle with spiders' webs clinging to it, the ruby liquid poured in the glass through a filter, [Fritz] Busch would say to some of the singers, 'Come, let's do it again!' The lights in the theatre would be turned back on, and at nine o'clock everyone would return to work. (If there was no work, Busch as likely as not would play four-hand piano duets with one of the other conductors, just to have music.) Everyone was committed, spiritually and physically –

there was no earthly reason to be at Glyndebourne unless one
wanted to be part of the best operatic production that could be
mounted. As Busch put it to the assembled *Magic Flute* company
after opening night, Glyndebourne had the advantage that 'even
work is more attractive than the night life of Lewes' . . .

To watch Busch work with an orchestra, using his personal
blend of firmness and kindly humour, was to learn something
about artistic leadership that only a master can teach. One of the
favourite stories at Glyndebourne dealt with Busch's very first
orchestral rehearsal, when he raised his baton, then dropped his
arms to his sides and before anyone had played a note said to the
men in mock reproach, and thickly accented English, 'Already is
too loud' . . .

The 1939 season ran from 1 June up to 15 July, with thirty-
eight performances, and after the final curtain fell on what was to
be the last performance of opera in that theatre for the next seven
years, Christie came before the curtain to utter an idiosyncratic
valedictory. There was, he told the audience, 'serious news'. With
rumours of war in all the papers, the audience stirred uneasily. But
the news which Christie felt could not wait until Glyndebourne's
patrons returned home was news from Lord's, not from Downing
Street: for the first time since 1908, the annual Eton–Harrow
cricket match had been won by Harrow.

Sir Rudolf Bing, *5000 Nights at the Opera*, Hamish Hamilton, 1972,
pp. 55, 64

*In Germany in the eighteenth century Dresden was the musical capital,
outshining Berlin itself:*

In 1756, the year of its zenith, the Dresden *Kapelle* included
nineteen singers and an orchestra of forty-six players, along with a
ballet of eight *premiers danseurs* and twenty-two *figurants*, and an
Italian comedy of fifteen actors and singers: what with the court
composers, the theatre architects and scene painters, the pensioners

and the miscellaneous officials the total personnel numbered no less than 146 ... The salaries of all the members of the *Kapelle* totalled over 100,000 thalers in 1756, and taking into account the cost of the operatic and theatrical productions, along with the incidental expenses of court concerts and serenatas, and the usual presents or 'gratifications' to the singers, we arrive at the round figure of 200,000 thalers, equivalent to about £90,000, as the amount the Elector spent on his music in a year. This was almost exactly equal to the expenditure of Charles Eugene in his heyday at Stuttgart, and both rulers were the scandal of Europe for the enormous sums they lavished on these evanescent pleasures. Nor did Frederick Augustus make any attempt to keep a check on these expenses ...

[In Berlin] an opera was the first requisite of a civilized court and Frederick [the Great] lost no time in dispatching [Carl Heinrich] Graun to Italy to collect a company of singers, and in commissioning Knobelsdorff to draw up plans for an opera house ... On 7 December 1742 the great opera house was opened with Graun's *Cesare e Cleopatra* ... It was a large building, with majestic Corinthian porticoes, 300 feet long and 100 feet broad, standing on a bastion of the old fortifications, free on all sides, so that a hundred coaches could draw up round it. There were large foyers and saloons ... and the staircases were so wide that sedan chairs could ascend right up to the fourth tier of boxes ...

During the Carnival, which usually began some time in December and lasted for two months, operas were performed twice a week, on Mondays and Fridays: two new operas were produced each season, so that each had some eight performances, or less, if they did not please the king. The performances began at six in the evening, lasting exactly three hours, and admission was free, by private invitation from the lord chamberlain. These invitations were distributed regularly, first to the civil and military authorities and the remainder to those of high rank and to distinguished strangers; but despite severe threats there soon grew up a considerable black-market traffic in the tickets ... The opera consisted almost entirely of female singers, usually sopranos, and castrati; for tenors and basses were quite insignificant ... It is obvious that a special place in Frederick's affections was reserved for the castrati, and for *Cesare e Cleopatra* there came from Italy three choice specimens, called with affectionate Italian diminutions Porporino, Paolino and Stefanino. Of these undoubtedly the best was Antonio Uberti *detto* Porporino, and Frederick became very excited about him, writing cantatas and arias for him and inviting him constantly to Potsdam for the evening concerts . . .

All the libretti, all the designs for the scenery and costumes had to be submitted to the king and approved by him . . . It was natural that Frederick should be meticulous over all the details of the opera management, for the opera was carried on entirely at the royal expense.

Alan Yorke-Long, *Music at Court*, Weidenfeld & Nicolson, 1954,
pp. 77, 79, 109–10, 116–17

Berlioz, always hypercritical, was underwhelmed when he sat through an opera in Berlin in 1843:

In Berlin, unhappily, as in Paris and everywhere else, there are days when there seems to be a kind of tacit agreement between artists and public that the performance shall be in greater or lesser degree trifling and perfunctory. Many seats in the house are empty and many desks in the orchestra unoccupied. These are the nights when the leading singers dine out, give balls, go hunting, etcetera. The musicians, half asleep, merely play the notes. One or two do not even do that; they snooze, read, draw caricatures, indulge in crude tricks at the expense of their neighbours, chat to each other in normal voices – but I do not need to tell you what goes on in an orchestra on these occasions.

The actors are too exposed to take such liberties (though even that can sometimes happen), but the chorus really let themselves go. They come on sporadically, in twos or threes. Some, having arrived late at the theatre, are not yet in costume; a few, having been on duty in church during the day, shuffle on exhausted, determined not to sing a note. Everyone relaxes. High notes are put down an octave or 'marked'. All expression disappears; a steady mezzo forte is established for the evening. No one looks at the conductor's beat, and as a result there are several wrong entries and as many ragged phrases. But what does it signify? The public never notice. The director knows nothing about it. If the composer complains, he is laughed at and waved aside as an interfering busybody.

Hector Berlioz, *Memoirs*, translated by David Cairns, Gollancz, 1969,

p. 323

Mark Twain commented flippantly on the German enjoyment of opera:

There is nothing the Germans like so much as an opera. They like it, not in a mild and moderate way, but with their whole hearts. This is a legitimate result of habit and education. Our nation will like the opera, too, by and by, no doubt. One in fifty of those who attend our operas likes it already, perhaps, but I think a good many of the other forty-nine go in order to learn to like it, and the rest in order to be able to talk knowingly about it. The latter usually hum the airs while they are being sung, so that their neighbours may perceive that they have been to operas before. The funerals of these do not occur often enough.

Mark Twain, *A Tramp Abroad*, 1880, Chapter 6

From 1927 to 1931 the manic-depressive conductor Otto Klemperer was the director of the innovative Kroll Opera in Berlin. The joint efforts of conductor, designers, and producers soon won the Kroll a reputation for radical productions. This made the Kroll a target for Nazis and extreme nationalists, who eventually succeeded in having the opera house closed down:

Klemperer's Kroll, as it was often called, so unmistakable was the personal stamp he put on it, arose out of a widely held belief that traditional opera was dying, together with the society that had given it birth. A new society demanded new forms of artistic expression, and it was in part as a means of bringing these into existence that the Kroll was set up as an artistically independent organization in 1927. At the same time it was to serve as the Volksbühne's opera house and no one seems to have paused to consider whether these aims were compatible. On both counts the Kroll became an object of controversy. Because it was regarded, by its foes as well as its friends, as an expression of a new regime and a new epoch, and because of its close links with the socialist Volksbühne, the Republikoper (as it was also called) aroused suspicion and even hatred among adherents of the old order, which had been destroyed by military defeat yet retained the loyalty of a large part of the population, especially among the middle classes.

Klemperer had been a supporter of the young republic since 1918 and vaguely radical in his political sympathies. But he was not in the least concerned with theories about art and society. His aims were at once more limited and more concrete. He wanted to abolish what he regarded as the abuses of repertory opera. He wanted to reform the staging of opera by bringing it into line with the innovations that had occurred in the spoken theatre. He wanted to introduce new works into a stagnant repertory. Above all, he sought a new unity of music and drama. Such aims were, however, sufficient to attract the wrath of traditionalists. That he himself was a Jew by birth and that of the group around him only [Ewald] Dülberg and [Ernst] Legal were 'Aryans', made it easier for the radical Right to depict the Kroll as an alien organism in German cultural life.

. . . It was only in the course of its second season that the Kroll began to fulfil its potential, notably in the production of *Der fliegende Holländer* and in Klemperer's concerts. Yet hardly had it done so than conservative and Catholic forces in the Landtag moved to close it. For the last year of its existence the Kroll was under sentence of death. That so much was achieved in such conditions says much for Klemperer's powers of leadership . . .

On 3 July [1931] the Kroll Opera finally shut its doors with a performance of *Figaro*, in which the music's underlying anguish overshadowed its merriment. As the curtain fell, the audience rose as a man. The entire company appeared on the stage, stage-hands as well as singers, musical staff as well as the orchestra, prompters as well as secretaries. Suddenly, a voice was raised above the tumult. From a proscenium box, Edgar Schmidt-Pauli, a friend of Klemperer from his Hamburg days, launched into a denunciation of the Landtag, the government, and, above all, the Finance Minister, Höpker-Aschoff. [Hans] Curjel replied from the stage and, whenever Klemperer's name was mentioned, it was drowned in cheers. But no word came from Buenos Aires [where Klemperer was conducting], [Heinz] Tietjen was in Bayreuth, and even the Kultusministerium did not trouble to send a representative. In its last hour the Kroll was abandoned by the men who had done most to launch it on its course.

Curjel wrote what must have been a bitter letter of reproach to Klemperer, who replied from Buenos Aires on 13 August at unwonted length . . .

'I wanted to send a telegram at the time of the final performance, but what was I to say? Every word seemed banal, even ridiculous. After all that I had *fruitlessly done* and *sacrificed* for our theatre, it seemed impossible to spin words. There are deaths at which one cannot even offer condolences. You reproach me on my tactics in my efforts to save our theatre. How unjust! If a tactic has no success that does not mean that it is wrong . . . In clear awareness that I was right, I brought my suit for *our opera* and my rightness is not lessened by the fact that so far I have failed *legally* and lost a lot of money . . . For the rest I can only say five words that even my enemies cannot deny: I did what I could.'

Peter Heyworth, *Otto Klemperer: His Life and Times, I: 1885–1933*, Cambridge University Press, 1983, pp. 372–5

CENTRAL EUROPE

In the late seventeenth century the Habsburg capital of Vienna, ruled by Emperor Leopold I, was a major centre of operatic activity:

It was apt and in character that he should have contributed music to the gigantic operatic spectacle provided to celebrate his own marriage in 1666 to the Infanta Margareta of Spain.

This wedding entertainment was a stupendous affair of a prologue and five acts by Antonio Cesti called *Il pomo d'oro* ... concerning the Golden Apple thrown by Discord among the Gods as a prize to be awarded to the most beautiful and which led to the situation familiar as and consequent on the Judgement of Paris . . .

For *Il pomo d'oro* [the stage architect Ludovico] Burnacini erected a theatre in the main square of the Imperial Palace . . . There was room for 2000 spectators, who were seated in a spacious parterre and in three tiers of galleries on three sides of the rectangular structure. The theatre stayed in position, a wonderfully luxurious example of theatrical baroque, until 1683 when, under the threat of Turkish attacks on the city, it was demolished.

Burnacini's day-to-day job, however, was not so much the construction of theatres as the designing of the scenes and machines for the productions which took place in them. These were on a splendid and lavishly imaginative scale which all the resources of Hollywood have barely equalled yet. A 'cast of thousands' was nothing; it was a daily occurrence. And if elephants could be dragged into the story on the slightest pretext then so much the better, for visual effect, the impact of the numerous intricately organized combats and cavalry movements, the spectacular sieges and cannonades, the triumphal cars and endless apotheoses which were always a feature of these productions were considered to be as important as, if not actually more important than the music. Some idea of the money spent by the emperor on a single opera like *Il pomo d'oro* to amuse his wedding guests can be gathered from the cost of the décor alone, which amounted to £50,000 – a really huge sum in those days . . .

Leopold I reigned for forty-seven years and in that time more than four hundred different operas were performed in Vienna, some of them importations from Italy, but the vast majority of them specially composed for the emperor. 'For the emperor': it is an important phrase, for opera at this time was entirely an entertainment for the court, and the works composed were nearly all intended for performance in connection with a variety of court festivities and occasions. They did not, in consequence, reach a very wide audience.

Spike Hughes, *Great Opera Houses*, Weidenfeld & Nicolson, 1956,
pp. 32–3

Outside Vienna standards were less sumptuous. In July 1864 Bedřich Smetana wrote a newspaper article attacking the conditions prevailing in Prague's Provisional Theatre:

Enthusiasts exclaim 'Thank God we have a Provisional Theatre!' But let us pray to God to deliver us from it soon! . . . How can we possibly play opera in a house as small as ours? In *Les Huguenots* the armies barely number eight on each side . . . and thus provoke laughter. The singers are pressed so closely together in the foreground that everyone must be careful not to hurt his neighbour when he turns. As for the chorus – they stand either in a straight line at the footlights or in a semicircle at the back packed tightly against each other, singing their parts without movement of leg or arm for fear of injuring the adjoining person . . . The narrowness of the stage is to blame, and behind it is even worse, for singers have no room to prepare an entrance. The acoustics are very different from those of our larger houses and when an artist has grown accustomed to a small stage area it takes many tiring hours and many errors before they become used to a larger one. Another evil is the orchestral pit – a space which barely deserves that name! Whoever hears the strings when their numbers are barely suitable for the production of chamber, let alone garden, music! There are four first violins, four seconds, two violas, two cellos and one double-bass only! We can never hear the musicians play as a body or in their correct proportions. The brass and wind smother the strings completely. In such conditions it is hard to speak of higher artistic standards. The most important ingredient of the opera house, the pit, they forgot when building the theatre. Perhaps they never considered opera at all . . . If we are to build a Czech opera

we must build a theatre which is suitable for opera and the sooner
the better.

Quoted in Brian Large, *Smetana*, Duckworth, 1970, p. 135

*Vienna was always notorious for its intrigues, which have brought the
careers of more than one director of the State Opera to an early close. Bruno
Walter was outmanoeuvred in the early 1930s:*

Toward the end of Schalk's directorial epoch, the voices of those
who wanted to see me at the head of the Vienna State Opera
became ever more urgent. Most weighty were the words of Dr
Julius Korngold, the musical critic of the *Neue Freie Presse*. As for
myself, my instinct made me keep entirely aloof – I did not lift a
finger. The voice of a large part of the press and the enthusiastic
demonstrations of the audiences at almost every one of my concerts
gladdened and touched me, but it was quite clear to me that the
Ministry of Education of a state ruled by the Christian Socialist
Party would not be likely to view my appointment with favour,
nor would it be at all convenient to me to have the ministry as my
superior authority. At any rate, the general demand for me was so
urgent that the minister could not very well ignore it. And so I
received a letter, addressed to me at his request, inquiring if I were
ready to enter into negotiations and suggesting that I should state
my terms. In a very guardedly written reply I confined myself to the
statement that I would not be averse to discussing the matter, but
I purposely refrained from saying a word about my terms. General
Director Schneiderhan, who had been exercising the functions of
the former general manager during the last years of Schalk's
incumbency, now wrote me requesting a secret personal discussion.
I replied by suggesting the restaurant of the Western Railway
Station as an inconspicuous place for our meeting. I was there, but
nobody showed up. Some time later, I received a written apology
from Schneiderhan, stating that my suggestion had reached him
too late. I naturally made no further reply. When I had left Vienna
again, a notice appeared in the papers to the effect that my

excessive financial demands had prevented my appointment. This
truly Viennese intrigue was launched by the same man who,
almost thirty years before, had doubted my ability to 'lead a
riflemen's band' and had in the meantime advanced from musical
reviewer to confidential man of the Ministry of Education. I wrote
to the Minister, asking for an official correction, but nothing came
of it.

Bruno Walter, *Theme and Variations*, translated by James A. Galston,

Hamish Hamilton, 1947, pp. 321-2

*Nor did the American conductor Lorin Maazel manage to survive as
director of the Vienna State Opera:*

It is widely rumoured that when Lorin Maazel finished conducting
Turandot last month, his last appearance as director of the opera,
champagne corks flew in a nearby hotel as those who forced him
to abandon his four-year contract before the end of his second
season celebrated his final performance in the Vienna house . . .

He had reduced the number of operas performed in the house
by a quarter in an attempt to raise standards. He had recklessly
promised, in a euphoric interview before arriving in Vienna, that
every night would be a gala evening.

His most unforgivable act of all for the Viennese was his claim
to be the second most important man in Austria. The first was the
Chancellor – no mention was ever made of Austria's President, Dr
Rudolf Kirschläger.

One mishap followed another, and the Viennese settled down to
their favourite pastime – the character assassination of maestros.
Spearheading this attack was Dr Franz Endler, the *éminence grise* of
Vienna's music critics and the cultural editor of the conservative
Vienna daily, *Die Presse*.

Dr Endler, who is quick to emphasize the role of his paper in
the termination of both Gustav Mahler's and Herbert von Karajan's
careers as opera directors in Vienna, feels personally grieved that
Maazel did not seek his support as soon as he arrived. Mahler, he

notes mournfully, saw the critic Hanslick within hours of his arrival in Vienna . . .

Dr Endler's theme was taken up, not least by the small but vociferous claques in the standing audience whose speciality – laughter alternating with boos resounding from the most resonant quarters of the house – became a regular feature at several of Maazel's performances.

The alliance cemented between Dr Endler and Herr Helmut Zilk, the Minister for Cultural Affairs, was more effective, if less public. Despite a lack of any musical experience, the minister accused Maazel of hiring singers who were untried on stage, although, according to Maazel, they turned out to have 200 performances and a Glyndebourne season behind them. Unabashed, Herr Zilk announced that the director's contract would be under review.

Maazel's reaction was to issue an open letter to five Austrian newspapers protesting at unwarranted interference in his affairs. Only one, the *Salzburger Nachrichten*, published the letter, while Dr Endler daily renewed his attacks in *Die Presse*.

Although, some disasters aside, Maazel's directorship had blown away the cobwebs which had gathered around the house, the conductor felt compelled to resign . . .

Maazel admits he underestimated his opponents and the great difference between the Austrians and the Germans. 'I never realized how Balkan this place is,' he says . . . Attempts to reform the house, confronted by a system of laws which gave most employees of the opera house the complacent diffidence of permanent civil servants, which in Austria they are, inevitably foundered.

Richard Bassett, The Times, 13 July 1984

SINGERS

3: Eighteenth-century Singers

Singing is near miraculous because it is the mastering of what is otherwise a pure instrument of egotism: the human voice.

Hugo von Hofmannsthal

Of the castrati who dominated eighteenth-century opera none was more acclaimed than Farinelli (1705–82):

Farinelli was pure singer and although tall and handsome, clearly made no attempt to act. Like a Flagstad or Melba, his genius lay in the perfect production of a glorious sound, built on a rock-solid musical foundation . . . A tiny doubt creeps in that he might have been a little dull after a while.

London fell: the opera orchestra were so thunderstruck when they heard him that they could not play; a noble lady in the audience cried out after an aria, 'One God, one Farinelli!'; Hogarth represents him in 'The Rake's Progress', surrounded by hangers-on; the Prince of Wales sent him 'a fine wrought gold snuff-box, richly set with diamonds and rubies . . .' In all, he probably made about £5000 a year while in London. Handel, in the rival opera house, was virtually ruined, but even Farinelli could not long stem the rot that had set into the Italian opera in London. The public were at bottom tired of it, and by 1737 the sensation of 1734 was said to be singing to £35 worth of takings.

Rupert Christiansen, *Prima Donna*, Bodley Head, 1984, p. 32

That omniscient historian of music, Dr Charles Burney, was also staggered by Farinelli's gifts:

No vocal performer of the present century has been more

unanimously allowed by professional critics, as well as general celebrity, to have been gifted with a voice of such uncommon power,
sweetness, extent, and agility, as Carlo Broschi *detto* Farinelli.
Nicolini, Senesino, and Carestini gratified the eye as much by the
dignity, grace and propriety of their action and deportment, as the
ear by the judicious use of a few notes within the limits of a small
compass of voice; but Farinelli, without the assistance of significant
gestures or graceful attitudes, enchanted and astonished his hearers
by the force, extent, and mellifluous tones of the mere organ,
when he had nothing to execute, articulate, or express. But
though during the time of his singing he was as motionless as a
statue, his voice was so active that no intervals were too close,
too wide, or too rapid for his execution. It seems as if the composers of these times were unable to invent passages sufficiently
difficult to display his powers, or the orchestras to accompany
him in many of those which had been composed for his peculiar
talent . . .

There was none of all Farinelli's excellences by which he so far
surpassed all other singers, and astonished the public, as his *messa
di voce*, or swell; which, by the natural formation of his lungs, and
artificial economy of breath, he was able to protract to such a
length as to excite incredulity even in those who heard him; who,
though unable to detect the artifice, imagined him to have had the
latent help of some instrument by which the tone was continued
while he renewed his powers by respiration.

Dr Charles Burney, *A General History of Music* (1789), Dover, 1957, II,
pp. 789–90

*Early in his career, Farinelli, in Rome, went into competition with a
trumpet:*

Here he performed the celebrated vocal feat which at once placed
him above all his competitors. In an opera which was then
performed, there was a song with obbligato accompaniment for
the trumpet, sung by Farinelli, and accompanied by a great per-

former on that instrument. Every night there was a contest between the singer and the trumpet-player . . . At length both
parties seemed resolved to bring it to an issue. After each of them
had swelled out a note, and tried to rival the other in brilliancy
and force, they both had a swell and a shake together, in the
interval of a third, which was continued so long that both seemed
to be exhausted; and the trumpeter at length gave it up, imagin-
ing, probably, that his antagonist was as much spent as himself.
But Farinelli, with the greatest apparent ease, and with a smile
on his face . . . broke out all at once in the same breath with
fresh vigour, and not only continued the swell and shake upon
the note, but started off into a series of rapid and difficult
divisions, till his voice was drowned by the acclamations of the
audience.

> George Hogarth, *Memoirs of the Musical Drama*, Bentley, 1838, I,
>
> pp. 415-16

A rival singer showed touching admiration for Farinelli on stage:

Farinelli and Senesino were both in England together in 1734, but
being engaged at different theatres on the same evenings, they had
not an opportunity of hearing each other sing, until, by some
sudden stage freak, they were both engaged to sing on the same
stage. Senesino had the part of a furious tyrant to represent:
Farinelli that of an unfortunate hero in chains; but in his first song
he so softened the obdurate heart of his oppressor, that Senesino,
quite forgetting his stage character, ran to Farinelli and embraced
him, much to the surprise of the audience.

> Frederick Crowest, *A Book of Musical Anecdotes*, Bentley, 1878, II,
>
> p. 31

*Handel prepares to take on the redoubtable Italian soprano Francesca
Cuzzoni (1698–1770):*

During the summer of 1722, Handel gave the earliest important demonstration of those capabilities in business which were at last to make him the first great operatic impresario. He understood that something more than a fine new opera was needed to re-establish his name with the patrons of His Majesty's ... He must introduce a new and unmistakable star, a star surrounded in advance by glamour and the clangour of elaborate publicity. He had heard good reports of a Parmesan soprano named Francesca Cuzzoni. She had, at the age of nineteen, made a brilliant Venetian début in 1719, since when she had been singing to notable acclaim throughout Italy. So Handel dispatched Sandoni, a cembalist from the opera orchestra, to fetch her from Italy, authorizing him to guarantee her £2000 a year if necessary. It was a daring, perhaps a desperate, gamble ...

When Handel first looked upon Francesca Cuzzoni, he must have felt his heart sink. He had already heard that the soprano was spoiled, headstrong, and silly. Now he saw that she was inordinately ugly as well. 'She was short,' Horace Walpole later wrote of her, 'and squat, with a cross face, but fine complexion; was not a good actress; dressed ill, and was silly and fantastical.' She did not appear a prima donna likely to capture the fickle hearts of the gentlemen out front at His Majesty's. But Handel had staked heavily on her, and he intended to win. He addressed himself immediately to the task of subjecting her to his will, of making her perform his music as he wished.

'Oh, Madame,' he is reported to have said to her in French, 'I well know that you are a veritable female devil, but I myself, I shall have you know, am Beelzebub, chief of the devils.' Then he told her to sing 'Falsa immagine', the luscious aria he had designed especially for her first appearance on the stage in Ottone. Cuzzoni sang it, but not as Handel had heard it in his imagination. So he told her how to sing it, and she refused. Handel was a big man, and Cuzzoni, though plump, was small. So he seized her around the waist and told her peremptorily that she would sing 'Falsa immagine' exactly as he wished it sung, or he would drop her out of the window, towards which he began to move her. Cowed, if not terrified, Cuzzoni agreed. And then Handel must have felt true delight, for the reports of Cuzzoni's voice had not been exaggerated: it was one of the most beautiful he ever heard.

Herbert Weinstock, *Handel*, Knopf, 1946, pp. 113–14

The rivalry between Cuzzoni and Faustina Bordoni (1697–1781) became more significant than the performances themselves:

It is told by Horace Walpole that his mother, Lady Walpole, had them at her house to sing in a concert at which an assemblage of the first people in the kingdom were present. She was under the greatest difficulty how to settle the precedence . . . The knot could not be untied, but it was cut by the following expedient. Finding it impossible to prevail on the one to sing while the other was present, she took Faustina to a remote part of the house under the pretext of showing her some curious china, during which time the company obtained a song from Cuzzoni, who supposed that her rival had quitted the field. A similar device was practised in order to get Cuzzoni out of the room while Faustina performed.

George Hogarth, *Memoirs of the Musical Drama*, Bentley, 1838, I,

p. 410

But Cuzzoni's career came to a miserable end:

In the *London Daily Post* of 7 September 1741, there appeared a startling piece of intelligence: 'We hear from Italy that the famous singer, Mrs C-z-ni, is under sentence of death to be beheaded, for poisoning her husband.' The sentence, if ever pronounced, was never put into execution. Seven years after this, in 1749, she appeared for the third and last time in England, when she took a benefit concert, on 18 May, at the little theatre in the Haymarket . . . She issued a preliminary advertisement, avouching her 'pressing debts' and her 'desire to pay them' as the reason for her asking the benefit; which, she declared, should be the last she would ever trouble the public with. Old, poor, and almost deprived of her voice in her infirmities, her attempt to revive the interest of the public in her favour was a miserable failure; her star was set for ever, and she was obliged to return to Holland more wretched than she came. She had scarcely reappeared there, when she was again thrown into prison for debt; but by entering into an agreement to sing at the theatre every night, under surveillance, she was enabled to obtain her release. Her recklessness and improvidence had brought her to a pitiable condition: and in her latter days, after a career of splendour, caprice, and extravagance, she was obliged to subsist, it is said, by button-making; she died in frightful indigence, the recipient of charity at a hospital at Bologna, in 1770.

Ellen Creathorne Clayton, *Queens of Song*, Smith, Elder, 1863, I,
pp. 62–3, 75–6

Caterina Gabrielli, born in 1730, handled herself with greater aplomb, displaying all the hauteur of the stereotypical prima donna:

Gabrielli quitted Vienna in 1765, laden with riches, and went to Sicily, where she excited the same enthusiasm, and exercised her caprice, regardless of consequences. Her insolence knew no bounds, yet no one dared to check her; she demanded and obtained whatever terms she chose, and sang when, where, and how she pleased; sometimes declining to sing altogether, or sending her sister, Francesca, whom she retained as second singer, to perform her parts. No matter with whom she came in contact, she compelled them to give way to her whims. On one occasion, the Viceroy of Sicily invited her to dine with him and with some of the highest nobility of Palermo, and at the appointed time, finding she did not make her appearance, the viceroy dispatched a servant to remind her of her promise. She was found lounging on her sofa with a book in her hand; and on the man respectfully presenting his message, she affected to have entirely forgotten the invitation: an insult which the viceroy was at first inclined to pardon; but when, during the opera, she acted with the most intolerable negligence, and sang all the airs *sotto voce*, he was so indignant that he threatened to visit her with some token of his displeasure. This did not make the slightest impression on the stubborn *cantatrice*: she declared that she might be forced to *cry*, but not to *sing*. The viceroy, exasperated by her impudent obstinacy, at length committed her to prison for twelve days. She gave costly entertainments, paid all the debts of her fellow-prisoners, and distributed large sums among the indigent, besides singing all the best songs in her finest style every day, until the term of her detention expired, when she came forth amidst the shouts and rejoicings of the grateful poor whom she had benefited while in jail . . .

[She] went to Russia, where Catherine II received her with every token of favour, and readily engaged her. But when the terms of her salary came to be discussed, the fair Italian demanded five thousand ducats. 'Five thousand ducats!' repeated the empress in amazement. 'Why, I do not give more than that to one of my field-marshals!' 'Very well,' replied the Gabrielli, with her customary nonchalance; 'your majesty may get your field-marshals to sing for you.' This audacious reply made the Empress laugh, and instead of dispatching the impertinent *cantatrice* to exercise her voice in the clear atmosphere of Siberia, she immediately granted the required sum.

Ellen Creathorne Clayton, *Queens of Song*, Smith, Elder, 1863, I, pp. 100–103

Nancy Storace was born in London in 1765, the daughter of a Neapolitan musician. She soon became a rival of the far more celebrated Marchesi:

[In Florence] the famous Marchesi was engaged at the Pergola Theatre, and Nancy was engaged as 'second woman' in the opera. She had not, apparently, all the qualities necessary to ensure success to a female singer; there was an unpleasant 'harshness' in her countenance, though her physiognomy was striking when lighted up by lively emotions; her figure was clumsy, her manner totally unfitted for serious opera, and there was a certain coarseness in her voice. Her natural style was, therefore, necessarily the comic, for which she had an innate humour; and she was an excellent actress; though her musical science was such that she could sing any kind of music.

Marchesi did not much like her, perhaps because she was not pretty; and soon they came to open warfare. It happened that Bianchi had composed for Marchesi the celebrated cavatina, '*Sembianza amabile del mio bel sole*'. Marchesi sang this with exquisite taste, and in one of the passages he ran up a flight of semitone octaves, giving the last note with such tremendous power, that it became famous under the title of '*la bomba di Marchesi*'. Immediately after he sang this in the opera, Signora Storace had to sing an air of a similar character, and fired with emulation, she took it into her head that she would throw out 'a *bomba*', and she executed her song with a brilliancy which amazed and enraptured the audience. Poor Marchesi was furious at being eclipsed, and indignant at anybody attempting even to rival him, more particularly the 'second woman'; and Campigli, the impresario, requested her to discontinue the air. She peremptorily refused. 'I have as good a right to show the power of my *bomba* as anybody else,' was her reply. Marchesi declared that if she did not quit the theatre, he would; and the manager, fearing to lose a singer of celebrity like Marchesi, sided with the imperious signor; so poor Nancy was dismissed.

Ellen Creathorne Clayton, *Queens of Song*, Smith, Elder, 1863, I,
pp. 210–11

4: Pasta and Malibran

The opera ain't over till the fat lady sings.

Dan Cook, *Washington Post*, 3 June 1978

Two sopranos in particular filled those who heard them with awe: Pasta and Malibran. Giuditta Pasta, born near Milan in 1797, did not have an immediately ingratiating voice. Her first appearances were not a success, so she returned to her vocal studies:

Madame Pasta was then laying the foundation of one of the most dazzling reputations ever gained by a prima donna. By sheer industry she had extended the range of her voice to two octaves and a half; from A above the bass clef note to C flat, and even to D in alt. Her tones had become rich and sweet, except when she attempted to force them beyond their limits; her intonation was, however, never quite perfect, being occasionally a little flat. Her singing was pure, and totally divested of all spurious finery . Her voice, though it had improved wonderfully, never appeared easy and clear in the emission of certain notes, and retained a veiled quality, from which it was only freed after the first scenes. Some of her notes were sharp almost to harshness, but this defect with the greatness of genius she overcame, and even converted into a beauty; for in passages of profound passion her guttural tones were thrilling. The irregularity of her lower notes, governed thus by a perfect taste and musical tact, aided to a great extent in giving that depth of expression which was one of the principal charms of her singing . . .

Outwardly calm and sustained, though poetical and enthusiastic in temperament, the crowning excellence of her art was its grand

simplicity. Sublime and terrible as she was in the expression of
vehement passion, there was yet a measured force in the display of
her power, which was always under the control of her taste and
judgement. She never wasted energy; nor in the expression of the
deepest pathos, or the most exalted passion, did she ever exceed
the bounds of art. She was always vigorous, but never violent;
always supremely graceful, but never artificial or affected; and she
was always greatest when she had the greatest difficulties to
encounter . . .

Her great triumph was in *Otello* . . . Her transitions from hope
to terror, from supplication to scorn, culminating in her vehement
exclamation '*Sono innocente!*' electrified the audience: no language
could convey an idea of the beauty, the intensity, the sublimity of
her acting. Indeed, throughout the final scene, her acting was the
perfection of tragic beauty: her last frenzied looks, when, blinded
by her dishevelled hair and bewildered with conflicting emotions,
she seems to seek fruitlessly the means of flight, were awful . . .

[On 15 May 1828] Madame Pasta attempted a daring experiment.
Selecting [Rossini's] *Otello* as the piece of the evening, she actually
appeared as the jealous Moor, Mlle Sontag being the Desdemona;
but the innovation was not liked: indeed the transposition of the
music of Otello from a tenor to a mezzo-soprano voice naturally
injured the effect of the concerted pieces; nor did the songs gain
by the change. But her acting was passionately grand.

Ellen Creathorne Clayton, *Queens of Song*, Smith, Elder, 1863, II,

pp. 4–10, 24

Stendhal was a discerning admirer of Pasta's art:

It was with astonishing skill that Madame Pasta wedded the head
voice with her chest voice. She exhibited supreme artistry in the
way she drew a vast range of delightful and thrilling effects by the
use of both types of voice. In order to brighten the colour of a
melodic phrase or alter its nuances in the twinkling of an eye, she
would use a falsetto technique right down to the midway point of

her vocal range; or she would cleverly switch from falsetto to her chest voice . . .

Pasta's head voice had characteristics entirely different from those of her chest voice. It was brilliant, swift, pure, effortless, and wonderfully light. As her voice descended, still using falsetto, the singer could *smorzare il canto* (diminish the tone) to the point that one wondered whether she was producing any sound at all . . .

She was always restrained in her use of *fioriture*, which she employed only to heighten the expressiveness of her singing. Moreover, she never used *fioriture* any longer than her artistic purposes required. I never found in her singing those lengthy embellishments that remind me somewhat of the ramblings of the garrulous and during which it seems that the singer loses her way or, having taken one route, wanders off in another direction.

Stendhal, *Life of Rossini*, chapter 35, translated by Stephen Brook

Henry Chorley appraised her with comparable astuteness:

Her voice was originally limited, husky, and weak, without charm, without flexibility, a mediocre mezzo-soprano. Though her countenance *spoke*, the features were cast in that coarse mould which is common in Italy. Her arms were fine, but her figure was short and clumsy . . .

She subjected herself to a course of severe and incessant vocal study, to subdue and to utilize her voice. To equalize it was impossible. There was a portion of the scale which differed from the rest in quality and remained to the last 'under a veil', to use the Italian term. There were notes always more or less out of tune, especially at the commencement of her performances. Out of these uncouth materials she had to compose her instrument, and then to give it flexibility. Her studies to acquire execution must have been tremendous; but the volubility and brilliancy, when acquired, gained a character of their own from the resisting peculiarities of the organ. There were a breadth, an expressiveness in her roulades, an evenness and solidity in her shake, which imparted to every

passage a significance totally beyond the reach of lighter and more
spontaneous singers . . .

There remains a strange scene to be spoken of — the last
appearance of this magnificent musical artist, when she allowed
herself, many years later, to be seduced into giving one performance at Her Majesty's Theatre, and to sing in a concert for the
Italian cause at the Royal Italian Opera. Nothing more inadvised
could have been dreamed of. Madame Pasta had long ago thrown
off the stage and all its belongings . . . Her voice, which at best
had required ceaseless watching and practice, had been long ago
given up by her. Its state of utter ruin on the night in question
passes description . . . A more painful and disastrous spectacle
could hardly be looked on . . . Among the audience, however, was
another gifted woman, who might far more legitimately have been
shocked at the utter wreck of every musical means of expression in
the singer, who might have been more naturally forgiven, if some
humour of self-glorification had made her severely just — not
worse — to an old prima donna; I mean Madame Viardot. Then,
and not until then, she was hearing Madame Pasta . . . The great
style of the singer spoke to the great singer. The first scene was
Ann Boleyn's duet with Jane Seymour . . . When, on Ann Boleyn's
hearing the coronation music for her rival, the heroine searches for
her own crown on her brow, Madame Pasta wildly turned in the
direction of the festive sounds, the old irresistible charm broke out;
nay, even in the final song, with its roulades, and its scales of shakes
ascending by a semitone, the consummate vocalist and tragedian,
able to combine form with meaning — the moment of the situation
with such personal and musical display as form an integral part of
operatic art — was indicated: at least to the apprehension of a
younger artist. 'You are right!' was Madame Viardot's quick and
heartfelt response (her eyes full of tears) to a friend beside her;
'You are right! It is like the *Cenacolo* of da Vinci at Milan — a wreck
of a picture, but the wreck of the greatest picture in the world!'

Henry Chorley, *Thirty Years' Musical Recollections* (1862), Knopf, 1926,
pp. 87–9, 92–3

Benjamin Lumley also recalls that ill-advised comeback in London in 1850:

A preliminary concert was given in the music-room of the establishment, before a select rather than numerous audience. Old admirers were there, who still recollected Madame Pasta when she was the greatest ornament of the lyric stage; younger dilettanti of the day assembled to catch the last rays of a genius which had once filled all Europe with its splendour ... She was done homage to as a queen by the circle around her: but the *artist* was, confessedly, a wreck. The fine qualities were still there, like the perfume of the spirit in the broken vase; the noble phrasing, the grandeur of expression, the classic severity of taste in the choice and use of ornament. But the voice, always thick and husky even in its prime, had lost all its volume and all command over correct intonation ...

A still severer trial attended the illustrious prima donna on the boards of the theatre. On Thursday 11 July she appeared (now 'for the last time on any stage') in a selection of 'scenes' from *Anna Bolena*. The part of the afflicted queen had been one of the greatest among her characters ... The spectacle was deeply interesting; yet it was melancholy, not to say painful, to all who could feel with true artistic sympathy. With the noble presence and the lofty air of the Pasta of old days, she moved like a mighty shadow of the past before the eyes of the spectators; but it was the 'shadow of a shade'. The qualities already mentioned – the faultless style, the finished phrasing, the grand declamation, were all greeted with something more than respect, whilst the imaginative among the audience may have figured to themselves, like clever geologists, out of the shattered remains of the great vocal Mammoth, a perfect creature of former times. But the general sentiment was one of disappointment and regret.

Benjamin Lumley, *Reminiscences of the Opera*, Hurst & Blackett, 1864,

pp. 283–5

*Maria Malibran (1808–36) was the daughter of tenor Manuel Garcia and
the sister of the soprano Pauline Viardot. When the family moved to New
York in 1826, Garcia assigned Maria the role of Desdemona in Rossini's
Otello:*

She was given six days to learn the part, and her protests were in
vain, for her father set about teaching her the role. The dress
rehearsal was fearful: Garcia's dissatisfaction with her acting in the
last scene invited a barrage of abuse. He outlined the scene as he
wanted it: 'You will do it, my daughter, and if you fail in any way
I will really strike you with my dagger!' Convinced that he meant
what he said, she played the part as he directed.

On opening night, as Otello advanced to murder her, she was
terrified to see her father holding a real knife, not the stage prop
she had expected. Forgetting the audience she screamed: *'Papa,
papa, por dios no me mates!'* She fought furiously with him, biting
his hand so hard that he screamed. Garcia later explained that he
had been unable to find the stage knife and at the last moment had
substituted one of his own. Perhaps he deliberately anticipated the
effect of a real dagger on his daughter's acting. The audience,
knowing neither Spanish nor Italian, thought this improvisation
part of the action and noticed nothing except the wonderful
realism of Maria Garcia's performance, for which she was highly
praised.

[*She repeated the interpretation two years later in Paris, thereby challenging
the supremacy of Pasta in the role.*]

Assuming the role of Desdemona on 15 April [1828] was even
more dangerous than singing Semiramide, despite the fact that it
suited her better, for to the Parisians Desdemona *was* Pasta. To
everyone's astonishment, Maria succeeded completely . . .

Maria did not attempt to duplicate Pasta's interpretation of
Shakespeare's heroine. Pasta had played her as a grown woman,
noble and resigned, in the classic tradition. Maria made her a
young girl of no more than sixteen. She gave her an innocence, a
touching weakness and vulnerability, a childish naïvety marked

with outbursts of terror and anger that sent shivers through an audience that had never before seen so realistic a conception of the part. She wept in the Willow Song, reduced her voice to an excruciatingly emotional pianissimo in the prayer – a pianissimo of such finesse that it was almost silence – and burst out 'like a thunderbolt' in the last duet with the murderous Otello. When the Moor approached with his dagger raised, Pasta had anticipated death, heroic in her virtue and courage; Maria ran from it, she leaped for the doors and windows. As Otello tried to grab her by the hair she attempted to climb the walls in her desperation and fright.

That Maria's vaunted superiority in singing was matched by an unprecedented histrionic talent stunned the Parisians. Fétis declared that the public was 'vanquished without return' by *Otello*, and Maria received the first of those hysterical ovations that would follow her to her final moment on the stage.

[*In June she chose the same part for her final performance of the season in Paris.*]

Maria was granted a farewell reception such as Paris had never before witnessed. In her own estimation she played the role of Desdemona 'better than I usually do', and she made a travesty of the law forbidding an artist to take curtain calls. At the conclusion of the second act someone threw a crown of flowers at her as she sang her aria '*S'il padre m'abbandona*' ... When the curtain fell the choristers, stage crew, and other artists crowded about her and tried to put the crown on her head, but she refused, thinking only of how she could thank the audience without breaking the law. As the curtain rose for the third act, she stood on the stage, head bowed, with the crown in her hands. The theatre exploded with an ovation that lasted for four minutes, and at the conclusion of the performance the audience remained, applauding and calling for La Malibran. The curtain was again raised so that the manager could explain the law regarding curtain calls, but no sooner had he opened his mouth than the audience booed and hissed him off the stage. The students in the theatre began smashing the benches together while the ladies stood in the boxes calling and waving their handkerchiefs. When the commissioner of police appeared and attempted to mount the stage, he was grabbed by the neck and dragged back before he could forbid Maria to reappear.

By this time [the impresario] Laurent had called the commissioner into the wings and demanded that he either address the uncontrolled crowd or accept liability for the havoc being done to the theatre. Frightened at the noise, and fearful of being attacked by the excited crowd, the official retreated, and in disgust Laurent told Maria to greet the audience. The hysteria that met her was such that she took the time to write [her husband] Eugène about it at two that morning. 'I can't let this moment pass without giving you the comfort of learning about the most beautiful triumph that has ever been seen in years,' she told him . . .

Maria Malibran was twenty years old.

Howard Bushnell, *Maria Malibran*, Pennsylvania State University Press,
1979, pp. 24–5, 72–3, 75–6

Maria Malibran's energy and determination were remarkable, even in circumstances when they were not called for:

One evening she had promised Mme Merlin to sing at a party, when [Edouard] Robert [the co-director of the Théâtre Italien in Paris] approached her about a benefit scheduled for that night at which she was expected to appear. An argument ensued and management won. 'Very well,' acquiesced the disgruntled singer. 'I will sing at the theatre because I have to, but I will sing at Mme Merlin's because I want to.' She kept her word. After singing *Tancredi* she arrived at the party, sang several songs for the guests, and partied until dawn. Returning home she slept until noon, rode horseback all afternoon, and appeared at the theatre again that evening. No sooner was she in costume as Arsace than she fainted from exhaustion . . . Robert, both furious and frantic, applied ammonia to her lips, and she regained consciousness, but her mouth was badly blistered. With the audience waiting, it was too late to change the programme. Rising from her couch Maria examined the damage in her mirror. 'Don't worry,' she said calmly. 'I'll fix this.' Picking up a pair of scissors she carefully broke the blisters and cut away the dead skin. A few moments later she was on stage, singing Arsace to Lalande's Semiramide.

Howard Bushnell, *Maria Malibran*, Pennsylvania State University Press,

1979, p. 130

Bellini wrote to his friend Francesco Florimo about his visit to London in 1833, where he saw Malibran interpret one of his own operas. The letter's authenticity is questionable, unfortunately:

I lack words, dear Florimo, to tell you how my poor music was tortured, torn to shreds, and – wanting to express myself in the Neapolitan way – flayed . . . Only when Malibran was singing did I recognize *La sonnambula*. But in the allegro of the final scene, and precisely at the words '*Ah! m'abbraccia*', she put such emphasis upon that phrase and expressed such truth by it that first it surprised me and then delighted me so much that, forgetting that I was in an English theatre, and not remembering the social customs and the consideration that I owed to the lady on whose right I was seated in her second-tier *loge*, and disregarding the modesty that a composer should show even if he doesn't feel it, I was the first to shout, at the top of my voice: '*Viva, viva, brava, brava*', and to clap my hands as much as I could. That southern, even volcanic, transport of mine, quite new in this cold, calculating, and stiff country, surprised and provoked the curiosity of the blond sons of Albion, who asked one another who the bold fellow might be who was permitting himself so much. But after some moments, when it was recognized (I wouldn't know any way of telling you how) that I was the composer of *La sonnambula*, I was given such a welcome that out of discretion I must be silent about it even with you. Not satisfied with applauding me frantically – even I cannot remember how often – or I with thanking them from the *loge* where I was, they wanted me at all costs upon the stage, whither I was all but dragged by a crowd of young noblemen ... The first person to advance to meet me was Malibran, and, throwing her arms around my neck, she said to me in the most exalted transport of joy, with those four notes of mine: '*Ah! m'abbraccia!*' and said nothing more. My emotion was at its climax; I thought that I was in Paradise; I could not utter a word, but stood there stunned ... The tumultuous and repeated plaudits of an English audience, which becomes frantic once it has warmed up, called me to the front of the stage; we presented ourselves holding one another by the hand ... From that moment, I became an intimate friend of Malibran; she shows me all the admiration that she has for my music, and I [show] her what I feel for her immense talent; and I have promised to write an opera for her on a subject to her liking.

Quoted in Herbert Weinstock, *Bellini*, Knopf, 1971, pp. 144–5

Malibran had irritated the impresario Alfred Bunn by skipping a rehearsal, but decided to make amends during the actual performance:

I went into her dressing-room previous to the commencement of the third act, to ask how she felt, and she replied, 'Very tired, but' (and here her eye of fire suddenly lighted up) 'you angry devil, if you will contrive to get me a pint of porter in the desert scene, you shall have an encore to your finale.' Had I been dealing with any other performer, I should perhaps have hesitated in complying with a request that might have been dangerous in its application at the moment; but to check *her* powers was to annihilate them. I therefore arranged that, behind the pile of drifted sand on which she falls in a state of exhaustion, towards the close of the desert scene, a small aperture should be made in the stage; and it is a fact that, from underneath the stage through that aperture, a pewter pint of porter was conveyed to the parched lips of this rare child of song, which so revived her, after the terrible exertion the scene led to, that she electrified the audience, and had strength to repeat the charm, with the finale to the *Maid of Artois*. The novelty of the circumstance so tickled her fancy, and the draught itself was so extremely refreshing, that it was arranged, during the subsequent run of the opera, for the negro slave, at the head of the governor's procession, to have in the gourd suspended to his neck the same quantity of the same beverage, to be applied to her lips, on his first beholding the apparently dying Isoline.

Alfred Bunn, *The Stage: Both Before and Behind the Curtain*, London, 1840,
II, pp. 68–70

Malibran's death was as spectacular as her life. Here is Sir George Smart's contemporary account of her final illness:

Malibran's death may have been accelerated by her extraordinary exertions whilst singing in a duet with Madame Caradori Allen; they settled the manner at rehearsal as to how it was to be sung, but when the time came Madame Caradori Allen made some deviation; this prompted Malibran to do the same, in which she displayed most wonderful execution. During the well-deserved encore she turned to me and said, 'If I sing again it will kill me.' 'Then do not,' I replied; 'let me address the audience.' 'No,' said she, 'I will sing it again and annihilate her.' She was taken ill with a fainting fit after the duet and carried into her room. Here she was partly undressed. She sent for me to say she would sing in the second act. Upon my reminding her of her undress she consented to be carried to her inn, and as I took hold of her arm, she said she had been bled by some medical man in the theatre, which I was informed by Dr Billing ought not to have been done but wine should have been given her. She was carried on her couch to the inn.

Malibran was brought on a couch to the church, intending to sing in the *Messiah* on the last day's performance, but was too weak to come into the orchestra; she was therefore carried back to the inn. Previous to leaving it, whilst in bed, she sent for the landlady to hear that she was capable of singing. She sang to her one of the songs in the *Messiah* and probably this was the last time her vocal powers were heard.

[*A week later she was dead at the age of twenty-eight.*]

Sir George Smart, *Leaves from the Journals of Sir George Smart*, edited by
H.B. and C.L.E. Cox, Longmans, 1907, pp. 282–3

The painter Eugène Delacroix encounters the celebrated musician Manuel Garcia, Malibran's brother, but refuses to share the adulation for the great soprano:

[27 January 1847:] Garcia in defending the role of sensibility and of true passion, thinks of his sister, Mme Malibran. He tells us as proof of her talent as a great actress that she never knew how she would play. Thus, in *Romeo* when she reaches the tomb of Juliet, she would sometimes stop at a pillar, on entering, in a burst of grief; at other times she would throw herself down sobbing before the stone, etc.; she thus achieved moments full of energy and seemingly full of truth, but it also happened that she would seem exaggerated and faulty in her timing, and as a consequence unbearable. I do not recall ever having seen her *noble* . . . It seems that she was endlessly seeking new effects in a situation. If one takes that course, one is never finished: that is never the way of consummate talent . . .

Mme Malibran, in *Mary Stuart*, is brought before her rival, Elizabeth, by Leicester, who implores her to humiliate herself before her rival. She finally consents to do so, and, falling on her knees, gives herself to the deepest supplication; but, outraged by the inflexible hardness of Elizabeth, she would rise up impetuously and throw herself into a fury which, he said, produced the greatest effect. She tore the handkerchief and even her gloves to tatters. There again is one of those effects to which a great artist will never descend: they are the kind which delight people in the boxes and afford a passing reputation to those who are willing to indulge themselves that way . . .

Garcia, in speaking of la Pasta, classed her among the cold and controlled talents, *plastic*, as he said. As to that word 'plastic', what he should have said was ideal. At Milan, she had created *Norma* with extraordinary brilliancy; people no longer talked of la *Pasta*, but la *Norma*. Mme Malibran arrives, she demands that role for her début, and she succeeds, with that piece of childishness. The public, divided in the beginning, carries her to the clouds, and la *Pasta* was forgotten; it was la Malibran who had become la *Norma*, and I have no difficulty in believing it. The people whose minds do not rise very high, and who are not at all difficult in matters of taste — which is to say, unfortunately, the majority — will always prefer talents of the type possessed by la Malibran.

Eugène Delacroix, *Journal*, translated by Walter Pach, Crown, 1948,

pp. 135–7

5: Early-nineteenth-century Singers

What nationality was Marietta Spinach, who sang in *Lucia* in 1840?

Spike Hughes, *Great Opera Houses*, p. 262

Angelica Catalani (1780–1849) made her début at the age of sixteen:

Tall, and of fine proportion, dazzlingly fair, with beautiful blue eyes, and lovely yet noble-looking features, she was like a painter's ideal ... Her voice was a soprano of the purest quality, embracing a compass of nearly three octaves, from G to F, and so powerful that no band could overwhelm its tones ... One of her favourite caprices of ornament was to imitate the swell and fall of a bell, making her tones sweet through the air with the most delicious undulation, and, using her voice at pleasure, she would shower her graces in an absolutely wasteful profusion. Her greatest defect was that, while the ear was bewildered with the beauty and tremendous power of her voice, the feelings were untouched: she never touched the heart ... With a prodigious volume and richness of tone, and a marvellous rapidity of vocalization, she could execute brilliantly the most florid notation, leaving her audience in breathless amazement; but her intonation was very uncertain ...

The immense volume of Catalani's voice was not liked by some. Queen Charlotte, being asked her opinion, replied with German emphasis: 'I was wishing for a little cotton in my ears all the time.' The predominating impression on the mind was its overpowering, almost terrific loudness ... Some wit was asked if he would go to York to hear her. 'I shall hear her better where I am,' he answered ...

Her excessive love of ornament proved a fatal stumbling-block, and ruined the beauty of this matchless voice. She cared for no simple air. Her delight was to take a bold and spirited piece, such as 'Non più andrai', even when written for a bass voice, in which she could bear down and overpower by sheer force of lungs the brazen instruments of the orchestra, amid rapturous thunders of applause. She preferred the music of the most inferior composers, written expressly for her, to the most exquisite productions of the greatest masters; which was greatly to be regretted, for all agreed that she could have become a perfect performer, had her noble gifts been guided by sound taste and judgement. She had a peculiar facility in running chromatic passages, placing on each note a trill which scintillated like a diamond in limpid water; she excelled in effects of contrast – now loud as an organ, then soft and penetrating as the lowest notes of the nightingale; and her skill in 'jumping' over two octaves at once, her rapidity in divisions, and the almost supernatural volume of tone which her throat was capable of throwing forth, created an increasing wonder. Her fantastical luxuriance and redundancy, her reckless daring, her defiance of all rules, disgusted connoisseurs as much as it astounded and charmed the multitude.

Ellen Creathorne Clayton, *Queens of Song*, Smith, Elder, 1863, I,
pp. 284, 305–6, 321

Napoleon's patronage proved a mixed blessing to Catalani:

Napoleon, whose musical ability historians have passed over, once heard Catalani at the Paris Opéra. He made up his mind that Paris should keep possession of her. Accordingly he commanded her to attend upon him at the Tuileries. Catalani was thunderstruck. She had never anticipated such an uncomfortable position; so with a trembling step she presented herself before him who, at the time, was terrifying all Europe.

'Where are you going, madam?' inquired the Consul.

'To London, sire,' replied the singer.

'But you must remain here,' retorted Napoleon; 'you shall have a hundred thousand francs a year, and two months' vacation. That is settled. *Bonjour, madame!*'

Catalani hurried away, and more dead than alive reached her apartments, without having dared to acquaint the Emperor that an engagement in Portugal would prevent her from complying with his wishes. In the meanwhile the Emperor quickly gave action to his word, and a document recording the arrangement was left at Catalani's house. This fired her: she resolved to escape the bondage at any cost. Accordingly she disguised herself as a nun, and, under the pretence of a pious errand, reached Morlaix, where there was a war-vessel exchanging prisoners. To the captain of this ship she offered £150, and strict silence, if he would take her on board. This was agreed to, and so the *cantatrice* made her escape. Luckily for her, affairs at Paris grew urgent. Apollo gave way to Mars; otherwise Catalani might have had cause to repent her evasion of the Emperor's commands.

Frederick Crowest, *A Book of Musical Anecdotes*, Bentley, 1878, I,

pp. 308–9

Catalani had a bizarre encounter with Goethe at Weimar:

Gifted with a voice of immense volume, compass, and flexibility, a throat of such size that a doctor who examined it declared that she might easily swallow a penny loaf whole, a perfect figure, and a beautiful face capable of every shade of expression, she seemed formed by Nature to be the queen of the lyric stage. Yet with all these advantages she was almost entirely uneducated even in music . . .

There is the story of a ludicrous scene which took place between her and the poet Goethe. Catalani, it must be remembered, was excessively talkative. Being once at the court of Weimar, she was seated at a dinner party as a mark of respect next to the great German poet. She knew nothing of Goethe, but, struck by his appearance and the attention paid to him, inquired of the gentleman on her other side who he was.

'He is the celebrated Goethe, madam,' was the reply.

'Oh! on what instrument does he play?' asked Catalani.

'He is not a musician, madam; he is the well-known author of *Werther*.'

'Oh! yes, yes; I remember,' said the vivacious lady; and turning to the venerable poet, she exclaimed, 'Ah, sir, what an admirer I am of *Werther*!'

A low bow was the acknowledgement for such a flattering compliment.

'I never,' continued she, 'read anything half so laughable in all my life. What a capital farce it is!'

'*The Sorrows of Werther* a farce, madam?' said the poet, looking aghast.

'Oh yes; never was anything so exquisitely ridiculous,' rejoined Catalani, laughing heartily as she enjoyed the remembrance.

It turned out, however, that she had been referring to a ridiculous parody which she had seen performed in Paris, and in which the great poet's sentimentality had been most unmercifully ridiculed!

Frederick Crowest, *A Book of Musical Anecdotes*, Bentley, 1878, I,
pp. 67–9

The tenor Nicolas Tacchinardi (1772–1859) had to reconcile a beautiful voice with an ungainly body:

Nicolas Tacchinardi, who was the great star of the Odéon under the Empire, was one of the most admired tenors of his day. He was not by nature formed for a stage hero, being short, with a large head sunk in his shoulders, and a repulsive face; but he had an exquisite voice and irreproachable taste, and was as capricious as he was ugly ... Being perfectly conscious that his personal defects operated against him in the estimation of those who were not familiar with his beautiful voice, he would beg those who wrote for him to give him parts which permitted him to sing at the side scenes before entering on the stage, that thus he might be heard before being seen. This expedient was not always easy to manage, however, so he invented another stratagem for concealing from the spectators some portion of his unfortunate figure; he would come on the stage standing in a triumphal car, looking even then a victor whose aspect terribly belied his supposed deeds. At his first appearance on the boards of the Odéon, he was saluted with the most insulting outburst of laughter and smothered ejaculations of 'Why, he's a hunchback!' Being accustomed to this kind of greeting, Tacchinardi tranquilly walked to the footlights, and bowed. 'Gentlemen,' he said, addressing the pit, 'I am not here to exhibit my person, but to sing. Have the goodness to hear me.' They did hear him, and when he ceased, the theatre rang with plaudits: there was no more laughter. His personal disadvantages were redeemed by one of the finest and purest tenor voices ever given by Nature and refined by Art.

Ellen Creathorne Clayton, *Queens of Song*, Smith, Elder, 1863, II,

pp. 257–8

The end of a career: the Parisian singer Cornélie Falcon (1812–97) comes to terms with the decline in her vocal powers:

Early in 1838, she left for Italy, where her energies revived; but only for a short time. She was beloved by her comrades, and a great favourite with the public; so that when she announced her reappearance for 14 March 1839 there was great rejoicing among her partisans. She chose for her benefit the second act of *La Juive*, and the fourth of *Les Huguenots*, and was supported by Duprez, Massol, and Madame Dorus Gras. The theatre was crowded – it was, a French writer says, like a family gathering to welcome the return of the *voix prodigue*. When the *bénéficiaire* appeared the house rang with acclamations, but the illusion was not of long duration. Some notes, by accident, yet remained pure; but the others were either veiled, stifled, or cracked.

'At first, firm and calm, Mlle Falcon assisted without faltering at the spectacle of her own agony,' says Charles de Boigne; 'but soon the general emotion infected her, her tears gushed forth, and her despair was evidenced in convulsive sobs, which redoubled the applause still more: the last homage to a fine talent which had ceased to exist. Leaning on the shoulder of Duprez, she remained some instants absorbed in grief; but then courageously resumed her duty: as she had commenced her part, she was resolved to finish it. As Rachel she accomplished her painful task, but as Valentine she had yet to drink the bitter chalice of failure to the dregs. When she returned in the fourth act of *Les Huguenots,* the music dragged painfully between the dying gasps of Valentine and the bravos arrested by the sight of so terrible a misfortune.' The phrase '*Nuit fatale, nuit d'alarmes, je n'ai plus d'avenir*' contained an allusion to her situation so poignant that the ill-fated *cantatrice* was scarcely able to pronounce them.

Such a desperate, agonizing struggle of Art against Nature has seldom been witnessed. The magnificent voice of Cornélie Falcon had fled.

Ellen Creathorne Clayton, *Queens of Song,* Smith, Elder, 1863, II,
pp. 129–30

Henry Chorley recalls one of the first tenors to achieve international stardom, Giovanni Battista Rubini (1794–1854):

He was in no respect calculated to please the eye; for the openness of his countenance could not redeem the meanness of features impaired by smallpox . . . He rarely tried to act, the moment of the curse in the contract scene of *Lucia* being the only attempt of the kind that I can call to mind. The voice and the expression were, with him, to 'do it all'.

Before, however, Rubini came to England his voice had contracted that sort of thrilling or trembling habit, then new here, which of late has been abused ad nauseam. It was no longer in its prime – hardly capable, perhaps, of being produced mezzo forte or piano; for which reason he had adopted a style of extreme contrast betwixt soft and loud, which many ears were unable, for a long period, to relish. After a time these vehemences (in themselves vicious) were forgotten for the sake of the transcendent qualities by which they were accompanied, though in the last years of his reign they were exaggerated into the alternation of a scarcely audible whisper and a shout; and it was said, not untruly, that it would be hardly possible to form any idea of a new tenor part were it presented for the first time by Rubini, so largely did memory and knowledge of his intentions aid his public . . .

There was never an artist who seemed so thoroughly and intensely to enjoy his own singing – a persuasion which cannot fail to communicate itself to his audiences. Again, there was never an artist more sure of his own effects than Rubini. He would walk through a good third of any given opera languidly, giving the notes correctly, and little more; in a duet, blending his voice intimately with that of his partner (in this he was unsurpassed); but when his own moment arrived there was no longer coldness or hesitation, but a passion, a fervour, a putting forth to the utmost of every resource of consummate vocal art and emotion, which converted the most incredulous, and satisfied those till then disposed to treat him as one whose reputation had been overrated.

Henry Chorley, *Thirty Years' Musical Recollections* (1862), Knopf, 1926,

pp. 21–2

Wilhelmine Schroeder-Devrient (1804–60) was the definitive Leonora in Beethoven's Fidelio:

Her face – a thoroughly German one – though plain, was pleasing, from the intensity of expression which her large features and deep tender eyes conveyed. She had profuse fair hair, the value of which she thoroughly understood, delighting, in moments of great emotion, to fling it loose with the wild vehemence of a Maenad . . . Her execution was bad and heavy. There was an air of strain and spasm throughout her performances, of that struggle for victory which never conquers.

But then, as an actress, the devouring suspense of the disquieted wife, throughout the first half of the tale, enabled the German Leonora to exhibit all her passion of byplay, in judicious interpretation of the situation. Her eyes, quickened by the yearnings of her heart, were everywhere; her quivering lip, even when her countenance was the most guarded, told how intensely she was listening. It was impossible to hear the 'Prisoners' Chorus' as given by the Germans in London during that year, and to see the eager woman as she unclosed cell after cell, and ushered its ghastly tenants into the fresh air, questioning face after face, all in vain, – without tears. Nor less earnestly wrought up was her scene in the vault, ending with her rapturous embrace of the rescued captive, for whom she had waited so long and dared so much. By no one has Madame Schroeder-Devrient been equalled in this opera.

Henry Chorley, *Thirty Years' Musical Recollections* (1862), Knopf, 1926,
pp. 38–40

The soprano Henriette Méric-Lalande (1799–1867) had created the leading roles in several operas by Bellini and Donizetti. When she made her London début in Bellini's La straniera *in 1832, Maria Malibran was in the audience and, in a letter to her lover Charles de Bériot, gave a bitchy account of the occasion:*

Let's see if I can dig up some news. Let's speak of the début of Mme Lalande . . .

Imagine a woman around forty, blonde, the face of a labourer, with a bad expression, bad figure, having in common with me the ugliest feet in the world, badly coiffed, and the same for her dress.

The recitative began . . . Her voice shook so badly that I could not judge whether it was sour, sweet, or otherwise. I patiently awaited the cavatina so I could judge . . . She finished her aria, which is very pretty and which she consistently sang with that bad wobble. She was well applauded. A thousand curtsies, the custom in London only, earning her prolonged salvos.

Next came the beautiful duet, which you know. She sang this coldly and always with the tremble. To make a long story short,

she finished the opera the same way she began it. She has a
beautiful aria at the end in the mad scene. Her husband and her
lover have both just been killed. She arrives with a little child,
who is yawning, because he would prefer to go beddy-bye than to
hear a lachrymose aria which has to be sung, and especially acted,
in a manner completely opposite to produce an insane effect. The
result of this was that she didn't make the least effect. However,
she was called for after the curtain, coming out to the most
anonymous applause, the most unanimous applause I mean, that
has ever been given, because the consensus is that she wasn't
good.

Howard Bushnell, *Maria Malibran*, Pennsylvania State University Press,
1979, pp. 111–12

*The impresario Benjamin Lumley on the high-handed and exasperating
ways of acclaimed singers:*

In the records of the theatre, beyond the reach of the public gaze,
Madame Grisi continually appears in the foreground, with 'indispositions', and refusals to sing such and such a part – Elisetta in
the *Matrimonio segreto*, for instance, which she had accepted in the
previous season; she complains of the monotony of the old *répertoire*, and yet speaks slightingly, if not with scorn, of the new roles
offered her ... At length comes a letter from Madame Grisi's
lawyer, complaining of the box not being at her disposal on an
extra night, and demanding the sum of twelve guineas, for which
sum it had been let on that occasion. I demur to the grounds upon
which her claims to the box on *extra* nights are based; assert that
the box had been hitherto placed at her service as a matter of
courtesy, not of right – a courtesy not intentionally discontinued –
deprecate the course that the lady has unadvisedly taken in applying
at once to a legal adviser, and leave her to find that remedy in the
law, to which in fact she has already had recourse; I take this
opportunity to remark upon 'the unseemly conduct pursued by her
on two recent occasions', and her general behaviour towards the

management, as forming a 'discreditable exception' to the 'otherwise orderly conduct of the company'. This storm, sharp and noisy as were the thunderclaps, was but a prelude to the strife of elements that was presently to ensue. Side by side with the irritable and ambitious lady, stands the other notable transgressor – whose 'indispositions' are, if possible, still more frequent, and who, on his own side, claims the right of refusing parts, in which, nevertheless, he had previously appeared . . .

On the night of Saturday, 26 April [1845], Signor Mario appeared as the Almaviva of the *Barbiere,* but only to disappear in the very first scene. An apology was made for 'huskiness', and he again came on, omitting his 'aria'. Discontent began to be manifest. The Rosina (Madame Grisi) came forward, but commenced her air in such 'admired disorder', that further manifestations of disapprobation arose. The prima donna, in her turn, came to a standstill, and confronted the audience with wrathful brow. The jollity of Lablache for a time restored something like composure; at the commencement of the celebrated finale, however, Almaviva having reappeared, and murmurs having been again heard, the indignant tenor left the stage, to return no more that evening. The inimitable humour of Lablache, expressed at this sudden flight, restored the audience to good temper by its irresistible comicality. Another apology was made – Signor Corelli had been sent for; and after some delay, the opera proceeded, with Corelli as the Almaviva of the night. An angry correspondence ensued between the management and the offending tenor: I, on my part, protesting that with but a slight display of goodwill, Signor Mario might have spared such an indignity to the subscribers and the public – the recalcitrant tenor imperatively asserting that on his part, with failing voice, and the burden of public disapprobation, he was wholly *dans ses droits* in leaving the stage abruptly. The breach between the management and two artists, with whom it was difficult to negotiate, and whom it was next to impossible to control, was thus widened more and more; until, with other elements of discontent (not apparently prominent until the ensuing season) the chasm became so wide and deep, so impossible to bridge over by concession, that a rupture was positively looked forward to as a relief.

Benjamin Lumley, *Reminiscences of the Opera*, Hurst & Blackett, 1864,
pp. 121–3

The careers of the great prima donnas such as Grisi and Malibran are well known. Less well documented is the career of the British soprano Anna Bishop (1810–84). After early successes in England and Denmark she moved to Sweden in 1840, where she packed the theatre every night:

On the morning she left Stockholm all the ministers and ambassadors assembled at her house to pay their respects, the Count de Rosen, sent by the king, conducted her to her carriage, and the Countess Tobey threw over her shoulders a mantle of superb ermine. At the University of Uppsala she was serenaded by 600 students. At St Petersburg in May 1840 she lived in the palace of Baron Chabot, with nine reception rooms, where she gave a private party every Wednesday, at which the imperial family, the Russian ministers, the foreign ambassadors and the whole court assembled. Then on again to Dorpat, Riga, Mitau, and Moscow. In June 1841 she was at Nijny Novgorod, singing to audiences of Chinese, Turks, Circassians, Cossacks, and Arabs gathered for the annual fair. Here she met the last king of the Georgians, 'who, in rapture with her beautiful singing, sent to her, by several of his dwarfs, presents of sweetmeats and a rich bracelet of turquoises'. Thence to Kazan, the capital of Tartary. Anna was always ready to surprise the natives by bursting into song in their own language; the Scandinavian tongues, Russian, Hungarian, all came alike to her; at Kazan she sang in the Tartar language. On she went, to Odessa, Yassy, Lemberg, Cracow, where Countess Potoski built a small theatre in her palace for the sole purpose of hearing Anna sing, to Brünn and Vienna in March 1842, with private concerts for the Emperor and Metternich, to Pressburg, with superb illuminations and a serenade arranged by Prince Esterházy and with the hospitality of the Bishop of Raab, then on to Budapest and Ofen, then Vienna again and Munich, where the King of Bavaria wrote the programme of her first concert with his own hand, and finally Italy . . . Anna Bishop sang at Naples for twenty-seven consecutive months, appearing 327 times in twenty operas, including thirty-six appearances in Verdi's *I due Foscari*.

Composers, it seems, were less enthusiastic than kings, queens and ambassadors. Verdi refused to have her in his new opera, and Donizetti, two years earlier, had rejected her equally emphatically: 'No, for Christ's sake, not la Bishop! Are you pulling my leg?' . . .

After singing in *La sonnambula* at Palermo, in the presence of the sovereigns of Russia and Naples, she returned to England, by way of Switzerland and Belgium, giving concerts everywhere. She appeared at Drury Lane in Balfe's *Maid of Artois* on 8 October, and in Louis Lavenu's *Loretta* on 9 November 1846. She delighted the provinces with 'her favourite last scene from *L'elisir d'amore*, composed for her by Donizetti at Naples' – a thumping lie! . . .

In 1849 she found Mexico a true El Dorado and in the following years the 'fair *cantatrice*' or 'wandering nightingale' seems to have sung at almost every city in North America . . . On 18 February 1866 she left Honolulu for Hong Kong . . . and was wrecked on a coral reef near Wake Island, losing all her clothes, jewellery, and music. After being marooned for three weeks on an uninhabited, waterless island, living on provisions salvaged from the wreck, the survivors made their way in an open boat to the Ladrone Islands, 1400 miles away. Anna and [her husband] Schultz landed on Guam on 8 April and thence made their way to Manila, where the interrupted routine of concert-giving was resumed . . .

She returned to New York, via Australia and England. She appeared in the Tabernacle at Salt Lake City, at the special invitation of Brigham Young, on July 1873. After another tour of Australia she spent a year in South Africa, travelling to places like Kimberley by rough roads and across or through unbridged rivers. At the end of 1876 she was in England again, where she stayed for three years, avoiding publicity and musical engagements, before returning to New York. She made her last public appearance there on 20 April 1883 and died of apoplexy at 1443 Fourth Avenue on 19 March 1884.

Frank Walker, *The Man Verdi*, Dent, 1962, pp. 137–8, 140–42

Giovanni de Candia, a popular nineteenth-century tenor known simply as Mario (1810–83), made his début as the Duke of Normandy in Meyerbeer's Robert le Diable *in Paris on 5 December 1838:*

Meyerbeer composed an air expressly for him in the second act which was so extremely difficult that none of his successors in the part ever attempted it. Mario relates that Rubini, the great tenor, looking at the manuscript of this song, asked with an air of evident astonishment: 'Do you propose to sing this?' 'I shall have to sing it as the master has written it for me,' was Mario's answer. 'Well, youth is rash,' replied Rubini. Later, when the opera was translated into Italian, Meyerbeer again added an extra song for Mario.

Mario, in relating the experience of his début, used to say that when he stepped on to the stage that night he felt as if he were ascending the scaffold ... As he moved into the full glare of the lights he heard an exclamation from a stage box, which in those days were actually on the stage itself, and looking up he recognized a young lady, a friend of his family, with whom he had often danced at Nice. The lady had no idea that Mario, the *débutant* singer, and Giovanni de Candia were one and the same person, and could not repress her astonishment. She was afterwards, however, begged to keep the secret from [Mario's father] Don Stefano, which she did, and the old man died unaware that the young tenor whose name was already beginning to reach Italy was his own son.

Mrs Godfrey Pearse and Frank Hird, *The Romance of a Great Singer:*
A Memoir of Mario, Smith, Elder, 1910, pp. 74–5

Many great singers were heavy smokers, Caruso for one and Mario for another:

His incessant smoking never affected his voice, although even in his dressing-room in the theatre and during the entr'actes he never was without a cigar. Once he narrowly escaped being caught with a cigar in his mouth on the stage. He was ready dressed for the second act of *Faust*, and was talking with friends in his dressing-room when the call boy told him the curtain was up, and Mario rushed on to the stage entirely forgetting his cigar, which was snatched out of his mouth by a scene-shifter before the audience saw him.

Mrs Godfrey Pearse and Frank Hird, *The Romance of a Great Singer:*
A Memoir of Mario, Smith, Elder, 1910, p. 141

The eccentric art of Sophie Cruvelli (1826–1907):

Though Mademoiselle Cruvelli proved, a year or two later, in London and in Paris, the most disappointing person whom I have ever heard, when she arrived in London for Mademoiselle Lind's second season [1848] she had more of the qualities which excite expectation than belong to ninety-nine out of a hundred stage singers – youth, a presence commanding, if somewhat peculiar . . . a superb voice, almost three octaves in compass, and a fervour and ambition which it could not be then foreseen would take their after-forms of reckless and perverse eccentricity. She gained, as time went on, some of the appearance, some of the reality, of a vocalist; but with every such gain in skill and in position there seemed to come a loss – an added inconsistency, wildness, disregard of such usages as belong to progress, justified by no temporary popularity, whether here or over the water. Towards the close of her theatrical career there were hazardous musical freaks ventured, at the Grand Opera of Paris, by Mademoiselle Cruvelli, hardly to be precedented. She thought it becoming to alter a rhythm, in a duet from *Les Huguenots*, from triple to common tempo. The curiosities of her reading of the striking temple scene in the second

act of Spontini's *Vestale*, where she turned her back on her duty to
the artists about to enter, and gesticulated to the stalls, are before
my eyes. But in the year of which I now speak, Mademoiselle
Cruvelli was rich in promise as few have been . . .

The change for the worse in Mademoiselle Cruvelli began to
show itself strongly this season [1852] . . . She was triumphantly
heedless of all her companions on the stage. In her great scenes she
was always too soon or too late. She preferred to fly into a fury
before the word was spoken that should set fire to the train. She
would fall into an attitude just after the moment for the attitude
had gone by. Then she performed strange evolutions with her
drapery by way of being statuesque, and exhibited things more
strange with her costume when it was not antique, by way of
being pictorial. So well were these propensities of hers known that
later, when, as Queen of the Grand Opera of Paris, she deliberately
altered the rhythm of the leading phrase of a grand duet in *Les
Huguenots*, the world said, 'Only Mademoiselle Cruvelli's way . . .'

Henry Chorley, *Thirty Years' Musical Recollections* (1862), Knopf, 1926,
pp. 215–16, 311

She outdid herself at the première of I vespri siciliani *in 1855:*

When Verdi's *I vespri siciliani* was to be given its première at the
Paris Opéra, the lady who was to sing the principal part, a Mlle
Sophia Cruvelli, suddenly vanished a few days before the performance. The Paris police went to work but two weeks after her
disappearance they had unearthed no trace of her whereabouts.
Verdi declared officially that he was ready to withdraw the opera.
A judgement was taken out against the singer. Since, like all opera
singers, she was an employee of the state, it was possible for the
state to set the fine, and this was fixed at the large sum of a
hundred thousand francs. The furniture of her apartment and her
personal property were seized. More days went by and nothing
was heard of her. The newspapers became furious . . .

Then, as mysteriously as she had disappeared, she returned. It seems that she had simply decided to go off on a holiday, though not alone. She had taken a trial honeymoon journey with a baron, whom shortly afterwards she married. Her only excuse was that the person who was to inform the management of the opera house of her departure had forgotten to do so. But here she was back and quite willing to brave the wrath of the Parisian public by singing again. The rehearsals of *I vespri siciliani* were resumed, and Mlle Cruvelli, refreshed by her holiday, threw herself into the work with passion. She made her reappearance before the Parisian public not in this opera but in Meyerbeer's *Les Huguenots*, as Valentine. When Valentine enters the Queen questions her; the first words she says to her are: 'Tell me the result of your daring journey.' When the Parisians heard the line they burst into laughter and Cruvelli was forgiven.

George R. Marek, *A Front Seat at the Opera*, Harrap, 1951, pp. 239–40

6: Late-nineteenth-century Singers

An unalterable and unquestioned law of the musical world required that the German text of French operas sung by Swedish artists should be translated into Italian for the clearer understanding of English-speaking audiences.

Edith Wharton, *The Age of Innocence*, chapter 1

Mad scenes were commonplace in nineteenth-century opera. Here is a real-life example, starring the tenor Antonio Giuglini (1827–65):

On the termination of my spring concert tour in 1865 we began a season of opera in the beginning of March at Dublin, Giuglini promising to join us at the conclusion of his St Petersburg engagement, which ended about that time.

One morning at breakfast I received a telegram from London; 'Come on at once. Giuglini arrived.' I was indeed delighted, and, having notified the good news to the Dublin press, left immediately for London. On my arrival at Giuglini's house in Welbeck Street I was told that he was very much indisposed in consequence of the fatigues of the journey, and that his mind did not seem quite right. I went upstairs to him at once. He was very pleased to see me, but to my astonishment he had no trousers on. Otherwise he was all right.

I talked with him some time, and advised him to put on the necessary garment, so that we might start that evening for Dublin. By force of persuasion I at last obtained his consent to let me put his trousers on for him, and in the course of an hour succeeded in getting one leg in. I then ordered some oysters for him, and talked to him whilst I was coaxing in the other leg. This I at length

managed to do, when to my horror I found the first leg had come
out again. After wasting the whole of the day I found myself too
late to catch the Irish mail, and the Signor still with one leg only in
his pantaloons . . .

On my return to London I went to pay Giuglini a visit at
Chiswick, Mlle Titiens insisting on accompanying me. We waited
some time, during which we were particularly cautioned not to
approach him. At length he entered; he was delighted to see us and
talked quite rationally . . . He afterwards sang us *'Spirito gentil'*
from the *Favorita*, followed by *'M'appari'* from *Martha*, singing
both airs divinely. The only thing peculiar was that his tongue was
drawn very much to the right, and that he had to stop after every
ninth or tenth bar to straighten it.

J.H. Mapleson, *The Mapleson Memoirs 1848–1888*, Remington, 1888, I,

pp. 84–6

*The bane of the backstage staff at opera houses must have been singers'
pampered pets. Ilma di Murska (1836–89) was the worst offender:*

The prima donna has generally a parrot, a pet dog, or an ape,
which she loves to distraction, and carries with her wherever she
goes. Ilma di Murska, however, travelled with an entire menagerie.
Her immense Newfoundland, Pluto, dined with her every day. A
cover was laid for him as for her, and he had learned to eat a fowl
from a plate without dropping any of the meat or bones on the
floor or even on the tablecloth.

Pluto was a good-natured dog, or he would have made short
work of the monkey, the two parrots, and the angora cat who
were his constant associates. The intelligent animal hated travelling
in the dog truck, and he would resort to any sort of device in
order to join his mistress in her first-class carriage, where he
would, in spite of his immense bulk, squeeze himself beneath her
seat. Once I remember he sprang through the closed window,
cutting himself severely about the nose in his daring leap.

The other animals were simple nuisances. But I must do the

monkey the justice to say that he did his best to kill the cat, and a
bare place on Minette's back showed how badly she had once been
clawed by her mischievous tormentor.

J.H. Mapleson, *The Mapleson Memoirs 1848–1888*, Remington, 1888, I,
pp. 164–5

*The rise to stardom in England of Jenny Lind, 'the Swedish Nightingale'
(1820–87), was deferred by protracted negotiations with a clutch of
impresarios, and the delays fuelled the curiosity of the public:*

Finally, she sang, in Meyerbeer's *Robert le Diable*.

Orchestra stalls went for five or six guineas, boxes for twenty.
The Queen and Prince Albert led an audience that included the
Duke of Wellington, Prince Louis Napoleon, Mendelssohn, and
Lablache, as well as the crush of nobility and fashion. Lind was
not making her début in a familiar opera . . . She had chosen the
'modern' music of Meyerbeer, which would be less immediately
telling of her technique. But after a superb trill at the end of her
first solo, Lablache let forth a stentorian '*brava*', and the rest of the
audience followed suit. By the end of the evening the enthusiasm
was maniacal, and the Queen herself threw down a bouquet . . . In
the ensuing months she sang in *La sonnambula*, *La Fille du régiment*,
and the unsuccessful première of Verdi's *I masnadieri*, her popularity
spreading far beyond the ordinary opera audience. Her private
virtue was as much praised as her singing. Horses, dogs, dolls, a
tulip, a pub, and a whistling kettle took her name in vain. She rode
along Rotten Row with the Duke of Wellington and was repeatedly
received at court . . .

Did her singing justify the fuss? Thackeray found her 'atrociously stupid. I was thinking of something else the whole time
she was jugulating away', and he could not wait to 'get out and
have a cigar' . . . [Music critic Henry Chorley] paid tribute to what
Garcia had nurtured – her extraordinary breath control, glorious
top register with its peculiarly beautiful pianissimo, and general
technical mastery. She was, however, limited in dramatic range to

the lyrical and pathetic, and even in the thickening atmosphere of adulation her Norma was considered pallid in a London with living memories of Pasta, and Grisi still in command at Covent Garden ... What finally gave Lind her appeal as a singer was a unique colour in the voice, an unmistakable and recognizable sound, which, like that of Supervia or Lotte Lehmann, immediately evoked a particular personality. Chopin described it as 'a kind of Northern Lights': others babbled of woodland freshness ...

Rupert Christiansen, *Prima Donna*, Bodley Head, 1984,

pp. 101–4, 106–7

The merchandizing of Jenny Lind was as thorough as that of any Hollywood blockbuster:

[Donizetti's] *La figlia del reggimento*, in which she made her first appearance [in Vienna] on 7 January [1847] ... struck just the light, sentimental note Vienna loved, and had a phenomenal success ... A print of her in the part of Marie, that had been published in Munich, was rushed to Vienna in thousands, and copies appeared in every house. Her portrait was displayed, in lithograph and engraving — some of them very poor, but she took no interest herself in her portraits, and let the engravers and daguerreotypists do what they pleased – in every bookshop and art shop window. Reproductions appeared on chocolate boxes, cigar boxes, scented soaps and toilet waters. A scent was on sale, labelled '*Extrait double de bouquet de Jenny Lind*', with her portrait and signature. Her name was everywhere ...

[During her tour of America in 1850] everything began to be called after her: gloves, bonnets, shawls, chairs, sofas, pianos, sausages, cigars, even a whistling kettle that sang when the water boiled. Her portrait appeared on water carafes, hotels served their choicest meals *à la* Jenny Lind. Songs and poems, polkas and quadrilles, were dedicated to her.

Joan Bulman, *Jenny Lind*, Barrie, 1956, pp. 148, 243

Lind was known for her prim moral rectitude, but the otherwise obscure
tenor Cardinali showed more interest in skirt than song:

At New York, as previously at Philadelphia, Chicago, and San
Francisco, lively complaints were made of the vanity and levity of
my tenor, Cardinali, who was an empty-headed, fatuous creature
unable to write his own name or even to read the love-letters
which, in spite, or perhaps in consequence of his empty-headedness,
were frequently addressed to him by affectionate and doubtless
weak-minded young ladies. Cardinali possessed a certain beauty of
countenance; he had also a sloping forehead, and a high opinion of
his powers of fascination.

At San Francisco he got engaged to a young lady of good
family, who was one of the recognized beauties of the city. A date
had been fixed for the marriage, and the coming event was
announced and commented upon in all the papers. The marriage,
however, was not to take place forthwith; and when my handsome
tenor got to Chicago he was much taken by one of the local
blondes, to whom he swore undying love.

At Philadelphia he got engaged to another girl, who became
furiously jealous when she found that he was receiving letters from
his Frisco fiancée. Not being able to decipher the calligraphy of the
former beloved one, he entrusted her letters for reading purposes
to the chambermaids or waiters of the hotel where he put up.

At New York Cardinali formed an attachment to yet another girl,
who fully responded to his ardour. He used to get tickets from me
in order that he might entertain his young women in an economical
manner at operatic representations; and one day, when he had taken
the girl whom he had met at New York to a morning performance,
he asked permission to leave her for a moment as he had to speak to
a friend. This friend turned out to be a lady with whom he had
arranged to elope, and the happy pair left for Europe by a steamer
then on the point of starting. He did not, as far as I know, change
his partner during the voyage, and I afterwards lost sight of him.

J.H. Mapleson, *The Mapleson Memoirs 1848–1888*, Remington, 1888, II,

pp. 152–4

Mapleson reflects on the habit of British singers of adopting bogus foreign names:

An English vocalist . . . will not hesitate to pass himself off, so far as a name can assist him in his enterprise, as some sort of foreigner. My old pal, Jack Foley, becomes Signor Foli, and the Signor sticks to him through life . . . Provincial managers have often entreated me to use my influence with Mr Santley in order to make him change his name to Signor Santalini, which they assured me would look better in the programme, and bring more money into the house A Mr Walker, being engaged to appear at Her Majesty's Theatre, called himself on doing so Signor Valchieri (Signor Perambulatore would certainly have been better); and a well-known American singer, Mr John Clarke, of Brooklyn, transformed himself on joining my company into Signor Giovanni Chiari di Broccolini.

J.H. Mapleson, *The Mapleson Memoirs 1848–1888*, Remington, 1888, II,

p. 275

Mapleson records the triumph of a second-rate singer:

Armandi, a tenor of doubtful repute, who resided at Milan, always awaited the result of the various fiascos of St Stephen's night (26 December) which marks the beginning of the Carnival season, when some hundreds of musical theatres throw open their doors. He had a large repertoire; and, after ascertaining by telegraph where his services were most in need, and where they would be best remunerated, he would accept an engagement as a kind of stopgap until another tenor could be found. Generally, at the close of the first evening he was paid for his six performances and sent back to Milan.

But on the occasion I am speaking of Armandi had stipulated in his contract that he should be paid the six nights and sing the six nights as well; for he was tired, he said, of being systematically shelved after a single performance.

The part in which he had to appear at Naples, where the leading tenor of the establishment had hopelessly broken down, was that

of Pollio in *Norma*; but every time he attempted to sing the public
accompanied him with hisses, so that he soon became inaudible.
At the close of the first act he came before the curtain, and after
obtaining a hearing begged the audience to allow him to finish the
opera in peace, when he would leave the city. If they continued
hissing he warned them that he would sing the remaining five
nights of his engagement.

The public took the candour of the man in such good part that
they not only applauded him throughout the evening, but allowed
him to remain the entire season.

J.H. Mapleson, *The Mapleson Memoirs 1848–1888*, Remington, 1888, II,
pp. 290–91

Theresa Tietjens (1831–77) in Fidelio:

Anyone who has had the good fortune to witness Mlle Tietjens'
performance of *Fidelio* will have seen one of the truest displays of
dramatic feeling, combined with grand singing, possible in our
generation. In the great prison scene it is scarcely possible to
conceive anything more touching and real than Mlle Tietjens'
impersonation. Yet to show what is possible even to excellent
singers when the 'sacred fire' burns low, it is related of Mlle
Schroeder that on one occasion (in the very scene which Mlle
Tietjens renders so 'telling') when she was offering the piece of
bread to the Florestan of the evening (Haizinger), he was rather
slow in taking it from her hand, whereupon the impatient 'Leonora'
whispered:

'Hang you! why the deuce don't you take it? Do you want it
buttered?'

Frederick Crowest, *A Book of Musical Anecdotes*, Bentley, 1878, II,
pp. 53–4

Herman Klein on her last appearance:

I heard her then in several operas, including *Norma* on the opening night [at Her Majesty's], and also in *Lucrezia Borgia*, on what proved to be her last appearance upon the stage. This latter risk she undertook against the advice of her doctors, who desired to perform an operation at once; but (it was on a Saturday night, 19 May 1877) she succeeded in persuading them to postpone their task until the following week.

The audience had little notion of the real state of affairs. Indeed, we should never have believed that a Lucrezia so glorious in every way was going through her part suffering pain at each step and every breath she took. Before the last act began someone told me that she had fainted twice during the evening. Then I watched more closely and could see that she was moving with difficulty. Moreover, her exclamation at the end, when Lucrezia discovers that Gennaro is dead, had in it a ring that sounded like the cry of one in actual bodily pain. She sank to the stage more heavily than usual, and I was not surprised to learn that, after the curtain fell, she had remained where she had fallen insensible for twenty minutes. After her fruitless operation she lingered on, suffering in patience, till the morning of 3 October when she passed peacefully away.

She was buried at the Kensal Green Cemetery, amid a display of mourning the like of which has never before or since paid tribute to a singer in this country.

Herman Klein, *Great Women-singers of My Time*, Routledge, 1931,
pp. 27–9

George Bernard Shaw damns a popular tenor with the faintest of praise:

Signor Nicolini [1834–98] is interesting as an exponent of a school of singing (if we may use the term) which has lately become popular, and which may be considered as a monument of the extraordinary gullibility of the world in matters musical. The education of a singer, according to the approved Italian method, has been facetiously described as consisting of two distinct processes: the destruction of the natural and the creation of the

artificial voice. This is at least half true, for the first operation is
generally accomplished to a nicety. Unfortunately, here the system
breaks down; and the student (should he possess a robust constitution, and survive) finds himself thrown on the world without any
voice, but with the consolation of being no worse off than most of
his profession. So he cultivates his head voice, in which register he
can sing florid music with tolerable fluency; pulls together any
ruins of chest notes which he happens to retain; and so manufac-
tures a compound sound which is neither the voice of man,
woman, nor boy, and which inflicts exquisite pain on all listeners
who can pretend to any purity of taste. Its common characteristics
are an impure and unsteady tone, an uncertain pitch, an undignified
expression, and a constant tremolo.

Nevertheless, the public listens, imputes its unpleasant sensations
to ignorance, applauds and encores as only the very ignorant can
do, and eventually has its judgement so corrupted by habit that
legitimate vocalization becomes actually repugnant to its ear.
Therefore, though we began by stating that Signor Nicolini is one
of our most popular tenors, we had no intention of implying any
artistic excellence on his part. Flattery itself could scarcely deem
his voice an agreeable one, or his style and presence impressive.
The list of his qualifications is soon exhausted.

G.B. Shaw, article of 20 June 1877, in *Shaw's Music*, Bodley Head, 1989,
I, pp. 139–40

*Luigi Arditi recalls how the tenor Ravelli came to be engaged by Mapleson
in 1880. Mapleson's own account is less colourful, so no doubt Arditi
spruced up his own version for publication:*

Poor Maas, whose ill-health often incapacitated him from appearing
when he was announced to sing, suddenly fell ill at the last
moment; in fact, on the very day he was to have appeared in
Lucia.

Mapleson, whose fate it was to be ever on tenterhooks concerning the vagaries or indispositions of his artists, never lost heart,

and was heard to exclaim, boastingly, 'Oh, I shall find another tenor today, never fear!'

It so happened that someone came into Mapleson's office at this moment, and said, 'Joking apart, there *is* a tenor walking about under the portico of the theatre, only waiting to be engaged. His name is Ravelli, and if you go down at once you may still find him . . .'

Mapleson was downstairs in a trice, and having spotted the tenor, who was strolling about with a huge cigar in his mouth, he assumed an indifferent air, managing, somehow, to enter into conversation with Ravelli. Both parties acted offhandedly with one another, as though each man was conferring an honour upon the other by conversing with him. When Mapleson casually observed that he was in want of a tenor for that night's performance, Ravelli replied by looking dubiously at his book of engagements, and saying that, oddly enough, he was free that evening, and would 'not mind' singing in lieu of Maas.

Thus Ravelli first trod the boards of Her Majesty's Theatre.

Luigi Arditi, *My Reminiscences*, Skeffington, 1896, pp. 242–3

But Ravelli was to prove a mixed blessing:

It was about three-quarters of an hour before the opening of the doors [for *Carmen*] when Ravelli sent word that he could not sing. It was then too late to change the opera. I therefore rushed off to his hotel, leaving word that the doors were on no account to be opened until I returned.

I found him in bed. Hearing me enter he slunk under the clothes, and I could not get him to answer my questions. I approached the bed to remove the sheets, when a dog sprang out at me, Ravelli's favourite dog Niagara.

'*Laissez-moi dormir!*' muttered the sluggard, as he turned over on the other side.

'Get up,' I exclaimed; 'don't you understand that you are

imperilling my enterprise by lying in bed and refusing to sing when there is nothing the matter with you?'

He told me that he was very tired, that he was quite out of sorts, that his voice was not in good order, and so on.

With the aid of his wife, I succeeded in making him get up. He dressed himself. Then taking him to the piano I tried his voice, and found that there was nothing whatever the matter with it. He could sing perfectly well.

Ravelli, however, for some minutes still hesitated. In his difficulty he determined to consult Niagara. Appealing to an animal whose superior intelligence he recognized, Ravelli said in the French language –

'*Est-ce que ton maître doit chanter?*'

The dog growled, and Ravelli interpreted this oracular response as an order not to sing. He tore his clothes off, sprang hurriedly into bed, and left me to my own resources . . .

I wrote a hurried notice which was put up in manuscript just as I had scribbled it down, to the effect that in consequence of Ravelli's refusing without explanation to sing, the theatre was closed for that morning.

The excitement outside was prodigious. Everyone, of course, said that it was through my fault the doors were shut . . .

J.H. Mapleson, *The Mapleson Memoirs 1848–1888*, Remington, 1888, I,

pp. 297–9

Some singers refused to be upstaged by mere composers such as Mozart. Emma Albani (1847–1930), singing in Figaro *in about 1880, was an example of this arrogant breed:*

The role of Susanna was allotted to an accomplished young soprano, Bianca Bianchi, who was afterwards a celebrity on the Continent, but had not yet become a favourite in London. In the duet, '*Sull'aria*', where the voices unite in a cadence towards the end, Susanna sings up to the high B flat whilst the Countess sings a third lower, so that for the moment, as Mozart has willed it, the voice of the mistress is outshone by that of the maid. But that would not do for Albani, who, being then the mistress in every sense, politely requested her youthful *comprimaria* to take the G whilst she appropriated the top note.

Herman Klein, *Great Women-singers of My Time*, Routledge, 1931,

pp. 110–11

In the Birmingham Post *Ernest Newman reviews Emma Albani's* Forty Years of Song *in 1911:*

Some day a book will have to be written on the psychology of the prima donna; and the author of it will have to find the solution of one problem that becomes more insistent with each book that is written by, or by authority of, a singer – how is it that these people, who are so interesting and occasionally so subtle in their art are so utterly uninteresting and inexpressibly simple the moment they take a pen in their hand? The lives of most of them could apparently be compressed into a single sentence: they were born, they learned to sing, they sang, they made money and bought diamonds, they got royalties to write in their autograph albums, and they died. Are certain great singers intellectually uninteresting by a law of Nature, or does their life make them so, or do they only pretend to be so? Intellectually uninteresting Madame Albani's book certainly is. Its tediousness is equalled only by its artlessness. For those who care about such things there are any number of details of the operas and oratorios Madame Albani sang in in this year or that, the presents that were made to her, the flowers that were hurled at her, the poems that were written about her, the great audiences that gathered to hear her, what the newspapers of thirty or forty years ago said about her, and so on and so on. For those who do not care a brass farthing for all this historical debris, what is there? What indeed! Madame Albani must have met hundreds of remarkable people in her time. Upon not one of them has she an original or even an ordinarily perspicacious reflection to make. She meets Brahms, for example, in Vienna, and can only record that 'his room was full of old furniture and precious things, and he had a very high desk at which he always wrote standing'. A sharp child could have noticed as much ... Some half-dozen honeyed adjectives suffice for them to characterize everyone whom they have met. Royal personages are, of course, always 'most gracious'; lesser people – but still great people in comparison with the ordinary run of us – are always 'most kind'.

The prima donna seems to swim in a sea of happiness; the public admires her, everyone is very courteous to her, the great of this world give her diamonds and lend her their houses for the summer, and, crowning joy of all, monarchs and princesses write their names with their very own hands in her autograph book! ... Even greater monarchs than those of Europe have not disdained to show Madame Albani honour. Did not that acute critic of singing, King Kalakua of the Sandwich Islands, compliment her, and was she not, as might be expected, 'very gratified by his kindness', and did he not decorate her with the Sandwich Islands Order of Merit? ... The heart of the bored reviewer goes out to his Serene Majesty King Kalakua and to the Chinese ambassador who went to sleep and snored audibly, to the scandal of everyone, at a concert at Buckingham Palace; they seem the only real, natural human beings in all these mellifluous saccharine pages.

Ernest Newman, *Testament of Music*, Putnam, 1962, pp. 95–7

Shaw takes a swipe at Herr Fritz Plank of Karlsruhe:

Unhappily, the preservation of figure and freshness up to fifty is not compatible with the main factor of German culture. That factor is beer ... An average German, with an average middle-class income – that is to say, one to whom the price of a fifth or sixth mug of beer is a matter of some concern – is too fleshy to play Romeo or Tristan gracefully when he is twenty-two. Make him an opera singer, with comparatively unlimited pocket money;

and what will he be by the time he becomes ripe for leading
business at Bayreuth?

Can you conceive the Klingsor of the Parsifal poem, the adroit
spearsman, the untiring intriguer, the personification of unrest,
eagerly weaving his enchantments, and sardonically chuckling over
the rout of his own despised slaves, otherwise than as an intensely
active man, lean, nervous, with perhaps a dash of the serpent, the
fox, the tiger in him, but certainly without a trace of the hippopot-
amus? Well, here is the Klingsor of Bayreuth – Herr Fritz Plank, of
Karlsruhe.

I submit that at least two thirds of Fritz's bulk, whether he
accumulated it himself or inherited it, must consist of the national
beverage, and only one-third of genuine Klingsor stuff. Plank is
celebrated at Karlsruhe for his impersonation of Wotan; but then
Wotan, if I recollect aright, had to empty a drinking horn, the end
of which was secretly connected with the sea; so that one can
conceive him as running a little to flabbiness. But I really do not
think Plank should have undertaken Klingsor without getting into
better physical training. And the fact that the matter is mainly one
of training is my justification for positively refusing to accept the
old plea that criticism should not be 'personal'. Criticism of artists
who offer their own persons as the material of their art cannot be
other than personal.

G.B. Shaw, in *Pall Mall Gazette*, August 1894, reprinted in *Shaw's Music*,
Bodley Head, 1984, III, pp. 314–15

*Verdi greatly admired Victor Maurel (1848–1923), but he was clearly
difficult to work with:*

One day, while talking with Giuseppe Verdi, I was lamenting the
scarcity of good artists as compared with the abundance of other
days. Interrupting me, the Maestro exclaimed:

'And Maurel? What have you to say about Maurel? When did
our fathers ever know so complete an artist? No; Maurel lacked
nothing! There was a unique artist – unique and perfect!'

Maurel, however, did not have the most dependable character for his managers. I recall that he once appeared in a season of three months of opera at La Scala that Corti directed. Maurel caused trouble at almost every moment of the season. He was arrogant, impertinent, difficult and almost everything you can imagine.

Corti kept his peace throughout the season, since he had his performances to give and his promises to the public to fulfil. After the final performance he called Maurel into his office. Maurel arrived. It was the same office that I occupied later.

There was a sofa in his room, and Corti, after saying 'Good day', asked Maurel to be seated on the sofa. Suddenly he grabbed Maurel at the throat and pushed him backward so that he lay on the sofa on his back. Corti was a little man, but a very strong one. Then, as quickly as he pushed Maurel back, he bent over him and his fists began to work. Bang! Bang! Bang! Bang! The blows did not cease to rain on poor Maurel's stunned face until Corti was thoroughly satisfied.

'Now,' said Corti, 'I am satisfied.' And he motioned Maurel to the door. The singer, still stunned, left meekly. And as the door closed, Corti cried after him, 'Now, dear Maurel, we are even.'

Giulio Gatti-Casazza, *Memoirs of the Opera*, Calder, 1977, pp. 192–3

Emma Calvé (1858–1942) was the definitive Carmen of her generation, but her performance failed to impress George Bernard Shaw:

I have no eulogies for her Carmen, which shocked me beyond measure . . . Her Carmen is a superstitious, pleasure-loving good-for-nothing, caught by the outside of anything glittering, with no power but the power of seduction, which she exercises without sense or decency. There is no suggestion of any fine quality about her, not a spark of honesty, courage, or even of the sort of honour supposed to prevail among thieves. All this is conveyed by Calvé with a positively frightful artistic power of divesting her beauty and grace of the nobility – I had almost written the sanctity – which seems inseparable from them in other parts. Nobody else dare venture on the indescribable allurements which she practises on the officers in the first act, or such touches as the attempt to get a comprehensive view of her figure in Lallas Pastia's rather small looking-glass, or her jealously critical inspection of Micaela from the same point of view in the third act.

Her death scene, too, is horribly real. The young lady Carmen is never so effectively alive as when she falls, stage dead, beneath José's cruel knife. But to see Calvé's Carmen changing from a live creature, with properly coordinated movements, into a reeling, staggering, flopping, disorganized thing, and finally tumble down a mere heap of carrion, is to get much the same sensation as might be given by the reality of a brutal murder.

> G.B. Shaw, article in *The World*, 30 May 1894, reprinted in *Shaw's Music*, Bodley Head, 1989, III, pp. 224–6

The pianist Ivor Newton felt greater admiration, but clearly found her hell to work with:

Something in every woman's nature makes her want to play Carmen, and it is amazing that, while each knows psychologically exactly how the role should be interpreted, few have discovered how to project the part across the footlights. Calvé most certainly could project it; she was a great singer and a great actress. She was not, unfortunately, even in the eyes of an admiring accompanist, a fastidious musician . . . But, to her, music was only a vehicle for her own remarkably attractive personality, not an art to which she could dedicate herself . . .

Completely wilful, she was a law unto herself; if she did not feel like singing, she would miss a performance with no apparent qualms of conscience. When, in one performance of *Carmen* at the Metropolitan Opera, New York, she skipped four bars in the first act, she was convinced that the conductor was to blame for the ensuing brief period of chaos. While her friend the composer Guy d'Hardelot spent the interval keeping the furious conductor away from her, she justified herself. 'Any conductor who knows his

job,' she explained, 'realizes that I'm uncertain in the first act.'
And she had no more to say of the contretemps.

Ivor Newton, *At the Piano*, Hamish Hamilton, 1966, pp. 107–8

Calvé, like other divas of her time, was initially reluctant to record her voice:

Madame Calvé, who endowed opera roles with an abundance of
Latin temperament, did not abate her vivacity when it came time
to make recordings. Taken to the door of the Maiden Lane building
in a luxurious four-wheeler by Landon Ronald, she at first refused
to budge from the carriage. Dismayed at the shabby appearance of
the building and the sinister atmosphere of the narrow street, she
cried out: 'Never in my life will I enter such a place. It is a tavern
– not a manufactory. I shall be robbed here. You have brought
me to a thieves' den.' Ronald was inured to the outbursts of prima
donnas and knew well how to cope with this one; he excused
himself for a moment, ran into the accountant's office, and returned
bearing the company's payment for Calvé's services (one hundred
guineas for six records). This acted as a strong restorative, and
soon she was upstairs – ready to perform for the gramophone. But
the troubles had only begun. She had the disconcerting habit of
commenting on her performance in the midst of a recording –
even uttering shrieks of joy or groans of disgust, depending on
whether she had turned a particular phrase to her liking – and in
'*Séguedille*' from *Carmen* she insisted on dancing in front of the
recording horn just as she was wont to do on stage. Despite her
antics, Calvé's 1902 recordings came off fairly creditably, though
their improvisatory quality seems rather grotesque beside the
studio-perfect renditions that we are accustomed to hearing on
records today.

Roland Gelatt, *The Fabulous Phonograph 1877–1977*, Cassell, 1977,
pp. 116–17

7: Three Divas: Patti, Melba, Tetrazzini

Once, passing a suite at the Savoy Hotel, London, while Melba was practising, Tetrazzini turned to Mrs Kate Butler, the Savoy's superintendent, and asked, 'Have you *many* cats in your lovely hotel?'

John Hetherington, *Melba*, p. 155

Adelina Patti was surely the most precocious of all prima donnas. She was born in Madrid of Italian parents in 1843. The family moved to New York, where she first sang in public at the age of seven:

That little girl was to sing 'by ear' Norma's great aria, '*Casta diva*', at a charity concert given in the city of New York ... and instantaneously to earn for herself a reputation as the most astounding vocal prodigy that had ever appeared on the American continent ...

Thanks to a miraculous ear, she could instantly repeat and remember whatever she heard; she could surmount without labour difficulties that took others hours and hours of study and hard striving. By the time Maurice Strakosch took her in hand at the age of seven, her mastery of vocal technique was well on the way to completion. Correct breathing, scales, shakes, ornaments, fioriture of every kind, all came naturally to her and required only the finishing touches. She just had to be shown the various roulades and cadenzas; to put them into her voice, as it were; then let them out again in a tone that resembled a nightingale's – pure, rich, luscious, warm, penetrating, and of a haunting beauty. It grew with her from childhood to womanhood, developing from year to year with ever-increasing loveliness and power . . .

Her fame grew like the spread of a conflagration, and with much the same rapidity. Her services were sought in every capital. The crowned heads of the Continent one and all lavished applause and presents and distinctions upon her. Her father and brother-in-law escorted her everywhere, besides rigidly supervising her studies and guarding her against overwork, annoyance or climatic exposure. Even at this period [1862] Strakosch began to insist that she should be spared the fatigue of rehearsing, except for operas that were new to her, and he frequently sang her parts at the ordinary *répétitions* in her stead.

Herman Klein, *Great Women-singers of My Time*, Routledge, 1931,

pp. 36–8, 41–2

The conductor Luigi Arditi tells of his first encounter with the young Patti:

The first time I ever set eyes on Adelina was in New York . . . Adelina's mother was anxious that I should hear the child sing, and so she brought her little daughter to my rooms one day.

Bottesini and I were highly amused to see the air of importance with which the tiny songstress first selected a comfortable seat for her doll in such proximity that she was able to see her while singing, and then, having said: '*Là, ma bonne petite, attends que ta Maman te chante quelque chose de joli*,' she demurely placed her music on the piano, and asked me to accompany her in the Rondo of *Sonnambula*.

How am I to give an adequate description of the effect which that child's miraculous notes produced upon our enchanted senses? Perhaps if I say that both Bottesini and I wept genuine tears of emotion, tears which were the outcome of the original and never-to-be-forgotten impression her voice made when it first stirred our innermost feelings, that may, in some slight measure, convince my

readers of the extraordinary vocal power and beauty of which little
Adelina was, at that tender age, possessed.

Luigi Arditi, *My Reminiscences*, Skeffington, 1896, pp. 80–81

*The Irish composer Charles Villiers Stanford recalls seeing Adelina Patti
at her most absurd:*

In [1862] I heard for the first time Madame Patti in the first opera
I ever saw, Flotow's *Marta*, that old warhorse of the early impresarios which was always trotted out when some other opera was
insufficiently rehearsed. I was strung up to a high pitch of dramatic
excitement about this piece of vapidity, and had a shock when the
diva, as an encore in an Italian opera, came down to the footlights
out of the picture, and interpolated 'Coming thro' the rye'. I
confess that it had much the same effect upon me as would have
been produced by a comic song in the middle of the anthem at St
Patrick's.

C.V. Stanford, *Pages from an Unwritten Diary*, Edward Arnold, 1914,
p. 62

*Mapleson records the passionate rivalry between Mesdames Gerster and
Patti during an American tour in 1883 and 1884:*

On the third night *Les Huguenots* was performed, with Mme Patti
as Valentine, and Mme Gerster as the Queen, when the following
scene occurred:

Prior to the commencement of the opera numbers of very costly
bouquets and lofty set pieces had been sent into the vestibule
according to custom for Mme Patti, whilst only a small basket of
flowers had been received for presentation to Mme Gerster. Under
ordinary circumstances it is the duty of the prima donna's agent to
notify to the stall-keepers, or ushers, as they are called in America,
the right moment for handing up the bouquets on to the stage.
That evening Mme Patti's agent was absent, and at the close of the
first act, during which Valentine has scarcely a note to sing, whilst

the Queen has much brilliant music to execute, he was nowhere to be found. There was a general call at the close of the act for the seven principal artists. At that moment the stall-ushers, having no one to direct their movements, rushed frantically down the leading aisles with their innumerable bouquets and set pieces, passing them across to Arditi, who sometimes could scarcely lift them. Reading the address on the card attached to each offering, he continued passing the flowers to Mme Patti. This lasted several minutes, the public meanwhile getting impatient.

At length, when these elaborate presentations to Mme Patti had been brought to an end, a humble little basket addressed to Mme Gerster was passed up, upon which the whole house broke out into ringing cheers, which continued some minutes. This contretemps had the effect of seriously annoying Mme Patti, who, at the termination of the opera, made a vow that she would never again perform in the same work with Mme Gerster . . .

On returning to her hotel she threw herself on to the ground and kicked and struggled in such a manner that it was only with the greatest difficulty she could be got to bed. The stupidity of the 'ushers' seemed to her so outrageous that she could scarcely accept it as sufficient explanation of the folly committed in sending up her bouquets, her baskets, and her floral devices of various kinds at the wrong moment. At one time when she was in a comedy vein, she would exclaim: 'It is all that Mapleson'; and she actually did me the honour to say that I had arranged the scene in order to lower her value in the eyes of the public, and secure her for future performances at reduced rates.

Then she would take a serious, not to say tragic view of the matter, and attribute the misadventure to the maleficent influence of Gerster. The amiable Etelka possessed, according to her brilliant but superstitious rival, the evil eye; and after the affair of the bouquets no misfortune great or small happened, but it was attributed by Mme Patti to the malignant spirit animating Mme Gerster. If anything went wrong, from a false note in the orchestra to an earthquake, it was always, according to the divine Adelina, caused by Gerster and her 'evil eye'. 'Gerster!' was her first exclamation when she found the earth shaking beneath her at San Francisco.

J.H. Mapleson, *The Mapleson Memoirs 1848–1888*, Remington, 1888, II,
pp. 33–5, 68–9

George Bernard Shaw pays tribute – in a typically double-edged way:

I never fully appreciated Patti until one night at Covent Garden when I heard her sing, not '*Una voce*' or anything of that sort, but 'God Save the Queen'. The wonderful even soundness of the middle of her voice, its beauty and delicacy of surface, and her exquisite touch and diction, all qualify her to be great in expressive melody, and to occupy a position in the republic of art high above the pretty flummery of newspaper puffs, flowers, recalls, encores, and so forth which makes it so difficult for people who take art seriously to do justice to the talent and the artistic pains with which she condescends to bid for such recognition.

I am so far from regretting that Time has stolen some of the five or six notes above the high B flat which she once possessed, and has made the rest hardly safe for everyday use, that I shall heartily congratulate her when the day comes when '*Bel raggio*' and '*Ah, non giunge*', in any key whatsoever, must be dropped, and replaced in her repertory by more such songs as '*Träume*'; for it is my firm belief that Patti is capable of becoming a great singer, though the world has been at such pains and expense to spoil her for the last thirty-five years.

G.B. Shaw, *The World*, 30 May 1894, reprinted in *Shaw's Music*,
Bodley Head, 1989, III, pp. 223–4

Wayne Koestenbaum astutely compares two photographs of Patti:

Two photographs of Adelina Patti, one as Norina in *Don Pasquale*, another as Lucia di Lammermoor, are identical: the same expression, angle of head, position of body within the picture's frame. Only the costumes are different. Patti imperiously refuses to alter her gestures from role to role; and her indifference to realism thrills us. She doesn't fall short of her role; she surpasses it. Our pleasure derives from her acting's insufficiency, its laxness, its willed remoteness from truth; realism is beneath Patti, for no diva needs to be realistic in order to achieve her ambitions.

Wayne Koestenbaum, *The Queen's Throat: Opera and Homosexuality and the Mystery of Desire*, Gay Men's Press, 1993, pp. 109–10

The record producer Fred Gaisberg visited Patti when she was sixty-three:

The year she celebrated the fiftieth anniversary of her début was the year she consented to make gramophone records.

When my brother and I went to Craig-y-Nos we travelled by a narrow-gauge railway to Penwyllt, now called Craig-y-Nos. Here a bus met us and we drove to the sombre and imposing edifice where the singer lived. There we were greeted at the door by her agent, Mr Alcock, and his wife. We soon discovered that every provision had been made for receiving us: two large bedrooms had been cleared and were placed at our disposal. Here we assembled our recording machine. We had a curtain over one of the doors, and through a hole projected the recording-horn. The piano was placed on wooden boxes, and when Madame Patti entered the room she was terribly intrigued as to what was behind that long horn. She had the curiosity of a girl, and peeped under the curtain to see what was on the other side.

It was an ordeal for her to sing into this small funnel, while standing still in one position. With her natural Italian temperament she was given to flashing movement and to acting her parts. It was my job to pull her back when she made those beautiful attacks on the high notes. At first she did not like this and was most indignant, but later when she heard the lovely records she showed her joy just like a child and forgave me my impertinence.

F.W. Gaisberg, *Music on Record*, Robert Hale, 1946, pp. 86 – 7

Rupert Christiansen places Melba (1861–1931) in her grandly Edwardian context:

Melba was anything but fey or vague ... She was brusque, businesslike, organizing, sometimes downright rude. 'I am Melba,' she would announce categorically to anyone who threatened to cross her will in any way. She was totally uninhibited. After a royal command concert at Windsor Castle at which a number of distinguished musicians performed, she turned to the Lord Chamberlain and complained in a loud voice, 'What a dreadful concert this would have been if I hadn't come' . . .

On stage, she moved pieces of scenery and discarded props which offended her. 'What's this bloody thing?' she would exclaim, and fling the unhappy object into the wings . . .

She knew that her real power lay not in having desserts named after her (Pêche Melba, as devised by Escoffier), but in her voice; just as her real palace was no ersatz Versailles, but Covent Garden. No one there crossed Melba, and her disapproval, expressed with a trooper's command of expletives, was said to have stifled the careers of Selma Kurz, Emma Eames (both Marchesi pupils), and Geraldine Farrar, though it is hard to find concrete evidence of this. If she did operate to get rid of rivals, she must have employed subtle rather than overt means. What did matter to her were her unique privileges. She had her own dressing-room to which she kept the key – 'MELBA. SILENCE! SILENCE!' was inscribed across the door; and her own fee – Caruso had to be content with £399 per performance as only Melba was permitted to earn £400. Her real power base was the loyalty of her audience, particularly its fashionable end, and from 1890 onwards 'Melba Nights' at Covent Garden were one of the major events of the fashionable calendar . . .

Melba was not a conventional singer, and her operatic repertory was substantially more contemporary than her nightingale predecessors. She sang no Mozart, no Bellini; Rossini and Meyerbeer only a little; Lucia was her sole major Donizetti role. The Italian nexus was fast giving way to the modern French one. It could be said that Gounod, Thomas, Delibes, and Massenet gave the world updated Donizetti . . . Melba studied with all three composers and made their music a cornerstone of her repertory. The only two roles she created, in now forgotten pieces, were also by Frenchmen, Saint-Saëns and Bemberg. She even sang some of the new *mélodies* of Debussy and Reynaldo Hahn. In late Italian opera, she briefly assumed Aida and Nedda in Leoncavallo's notorious *I pagliacci,* but her two most famous parts here were Desdemona in Verdi's *Otello* and Mimi in Puccini's *La Bohème* – both of which, again, she studied with the composers, and which she sang until the very end of her career.

Rupert Christiansen, *Prima Donna*, Bodley Head, 1984,
pp. 123–4, 127–9

Melba worked hard to achieve her immense popularity – and just as hard to retain it:

Every action of her public life was carried off in the grand manner, and when she travelled the world was aware that this was Melba passing by. In the early years of this century the famous New York–Chicago railroad train, the Twentieth Century Limited, carried many passengers with a taste for Arabian Nights luxury and the means to satisfy it, and Melba was to the fore among them. Writing of the year 1902, in his history of the train, Lucius Beebe said: 'Melba acted the part of the star performer both on stage and off, and travelled in a cloud of hothouse flowers, couriers, personal attendants and the gastronomic prejudices of the well-placed and determined of the world. One of her favourite dishes, plover's eggs *en croûte* with fresh caviar, she was unable to get in New York, but The Century lived up to her standards. Before she boarded the train, her personal staff remade her bed and toilet appointments with the diva's own specially scented bedlinen and towels, and the adjacent drawing-room which she used as a sitting-room was decorated with Melba's own sofa pillows, silver candlesticks and a few gold-framed and autographed likenesses of crowned heads for company to Chicago where she was to sing *La Bohème*. It was all approximately as Bohemian as life in Buckingham Palace' . . .

For many years opera appearances and concerts earned her not less than £1000 a week, and in some years her earnings were considerably higher; her share of the profits of an Australian opera season in 1911 was £46,000, at a time when taxation was negligible, and for many years her gramophone records earned her about £18,000 a year . . .

In grand opera, as in any other branch of the theatre, a man or woman gains a topmost place only by means of artistic excellence, but rarely, perhaps never, holds it by means of artistic excellence alone. As the years cause the individual's powers to decline, a willingness to crush challengers is indispensable. Melba, like Caesar, would brook no rivals . . . In her time she routed many challengers, and did it without a qualm, knowing that if any of them had prevailed against her she would have been destroyed . . .

In a performance of *Bohème* in 1903 the Musetta was a young Austrian soprano, Fritzi Scheff. She was not a potential rival of Melba, but perhaps the audience's response to Fräulein Scheff's singing irritated the diva. At all events near the climax of Musetta's second-act aria an unmistakable voice came sailing out from the wings when Scheff was singing the high B, and finished the phrase with her. The second singer was of course Melba, and Percy Colson, who was in Melba's box that night with Herman Bemberg, reported that Scheff 'tried to scratch Melba's face, and then had hysterics'. Fräulein Scheff was unable to go on with the performance, and an announcement was made that she was indisposed, so that night *Bohème* ended with the unrehearsed duet between Mimi and Musetta. To compensate the audience for the loss of the last two acts Melba, ever self-possessed, sang the Mad Scene from *Lucia*.

John Hetherington, *Melba*, Faber & Faber, 1967,
pp. 78–80, 84, 138

But even Melba sometimes got her comeuppance:

The great French *diseuse*, Yvette, who had made her reputation in the *café-concert* world of Paris, was appearing in New York when Melba was singing in the 1895–6 season at the Metropolitan Opera House. Someone suggested to Melba that she should lunch with her sister celebrity from the other side of the tracks.

'With that *chanteuse*?' Melba scoffed. 'At the most, she might have been invited to come for dessert, for a fee, to sing one of her couplets.'

Yvette had a sharp tongue, too. 'I quite understand,' she replied with mock humility when Melba's words were reported to her. 'I am of humble birth, but Madame Melba of course belongs to the royal family of France.'

Remembering that the Australian was the former mistress of the French pretender, New Yorkers hooted with joy.

John Hetherington, *Melba*, Faber & Faber, 1967, p. 95

How Melba played to the gallery – literally:

When she paid a visit, well before the season started, to Her Majesty's Theatre, Sydney, the stage-hands stood all about staring at her, hardly able to believe they were looking at the great Melba in the flesh.

'Like to hear me sing, boys?' she asked.

She spoke a few words to the conductor, and the orchestra went into the opening of '*Ah fors'è lui*'. Melba sang it through to the end, and walked off into the wings, then came back and bowed to the stage-hands. They were her devoted slaves everafter.

She also won the hearts of the gallery in Sydney with a like gesture. The gallery was packed out by two o'clock every afternoon for the evening performance and the management found a corner there for a piano, so the waiting people could entertain themselves. Melba was persuaded to climb to the gallery one afternoon and show herself. It was a tiring climb but she recovered her wind by the time the ovation died down. Then she sat on the piano stool and, playing her own accompaniment, sang while the gallery sat, hardly breathing. When she got up to go they stood and yelled their adulation.

John Hetherington, *Melba*, Faber & Faber, 1967, p. 171

Melba scorns the views of emperors:

She was summoned to the imperial salon after a performance of *Faust* [in Berlin], and received by Wilhelm II, resplendently uniformed, and the Empress Augusta. The Kaiser, who fancied himself an authority on opera singing, as well as military strategy and tactics, international politics, and all other matters which came under his eye, congratulated Melba on her performance, but then demanded, almost accusingly, 'Don't you think, Madame Melba, you took the Jewel Song at much too fast a tempo?'

'No, your imperial majesty,' Melba replied, at least in her own version of the episode, 'I do not. I sang the part of Marguerite according to the instructions of the composer himself, M. Charles Gounod, who was pleased to express his entire satisfaction with my interpretation and to compliment me on it.'

The Kaiser's spiky moustaches bristled, his eyes flashed, and he turned on his heel and strode to the door, snapping his fingers for the Empress Augusta to follow him.

John Hetherington, *Melba*, Faber & Faber, 1967, p. 176

How Melba dealt with her critics:

Like most public performers she always pretended to care nothing for what critics said of her, yet she was an avid reader of the opinions on her singing published even by nonentities, in obscure newspapers where the music critic was likely to be also the court reporter, the agricultural correspondent, the assistant football writer and the religious editor. When she toured New Zealand in 1903 her singing at a recital in Christchurch on the night of 20

February was adversely criticized in the *Lyttleton Times*. The writer
applauded her technical mastery, but regretted the 'soullessness' of
her numbers, and was trenchant on the standard of some of the
supporting artists. Melba went along in person next day to the
Lyttleton Times office, swept in to see the editor, and demanded
that the critic should be publicly thrashed. The critic evidently had
either a showman's sense or a gift of mordant humour, and 'agreed
to this on condition that she did the thrashing herself, that it
should take place in a public hall, and that he would receive the
whole of the takings. The case did not proceed.'

John Hetherington, Melba, Faber & Faber, 1967, p. 73

Melba was proud of the fact that she retained, virtually in perpetuity, her
own dressing-room at Covent Garden. Before the 1918 season, Sir Thomas
Beecham had the room repainted. Melba was not amused:

It was a few weeks before its opening that an angry figure
stormed into my office and asked what the deuce I meant by
painting her room green. It was Nellie Melba, and very upset she
seemed to be. I had never before come into working contact with
this imposing personality, although I had heard something of her
autocratic ways; and considering the best method of defence here
to be attack, I pretended not to remember who she was, and
asked what the deuce she meant by entering my office unan-
nounced, adding that I knew nothing of private ownership of
rooms in the building. This produced a fresh explosion of wrath
which, as I remained grimly silent, gradually subsided and was
eventually succeeded by an aspect of resignation and the mild
complaint that she would not have minded so much if the green
had been of a cheerfully light instead of a depressingly dismal
hue . . .

As she was going to sing on the opening night under my
direction, I decided to be magnanimous as well as diplomatic
to the extent of offering to repaint 'her' room any colour she
liked. This little concession delighted her more than the most

costly present could have done and we soon became excellent friends.

Sir Thomas Beecham, *A Mingled Chime*, Hutchinson, 1944, pp. 170–71

The pianist Ivor Newton recalls her imperiousness and wit:

Working with Melba was not easy; her strictness, perfectionism, and technical mastery made demands on her colleagues and accompanist as exigent as those made on her own skill and temperament . . . No one could have called her an intellectual singer, in spite of her strictly disciplined approach to her art. 'I shall sing the opera exactly as Gounod wrote it; I hope that you'll conduct it in the same way,' were her words to the young Eugene Goossens when, before a performance of *Faust* which he was unexpectedly called upon to conduct, he went to ask her how she would sing Marguerite and if there was anything about her interpretation he ought to know. On the other hand, she was certainly not an emotional singer; the extreme purity of her voice prevented that, and as for acting, someone unkindly said her 'quaint little gestures' were her substitute for it . . .

For a long time her contract contained a clause declaring that no artist appearing at Covent Garden was to receive more than she did, so that she was paid in guineas to Caruso's pounds. This was the age when every well-dressed man wore a tie-pin, and it was with tie-pins that Melba rewarded her male colleagues and subordinates. A tenor or baritone high in her favour would receive a tie-pin with her initial 'M' in diamonds; the less exalted found that the initial was in gold, while for attentive stage-door keepers it was in blue enamel . . .

Only once did Melba shake the Australian people's devotion to their star. When Clara Butt and [Butt's husband] Kennerley Rumford were about to tour Australia for the first time, draining the country of money with fourteen concerts in Sydney, another fourteen in Melbourne and as many in every other city as its population warranted, the Rumfords asked Melba's advice. What

sort of programmes, they wondered, would Australians like? 'Sing
'em muck,' said Melba, bluntly. 'It's all they understand' ... A
mutual friend asked Melba if it were true that she had really given
Clara Butt this dangerous advice. 'Of course not,' retorted Melba;
'in Clara's case, it wasn't necessary.'

Ivor Newton, *At the Piano*, London, 1966, pp. 100–103

It was Luisa Tetrazzini (1871–1940) who gradually supplanted Melba:

When, in her eighteenth year, a soprano celebrates her fiftieth
performance of *Lucia* with a gala night it is something to boast
about, but when in addition each performance is sold out and at
every one of them the president of a great republic is in the
audience, it is enough to turn any singer's head. This is what
happened to Luisa Tetrazzini in Buenos Aires in 1890. It must
have spoiled her a bit, because when she could not find an
impresario bold enough to tour her in the provinces and follow up
her success, she stubbornly formed her own company, went barn-
storming and reaped a harvest. Her self-confidence dates from the
day when, as a girl of sixteen, she sang the important role of Inez
in *L'Africaine* at short notice in the Fenice ...

The scene shifts to Buenos Aires. There, by great luck, she
found no reigning diva in occupation. She created a furore at
£1500 per month and was the talk of the town for five years.
Supposed love escapades and adventures, even involving the name
of President Saenz Peña, added spice to her sojourns in
Argentina ...

One foggy Saturday evening in November [1907] she made her
[London] début in *La traviata* before a half-empty house. One
could barely see the platform, so dense was the atmosphere. The
few bored critics of the Sunday press opened their eyes in amazement when they heard her wonderful singing, and next morning
the papers went wild about her ... To his dying days [Covent
Garden manager Harry] Higgins considered her the greatest prima
donna of his time. He said nothing ever excelled the brilliance of

her attack and the *abandon* of her cadenzas. Of this her gramophone records alone are proof enough.

F.W. Gaisberg, *Music on Record*, Robert Hale, 1946, pp. 97–8, 102

Tetrazzini refused to play second fiddle, as it were, to a mere harp, whatever the score says:

Cleofonte Campanini married Eva Tetrazzini, the elder sister and teacher of the internationally famous Luisa who was concerned in a typically Parmesan incident at the Teatro Regio. Luisa Tetrazzini, doing her brother-in-law a favour and singing for her bare expenses in *Lucia di Lammermoor*, arrived in Parma having heard that the orchestra boasted a great woman harpist, Rosalinda Sacconi, whose long solo introduction to the scene and cavatina '*Regnava nel silenzio*' in Act I of *Lucia* was played so beautifully that it invariably had to be repeated not once but several times. The introduction was played with the curtain raised and Lucia waiting to sing.

'What,' asked Tetrazzini, 'am I supposed to do until the harpist has finished her encores? Count the seats in the stalls?' The singer pointed out that Lucia, not the harpist, was supposed to be the protagonist in the opera, and she did not propose to provide a living tableau to an instrumental display. Either – Tetrazzini was getting rough by now – there was no star harpist or there was no star singer.

Signora Sacconi saw the point and good-naturedly retired from the scene; and a deputy was found for the performances of *Lucia*. The deputy, although himself a distinguished professor of the instrument, did not arouse the audience to more than a little polite applause at the end of his solo and the opera proceeded.

Spike Hughes, *Great Opera Houses*, Weidenfeld & Nicolson, 1956,

pp. 133–4

8: Caruso

Once after [Caruso] had sung a duet with a celebrated soprano, more noted for her beauty than her voice, I asked how he liked her singing. 'I don't know,' he answered. 'I've never heard her.'

Dorothy Caruso, *Enrico Caruso*, p. 69

In her devoted, almost pious memoir, Caruso's widow, Dorothy, whom he married towards the end of his life, portrays the great tenor's character in idealistic terms:

Being so full, so rich in himself, he could not absorb the kaleidoscopic life of other people. This is the reason why, when I am asked what Caruso thought of his contemporaries, I cannot answer. He didn't think of them – he greeted them. Only when their orbits crossed his, as on the stage, did he feel their proximity. He didn't speak of them to me except in relation to his work. Even then he neither praised nor criticized their singing; nor did he express a preference for singing with one artist rather than another. His complete absorption in his own work left him neither the time nor the desire to indulge in the usual and useless commentaries on events and people . . .

Enrico could never hear the lovely quality of his voice when he sang – he simply felt something inside when the notes came out well. Only by listening to his records could he hear what others heard. 'That is good, it is a beautiful voice,' he would say in astonishment. But he always added, a little sadly, 'With a beautiful voice it is not hard to reach the top. But to stay there, that is hard.'

I realized that it was more than hard – it was a sort of slavery.
The more he sang, the more people demanded of him. He could
never let them down and he drove himself beyond endurance. He no
longer sang because he loved it, but because it was something he
had to do. And because he was a perfectionist he had no satisfaction
within himself; perfect as he tried to be, he knew there was
something beyond   a place better than his best. He got no
comfort or food from music, but he gave both. I have seen him
come home to supper after a magnificent performance and sit,
unable to eat, his eyes full of tears. 'What is it?' I asked. He held
out his palm   'Ashes.' It was no use to say, 'But it was divine
and you had fifteen curtain calls.' It was because of that he wept.
And because I understood that these things were beyond words, I
said nothing. My silence was a comfort to him.

Dorothy Caruso, *Enrico Caruso*, Simon & Schuster, 1945, pp. 60–61, 73

Caruso enjoyed telling stories about his early career:

He told us of the night in Brussels when there wasn't even
standing room left and music-loving students of the university,
unable to get into the theatre, gathered in the street and shouted
up to his dressing-room; he opened the window and sang his aria
to them before going down to the stage. There was also his story
of the first time he ever sang in a theatre in a little town near
Naples when he was just nineteen. He was hissed off the stage
because, not having expected to sing that night, he had drunk too
much good red wine with his supper. He returned to his little
room, certain that his career was ended, and his despair was so
great that he even thought of killing himself. But the following
night the audience so disliked the substitute tenor that they called
for 'the little drunkard'. Enrico was sent for in haste and made his
first success that night. The next morning, when photographers
arrived to take pictures of the promising young singer, they found
him naked in bed – he had sent his only shirt to be washed. He
draped the bedspread around his shoulders and posed for his

photograph with a proud and stern expression. This picture was the first ever published of Caruso.

Dorothy Caruso, *Enrico Caruso*, Simon & Schuster, 1945, p. 143

Caruso performed in the Egyptian première in 1895 of Puccini's Manon Lescaut *but he was overworked and thus insufficiently prepared:*

The Manon of that occasion, Elena Bianchini Cappelli . . . reveals something of the rough and ready circumstances in provincial touring companies of those days; in the last act, when Caruso had gone off-stage, she was suddenly surprised to hear him calling from the wings, *sotto voce*, telling her not to move because he was going to put the score behind her back, for otherwise he could not go on. She describes how embarrassed she felt before the public, for she was supposed to be dying, and she had appropriate gestures to make. But with the score propped up against her she was helpless to do more than just hold as still as possible, serving as a music stand for Caruso. Great was her fury when she realized that he was longing to laugh. Finally, when the curtain came down, she pursued him, hurling after him the score, which he had dropped in his flight. But no one in the audience was any the wiser and after the last performance Caruso created such a furore that Bracale [the impresario] made him a gratuity of £20.

Michael Scott, *The Great Caruso*, Hamish Hamilton, 1988, p. 19

In 1901 La Scala revived Donizetti's L'elisir d'amore *under Toscanini's baton. The opera house's director Giulio Gatti-Casazza recalls how Caruso came to the rescue:*

[Toscanini] takes his place at the desk and the opera commences. The chorus sings its strophes; Adina relates with grace and feeling the story of the love of Queen Isolde and the magic philtre; Nemorino in a song sighs deliciously; but the public takes no interest and remains cool. Not even Belcore, whom the baritone Magini-Coletti impersonates in a masterly manner, succeeds in winning the approval of those terrible subscribers of the Scala. The second act with the concerted scene of Adina, Nemorino, Belcore and the chorus, ends almost in silence. An ugly state of affairs.

Back on the stage I feel my blood freezing and I begin to fear that the evening will end disastrously. Through a peep-hole I watch the public and I see that it is in ill humour and bored. I glance at Toscanini. He has regained his composure and is directing with his customary elegance and masterly style.

The duets begin and Adina is delivering her phrases delightfully, but when she finishes some murmurs of approval are suddenly repressed. Now it is Caruso's turn. Who that heard him would not remember? Calm and conscious that at this point will be decided the fate of the performance, he modulated the reply, '*Chiedi al rio perchè gemente*', with a voice, a sentiment and an art which no word could ever adequately describe. He melted the cuirass of ice with which the public had invested itself, little by little capturing his audience, subjugating it, conquering it, leading it captive.

Caruso had not yet finished the last note of the cadenza when an explosion, a tempest of cheers, of applause, and of enthusiasm on the part of the entire public saluted the youthful conqueror. So uproariously and imperatively did the house demand repetition that Toscanini, notwithstanding his aversion, was compelled to grant it. When the curtain fell, Nemorino and Adina had a triple ovation. During the intermission only Caruso was talked about and the old subscribers compared him to Mario, to Giulini, to Gayarre, and recalled their glory . . .

The evening is a triumph in crescendo. Every number is applauded from now on. The *romanza*, '*Una furtiva lagrima*', interrupted at every phrase by exclamations of admiration, has to be repeated by Caruso, and the public almost insists upon its being sung a third time. The curtain falls for the last time . . .

Toscanini, radiant, as he was going before the curtain with the artists to thank the public, embraced Caruso and said to me:

'*Per Dio! Se questo Napoletano continua a cantare così, fara parlare di*

se il mondo intero!' (By heaven! If this Neapolitan continues to sing
like this he will make the whole world talk about him!)

Giulio Gatti-Casazza, *Memories of the Opera*, Calder, 1977,
pp. 106–8, 110

Caruso soon became an ornament of English society:

On 24 May [1902] he appeared in a command performance of *La
Bohème* with Melba in the presence of Edward VII and Queen
Alexandra. Suddenly he was famous everywhere. It took him some
weeks to become accustomed to the pressure of social engagements,
and in a relatively short while he was inundated with invitations to
dinner, at which it was hoped that he might be prevailed upon to
sing a song. If the mood took him, he would eagerly open the
piano and once comfortably ensconced he would sing away for
hours on end, accompanying himself, but he soon learned to be
canny. At one stately home he was received by the butler and
ushered into a drawing-room and there left to cool his heels. He
had the time, however, to spy the piano, and turning the lock he
quickly pocketed the key before at last his hostess made her
appearance. Great was the anticipation when he acceded to her
gracious request and agreed to sing a song, but greater still was
her chagrin when all attempts to open the piano failed; as he was
leaving he contrived to drop the key into an ashtray.

Michael Scott, *The Great Caruso*, Hamish Hamilton, 1988, pp. 62–3

*Caruso's recording career began after Fred Gaisberg, recording manager for
the Gramophone and Typewriter Company, heard him sing at La Scala in
March 1902 in Franchetti's new opera* Germania:

Afterwards he and his brother forced their way into Caruso's
dressing-room, pumped his hand and explained breathlessly,
through a grinning interpreter, that they wished him to record a
few arias.

  Some of the tenor's entourage jeered and urged him not to

waste his precious voice on this new toy, but Caruso took an instant liking to Fred Gaisberg's good-natured face and invited him to lunch at his flat next day. He thought a fee of £100 for ten songs more than generous and signed without hesitation when the Gaisbergs hinted astutely that the records could be on sale in London before his Covent Garden début, which was already making him feel nervous. Fortunately, he was kept in ignorance of a last-minute complication. Fred Gaisberg had gleefully forwarded details of his coup to the London office, which, to his dismay, wired back: 'FEE EXORBITANT. FORBID YOU TO RECORD.' He decided to go ahead anyway.

Caruso looked 'debonair and fresh', according to Gaisberg, when he arrived at their suite in the Grand Hotel, exactly above the suite in which Verdi had died. His first recording would be *'Questa o quella'* from *Rigoletto*. It was a sunny and very warm afternoon and he complained ruefully of having to delay his lunch, but otherwise he seemed to be treating the whole affair as an amusing outing.

Accompanied by a pianist perched on a packing-case, he sang for two hours into a bell-shaped tin horn hanging five feet from the floor. The programme, effortlessly delivered, included *'Una furtiva lagrima'*, *'E lucevan le stelle'* and *'Celeste Aida'*. He then pocketed his cheque, shook hands with the Gaisbergs, embraced the accompanist and hurried off, whistling cheerfully, to join Ada for a late lunch. The waxes were rushed to Hanover and processed without a single failure. They would yield around £15,000 in net profits for the company.

Stanley Jackson, Caruso, W.H. Allen, 1972, pp. 91–2

The Neapolitan Caruso assumed he would be immune from the intrigues for which the San Carlo opera house was notorious:

He had of course experienced claques in Milan and elsewhere but seemed oddly ignorant of San Carlo's quite exceptional hierarchy. Two rival bands of patrons, known locally as the *sicofanti*, were led by noblemen powerful enough to make or break any singer. Even giants like Tamagno and de Lucia had suffered at their hands and now took good care to placate either or both of these ruthless groups, particularly that ruled by an effete dandy, Prince Adolfo di Castagneto, whose retinue included several leading critics. His monocle, screwed into a supercilious eye or more often removed in disapproval, had all the authority of the imperial thumb.

As a native son who had conquered La Scala and been honoured by the Tsar of Russia himself, Caruso had naïvely expected something like a hero's welcome. He was a little hurt but not too alarmed when the critics failed to call on him for interviews. A good manager would have advised him to entertain them or at least leave his card at their newspaper offices. He tippled instead with back-slapping acquaintances and was deceived by the hypocritical politeness of some of his fellow artists at rehearsals.

He had taken an even greater risk in ignoring the *sicofanti* and failing to bend the knee to either Prince Adolfo or the Cavaliere Monaco, ruler of the opposing claque. He was also handicapped by his previous début at La Scala, a theatre traditionally hated and envied by all good Neapolitan opera goers. Moreover, instead of appearing in a new opera, which might have soothed local pride, he would open in *L'elisir*, already blessed by Milan. San Carlo therefore decided to sit on its hands while this strutting expatriate and former street-singer demonstrated exactly why he now thought himself worth 3000 lire (£120) a night.

The result is now part of operatic history. On that night of terror the comic bumpkin, Nemorino, failed to raise a single chuckle. A spatter of welcome from Daspuro and other staunch friends was at once squelched by the *sicofanti*, who called ominously for silence. When the Cavaliere finally gave modest approval, his enemy's monocle was whipped out to signal a counterblast of hisses. Caruso struggled on with his stage clowning, but not even the normally fireproof '*Una furtiva lagrima*' could survive such an audience . . .

Daspuro saw him off at the station and wished him success in Monte Carlo. He added consolingly that the tenor's next appearance at the San Carlo would no doubt be happier.

'I'll never sing again in Naples,' Caruso declared emphatically. 'When I come here in the future it will be only to eat spaghetti.'

Stanley Jackson, *Caruso*, W.H. Allen, 1972, pp. 84–5

Travelling to a performance of Bohème *in Philadelphia, the bass Andrés de Segurola told Caruso he was rapidly becoming hoarse:*

There was no understudy for the role of Colline and the loss of his voice would mean a disaster. Enrico advised him to hold back as much as possible for the first three acts and save himself for his big aria, '*Vecchia zimarra*', in the fourth. Although Andrés had agreed, when he went on the stage the idea vanished and from the very beginning he held back nothing at all. Consequently after the third act he stood backstage shaking and as hoarse as a crow. Polacco, who was conducting, knew nothing of the desperate basso's situation and gave the signal for the fourth act to begin. He saw Colline enter with his broad felt hat pulled over his face; watched him bring a chair to the footlights, take off his greatcoat, place his foot on the seat of the chair and sing the famous farewell song to his coat. At the end of the aria there was great applause as Colline left the stage; then Caruso came on as Rodolfo and the act finished as usual.

Hardly had the curtain descended when Polacco rushed to Enrico's dressing-room in a rage. 'Are you crazy?' he shouted. 'If the audience had recognized you as Colline it might have ruined the performance.'

'It was a good joke on Polacco,' Enrico said. 'He did not know I was such a good basso.'

After this *tour do force* the Victor Company asked Enrico to make a record of the coat aria for their private files. Naturally neither he nor Mr Child would permit it to be published. 'Besides,' Enrico beamed, 'it would not be fair to the other bassos.'

Dorothy Caruso, *Enrico Caruso*, Simon & Schuster, 1945, pp. 208–10

Caruso could not resist deflating the imperious Melba from time to time:

Caruso's sense of fun, which had an exuberant peasant simplicity, did not amuse her much; for one thing he did not keep his jests off the stage, and Melba was too businesslike a singer to find pleasure in practical jokes which threatened the quality of her performance. Once in *Bohème*, while singing '*Che gelida manina*' to her, he pressed into her hand a hot sausage which he had had his dresser heat over a spirit lamp in the wings. Yelping with shock, Melba flipped the sausage into the air and it bounced across the stage. She gritted out a few choked words of anger, but Caruso's superb voice continued with the love song. Then in a pause for breath he whispered, 'English lady, you like sausage?' Caruso also laughed too heartily once when her dignity – and taste buds – were hurt. She habitually chewed chewing-gum, or for preference a piece of Australian wattle gum, on opera or concert nights to keep her mouth and throat moist. Making an entrance at Covent Garden, she took her gum from her mouth and put it on a little glass shelf, provided for the purpose in the wings. When she came off the stage she went to the shelf, picked up her piece of gum, as she thought, and put it in her mouth. She spat it out and two or three strong words with it. A stage-hand had substituted a quid of tobacco for the gum. Melba demanded that all the stage-hands should be sacked, but she was probably less furious with them than with Caruso, who thought the incident was the best joke of the Covent Garden season and went about backstage bellowing with laughter, his eyes shining with tears of joy.

John Hetherington, Melba, Faber & Faber, 1967, pp. 101–2

Indeed, he adored practical jokes:

Nobody was immune, and he took a special delight in baiting Melba, whose high-and-mighty attitude to Titta Ruffo and other of his friends invited reprisals. She would never forgive one episode when, as Mimi, she was expiring with dignity and in perfect pitch only to hear a sudden guffaw from the audience. Caruso had bribed a stage-hand to place a chamberpot by her bed . . .

La Bohème became Caruso's favourite playground for high jinks in low taste. His old friend Arimondi once delivered Colline's Overcoat Song to find his stovepipe hat half filled with water. Another Colline, this time Caruso's Neapolitan Pasquale Amato, was preparing to go out into the cold night to buy medicine for Mimi when he found he could not put on his coat as the tenor had sewn up the sleeves. Frances Alda also had a most unnerving experience in Philadelphia. Instead of snowflakes, a shower of string, paper and old buttons descended on Mimi's deathbed. Her decanter was also filled with ink instead of water and two castors had been removed from the four-poster, so that the luckless soprano had to expire in a bed which rolled like a hammock in a storm.

At the Metropolitan, not long afterwards, he gave poor Alda another playful nightmare in the same opera. Stooping to pick up a key, she had the misfortune to unhook her white pantalettes, which collapsed like a concertina below her crinoline. She retrieved the situation by slipping out of them behind a sofa but Caruso, without interrupting his singing, scooped them up and laid them carefully on the sofa. The audience shrieked with laughter until Alda's blushes inflamed the pale cheeks of tubercular Mimi.

Stanley Jackson, *Caruso*, W.H. Allen, 1972, pp. 116–17

Osbert Sitwell recalls hearing Caruso and Melba:

Caruso and Melba, when, fat as two elderly thrushes, they trilled at each other over the hedges of tiaras, summed up in themselves the age, no less than Sargent netted it for others. Not only was Caruso as natural a singer as the thrush he resembled, the blackbird, or the conventional nightingale to which he was compared, but contradictorily, for all its lack of art, his voice carrying in its strains, in the sound of those notes which he was able to attain and hold as could no other singer, of that or of a later day, the warm breath of southern evenings in an orange grove, and of roses, caught in the hush of dusk at the water's edge, possessed, as well

as a high degree of technique, a certain kind of art. Of Melba
the same cannot be said. Her magnificent voice was not invariably true, having about it something of the disproportion of the
Australian continent from which she had emerged. But at least
it can be claimed for her that, with her ample form lying on a
couch, she made a surprising and unforgettable type of romantic
consumptive.

Osbert Sitwell, Great Morning!, Atlantic Monthly Press, 1947, p. 151

In 1918 Caruso began to make movies:

A fee of $100,000 proved irresistible, and between 15 July and 10
September, he agreed to make a couple. The first, *My Cousin*, had
him playing two roles. But hardly surprisingly – it was *silent!* – the
reception was equivocal. It was unfortunate that he did not, as was
originally planned, play Canio in a film of Leoncavallo's *Pagliacci*,
for had he mimed '*Vesti la giubba*' or '*No! Pagliacci non son!*' these
excerpts might at least have been dubbed with his records. One
wonders what Jesse Lasky, the film's director, was thinking of;
phonograph records of Pavlova dancing or Picasso painting could
hardly have been less revealing. Needless to say, his second film,
A Splendid Romance, was released only in Europe and South
America.

Michael Scott, The Great Caruso, Hamish Hamilton, 1988, pp. 160–61

*Caruso, plagued by migraine-type headaches and throat ailments, did not
enjoy perfect health. At one performance of* L'elisir d'amore *at the
Brooklyn Academy of Music, on 11 December 1920, Caruso displayed
symptoms of the pleurisy that would lead to his death some months later:*

My seats were in the front row. The curtain rose a quarter of an
hour late, and I knew that the doctor must have arrived. The four
long acts of gaiety began, on a stage filled with moving colour and
bright melody. Enrico came running out over the little rustic
bridge, laughing and looking as foolish and stupid as possible. He

wore a red wig, a pongee smock, brown breeches and striped stockings; a big red cotton handkerchief hung out of his pocket and he carried a little basket over his arm. The audience applauded wildly. Standing close to the footlights, he began at once to sing. When he had finished he turned his back and reached for his handkerchief. I heard him give a little cough, but he came in on his cue, finished the phrase and turned away again. When he faced the audience I saw that the front of his smock was scarlet. A whisper blew through the house but stopped as he began to sing. This time it was an aria and he couldn't turn his back. From the wings Zirato's hand held out a towel. Enrico took it, wiped his lips and went on singing. Towel after towel was passed to him and still he sang on. All about him on the stage lay crimson towels. At last he finished the aria and ran off. The act was ended and the curtain came down.

Cold and blind with terror, I sat without moving. For long moments the theatre was as silent as an empty house. Then, as if a signal had been given, a thunder of sound and movement shook the audience. I heard shouts and screams, voices crying 'Stop him!' 'Don't let him go on!'

Someone touched my shoulder. 'I am Judge Dyke, Mrs Caruso. May I escort you to the dressing-room?' I rose and took his arm. We walked slowly up the aisle but when I reached the corridor I began to run.

Surrounded by terrified faces, Enrico was lying on a couch. Dr H. was explaining that a little vein had burst at the base of the tongue, and Mr Ziegler, assistant manager of the Metropolitan, was pleading with Enrico to go home. For the first time in his life he didn't protest but consented that the audience be dismissed.

Dorothy Caruso, *Enrico Caruso*, Simon & Schuster, 1945, pp. 237–8

His widow Dorothy portrays his curiously self-contained personality:

Enrico was a musician who had no time for music. We never went together to hear opera. I don't believe he had heard one for twenty

years, except those in which he himself sang; and even then he
never stood in the wings to listen to the other singers. We never
went to symphony concerts either. Once we went to a recital – the
début of Tito Schipa, who was giving a programme of Neapolitan
songs. We arrived late, sat in the back of the hall where no one
could see us and left in fifteen minutes. 'Why did we go at all?'
I asked. 'Because he is a tenor. But it's all right,' he said
cryptically . . .

No amateur accompanist ever played for him, nor did he ever
sing 'for fun' at parties. His contract with the Metropolitan forbade
his singing anywhere unless he had official permission. I know of
only one time that he broke this rule. We had gone to a benefit
vaudeville performance, given for soldiers and sailors, at the
Manhattan Opera House. We thought no one could see us, seated
in the back of a stage box, but a boy in the front row called out,
'There's Caruso!' The performance stopped, the audience shouted
and stamped and the manager came to our box. 'Mr Caruso, they
want you to sing "Over There".' Enrico didn't hesitate but left me
immediately and went on to the stage. When he had finished, the
audience wouldn't let him go. Finally, waving and calling 'No
more,' he hurried back to me. 'We must leave quickly,' he whispered. 'I must go and tell Gatti* I broke my contract.' I waited in
the car outside the stage door while he talked with Gatti. When he
came out he was beaming. 'He excuse me,' he said . . .

Enrico was ruthless when singers came to him for criticism, and
scarcely a day passed without his listening to an audition. Some of
the voices were good, others frightful. Society women were the
most trying – I remember one who insisted on singing her entire
repertoire, even after Enrico had told her that her voice wasn't
suited for opera. 'But what is wrong with my voice?' she insisted.
'It is too old,' he said bluntly.

One day the Marchesa C., a ravishingly beautiful woman, and
her little husband came to see us. Enrico had known them both in

---

* Giulio Gatti-Casazza, then director of the Metropolitan Opera House, with which
Caruso had an exclusive contract.

Italy. She had sung professionally throughout Europe, accompanied at the piano by her husband. She was to give a Debussy recital at the Princess Theatre for a smart audience, and hoped to be engaged for private soirées later on. If Enrico would only go to her concert, she was sure it would be a success.

We went and sat in the front row . . .

The audience sat hypnotized – all but Enrico. He rolled his eyes and pushed up his nose with the knob of his cane. After it was all over the husband met us in the lobby, trembling with excitement.

'Come with me,' he said, 'there are crowds waiting, but she will see you.'

'I go home,' said Enrico.

'But –' said the little man.

'I go home,' said Enrico again and added over his shoulder, 'You can come to dinner tonight.'

At dinner Enrico laughed, talked and told stories without stopping. He never mentioned the concert. The Marchesa became more and more unresponsive. She waited until the coffee was served to say, 'Well, Caruso, what did you think of my recital?'

'Beautiful,' said Enrico without hesitation. 'You had a great success.'

'Yes, but what did you think about me?'

'You were very effective – the chair – the muff – everything. I tell you they liked very much.'

'But what about my voice, my singing?'

Enrico's expression changed. 'You want to know my opinion of your voice as Caruso the artist or Caruso the friend?'

Her voice was high as she answered, 'Artist, of course.'

'Well, then, I tell you. You do not sing because you do not know how.'

She was furious. 'How can you say that? I have studied seven years with Jean de Reszke!'

'Then, madame, you both wasted seven years. You have no voice, you know nothing about singing. But you will be engaged because you look nice.'

Immediately she rose from the table and left the house.

The next day Mrs Belmont and Mrs Reginald de Koven called
on us. They had been to the recital and wanted to know what
Enrico thought of it. If he said it was good, they would ask the
Marchesa to sing in their houses.

'She is most effective and made a great success,' said Enrico.
'You not make a mistake.' They had thought so too, they said, and
went away pleased.

'You see, Doro, she get the work. But she had not the sense to
keep quiet after I show I not want to talk. She made me hurt her,
otherwise she repeat to someone that I say she sing well and they
maybe know singing and say, "Caruso is a stupid – he cannot tell
good voice from bad." This I cannot let happen for my name as an
artist. Always I must tell the truth – if they insist.'

Dorothy Caruso, Enrico Caruso, Simon & Schuster, 1945,
pp. 144–5, 154–6

*Gatti-Casazza, director first of La Scala and then of the Metropolitan
Opera, pays tribute to this unsurpassed singer:*

I have heard all the great tenors of my time, over and over again.
Many of them were wonderful artists, with exceptional voices; and
all sang, I remember, some marvellous performances. Yet not one,
in my judgement, ever sang an entire role with the vocal or artistic
consistency of Caruso; and certainly no other tenor I can call to
mind remotely compares with him in having continued to sing –
week after week and season after season – with the same almost
unvarying achievement of supremacy, almost never disappointing
an audience through inability to appear.

Giulio Gatti-Casazza, Memories of the Opera, Calder, 1977, p. 234

9: Chaliapin

You are to music what Tolstoy is to literature.

Letter from Maxim Gorky to Feodor Chaliapin

The great Russian bass Feodor Chaliapin (1873–1938) prepares for his most celebrated role, that of Boris Godunov in Mussorgsky's opera:

Boris Godunov appealed to me to such an extent that, not content with learning my role, I sang the whole of the opera, all parts, male and female . . .

Apart from this thorough exploration of the Mussorgsky music, I began to look at him from the historical angle. To this end I began reading Pushkin and Karamzin. But this was not enough, I wished to go farther, and consequently I enlisted the aid of the famous historian, Klyuchevsky . . .

The rehearsals for *Boris Godunov* began. At once I realized that my colleagues did not see things my way and that the existing school of opera did not meet the requirements of such a work. There seemed a deficiency, even in the performance of an opera like *The Maid of Pskov*. I myself, of course, was a product of the same school, a school of singing, and nothing more. This school taught how to hold the sound, how to broaden or reduce it, but what it did not teach us was the psychology of the character portrayed. Certainly nobody was ever instructed to make a study of the epoch in which a character had lived. The professors of this school were wont to use the most baffling terminology, often incomprehensible. They talked of 'holding the voice in the "masque"', of 'placing it on the diaphragm', or of 'pressing down'. It may have been necessary, but it was not the essence of the matter. To me it seemed not enough to teach a man to sing a cavatina, serenade, or ballad; he must be taught to understand the meaning of the words he sings, the feelings they evoke . . .

The day of the performance arrived. Since the production of *The Maid of Pskov*, I had become perhaps the most popular artist in Moscow, and the public flocked to productions in which I took part. In the beginning *Boris* was greeted coolly, apathetically, and I was worried. But suddenly the hallucination scene electrified the audience, and the opera ended in triumph. It seemed strange to me that this opera had never before made such an impact, and yet this work is Shakespearean in its power and beauty. The performances that followed brought the public nearer to it, and now from the very first act they seemed to fall under its enchantment.

Prepare as I might, study and strive as I might, I never once walked on to the stage with the feeling of mastery. That was something that grew in the act itself; and the reward and the knowledge arose out of my performance. It was this living of the role that, with each production, I broadened and deepened the character.

Feodor Chaliapin, *Chaliapin: An Autobiography as Told to Maxim Gorky*,
ed. Nina Froud and James Hanley, Macdonald, 1968, pp. 128–30

Sir Isaiah Berlin reminisces about Chaliapin, whom he, as a child of seven, heard singing in Boris Godunov *in pre-revolutionary Russia:*

'It's not the death scene in which I remember Chaliapin,' he told me. 'About that I remember only that one of the chorus forgot to rush forward and support him as he tottered down the steps, and was kicked sharply by another boyar. That I enjoyed very much indeed. What haunts my memory is the ghost of Dimitri, or rather, Boris's hallucination. Chaliapin seemed physically to contract as he clutched the tablecloth of the table on the extreme left of the stage, behind which he stood. His features contorted, and his voice in some miraculous fashion seemed at the same time to sing magnificently while sounding distorted and strangled. He gradually disap-

peared or nearly so, behind and underneath the table, half pulling
the tablecloth over himself. The whole thing was most terrifyingly
hypnotic.

'I don't think that at that age I could have known what was
being represented, only that a huge, marvellously dressed man was
going through an agony of terror or some abnormal and very
frightening condition. His dilated eyes and the violent, twisted,
continuously expressive miming remain with me to this day. He
was certainly the greatest actor that I've ever seen.'

Ivor Newton, *At the Piano*, Hamish Hamilton, 1966, pp. 87–8

Sir Thomas Beecham mounted a production of Boris Godunov *by the
Russian Opera Company in London in 1913. At one performance he
noticed that the Russian chorus had absented itself from the stage:*

I hurried behind at the fall of the curtain and found everything in a
state of wild confusion ... The cause of the disturbance was an
acute disagreement between Chaliapin and the choristers. Hard
words had been exchanged between the contending parties, tempers
had run high; the only person who might have put the matter
right was the manager, and he had fled before the storm. Eventually
the indignant malcontents were persuaded to leave the stage and
retire to their dressing-rooms, as they did not take part in the next
act; but at the close of it, and just as Chaliapin was about to leave,
they reappeared. One of their leaders approached him, and a brief
altercation took place which ended dramatically with Chaliapin
knocking the man down. Like a pack of wolves the rest of the
chorus flung themselves upon him, brandishing the tall staves they
were to use in the next scene, the small English group rushed to
his assistance and the stage-door keeper telephoned for aid to the
police station, which luckily was hardly a stone's throw from the
theatre. The struggle was still raging when a few minutes later
Drury Lane beheld the invasion of about a dozen familiar figures
in blue, and very soon something like order was re-established ...
By undertaking that their grievances should be investigated and

remedied I secured the presence of the chorus for the rest of the work. So far from being upset by what had taken place, they went through the great Revolution Scene with more than usual fire and enthusiasm; but at the close of the performance nothing would induce them to leave the stage, and they refused to budge a step until they had had it out with Chaliapin himself. The latter at first declined to emerge from his room, but, on being assured that he would be well guarded, finally came out with a loaded revolver in either pocket. By this time the warm reception given to the chorus for their magnificent singing had allayed somewhat their exasperation, and they seemed inclined to carry on the dispute in more orthodox fashion.

It was certainly a strange sight: the principal character still in his royal costume and fully armed for warfare; the choristers who had just played the part of an insurgent peasantry, wild and savage in appearance; the stolid English contingent in its everyday working dress; and the cohort of police silent but alert in the background. The proceedings began with a speech of immense length from one of the chorus leaders, and this was answered by Chaliapin in another of even greater length. A third speech followed from a female member of great eloquence and volubility, to which Chaliapin again replied in like manner. I began to wonder if this was how business was transacted in the Duma, for it seemed that this sort of thing might go on for ever. But all at once there was a huge shout of joy, and the next moment Chaliapin was being hugged and kissed by every member of the chorus, male and female.

Sir Thomas Beecham, *A Mingled Chime*, Hutchinson, 1944, pp. 120–21

Giulio Gatti-Casazza, the director of La Scala, hired the unknown Chaliapin on the basis of a recommendation from the Inspector of the Imperial Russian Theatres:

The telegram was sent off to Moscow offering ten performances and asking what compensation he would demand. The telegram having been sent, I communicated again with Boito, who, much to my surprise, this time showed himself satisfied.

'I have heard some talk about this Chaliapin,' he said, 'and very favourable. I have an idea that this Scythian barbarian will do very well.'

Three or four days later the telegram in reply was received. Chaliapin agreed to the proposition and asked 1000 lire per performance. If we accepted, he would come to Milan to sign the contract himself and to meet Boito and the rest of us. About a month after receiving our favourable reply, he arrived at Milan . . .

The contracts were signed and exchanged, and the newspapers announced the revival of *Mefistofele* and the engagement of the basso from the Moscow theatre.

Then, like a bolt from the blue, the whole theatrical world vented its indignation. In the famous Gallery Victor Emmanuel nothing else was talked about, and particularly they spoke of the director of the Scala as of a traitor to his country . . .

Chaliapin studied and prepared his role with that attention and diligence that characterize the few members of that select company of artists who look after everything, think of everything, with perfect conscientiousness. His Mefistofele turned out a new thing, without precedent, breaking all traditions. His make-up and costume have since been copied by everyone; but above all were his great authority, mobility of countenance, richness of expression and incredible acting. In a word, it was one of those few occasions when the much-abused word 'creation' could be applied with perfect justice . . .

To say that Chaliapin won a success at the première is to put it mildly. He won the battle to such a degree that the public, which had come to the theatre full of diffidence, and even prejudice, against him, finished by driving out of the theatre some disturbers who dared attempt to hiss.

Giulio Gatti-Casazza, *Memories of the Opera*, Calder, 1977,

pp. 112–15, 118

Chaliapin gave his own account of his 1901 début at La Scala, where he encountered some curious local customs:

I received a telegram from La Scala, Milan, inviting me to sing in Boito's *Mefistofele*, and asking my terms. At first I treated it as a practical joke, but my wife persuaded me to treat the matter seriously . . . I was afraid of it, since I could not speak Italian, and certainly could not sing it, besides which I did not know Boito's opera. I felt I dare not reply in the affirmative. For two whole days I was in such an agitated state of mind that I could neither eat nor sleep. Finally I found a score of the opera, and saw that it was easily within my range. Even this did not supply the confidence required, and I sent off a telegram asking for what I thought to be impossible terms, secretly hoping they would refuse them, and so let me out. But they actually agreed to them . . .

The conductor, a young man named Toscanini, spoke in a hoarse and colourless voice, informing me that the theatre had formerly been a church, Madonna della Scala. I was amused by this. In Russia the transformation of one temple into another would have been quite impossible. I examined everything I was shown with great interest, and I must confess that an involuntary tremor passed through me. How would I sing in this colossal theatre, in a strange tongue, before a strange people? The rehearsals began almost as a murmur, the artists, among whom I found Caruso, then a young man just starting his career, sang in a low voice. I followed his example, being tired and feeling that it would be wrong for me to use full voice when no one else did.

The conductor looked quite ferocious to me. A man of few words, unsmiling, he corrected the singers harshly, and spared nobody. Here was a man who really knew his job, and one who would brook no contradiction. I remember him turning to me in the middle of rehearsal, and asking in rasping tones if I intended to sing the opera as I was singing it then.

'No. Certainly not,' I said, embarrassed. 'Well,' he replied, 'I have not had the honour of going to Russia and hearing you there.

Thus I don't know your voice. Please be good enough to sing as you intend to do at the performance.'

I saw that he was right, and I sang in full voice. Often he would interrupt the other singers, offering advice, but he never said a word to me. I didn't know how to take this, and it left me with a feeling of uncertainty.

Again the next day there was a rehearsal in the foyer ... [It] began with the Prologue. I gave it full voice, and when I had finished Toscanini paused for a moment, his hands lying on the piano keys, inclined his head a little, and uttered one single word in a very hoarse voice.

'Bravo.'

It was quite unexpected, and had the effect of a pistol shot. I hardly realized this praise was meant for me. Elated by this success, I sang with tremendous enthusiasm, but Toscanini never uttered another word . . .

Opening night approached. Milan became a hive of activity for various theatrical parasites. In no other country in the world are there so many people engaged in speculation. Nowhere on earth can one find such importunate and brazen claques. The unknown artist is forced as by a law to pay a contribution to the claque, the sum being dependent on the fee received by the artist. I, of course, was quite ignorant of this institution, never having heard of its existence.

Imagine my surprise when a group of people suddenly appeared announcing that they had taken it upon themselves to 'ensure my success', and requesting me to provide them with several dozen tickets, and the sum of 4000 francs for their guaranteed applause on the opening night . . .

I told them to go to hell, and they made their exit, warning me that Signor Chaliapin would have cause to regret this. I felt angry about this and stamped into the director's office.

'I have come to La Scala,' I said, 'with much the same feeling as a Christian approaches Communion. But these people disgust and depress me. I cannot sleep at night for thinking about it, dreading a failure. Perhaps I should return to Russia where such things do not happen.'

This went right home, and he made great efforts to calm me, and promised me full protection from the claque . . .

When the day of the actual opening arrived I set out for the theatre with a heavy heart . . . The performance began . . . I sang without feeling anything, simply singing the words that I knew by heart, and giving as much voice as I could.

My heart fluttered. 1 seemed not to have enough breath, there was a mist before my eyes, everything appeared to float past me. The moment I finished, after which the chorus enters, there was a sudden loud crash. I thought a piece of scenery had fallen, or that the wheels on which I stood had broken. Instinctively I ducked, and only then did I realize that this great wave of noise was coming from the auditorium. Something quite unimaginable was going on out there. Those with experience of Italian opera houses will know what the quality of Italian praise or protest is like. The public literally went mad, interrupting the Prologue halfway . . . .

After this it was easier to sing, yet after the Prologue I felt flat, drained. The opera was a great success. I kept on waiting for some form of demonstration from the claque I had offended, but there wasn't a single whistle, boo, or hiss. Later I was told that even claques loved art.

Feodor Chaliapin, *Chaliapin: An Autobiography as Told to Maxim Gorky*,
Macdonald, 1968, pp. 144–50

Chaliapin remained at the peak of his powers well into middle age. Vincent Sheean heard him in the early 1920s:

At this time Chaliapin was getting toward fifty but had lost none of the round, ringing power of his incomparable voice. It was a voice capable of almost any variety of expression, emphasis or suggestion. Except that he was a basso by decree of nature, it would have been impossible to assign limits to his musical and dramatic power. When that gargantuan voice was reduced to a whisper, it could still be heard in the remotest part of this or any other house. With such an unequalled endowment he combined an infallible sense for stage action in the representation of character. For this he never had an equal, so far as I know, except Mary Garden. Neither could have created character in this way – *lived* character, *been* character – in the ordinary theatre, with its totally different demands, but in the lyric theatre, where everything up to and including the innermost soul of the personage is a function of music, they were the first and so far the only examples of their kind . . .

He was a childlike creature by temperament – I knew him later – and I have no doubt he enjoyed every minute of it. He had retained his youthful powers, I think, precisely by means of this childlike temperament, which did not permit him to worry or even to think except about the ferociously serious business of the 'creation'. Where the 'creation' was concerned he was adult in the extreme, fanatically concentrated and incapable of compromise. Each of the great 'creations' – not only Boris itself but Basilio in *Il barbiere di Siviglia* and all the others – was the work of years, but once it was fixed, it had the permanence of sculpture or architecture.

Vincent Sheean, First and Last Love, Gollancz, 1957, pp. 59–61

Chaliapin's visit to New York in 1922 was marred by sickness:

He had no sooner arrived in New York than he was attacked by severe laryngitis. I was in his bedroom at the Waldorf-Astoria Hotel on a Sunday evening, half an hour before he was due to make his post-war début in New York . . . He was surrounded by the impresarios Solomon Hurok and Frederick Coppicus, his accompanist Rabinovitch and myself. The air was charged with anxiety. Chaliapin with his laryngoscope, seated in his underwear before a mirror, was inviting us to look down the instrument to convince ourselves that those inflamed spots on his vocal chords made it impossible for him to sing. The concert had already been postponed twice on account of his laryngitis. The two American impresarios were wringing their hands, saying they would be ruined by another cancellation and begging him to go to the concert if only to apologize to the audience. Chaliapin in despair threw himself on to the bed and moaned, 'Bozhe, Bozhe, what have I done to deserve this?' He paced the room, knocking his head on the wall and again cried to God, 'Why should I be so punished?' Then suddenly Nicolai, his little valet, said in Russian, 'Feodor Ivanovitch, go to the concert; God will give you back your voice when the moment comes.' Chaliapin stopped short, and with a look of scorn at the valet said, 'What has God got to do with my voice?'

It was already past the hour for the commencement of the concert when we made a combined effort and started to dress him, in spite of his continued resistance. I put on his socks and fastened up his boots. Hurok tied his tie and we dragged the protesting giant downstairs, thrust him into a taxi, and started for the Manhattan Opera House . . .

Chaliapin tried to persuade the doctor in attendance to go on to the platform and announce to the waiting audience that Chaliapin was going to appear, in spite of his warning that his septic throat made it impossible for him to sing, and that if he attempted to do so he would probably lose his voice for ever. This the doctor was too shy to do . . .

I was placed in the middle of the stage with the curtain down, alone in that vast space. I could hear the yells of the audience from the other side, like those of hungry lions in a den. In a moment the curtain quickly rose and I looked out on a sea of faces. There was a hushed silence. Closing my eyes I cried out the apologies of Chaliapin and asked the indulgence of the audience. There was a great roar as I retreated to the wings.

Then Chaliapin strode forth, followed by his accompanist, and for the next five minutes the cheering was continuous. Through his superb acting he made it plain that he was suffering; he even produced tears to win the sympathy of the public. Then he literally barked out, in a sick voice, five songs. It was indeed a pitiful performance, but the audience had to be satisfied as there certainly would be no money returned.

By a back door he and I fled from the theatre to a quiet Harlem speakeasy, where I did my best, through a long evening, to console him. Early next morning I hustled him down to a secluded farm in the heart of New Jersey, on the outskirts of Jamesburg, before reporters could get at him, and I kept him there until his throat was well. It was not long before the villagers' curiosity was aroused by this blond giant who took his daily walks through the village streets. The enterprising proprietor of the local movie house soon discovered that this stranger was a singer, and one morning stopped Chaliapin in the street, suggesting that as he was doing nothing else, he might earn a little money if he would sing a few songs on Saturday night at his theatre. For this he boldly offered three dollars! Chaliapin suggested that he could pay four, but the proprietor replied that his house only held twenty when it was full, and that was the end of their negotiations. Chaliapin had that very day refused an offer for twenty performances in South America at $2500 a performance.

F.W. Gaisberg, *Music on Record*, Robert Hale, 1946, pp. 223–5

Chaliapin reports on the ingenious measures taken by the management of the Metropolitan Opera House in New York to dissuade singers from outbursts of temperament. On this occasion the first night of Mefistofele *was imminent:*

My nerves were on edge, and on the first night, feeling really ill, I sent in a note to the administration informing them that I was unable to appear. The reply to this note was startling.

In my room I was suddenly confronted by a long, bony lady wearing spectacles, with frowning eyebrows, and a turned-down mouth. Pointing her finger at me, she said something in English. I gathered she wanted to know if I was Chaliapin and I replied in the affirmative, apologizing in my best Russian for appearing in a dressing-gown. With eloquent gestures she then bade me to lie down on the bed. I did so, and to my horror saw her removing instruments from her doctor's bag.

She ordered me to go to bed, and then to my further alarm I

saw that I was to have a colonic *lavage*. This scared me and I yelled
for the valet, who spoke French. He explained that the lady was a
doctor who would cure me within twenty-four hours. I asked him
to convey my respects to her, but that I was not requiring her
services. In spite of this she insisted that I should go to bed. The
instrument for *lavage* hung in the air; I pleaded with her to go
away.

'I will sing. I will sing! Just go away. Please.' And she went.
The scene made me laugh, and in fact calmed me down a little.
Although that night I was feeling exhausted, I sang well.

Feodor Chaliapin, *Chaliapin: An Autobiography as Told to Maxim Gorky*,
Macdonald, 1968, p. 173

Osbert Sitwell encounters Chaliapin's wrath:

One evening, in after years, when I had grown to know Chaliapin
fairly well, Lady Aberconway and I went to congratulate him, in
his dressing-room, after he had taken the part of Salieri in Rimsky-
Korsakov's *Mozart and Salieri*. Mozart had been played by a young
Italian tenor, of whom Chaliapin was a warm supporter, having
proposed him for the part, and to a certain degree coached him at
the rehearsals. The Italian was small – or perhaps not, for one of
Chaliapin's attributes was that, though a giant, he never looked
over life-size, but merely reduced the scale of others, even tall
men. At any rate, on this the first night, this protégé had enraged
Chaliapin by the lightness of his singing, and by the airy way he
played the harpsichord on the stage, lifting his hand up and down
in a fashion against which he had been warned by the great singer.
When, therefore, we arrived, and opened the door, we found the
enormous Russian shaking the young Italian, as a mastiff might
shake a griffon. After we entered the room, he desisted, saying in
explanation, 'And the plot of this opera is that *I* have to be jealous
of *him*!'

Osbert Sitwell, *Great Morning!*, Atlantic Monthly Press, 1947,
pp. 264–5

Chaliapin's funeral:

To Paris I journeyed in April 1938 to pay my last respects to the great artist, and there mingled with the thousands of Russians of every degree who filled the small Russian Cathedral in rue Daru and overflowed into the streets. I saw real, unabashed grief. For six days Chaliapin lay in state in his home in the avenue d'Eylau while a constant stream of friends and fellow-countrymen as well as fellow artists looked their last on him. On the day when he was buried the funeral cortège stopped at the cathedral where a Mass for the Dead was read, with an unaccompanied chorus consisting of the famous Afonsky Choir and the Aristoff Russian Opera Chorus . . . Many of his old colleagues sang as choristers . . . It was the most wonderful choral singing I have ever heard, and everyone was profoundly moved. After the custom in France, about midday the long funeral cortège, with many vehicles of floral tributes, began its journey to the cemetery. Members of the Paris Opéra, headed by Serge Lifar, had arranged to honour their colleague. The procession paused in the courtyard of the Opéra, where, in the open air, amidst the hum of the Paris traffic, a prayer for the dead was read and the choir intoned a chorale. I had not expected such a display of emotion by these choristers and former colleagues, and turned to my neighbour, Prince Zeretelli, for an explanation. 'Chaliapin dead,' he said, 'all is forgiven. They realize now that there will be no other like him. Whatever his faults, for them he was Russia.'

F.W. Gaisberg, *Music on Record*, Robert Hale, 1946, pp. 230–31

10: A Clutch of Tenors

Singers fear the inevitable day when the organism will betray them, and they fend off that retribution by muffling their throats, whispering in rehearsal, or trusting in charms: Caruso wore an amulet of anchovy round his neck, Pavarotti grubs for bent nails backstage. They all know their high Cs are numbered. When one is let out, it's gone for ever, and must be deducted from the total.

Peter Conrad, *A Song of Love and Death*, p. 357

In 1897 Leo Slezak (1873–1946) made his début at the Royal Opera House in Berlin:

Young Richard Strauss was the conductor and the famous Emmy Destinn was Elsa. Papa was shaking with nerves and the début was not too auspicious. One of the reviews the next day read: 'A Mr Slezak from the Civic Theatre in Bruenn sang Lohengrin. He did not wear a beard; he looked like a child and sang like an old man.'

[*Years later* Lohengrin *was to provide Slezak with a famous opportunity to demonstrate his wit and coolness under fire:*]

It was just before his first entrance. He was ready to step into the boat, which, drawn by a swan, was to take him on-stage. Somehow the stage-hand on the other side got his signals mixed, started pulling, and the swan left without Papa. He quietly turned around and said: 'What time's the next swan?'

[*In 1933 Leo Slezak was still singing:*]

On 26 September 1933, Papa sang *I pagliacci* at the Vienna Opera House. He was then sixty years old.

'I felt like a twenty-five-year-old,' he wrote me. 'My voice sounded as young as ever, without any strain or effort. It was one of those rare evenings and the spark of my happiness must have jumped across the footlights and the orchestra pit into the audience. Rarely have I had such an ovation after the aria *"Ridi Pagliacci"*. They applauded right through the intermission. As I was waiting for my second-act entrance, I thought: Wouldn't that be a wonderful way to leave, to end my career in opera on such a high note; maybe I will never be able to sing so well! By the time the final curtain had rung down, my mind was made up. I had sung my last opera! . . . The next morning, I called on Clemens Krauss, the general manager, and informed him that I had retired. "But that's impossible, that's unheard of," he protested. "You cannot simply walk away from a career such as yours without giving at least a farewell performance." "My dear Herr Director," I laughed, "I don't go to other people's funerals; I am certainly not going to my own."'

A few weeks later Papa got an official document from Chancellor Dollfuss, informing him that he would receive the highest decoration the state of Austria can bestow on a civilian, and that the ceremony of presentation would be held on the stage of the Opera House, the place of his great triumphs, surrounded by all his colleagues, the orchestra, and assorted functionaries.

So Papa wrote him a very nice letter, thanking him for the great honour: '. . . but, your excellency, I know how these official interments are handled: I have attended a few of them myself!

'It's eleven in the morning, everybody has to appear, dressed in cutaway or something equally uncomfortable. The "dear departing one" is led up an elevated platform and seated on a "throne" that has been brought up from the property room, dusted and decorated with laurel leaves. Then begin the speeches: I will be informed that my name will be entered into the illustrious annals of the Vienna Opera House as one of their immortals, that my contribution will never be forgotten and that the memory of my performances will live on as an inspiration to coming generations of singers! Believe me, your excellency, it's the bunk! The other tenors are already waiting in the wings and the annals are read by nobody. The singer is a torch-bearer: as long as the torch burns brightly, the crowd will follow him. Once it's extinguished, he is alone. But I am just sentimental enough to get very emotional and possibly burst out in tears, and I would like to spare you and me that spectacle. Permit me to come to your office, where you will hand me the greatly appreciated medal; I will tell you a few good stories and that will be it!'

Dollfuss wrote back: 'All right, if that's the way you want it!' Clemens Krauss and Papa rode to the Chancellery. At the presentation, the Chancellor, who was a tiny man and reached just up to Papa's navel, said: 'Herr Kammersänger, I hope you will forgive me, but I cannot just hand you that medal; I will have to say a few words.' He then began a speech and inadvertently slid into the phrase about the annals, then the never-to-be-forgotten contributions and the inspiration to coming generations. Suddenly, all burst out laughing. Dollfuss gave Papa the box with the medal. 'Go home,' he said, 'you are incorrigible.'

Walter Slezak, *What Time's the Next Swan?*, Doubleday, 1962, pp. 58, 178–80, 210

Sir Thomas Beecham was a great conductor and wit, but he had tyrannical ways. So it's heartening to find him, just for once, firmly put in his place by Richard Tauber (1891–1948):

Tauber was a highly intelligent, cultivated and amusing companion, one of the few who can be said to have successfully scored off Sir Thomas Beecham. At a rehearsal of *The Bartered Bride*, with Beecham conducting and Tauber singing the role of Jenik, things were not going well. Tempers had been lost and a prima donna was in tears at the violence of the conductor's strictures when Tauber walked casually down to the footlights. 'You must forgive us, Sir Thomas,' he said. 'We have all sung this opera incorrectly so often in Vienna and Berlin that you can hardly expect us to get it right now in one rehearsal.'

Ivor Newton, *At the Piano*, Hamish Hamilton, 1966, p. 209

Beniamino Gigli (1890–1957) contentedly records his début at the Metropolitan Opera in November 1920:

I had thirty-four curtain calls to myself. Next morning, [director] Gatti-Casazza added a further three months to my contract. Caruso sent me a generous message of congratulation. Then someone brought me an imposing pile of incredibly voluminous newspapers. A headline in the Pittsburgh *Despatch* declared: 'Tenor with Queer Name Ranks Next to Caruso.' The New York journals, while more dignified in tone, were still far more enthusiastic than I had dared to hope for. I was especially pleased by what the *Herald Tribune* said about me: 'A loyal Italian, possessed of full faith in the Boito tradition, he disclosed himself as a servant of art and not a mere seeker after personal glory.' The *New York Times* reproached me with 'a persistent disposition to sing to the audience instead of to Margherita', but conceded that I had 'a voice of really fine quality, which he does not often force, still fresh and possessed of colour'. The *World* was cautiously noncommittal: 'Gigli may never set the river on fire, but he will certainly prove himself of value at the opera house.' The *Evening Mail* noted 'occasional hints of tremolo, and a certain breathless effort'. But the *Sun* thought that 'Gigli comes very near to the younger Caruso.'

Beniamino Gigli, *Memoirs*, translated by Darina Silone, Cassell, 1957,

p. 113

Gigli was usually regarded as a generous singer by his colleagues, but Maria Caniglia had a different experience:

'As modest and cosy as [Tito] Schipa was, the same cannot be said of Gigli, with whom I sang over five hundred times and recorded various operas. He did not speak to me for two years. Then suddenly his anger was spent, and he invited me and my husband to dinner as if nothing had ever happened. "*Cara Maria*" and all of that! You can imagine how convincing our love scenes were during those twenty-four months when, offstage, he cut me dead. The rage was sparked by a performance of *Tosca* in Rome with

Tito Gobbi as our Scarpia. After "*Vissi d'arte*" I received an
endless ovation. Although there were insistent demands for a
repeat, I did not grant the encore. But at the end of the second act,
when I was invited by the intendant to take a curtain call alone,
Gigli declared that if I acceded to this request, he would not
continue to sing, accusing me of having a claque. To this I replied,
"Then, my dear Beniamino, you are implying that I bought every
seat in the house!"'

Lanfranco Rasponi, *The Last Prima Donnas*, Gollancz, 1984, p. 244

How Gigli came to terms with his lack of ability as an actor:

Chaliapin was a great Mefisto and a great Boris Godunov not only
because he could sing – although that, of course, was the primary
requirement – but also because he could act. Caruso was a great
Canio, a great Rodolfo, a great Eleazar, a great John of Leyden for
the same reason. Yet when all is said and done, opera is generally
too implausible to be a realistic vehicle for acting. This is the
anomalous situation in which every singer finds himself; this is
the problem which every singer has got to work out for himself.
How can Romeo die convincingly when, having taken poison, he
must linger on and on, in a semi-recumbent position, singing as
exquisitely as possible?

One can only compromise. The music is the all-important thing;
for its sake one must try to act in spite of the absurdities. A good
libretto helps. The rest is illusion. The audience must be hypnotized
into accepting the make-believe.

For me the problem was more difficult than it can have been for
either Chaliapin or Caruso because, although fully aware of its
implications, I lacked the talent which helped them to solve it. I
was no actor . . .

Whenever a role was assigned to me, I accepted it as a reality –
or tried to – blindly and totally, no matter how improbable or
inconsistent it might be. I tried to identify myself with it, to
become, for the time being, the character I was supposed to

impersonate; or if that was impossible, then at least his twin brother, or his dearest friend. I tried to imagine his reactions, to feel with his feelings. I would find myself talking to him, arguing with him. Feeling! That was the keynote of my method, if it can be called a method. I tried to pour feeling into the role, to make it come alive through feeling. Not every opera responded to this treatment. *Gianni Schicchi* never did, for instance, nor *Iris*. Some roles defeated me. Others, such as Andrea Chénier, or Puccini's Des Grieux, required practically no effort whatsoever; these were generally (but not always) the roles I sang best.

Rehearsals, apart from helping me to learn positions on the stage so as not to fall over other people, were never of much use to me. I needed the footlights and the inspiration of the audience, and then I could trust to impulse and throw myself completely into the part. Of course I could and did think out certain fundamental aspects of a role beforehand ... but I could never foresee exactly how it would work out afterwards, and it never worked out the same way twice. Even when, in giving an encore, I had to sing the same aria over again after a few minutes, I always gave an entirely different version of it the second time – not deliberately, but simply because the first moment had passed and my feelings had now flowed into a different mould. This can scarcely be called acting; but whatever it was, it served my purpose. It enabled me to shed real tears on the stage, to feel real passion and real despair.

Beniamino Gigli, *Memoirs*, translated by Darina Silone, Cassell, 1957,

pp. 131–3

Gigli arrives in London in 1933 and is mistaken for a soprano:

A certain atmosphere of comedy had surrounded my arrival at Victoria Station. A large crowd of people, mostly Italian, had come to meet me, and the moment I stepped off the train they clamoured for me to sing. I tried to comply, but a majestic station official intervened. 'What's all this about?' he demanded. 'It's Gigli singing,' someone explained. 'Well, I don't care who it is,' said the official, 'he can't sing here. This,' he added importantly, 'is Victoria Station.'

I was sorry to have to disappoint the people who had waited for me; and as my taxi drew away from the kerb, I sang a few high notes, for fun, as a farewell. Just then a couple passed by. They had not seen me, but they heard my voice.

'I told you so, dear,' said the woman to the man. 'It *is* Tetrazzini.'

Beniamino Gigli, *Memoirs*, translated by Darina Silone, Cassell, 1957,
pp. 183–4

Gigli patronizes the young Giuseppe di Stefano (1921–):

[Giuseppe di Stefano's] boyhood hero was Beniamino Gigli, and one day when he was sixteen he saw the great man strolling in the famous Galleria in Milan. Rushing up, di Stefano tried to address him. 'Commendatore,' he wished to say, 'can I sing to you?' Overcome by shyness and hero-worship, and stammering nervously, he found it almost impossible to get the words out, so that Gigli dismissed him. 'Before you learn to sing, shouldn't you learn to talk?' he asked.

Years later, di Stefano appeared at the Theatre Colon, in Buenos Aires, in the same season as Gigli, and was disturbed to find that on one of the many bills, his name appeared in larger type than Gigli's. He told the great man at once how this apparent slight was none of his doing and that it distressed him to see himself given such precedence. 'Don't worry, my young friend,' Gigli loftily told him, 'as soon as the public hear us both, they will realize which billing is correct.'

Ivor Newton, *At the Piano*, Hamish Hamilton, 1966, pp. 203–4

Jussi Björling (1911–60) had a stunningly beautiful voice, but his career was blighted by alcoholism and a distinctly unappealing personality:

He was a man of surprising contradictions: as an artist, he was superb, with a remarkable range and an impeccable style that permitted no musical mistakes and no lapses of memory in its strict fidelity to what the composer had written. As a man, he was obstinate, difficult, taciturn and unusually lazy.

He hated to rehearse, and would find endless excuses – his health, the weather, and all varieties of ingenious reasons – to avoid doing so. Unlike most other singers with whom I have worked, he never vocalized to get his voice into trim before going on to the stage. When I asked him the reason he simply shrugged his shoulders. 'When I'm well, it's not necessary. If I'm not well, what good does it do? . . .'

To the singer's normal anxieties and idiosyncrasies he added a concern about draughts that would move him from table to table in a restaurant, finally to subside gloomily complaining of a cold wind which everyone else found completely imperceptible. In addition he disliked travel and never showed the remotest interest in whatever was happening. Björling could maintain an apparently bored silence for longer than anyone else I have ever known.

Ivor Newton, *At the Piano*, Hamish Hamilton, 1966, pp. 199–200

He was often reluctant to attend rehearsals at the Metropolitan, so eventually director Rudolf Bing read him the riot act:

[My] despairing letter made its effect, and Björling did indeed attend rehearsals; but he grumbled about it, and later in the season began to talk about being 'unable to afford' to continue singing at the Metropolitan. He did continue, but his participation in our efforts to improve staging was always grudging, as little as he could get away with. He was, unfortunately, a very irresponsible artist. One of the most astonishing things I ever saw on an opera stage was the last act of Puccini's *Manon Lescaut* during my observation year, on a night when Björling, as Des Grieux, was troubled with a backache and didn't feel like getting up to fetch some water for the dying Manon. The ever-obliging Licia Albanese, at his suggestion, got up and fetched the water for him.

Sir Rudolf Bing, *5000 Nights at the Opera*, Hamish Hamilton, 1972, p. 128

Bing also had to learn how to deal with the unreliable Giuseppe di Stefano:

One of the most erratic artists with whom I had to work at the
Metropolitan Opera was also one of the most gloriously talented:
Giuseppe di Stefano. The most spectacular single moment in my
observation year had come when I heard his diminuendo on the
high C in '*Salut! demeure*' in *Faust*: I shall never as long as I live
forget the beauty of that sound. For my first season, I was
counting on him to do a number of Almavivas in *Barbiere*, and
ultimately he did do most of them, but we never knew from day
to day whether he would show up. Once his wife called on the
afternoon of a performance to tell me how sick he was, and I
said that if he was that sick he should not be permitted to
remain at home, I would immediately call an ambulance at the
expense of the Metropolitan Opera. In an hour he was at the
theatre.

Sir Rudolf Bing, *5000 Nights at the Opera*, Hamish Hamilton, 1972,

p. 145

Dealing with singers' wives can be more tricky than dealing with the artists
themselves. John Culshaw had to placate Lauretta, spouse of the tenor
Franco Corelli (1921–), who was having trouble mastering French for his
portrayal of José in Carmen:

Until I met Lauretta Corelli I did not think anyone in the world
could rival Rina del Monaco, Mario's wife, in certain characteristics. Rina had a louder voice – louder, if she cared to use it so,
than her husband's. She did not care much about how she looked
or spoke. Her sole concern was that her husband's voice should be
not just a little but a very great deal louder than any other musical
element in whatever piece he was appearing in. It did not matter a
fresh fig to her that Verdi, for example, frequently wrote, '*ppp . . .*
morendo' (very quietly . . . dying away), or, '*pppp . . . voce soffocata*'
(extremely quietly . . . as if suffocating), in the score of *Otello*; what
Rina wanted at all times was that Mario should be as loud and
clear as a station announcer with a good amplifier, and to hell with

what the words were about. That he did not always take notice of her was greatly to his credit, but it did not stop her . . .

Around midnight one evening — which would have been five or six hours earlier in New York — I had an agitated call from RCA. Lauretta had called reverse charge from the hotel to say that Franco had been working so hard for months on his French pronunciation that his studies justified an increased fee. I am afraid I burst out laughing and told RCA the truth, which was at least unwelcome. What it all came to was that unless RCA provided an extra fee for the French 'studies' there would be no Flower Song. I said it was appalling, but, in such a situation, I thought it would be wise to pay up. The amount was one thousand dollars, which, although no kind of fortune, was worth a great deal more in 1963 than it is now . . . I also added that if we did not finish it would cost not one but many thousands of dollars to reassemble the cast in the future.

I soon realized that I had made a psychological mistake, for the RCA lawyer assumed that I was on Corelli's side, whereas I was just trying to be practical . . . I also knew that companies the size of RCA do not go into litigation against Italian tenors on an issue of a thousand dollars. Lauretta was on a winning run, and she knew it. Franco, as usual when she was in action, made no comment and did not show himself.

By the next afternoon RCA had tracked down the French lady and she had confirmed the story . . .

The next day was the last session, which included the Flower Song, and that evening the telephone calls between RCA and Vienna hardly seemed to stop at all. Finally, I had had too much. I told the lawyer that although I had not been keeping a record, I felt certain that by now the calls alone, given their length, must be adding up to something not far off a thousand dollars. RCA decided to concede defeat, and to ring Lauretta with the news. I thought that was the end of it, but an hour later RCA was back on the line again to say that she wanted the money the next morning, and *in cash* . . .

The money turned up in the morning. Franco turned up for the afternoon session minus his tie and also minus Lauretta. He sang an excellent Flower Song and ordered some champagne for the crew and the cast.

John Culshaw, *Putting the Record Straight*, Secker & Warburg, 1982,
pp. 330–31, 336–8

The conductor Leopold Stokowski took a free-wheeling approach to operatic conducting in a Metropolitan production of Puccini's Turandot, *as Bing and Corelli discovered:*

He was especially concerned with the lighting, and how it might affect the appearance of his hands while he was conducting. At performances, he often just luxuriated in his role, failing, for example, to tell his soloists when to end a sustained high note which the score allowed them to hold *ad lib.*

In Boston, on tour, this situation exploded. In the second-act finale, Franco Corelli ran out of breath while Birgit Nilsson was still sustaining her note, and he just walked off the stage. I was not in the hall: an emissary came to me in the lobby and said, 'Mr Bing, we are losing our tenor.' I went backstage, and even before I neared Corelli's door I heard him screaming, his wife screaming, the dog barking. He had slammed his hand on the dressing-table, and had picked up a minuscule splinter. There was a drop of blood on the table, and Mrs was calling for an ambulance. I calmed them down as much as I could, and suggested to Corelli that in the love scene in the next act he could get even with Miss Nilsson by biting her ear. That cheered him up a great deal; in fact, he liked the idea so much that he told Miss Nilsson about it, which gave him all the satisfaction of actually biting her without doing it, thank God. Meanwhile, I went to Stokowski's dressing-room to apologize to him, and found him entirely unconcerned.

Sir Rudolf Bing, *5000 Nights at the Opera*, Hamish Hamilton, 1972,
pp. 136–7

Jon Vickers (1926–) was, for many, the greatest Florestan and Tristan of the post-war years. He was also a devout Christian Scientist, and producer Walter Legge revealed, in a letter to Robert Jacobson, some of the consequences of his beliefs:

Vickers' cancellation – on religious grounds! – of *Tannhäuser* has put Covent Garden in a nasty spot. Considering that his religious convictions allow him, in other roles, to screw his sister and his aunt and murder his white wife, the *Tannhäuser* cancellation story is a bit thin.

Elizabeth Schwarzkopf, *On and Off the Record: A Memoir of Walter Legge*, Faber, 1982, p. 77

11: Lotte Lehmann

'I am an inexact artist. When I go out on the stage, I live the music, and this is what counts for me. Technique has never concerned me, for I am a creature of instinct.'

Quoted in Lanfranco Rasponi, *The Last Prima Donnas*, p. 479

The German soprano Lotte Lehmann (1888–1976) turned her technical failings to her advantage by the sheer radiance and passion of her singing, qualities that remain evident in her many recordings. Here Lehmann recalls her early days in Hamburg:

One day [Otto] Klemperer called me. I still had my old passion for him, and stood before him in some confusion.

'Do you think you could manage to take on Elsa's part [in *Lohengrin*]? You'd only have a week. Frau Wagner is on holiday, Fleischer-Edel is away too at the moment, and we're in a fix. I've persuaded Dr Loewenfeld to let you risk it. Well – do you think you can do it?'

Did I think I could do it!

I had, of course, studied Elsa's part by myself, and came proudly to the rehearsal. But if I thought I knew the part, I realized my mistake after the first five minutes. Klemperer sat at the piano like an evil spirit, thumping on it with long hands like tigers' claws, dragging my terrified voice into the fiery vortex of his fanatical will. Elsa's dreamy serenity became a rapturous ecstasy, her anxious pleading a challenging demand. For the first time I felt my nervous inhibitions fall from me, and I sank into the flame of inner experience. I had always wanted to sing like this – it was like flying in a dream: a bodiless gliding through blissful eternity . . . But usually one wakens from this lovely kind of dream with the terror of falling. And so I was dragged back from those ecstasies by Klemperer's voice saying:

'No idea of the part. We must work hard if you're to manage it.'

I managed it . . .

Theo Drill-Orridge was singing Ortrud on a visiting engagement, and her eyes grew wider as she noticed at the rehearsal how simply everyone was against me – even Klemperer, who grew furious every time I forgot anything, seemed to lose all confidence in me and shouted up:

'What's the matter? Has the big part gone to your head and made you forget everything?'

But now I set my teeth, and plunged into the hazards of this great undertaking.

I didn't see the audience – probably a sceptical one, expecting nothing very special   on the evening. Nor did I see Dr Loewenfeld's dreaded face spying from the box . . . I was just Elsa! I felt only the blissful pulsation of my voice, I forgot everything that conductor and producer had pumped into me – I was just myself alone. Tears stood in my eyes as I passed down the minster steps through the bowing throng.

'Hail to thee, Elsa of Brabant,' sang the chorus – and 'Hail to thee' my whole heart sang, greeting this day that was the real beginning of my rise to fame.

Lotte Lehmann, *Wings of Song*, translated by Margaret Ludwig, Kegan
Paul, 1938, pp. 105–6, 117–19

In 1912 the young Lehmann made the acquaintance of Caruso at the Hamburg Opera:

I received a telegram. Would I sup with him in a hotel after the performance of *Carmen*. What to do? I was still half a child, and sat there with my telegram in my shaking hands. Oh, how I should have loved to go! It was such a temptation, to be seduced by perhaps the greatest tenor in the world, in some dangerous *chambre séparée*. But I did not dare. Too many fragments of the eggshell of parental control were still attached to my newly spread wings. So, with the help of a dictionary, I wrote him a polite letter, and explained that my parents would never allow me to go, and would he please not be angry with me.

I was on my way to post this letter, which had cost me many tears, when I chanced upon some colleagues, and overheard one say: 'Are you also going to Caruso's this evening?' I stopped dead as if struck by lightning, and asked them whether there was a party at Caruso's that night. Well, he had invited the entire company, and my nightmare of a seduction in a *chambre séparée* was all nonsense. How lucky that I heard in time! I should never have lived it down if they'd found out that I'd been arrogant enough to presume that Caruso had wanted to seduce anyone as stupid as me.

I felt quite relieved, and yet – what a pity.

> Lotte Lehmann, 'Twelve Singers and a Conductor', in *Opera 66*,
> ed. Charles Osborne, A. Ross, 1967

Lehmann played a starring role in many feuds and rivalries. Here is an account of her long-standing rivalry with Maria Jeritza:

As such rivalries go, theirs was a sadly serious matter, fanned not by the press but by an artistic competitiveness centring on [Richard] Strauss.

They entered the [Vienna] opera house by different doors on the nights on which they sang together, in *Die Frau [ohne Schatten]*, *Ariadne*, *Carmen*, or *Die Walküre*; Lehmann refused to sing in a later opera of Strauss's, *Die Aegyptische Helena*, because Jeritza had cornered it before her, while Jeritza always claimed that Strauss had offered her either of the leading parts in *Die Frau*, and Lehmann had been handed her cast-off. Later, their territories separated: Lehmann never reached the Met until past her operatic prime, in the season after Jeritza had completed her thirteen-year sojourn there, and Jeritza never sang at Covent Garden after 1926, during Lehmann's legendary seasons. In her autobiography, Jeritza

makes no mention of Lehmann whatsoever; Lehmann, in one of
her many books, makes much of Jeritza, granting her genius but
making a number of back-handed comments on her general
deportment . . .

Much of the Lehmann–Jeritza feud went on unpublicized, but
in 1925 Jeritza caused a real public scandal, when she clashed with
the notoriously sensitive and excitable contralto Maria Olczewska
during a performance of *Die Walküre* in Vienna. Jeritza stood in
the wings with another singer, Hermine Kittel, waiting for her Act
II entry. Olczewska was on stage singing Fricka, deep in the
debate with Wotan, sung by her fiancé who was widely suspected
of dallying with Jeritza. In the circumstances, it was not surprising
that Olczewska became thoroughly distracted by the sound of
Jeritza's laughter and conversation. She hissed at her to stop, but
Jeritza continued her merriment. Finally Olczewska marched towards the wings while Wotan was addressing her and spat at
Jeritza. Unfortunately the force of the insult landed on the innocent
Kittel, who was understandably outraged. Olczewska was immediately dismissed from the Vienna Opera.

Rupert Christiansen, *Prima Donna*, Bodley Head, 1984, pp. 243–5

*In 1933 Lehmann, a star of the Vienna Opera, was courted by the new
Nazi regime in Germany. When she was invited to lunch by Hermann
Göring, then Minister of Education, the director of the Berlin Opera urged
her to be tactful:*

Göring came straight to the point. 'I read about your success in
America,' he said, between mouthfuls . . . 'and you caused me a
sleepless night. Yes. I thought of your future. You had earned a
good deal of money, and you are likely to pay it into a bank in
Vienna, where the Jews will deprive you of it.'

'Nonsense, my money would be perfectly safe. Anyway, I don't
need other people to lose my money for me. I spend it fast enough
myself. I have no talent for saving.'

'But what about your future? What will become of you – later?'

'Oh, good gracious, I've got plenty of time to think about that. In any case I shall be getting my pension from the Vienna Opera.'

He laughed about that. It was a most unpleasant laugh, and I began to feel very uncomfortable. 'The Vienna Opera! You surely don't enjoy singing for Schuschnigg?'

'But I don't sing only for Herr Schuschnigg, I sing for the whole world. In any case, I find Schuschnigg simply charming.'

The director of the Opera seemed to be suffering from a severe cold. He coughed violently, and I saw that he had to wipe the sweat from his brow.

Curiously enough, Göring reacted not at all to my thoughtless remark. He placed the knife and the riding crop on the table, looked at me smiling, and said, in quite a friendly manner, 'Let's forget Vienna for a moment. Let's talk about your contract!'

'What contract?'

'With the Berlin Opera.'

I don't know what made me so dangerously imprudent, despite all previous warnings. I ignored the imploring looks of the Opera director, and said very quietly to Göring:

'I am not in the habit of discussing contracts between a knife and a whip.'

Later, the Opera director informed me that I might have had ample opportunity to bitterly regret my audacity had Göring not taken a liking to me . . .

Göring had only smiled. He himself proposed a fee. I have forgotten how much it was, I only know that it was a fantastic amount. I think I could have asked double, and he would have granted it, but I was speechless at the offer.

Again and again he asked me whether I did not have any particular personal requests to make, and explained that, as well as my salary, I should be given a villa, and, naturally a life pension of a thousand marks per month (at that time a respectable sum) . . .

Of course Göring also had a few wishes: he expected me, as a matter of course, never to sing outside Germany again. 'You should not go out into the world,' he said dramatically. 'The world should come to us, if it wants to hear you.'

'But an artist belongs to the whole world. Why should I limit myself to one country? Music is an international language, and as one of its messengers I wish to sing everywhere, all over the world.'

Blushing furiously Göring looked at me with icy contempt. 'First and foremost, you are a German. Or perhaps not?'

As I was about to answer hastily and thoughtlessly, I happened to glance at the director of the Opera. His look of deathly terror stopped me.

So I half-agreed to the contract with Berlin. The warning that I would be allowed to sing only in Germany I did not take very seriously. Nor did I take seriously some of the remarks that had sounded like hidden threats. I gathered only that this was a contract which it would have been sheer madness to refuse. Göring, highly delighted, ordered the contract to be drawn up at once, adding: 'I personally stand guarantee for everything that I have promised you!' We then somehow came to speak about the critics. I don't exactly remember how we got on to the subject, and Göring said with a curious smile: 'And in Berlin you will never get bad notices!'

'Why? I may give a bad performance, and not deserve praise.'

'If I myself think you are singing well, no critic will have a different opinion. And if he dares, he will be liquidated.'

This sounded so absurd to me that I simply laughed. I didn't dream that he could be in deadly earnest . . .

When I received the contract it contained no word about all that Göring had promised me, and so I wrote the Opera director, as has always been my way, a very honest and frank letter . . . My letter stated that I refused to sing only in Germany. And where was the guarantee for all the extravagant promises made? And what would happen if Göring were to lose his position? And where were the opportunities for guest appearances in America? And in my beloved Vienna?

The result of all this was that I was *forbidden* to sing in Germany . . . Göring himself dictated a reply to me. It was a terrible letter, full of insults and low abuse. A real volcano of hate and revenge poured over me.

That was the end of Germany for me. Hitler's Germany! Later, they tried to get me back with promises. Everything would be forgiven and forgotten and I would be welcomed with open arms. But by then I knew better. My eyes had been opened to their crimes, and nothing could have induced me to return.

Lotte Lehmann, 'Göring, the Lioness and I', in *Opera 66*,
ed. Charles Osborne, A. Ross, 1967

Viorica Ursuleac, Richard Strauss's favourite soprano, on Lehmann's hatred for her:

'I believe her hatred for me originated when I exploded on the Viennese horizon with my easy top register just when she was beginning to have a very difficult time with hers. One must remember that at that time, with Jeritza in the United States, she considered herself to be the undisputed queen, and in many ways she was.

'I will only speak briefly of all the miseries she subjected me to at the Salzburg Festival, where I was engaged for the Countess in *The Marriage of Figaro* and she for the Marschallin, which I was to sing later for a total of a hundred and fifty-two performances.

'At that time I had never sung *Der Rosenkavalier* and was asked to learn the role in a hurry, for Lehmann would not sing one of the performances scheduled. I forget now the reason, but it was a valid one. But when she learned that I was the one chosen to replace her, she changed her plans and insisted on being available that night so that I should not sing it. She started loathing me when Strauss began to single me out for certain assignments, as she considered him her personal property.

'But this is a trifle compared with the trouble she made for me on a political level. Göring heard Lehmann in Germany and was very impressed with her; and as he was anxious to make the Berlin Staatsoper the most important in Europe, he contacted her to offer her a highly lucrative engagement. She rushed to Berlin to discuss this with him, but made it a condition that Chrysothemis, Arabella, and Sieglinde be sung only by her. It so happened that my contract was already in operation and that among the roles assigned to me were those she asked for. I did not have the exclusive rights to them, but they were on my list. She had a fit of hysteria when she heard this, walked out of his office, and returned to Vienna. From then on she did nothing but spread stories that I was a dedicated Nazi. Nothing could have been further from the truth.'

Lanfranco Rasponi, *The Last Prima Donnas*, Gollancz, 1984, p. 136

Lehmann sang in the Viennese première of Strauss's Arabella the day after her mother's death in October 1933:

[Clemens Krauss] called at once to say that everyone understood what this death meant to me and that therefore he scarcely dared to ask if I would consider going on just the same. However . . . as there could be no possible substitution for a Strauss première – the house for the first time in history would have to be closed if I refused . . .

Crushed as I was by the burden of my loss, by the death of the person who was to me the best mother in the world, I could react only with a lethargic assent: 'I'll go on.'

It was an experience I shall never forget. No power in the world is greater than that of music. For two brief hours it enabled me to forget my deep personal grief, to be Arabella rather than my own tormented, pain-racked, and mourning self . . .

The crowd waiting at the stage door for the artist after the show is usually rather a noisy and unruly group, and it was especially so after a Strauss première. My nerves that night were stretched taut, ready to snap, and I dreaded having to face them. But for once I had done the Viennese a grave injustice by underestimating their tact. To a man they felt with me and for me, standing by in absolute silence, hats off, as I passed, in one of the most moving tributes I have ever received.

Lotte Lehmann, *Singing with Richard Strauss*, translated by Ernest Pawel,
Hamish Hamilton, 1964, pp. 84–5

Lehmann's famous truncated Rosenkavalier *at Covent Garden in 1938:*

Covent Garden seemed the same as ever, a friendly and familiar place; but all the roles in *Der Rosenkavalier* had been reassigned, with only myself as the Marschallin representing the Old Guard. Octavian was sung by Tiana Lemnitz, an excellent and exceedingly ambitious young singer. The entire cast had come from Berlin so that I, an unequivocal and staunch opponent of the Nazi regime, felt surrounded by enemies, with only Sir Thomas Beecham, the conductor, as my friend.

On the day of the performance, moreover, I had received bad news. My husband had fallen ill with tuberculosis, the dread disease that was to kill him within a year, and the children of his first marriage, being half-Jewish, were in acute danger now that Vienna had been taken over by the Nazis.

The convergence of fear and suspicion must have brought about an hysterical paralysis of the vocal cords. During the first act I felt my voice gradually giving out. Finally I stood there absolutely mute, unable to control myself; I left the stage, and the curtain was lowered, whereupon for the first and last time in my life I fainted. At least I think I must have fainted, for I do not remember anything until I found myself sitting in my dressing-room with a doctor in attendance. He diagnosed an hysterical paralysis of the vocal cords and predicted a quick and spontaneous recovery. I could not, of course, go on that night, and I do not recall who took my place; the entire episode is blurred even in memory.

Lotte Lehmann, *Singing with Richard Strauss*, translated by Ernest Pawel,
Hamish Hamilton, 1964, pp. 155–6

In fact it was Hilde Konetzni who stood in for Lehmann:

'Perhaps the most incredible experience I ever had was in London in 1938, when I was engaged to sing at Covent Garden, and it made me internationally famous overnight. I was due to make my début as Chrysothemis and had gone to the theatre by myself very

inconspicuously the night before to hear *Der Rosenkavalier* with
Lotte Lehmann as the Marschallin. Suddenly she stopped in the
middle of the act and walked out. There was pandemonium and
the curtain came down. She simply announced she did not feel in
good form and could not continue. Someone remembered that I
had asked for a ticket so I must be in the house. I had been very
successful in this part even in Salzburg. My name was called out,
and I left my seat to see what was wanted . . .

'As I told you before, I have always enjoyed challenges, and this
was the greatest ever. Lehmann's Marschallin was considered,
right or wrong, the greatest, and no one in London knew me, I
accepted. But there were no costumes. Lehmann had left the
theatre in a tearing hurry, and, amazingly enough, had carried
them off with her. But that was Lotte! She only thought of herself.
So while the public patiently waited, having been told that a
replacement had been found, the management was desperately
looking for something that I could wear . . . Somehow they also
found a white wig for the final scene. You cannot believe the
triumph I had. I thought they would never allow me to go home
and have a good sleep before the *Elektra* the next night. When I
awoke late in the morning, I had to move out of my room and
take another one, for there were literally dozens and dozens of
bouquets and baskets of flowers, including a bunch of roses from
Lehmann herself. And all the critics had raved.'

Lanfranco Rasponi, *The Last Prima Donnas*, Gollancz, 1984, pp. 103–4

Lehmann's account of why she walked off the stage is not the only one:

The audience was told that Madame Lehmann was suffering from
seasickness, but a doctor diagnosed hysterical paralysis of the vocal
cords. Walter Legge, then assistant director at Covent Garden,
remembers it rather differently. 'Next day, Lotte, in good spirits,
gave a small lunch party. She said she needed a rest and explained
privately . . . that a few minutes before the performance she had
been told that relations of hers who were trying to smuggle

valuables out of Austria had been held up at the customs, but now
she knew they were safely through.'

Rupert Christiansen, *Prima Donna*, Bodley Head, 1984, p. 253

Lehmann on herself:

'Phrasing, for me, is the clue to an interpretation, and the knowing
audience has always appreciated very much the fact that it never
misses what I am saying. Inaccuracy in the notes here and there –
that they can accuse me of; but of betraying the text, never. I have
given of my voice with no restraint, and I am fully aware that this
has to be paid for dearly. But I cannot restrain myself, for I
become tremendously involved with characterization or a song,
and the reason for my success has always been that the public
knows I am handing it all I have. Actually, considering how much
of my vocal resources I have squandered away, it is a miracle that I
still have an instrument in fairly good shape.'

Lanfranco Rasponi, *The Last Prima Donnas*, Gollancz, 1984, p. 479

12: Maria Callas

Callas saw her art as a servitude. She was an aggressor toward
her audiences, assuming that her voice would be disliked when
first heard ... With disciplinary sadism, she castigates a voice
which is self-indulgent, interested only in being beautiful. The
image she uses is revealingly destructive: 'it isn't enough that
you have a beautiful voice; you must take this voice and break
it up into a thousand pieces, so she will serve you'.

Peter Conrad, *A Song of Love and Death*, p. 322

*Maria Callas (1923–77) did not single-handedly revive the art of bel canto
singing, but she did transform coloratura technique into a vehicle for singing
of the utmost dramatic intensity. She dominated the operatic stage throughout
the 1950s, and for many who heard her, and for many who did not, she was
the greatest operatic interpreter of them all. Unfortunately she is often
remembered more for her volatile personality than for her genius, and her
ex-husband Giovanni Battista Meneghini contributed to this preference for
gossip over appreciation. Here is his account of Callas in murderous mood.
In September 1951 she was engaged to sing Tosca in Brazil, alternating
with Renata Tebaldi, but found it difficult to get on with the administrator,
Barreto Pinto:*

The morning of the day she was scheduled for her second *Tosca*,
Maria and I left the hotel, and passing in front of the theatre, we
stopped to look at Barreto Pinto's poster. 'Let's see who will be
singing with you this evening,' I said. But we realized with
astonishment that she was the only member of the cast who was
changed. Incredulously, Maria read the broadsheet without her
name. After a couple of moments of silence, she said, 'Let's see
Barreto Pinto.'

Walking with the stride of a Valkyrie, she set out for the office
of the superintendent . . . Pinto was behind his desk. Maria asked
him, 'Listen here, why have you replaced me?'

'Because you were lousy the other night,' he replied.

'Ah, in your opinion I was lousy?' she repeated in a rage. On his
desk was a large bronze inkstand and paper holder. It weighed
over twenty pounds. Maria picked it up and, holding it in the air,
said, 'Repeat what you just said, if you have the nerve, and I'll
smash your skull.'

She had fire in her eyes. Limitless strength seemed to emanate
from her entire body. I had never seen her so furious. I rushed
forward to restrain her. The other people present also intervened
and managed to hold her, but only with difficulty. Barreto Pinto,
terrified, had sunk down into his chair. Maria continued to revile
him with the most abusive insults. When Pinto was certain we had
managed to remove the inkstand from her grip, he said, 'Now I
am going to call the police and have you arrested for threatening
me.'

He should not have said that. Maria pushed us aside, and threw
herself on Pinto, striking him in the stomach with her knee. It
could have been a fatal blow. Maria at that time weighed more
than two hundred pounds, was twenty-eight years old, and had the
power of a young bull. I heard Pinto emit a moan, and then I saw
him close his eyes and double over. 'Oh, my God, he's just
breathed his last,' I thought. Asking the others to look after the
unfortunate man, I took Maria by the arm and we hurried back to
our hotel.

The situation was serious. Barreto Pinto had many friends in the
government and he could have had us arrested; no one would have
been able to stop him. I was extremely worried. Maria, however,
was now very calm. She walked about the room humming, totally
pleased with what she had done. 'Don't you think you overdid it?'
I asked.

'I only regret not having broken his head,' she said with a smile.
'I don't like that man and I will never again consider singing in
this country.'

Immediately after noon, the hotel desk announced that there was a person asking to speak with us. 'There we are,' Maria said. 'It's the police. Now be good, don't open your mouth, for goodness' sake. Let me do the talking.'

I had the visitor come up. It was not a policeman, but rather a messenger from Pinto. In one envelope he had the money for Maria's fee, including the performances stipulated in her contract but which she had not yet sung; in another envelope were two plane tickets for our return to Italy. 'The plane leaves in two hours,' the envoy said. 'Barreto Pinto has already reserved your places. In front of the hotel is a car ready to take you to the airport. Barreto asks if he must send along another one for your luggage.'

'Certainly,' said Maria.

'One will be here immediately,' the man said.

We hurriedly packed our bags. Two hours later we left Brazil, never to return.

> Giovanni Battista Meneghini, *My Wife Maria Callas*, translated by
> Henry Wisneski, Bodley Head, 1983, pp. 153–4

In December 1951 Elisabeth Schwarzkopf and her husband, the recording producer Walter Legge, saw Callas in La traviata:

When Walter had heard Maria, he insisted that at the earliest moment I should hear her in person too. So we went on a pilgrimage to Parma, where she was singing *Traviata*. She was then still more than robust and healthy looking, far from the fragile, delicate Violetta of her later years. The house was already seething with anticipation when we took our seats. To our amazement the back of the orchestra was lined with police, firemen, and nurses, anticipating things to come. And already during the overture when the conductor took a few measures too fast, a chorus of hissing began. Apart from the conductor, there was the elder Germont who had a slight frog and several others who never dared show themselves before the curtain. And even

Maria had a moment's opaqueness on a top note. Still, we all witnessed a major victory for Callas. As everyone knows, there is no victory in Italy like being acclaimed in Parma in a Verdi role! Walter and I went backstage and quite spontaneously I said to Maria, 'There is no point in my singing this role again.' And I didn't.

Elisabeth Schwarzkopf, *On and Off the Record: A Memoir of*
Walter Legge, Faber, 1982, p. 192

Callas's relationship with her audience was often as tempestuous as every
other aspect of her life – and she thrived on it:

The challenge of a great conductor and/or stage director curiously paralleled her reactions to a less enthusiastic reception than she expected and felt she deserved after a first act. She would pace her dressing-room with a hard glint in her eyes and mutter, 'I'll teach those stinkers out there,' or sometimes, 'Don't worry! When I'm furious I'm always at my best.' Then she would sing the rest of the performance with incandescent inner fire and aggressive flamboyance. During several *Sonnambulas* I sat in [La Scala manager Antonio] Ghiringhelli's box watching her move down to the footlights to hurl '*Ah, non giunge*' into the very teeth of the gallery. The Scala gallery was a vital factor in Meneghini's operations, especially the seats near the proscenium, which he infiltrated with young fans to throw bouquets to his wife when she took curtain calls. One evening the opponents got there first: fewer floral tributes were mixed in the rain of bunches of small vegetables from the gallery. Callas, trading on her well-known myopia, sniffed each bunch as she picked it up; vegetables she threw into the orchestra pit, while flowers were graciously handed to her colleagues.

Elisabeth Schwarzkopf, *On and Off the Record: A Memoir of*
Walter Legge, Faber, 1982, p. 200

*Rudolf Bing recalls Callas at the Metropolitan Opera House in 1956.
Vegetables make yet another appearance:*

Two moments of terror remain in the memory from that first
Callas season. The Saturday matinée following her début, she sent
word from her dressing-room during the overture that she would
be unable to go on. I literally ran to her room, and found her
genuinely ill, with Meneghini and a doctor in solicitous attendance;
by the time I got there, I suppose, I looked sicker than she felt,
and after a few encouraging words from me she agreed to go on,
saving us from what would have been a riot. (It was at the close of
this performance that some idiot threw radishes on the stage;
fortunately, Miss Callas was so short-sighted she thought they
were tea roses.) Then, in a *Lucia*, an Italian baritone held a high
note beyond the value Donizetti had given it, making Miss Callas,
who had sung her part of the duet correctly, look short of breath.
She said '*Basta!*' (which was misinterpreted by the audience in the
orchestra rows that heard her); and so did I: I ordered the balance
of the baritone's Metropolitan contract cancelled. He got on the
front page of the newspapers tearing up her picture, and then
booked space on the plane that was taking her back to Italy. She
said, with her typical honesty, 'I don't like this man taking
advantage of my publicity.' During her nine weeks she cancelled
only one performance, which is at least par for the course in a New
York winter.

Sir Rudolf Bing, 5000 Nights at the Opera, Hamish Hamilton, 1972,

p. 184

*Callas could be petty and vindictive, with Renata Tebaldi a frequent
recipient of her malice:*

Callas never failed to appear in a proscenium box at La Scala when
Tebaldi sang *La forza del destino*, and she attended many of Tebaldi's
*Aida*s at the Chicago Opera. At one of these performances, just as
Tebaldi began to sing the fiendishly difficult '*O patria mia*', Callas
created quite a stir by summoning an usher with a flashlight to

find a bracelet she had dropped by her seat. One wonders why someone who so respected art would stoop to such a cheap trick to disturb a fellow artist.

Lanfranco Rasponi, *The Last Prima Donnas*, Gollancz, 1984, p. 582

Meneghini gives his account of one of the most controversial nights in a very controversial career:

On 2 January 1958, my wife became embroiled in another situation, the ugliest of her entire career, and one which is still remembered as the most publicized scandal in the history of opera in this century. On that day Maria was to open the season of the Rome Opera with a performance of *Norma* (it was also to be broadcast throughout Italy). It was an especially gala affair because President Giovanni Gronchi of Italy was to be there with his wife, along with other dignitaries . . .

The days immediately preceding that evening were trying for us because Maria was not feeling well, but with the help of various medications the doctors managed to ameliorate her condition enough that she felt she could fulfil the assignment. The human voice, however, is not like a string or keyboard instrument, and it is always subject to unexpected changes. At the end of the first act, my wife said that she was not well enough to finish the performance. The situation was certainly regrettable, but it need not have been desperate . . . It would have sufficed if the Rome Opera's administration had moved quickly, announced that she was sick, and replaced her with another singer . . . But it was not the case of just any singer, but Maria Callas. They had banked everything on her name and had not even considered arranging for a cover.

What to do? . . . The intermission was stretching to embarrassing lengths. President Gronchi was becoming nervous and some members of the audience were whistling for the commencement of Act II. In the meantime, the theatre's superintendent and other officials had gathered in Maria's dressing-room, trying to convince her to continue. 'You are a great actress,' they told her. 'You can go on even without a voice. It's fine if you just go out there and declaim your lines.'

Maria understood the gravity of the situation, but there was nothing she could do. Her high notes had started to slip away, and she was even having difficulty producing notes in her middle register. She had almost cracked on a note during the '*Casta diva*' and someone in the audience had shouted: 'Go back to Milan. You cost us a million lire!' If Maria went out and started reciting, instead of singing her lines, God only knows what would have happened. And especially with Gronchi present, it was unwise to take any chances. Maria was adamant; she could not go on.

After an interval of almost an hour, Gronchi was informed that the performance was being suspended. The President and his wife quickly left the theatre. Immediately, the public was informed by loudspeaker that the performance had been terminated. It is impossible to convey how explosively the news was received in the auditorium. Outside the stage door, hundreds waited hours for my wife, threatening to lynch her. We left the theatre after midnight through a passageway that leads from the opera house to a nearby hotel. Groups of fanatics stood under the windows of our hotel room throughout the night, shouting insults and obscenities.

The lynching of Maria continued the next day, in the press . . . The blame was ascribed exclusively to Maria. No one chose to believe that she was sick. The newspaper articles implied that she had broken off the performance because the applause accorded her after Act I was not sufficiently enthusiastic. Others postulated that Maria had lost her voice from having celebrated the New Year at parties in the homes of Roman patricians . . .

The actual circumstances leading to the débâcle require explanation. We arrived in Rome on 27 December and Maria began rehearsals immediately in the opera house, which was unheated. All the singers protested, but to no avail. Fedora Barbieri became ill and they had to replace her before the dress rehearsal. Then Maria caught a cold and was obliged to go to bed. The head of the Rome Opera came to the hotel. 'Maria, you must get better, you absolutely must sing,' he pleaded.

My wife did everything she could, taking medicine, and using hot compresses and vaporizers. She was attended by the house doctor and was also in touch by telephone with her personal physician in Milan. She managed to get back on her feet. Although she knew that she was not in her best form, she was confident she could manage to sing.

She was examined an hour before curtain time and her condition seemed to be satisfactory. However . . . by the end of Act I, she had lost her voice and could not continue. This is the story behind the imbroglio, but the newspapers did not want to accept it.

Giovanni Battista Meneghini, *My Wife Maria Callas*, translated by
Henry Wisneski, Bodley Head, 1983, pp. 262–5

In May 1958 Callas gave a series of performances of Bellini's Il pirata *at La Scala, even though she had just been through an operation. Under pressure from the Italian government, according to Meneghini, the director of La Scala, Antonio Ghiringhelli, who had long been hostile to Callas, decided to stop hiring the singer. It became apparent that the performance scheduled for 31 May would be her last at La Scala for the foreseeable future:*

Her most faithful admirers had surmised that this was her final appearance, and they arrived at the opera house on 31 May with great masses of flowers to pay homage to her. The police, however, refused to allow them to bring them into the theatre. The evening began with the atmosphere of a bullfight. Maria was very tense. She wanted to bid farewell to her public but at the same time call attention to Ghiringhelli, his resentment and his spitefulness. That night the superintendent was sitting towards the back of his box. In the mad scene, which is the culmination of the opera, Imogene has just learned that her lover, Gualtiero, has been condemned to death for murder. She loses her reason and imagines she sees her love ascending the steps of the scaffold, at which point she launches into the cabaletta *'O sole! ti vela di tenebra fonda'* ('Oh, Sun, veil yourself in darkest gloom'). Maria usually delivered these lines facing the audience, with a wild look in her eyes, and a vocal quality that gave one chills. That night she turned towards Ghiringhelli's box, and as she extended her arm in the direction of Ghiringhelli she sang the line, '*La vedete il palco funesto*' ('There, see the fatal scaffold [or theatre box]'). She continued to sing, pointing menacingly at his box. The public understood the allusion and all heads turned towards the box with curiosity. Ghiringhelli got up and left.

At the end of the performance, Maria was accorded an incredible ovation which lasted almost thirty minutes. The public did not want her to leave. People were shouting, 'Come back, Maria, return to us.' Many were weeping. Ghiringhelli, angered by this display of affection, had the fire curtain lowered while Maria was still on stage acknowledging the applause.

Giovanni Battista Meneghini, *My Wife Maria Callas*, translated by
Henry Wisneski, Bodley Head, 1983, pp. 269–70

For her admirers, each Callas performance was to be savoured, assessed, and ranked, for her interpretations and her vocal prowess altered from night to night. Harold Rosenthal recalls her Violettas at Covent Garden in 1958:

She sang five Violettas that summer in London, I saw four of them. One I was fortunate enough to witness from the side of the stage, and this taught me even more about that remarkable singer's art than the performances I heard from my usual seat in the stalls. I wrote about three of the performances in the longest review of an opera I ever contributed to the magazine [*Opera*]. The way Callas found the right 'tone colour' for certain phrases marked her as someone unique in our day. Single words and phrases would take on a new meaning – the emphasis she put on the word '*due*' in the phrase '*Di due figli?*' when Alfredo's father, Giorgio Germont, tells her that Alfredo is not his only child; or '*È vero, è vero*', uttered in a resigned tone when Germont pointed out that one day she would grow old and that Alfredo would tire of her, will, I know, never be equalled. Nor the way she started '*Dite alla giovine*' when the phrase sounded as if it was suspended in mid-air.

Callas's last act was superb. One suffered with the dying Violetta as she dragged herself from bed to dressing-table, from dressing-table to chair; '*O come son mutata*', she gasped, as she looked at her wan reflection in the mirror. When her faithful maid, Annina, told her that Alfredo had arrived, she hurriedly tried to tidy her hair and look her best; then came the reunion of the two lovers, with Violetta's hands (and how Callas had made use of her beautiful long fingers throughout her performance) clasping at the longed-for happiness and hardly believing that Alfredo was really a flesh-and-blood figure. '*Ah! Gran Dio! Morir si giovane*' (Oh God, I am too young to die) was sung with terrific intensity – and at the final performance Callas took the whole phrase in one breath. As the drama moved to its close and Violetta gently gave Alfredo her locket, it was impossible to keep back my tears. The death scene was almost horrific, the last '*È strano!*' was uttered in an unearthly voice, and as Violetta rose from her chair to greet what she thought was a new life, a glaze came over her eyes, and she literally became a standing corpse.

If I have devoted too much space to describing one of the greatest operatic performances it has been my privilege to experience it is because I believe that Callas's Violetta deserves to be recorded in detail, for I am as sure today as I was in 1958 that we will not hear another like it.

Harold Rosenthal, *My Mad World of Opera*, Weidenfeld & Nicolson,

1982, pp. 137–8

Tito Gobbi recalls her Covent Garden Tosca *in 1964:*

Maria stayed away from a rehearsal of Act II one day because of a slight cold, and John Copley stood in for her. On this occasion it so happened that a distinguished titled lady came to the box office to pick up her tickets and, realizing that a rehearsal was in progress, she implored Sergeant Martin [the colossal doorkeeper at

Covent Garden] to allow her just one glimpse of the diva: if he would just open the door a single crack ... The poor man, with all the solemn authority for which he was famed, explained that he simply could not do so, not even for such a distinguished lady. Well, would he just for one moment open the little window connected with the house so that she might at least hear a note or two from that famous voice?

With this request Sergeant Martin complied and at that moment John Copley, lying in my arms with beard and glasses, let out an excruciating shriek: '*Ah più non posso, ah che orrore.*'

'Ah, the unmistakable voice!' whispered the delighted lady to Sergeant Martin. 'Thank you, thank you.' And she went away quite satisfied ...

In spite of her tremendous, unparalleled triumph [Callas] remained desperately nervous. On each day of performance she would phone me to say she could not sing – she had no voice left, or else she must change everything in the second act. I would be half an hour on the telephone consoling the poor girl and encouraging her. 'All right,' I would say, 'you don't sing. It is enough for you to appear. You just act and I'll do the singing. All right, you change whatever you want. You know we understand each other –' and so on.

In the evening she would come by my dressing-room before going on stage and I would take her to the wings, holding her icy hand and whispering encouragement while rivulets of perspiration would be running down her neck and the edge of her dress. Yet when she came off-stage after her exquisitely sung duet with Cioni she would clasp my hand and wish me luck and stand there waiting until my first phrase had been sung. Indeed, there was something utterly touching in the way she would show endearing flashes of concern for others however deeply absorbed she might be in her own ordeal.

Tito Gobbi, *Tito Gobbi on His World of Italian Opera*, Hamish Hamilton,

1984, pp. 211, 212–13

Two assessments of Maria Callas, first from Rupert Christiansen:

It is important not to romanticize Callas. She was a martyr rather
than a saint, and was fuelled by an overweening morality – 'I am
Victorian,' she told an interviewer – of discipline and self-restraint.
Every failure was taken hard; she alone was responsible for her
shortcomings. All this made her cold, withdrawn, and quintessen-
tially egocentric. One searches her biography in vain for any
instances of spontaneous generosity or kindness. Instead one finds
the persistent insecurity of the unloved child, the anxiety to find
people she could depend upon, and a proud automatic mistrust of
anyone not completely dedicated to her. 'We are all vulnerable,'
she told *Life* in 1964. 'I am extremely so and have naturally tried
not to show it for my own self-preservation. My shyness and
insecurity have often made me seem arrogant – it's a form of self-
protection for timid people.'

Rupert Christiansen, Prima Donna, Bodley Head, 1984, pp. 312–13

And from Walter Legge:

Callas suffered from a superhuman inferiority complex. This was
the driving force behind the relentless, ruthless ambition, her fierce
will, her monomaniacal egocentricity and insatiable appetite for
celebrity. Self-improvement, in every facet of her life and work,
was her obsession. When she was first pointed out to me, a year or
two before we met, she was massive, shabbily dressed in a nondes-
cript tweed coat, and her walk had the ungainly lurch of a sailor
who, after months on rough seas, was trying to adjust himself to
terra firma. At our first meeting I was taken aback by her rather
fearsome New York accent, which may have had a booster from
GIs when she worked as interpreter for the American forces in
Athens. Within months Callas was speaking what the English call
the King's English until the BBC murdered it. A gifted linguist,
she soon learned good Italian and French. When she had slimmed
down from over 200 pounds to less than 140, she became one of
the best-dressed women in Milan . . .

Our first recordings together were made in Florence after a series of performances of *Lucia* there with Serafin. The acoustics of the hall our Italian branch had chosen were antimusical and inimical. I decided to make a series of tests of '*Non mi dir*' with Callas for two purposes – to get the psychological feel of working with her, sensing how receptive she would be to criticism, and to find placings to give at least a decent sound. It was soon clear that she would take suggestions without a murmur. I had found a fellow perfectionist as avid to prove and improve herself as any great artist I have ever worked with. Ten years later we were to spend the best part of three hours just repeating the last dozen bars of the *Faust* Jewel Song to get a passable end to it. I have never known anybody to have such a will to repeat. She was always so critical; on one occasion we were recording, and she called over the microphone, 'Walter, is that all right?' I said, 'Maria, it's marvellous, you can go on.' 'I don't want to know if it's marvellous, is it good?' . . .

Even in the most difficult fioriture there were no musical or technical difficulties in this part of the voice which she could not execute with astonishing, unostentatious ease. Her chromatic runs particularly downwards, were beautifully smooth and staccatos almost unfailingly accurate, even in the trickiest intervals. There is hardly a bar in the whole range of nineteenth-century music for high soprano that seriously tested her powers, though she sometimes went sharp on sustained high notes or took them by force . . .

Her legato line was better than any other singer because she knew that a legato must be like a telegraph wire or telephone wire, where you can see the line going through and the consonants are just perched on it like the feet of sparrows. She used the consonants with great effect, but basically the legato line was held so that you could hear that all the time and were not aware of the interruption of the consonants except for their dramatic purpose.

Callas had an absolute contempt for merely beautiful singing. Although she was preoccupied all her career with bel canto, that is, beautiful singing, she was one of the few Italian artists in my

memory who quite deliberately produced significant sounds of a
particular dramatic intensity or meaning on a syllable or even on a
single consonant — sometimes over a long phrase to convey
dramatic meaning. She herself often said, 'After all, some of the
texts we have to sing are not distinctive poetry. I know that to
convey the dramatic effect to the audience and to myself I must
produce sounds that are not beautiful. I don't mind if they are ugly
as long as they are true' . . .

Most admirable of all her qualities, however, were her taste,
elegance, and deeply musical use of ornamentation in all its forms
and complications, the weighting and length of every *appoggiatura*,
the smooth incorporation of the turn in melodic lines, and accuracy
and pacing of her trills, the seemingly inevitable timing of her
portamenti, varying their curve with enchanting grace and meaning. There were innumerable exquisite felicities — minuscule portamenti from one note to its nearest neighbour, or over widespread
intervals — and changes of colour that were pure magic . . .

She could be vengeful, vindictive, malicious in running down
people she was jealous of or had taken a dislike to, often without
reason. She was ungrateful: for years she refused to work with or
even talk to Serafin, who had been her invaluable help and guide
since her Italian début, after he recorded *La traviata* with Antoni-
etta Stella.

She learned more from Serafin of the qualities that made her
what she was than from anybody else. The old man was a great
master of that particular sort of repertoire that Callas was to do
better than anybody — Rossini, Bellini, Donizetti, Verdi. And
nobody else, apart from Toscanini, knew such an enormous amount
about singing. After all he had produced — he made — Ponselle.

She was convinced that sooner or later she would quarrel with
every friend.

She said to me one day, 'You know when we have our quarrel,
it's going to be hell, because you know how to hurt me and I
know how to hurt you.' I said to her, 'Maria, there is no need for
us to quarrel. Why should we ever quarrel?' She said, 'People of
our strength of will and personality always quarrel eventually.'

She quarrelled with me because I resigned from EMI, which she claimed I had done solely to ruin her recording career. That did not stop her from begging me, after years of non-communication, to share her Juilliard master classes with her, 'because we are the only two people who know what bel canto is, and you can talk'.

Elisabeth Schwarzkopf, *On and Off the Record: A Memoir of Walter Legge*, Faber, 1982, pp. 193–6, 198–9, 202

13: Some Singers of the Twentieth Century

[Birgit] Nilsson seized the notes from the sky. Hers was the voice of hubris, as superhumanly proud as the chaste Brünnhilde on top of her mountain or the frigid Turandot on top of her staircase.

Peter Conrad, *A Song of Love and Death*, p. 338

Lina Cavalieri (1874–1944) clambered up from rags to riches, earning this dismissive assessment of her art:

[She] arrived at the Met in 1906, the same year as Farrar, but ... failed to establish herself in a comparable repertory. Cavalieri let it be known that she was the barefoot daughter of a Roman washerwoman and a newspaper vendor, that she had slept in the gutters and sold oranges in the Piazza Navona, that she had begun by singing outside cafés. It may have been true, but supposition becomes verifiable fact in the mid 1890s when she became the mistress of Prince Alexander Bariatinski and then, from 1900, a prima donna. At the Met she sang with Caruso in the first house performance of Puccini's *Manon Lescaut* and Cilea's *Adriana Lecouvreur*, but her art was a fragile thing. By 1909 she was concentrating her activities on a Fifth Avenue atelier where she sold cosmetics made according to the recipes of Catherine de' Medici, and in 1910 she married one of the Astor clan, from whom she was separated less than three months after. A brief film career was curtailed by the damage that studio lights did to her eyes. With the outbreak of war, she returned to Europe and lived off her jewels and divorce settlement. There were two more marriages, out of a total, she claimed, of 840 proposals.

Cavalieri had an insubstantial but pretty little voice which went well with her diaphanous beauty. As a singer she could not be taken very seriously, but as a late manifestation of the courtesan – a courtesan with a career and a press agent – she was magnificently successful.

Rupert Christiansen, *Prima Donna*, Bodley Head, 1984, pp. 195–6

Vera Stravinsky, in 1970, often recalled Cavalieri for her private life rather than her singing:

V. recalls that she first saw [*La traviata*] with Lina Cavalieri, 'the mistress of a grand duke who rewarded her, a little too specifically, perforce, with a gold bidet whose fountain was diamond-studded'.

Robert Craft, *Stravinsky: Chronicle of a Friendship,* Vanderbilt University
Press, 1994, p. 524

Geraldine Farrar (1882–1967) was so popular at the Met that her hordes of female fans became known as Gerry Flappers:

Her personality was more remarkable than her voice by the time I heard her. The voice had grown wiry thin in all its upper reaches and it never could have had much to offer in the lower part. By compensation there were wonderfully expressive tones still at her command in the middle voice, and she actually did have something to express. She was not always good – a spoiled darling of the public, with flowers scattered over her wherever she went, and by some accounts a capricious termagant to those who opposed her, she had no single-minded aesthetic purpose and thus could not become a great artist. She had made films, some of them very bad, had conducted a good many of her personal and professional quarrels in public, had pushed out her repertoire in all directions without regard for her special gifts, and was quite capable – as in Leoncavallo's *Zaza* – of an exhibitionism which had nothing to do with play, music, character, or the lyric theatre in general. She almost seemed to be winking at the audience as a circus clown does. She liked silks, satins, and trains, and she wore them; even the village maiden in *Faust* had acquired a train by the time I saw her, and the dresses for *Madama Butterfly* must have cost a fortune. Her famous Carmen was a soprano, of course, and she used all the customary soprano substitutions of notes as well as some (if I mistake not) which were all her own. And yet, much as I dislike a soprano in a part which is not only mezzo or contralto in music but also by character, I think even now that Farrar's Carmen was one of the very best I ever saw or heard.

Vincent Sheean, *First and Last Love*, Gollancz, 1957, pp. 56–7

At the Met in 1908, the exuberant Farrar had a fight on her hands when confronted by Arturo Toscanini:

Farrar came to her first rehearsal with Toscanini from a series of triumphs in Berlin in the role she was to sing with him: Cio-Cio-San in *Madama Butterfly*. It is likely that her phrasing was influenced by the fact that she had been singing the role in German, equally likely that she had mannerisms and vocal tricks not indicated in the score. (Puccini, one recalls, had disliked her Butterfly two years before; and to her fury he would not offer her the creation of Minnie in *The Girl of the Golden West* two years later.) Toscanini was having none of her mannerisms, and his contract gave him complete authority – 'right of use,' it read in the awkward English translation, 'of all that concerns the performing of the art'. In one of the most famous contretemps in opera she halted his rehearsal to tell him that he would have to follow her lead in *Butterfly*, because she was the star. In the earliest printed version of Toscanini's reply, which appeared on the front page of the *American* on 7 December, the maestro says, 'The stars are all in the heavens, mademoiselle. You are but a plain artist, and you must obey my direction.' This provoked a demonstration that Miss Farrar had a temper too, and an appeal by the soprano to [director]

Gatti-Casazza, who dealt with her disturbance as he would later deal with nearly all artists' complaints: by hearing her out and grunting a noncommittal comment at the end. Farrar then took further appeal to [Otto] Kahn, requesting to be released from her contract, which of course Kahn refused. Miss Farrar thereupon sang Cio-Cio-San as Toscanini wanted.

> Martin Mayer, *The Met: One Hundred Years of Grand Opera*, Thames & Hudson, 1983, p. 102

The confrontation turned out to be the prelude to a love affair:

They became embroiled in a long and passionate love affair, kept a close secret from the press. Farrar finally demanded that Toscanini leave his wife and marry her: Toscanini, with his Italian conception of *la famiglia*, refused, and Farrar terminated the relationship. Toscanini's sudden and apparently unmotivated departure from the Met is now thought to be largely explained by his pain at the unavoidable encounters with his lost lover. Many years later Farrar invited him to dinner, at which caviare was served. Toscanini was furious, and whispered to his neighbour, 'I slept with that woman for seven years. Wouldn't you think she'd remember that I hate fish?'

> Rupert Christiansen, *Prima Donna*, Bodley Head, 1984, p. 193

Farrar gets carried away:

Whatever could be said of her Carmen on 17 February [1916], it could not be called 'dull'. Musically it conformed to convention, but she slapped Caruso smartly in the face during Act I, pushed one of the chorus girls roughly in Act II, and scuffled about in Act III with such vigour that she found herself in a position more singular than singable. At the end, Farrar let it be known that if Caruso didn't care for this 'realism', the company could find another Carmen. 'No,' the tenor gallantly replied, 'we can prevent a repetition of the scene by getting another José.' Apparently

conciliatory words had been spoken on both sides, for the awaited
repetition on 25 February went without incident.

Irving Kolodin, *The Story of the Metropolitan Opera*, New York, Knopf,

1953, p. 305

*The Polish soprano Ganna Walska, engaged to the enormously rich Harold
McCormick of Chicago, was signed up by Raoul Gunsbourg of the Monte
Carlo Opera in 1922:*

Later, in 1923, she was to have a disastrous début as Gilda at the
Paris Opéra (a charity performance paid for by her husband) and
in 1925 made an equally unhappy appearance as Cio-Cio-San at
Nice. The astute Gunsbourg may have achieved her survival as the
only vocal soloist in the four performances at Monte Carlo [of the
trivial opera *Le Soleil de minuit*], firstly by surrounding her with
three ballet dancers to distract the audience's attention, and also by
having what one might describe as a 'back-up' chorus accompany
most of her singing. Of course, that she was shortly to become
Harold McCormick's wife was not a disadvantage, especially in
Monte Carlo. But as an artist? To quote *Time* news magazine
following her appearance in Paris: 'Ganna Walska is beautiful; she
exerts a powerful fascination; she has wealth. What more can she
want? She wants, with all the passion of a strong, ambitious
nature, to sing in opera. And she has no voice.'

T. J. Walsh, *Monte Carlo Opera 1910–1951*, Gill & Macmillan, 1975,

p. 92

*When Beniamino Gigli stood in for Giovanni Martinelli in a performance
of Giordano's* Fedora *at the Metropolitan Opera on 14 January 1925, he
was cast opposite the Viennese soprano Maria Jeritza (1887–1982):*

Between this lady and myself there had existed, ever since we
began to sing together at the Met, what I can only presume to
have been a latent conflict of temperaments. In her presence, I
always felt tension. I never had any psychological difficulties with

my other colleagues, but Madame Jeritza's legendary 'temperament' had a disastrous effect on me. At the least sign of it, something would boil up inside me, and I would suddenly feel capable of becoming every bit as temperamental as she was.

On the night of the *Fedora* première, she hurled herself on me with such abandon in the betrothal scene at the end of Act II that I was able to withstand the impact only by bracing myself firmly against a wing support. At the next performance, she wriggled so violently in my supposedly loving arms that I did actually stagger, making the audience roar with laughter at what should have been an intensely tragic moment . . .

Then came the evening of 26 January. The opera was drawing to an end; it was the scene of my final interview with Fedora; having discovered her to be a spy, I was supposed to spurn her. What happened then exactly I really cannot say. Did my suppressed resentment at the way in which, on all these previous occasions, she had managed to ridicule me on the stage suddenly find an outlet? Did I miscalculate the force with which I pushed her away from me? Or did she simply slip? All I knew was that she was reeling towards the edge of the stage, and barely saved herself from tumbling over into the orchestra pit. I saw that she was hurt, and tried to help her to her feet, but she rejected my offer violently. She sang on to the end of the scene, and then rushed from the stage in a paroxysm of sobs.

She had wrenched her right wrist in falling on the glass and metal of the footlights, and had abrasions on both legs. 'He did it!' she shrieked, pointing at me. I was really sorry; I apologized profusely and assured her that it was an accident; but in vain. 'He did it! He wanted to kill me! Murderer! Murderer!'

This was too much; I protested.

'Listen to him! First he tries to murder me, then he insults me!' She turned to her husband, Baron Leopold von Popper, a tall, martial-looking Austrian, who always waited for her backstage. 'Defend my honour!' she commanded him. 'Challenge that man to a duel!'

To my relief, I received no challenge from the level-headed

baron; but next day there was an uproar of speculation, both in the newspapers and in the corridors of the Metropolitan, as to whether or not I had 'done it on purpose'. Things went so far that Gatti-Casazza, who normally refused to listen to gossip about any of the Met squabbles, much less intervene in them, felt obliged to issue a statement explaining that I had *not* done it on purpose; but for once, nobody paid any attention to him – it was more fun to let the battle rage.

Beniamino Gigli, *Memoirs*, translated by Darina Silone, Cassell, 1957,

pp. 146–7

Rosa Ponselle (1897–1981) was adored by the New York audience, but the appeal of her seamless yet agile voice, so evident from her recordings, has proved difficult to define in words:

[Her] performance in *Norma* from 1927 onwards was probably the best thing the Metropolitan had to offer for several years. Hers was a wonderfully smooth voice by now, smooth as very thick silky velvet all the way from the top to the bottom, no breaks and no alterations of quality either by reason of breathing or extreme notes at either end. She had in her throat a more evenly integrated homogeneous voice than any other that easily comes to mind and it was also of ravishing beauty as sheer sound. The demerit of her performances, or at least the aspect of them that may be said to have kept her from true greatness, was an absence of dramatic urgency. All the desperate situations and horrendous tragedies to which the heroines of Italian opera are subjected could not wring from her anything less (or more) than wonderfully beautiful singing. She never imperilled her vocal cords by a cry of desperation. The absence of urgency in her operatic emotion, by the way, was never felt in New York so far as I know, except by me, and it is no doubt heresy to mention it.

Vincent Sheean, *First and Last Love*, Gollancz, 1957, pp. 85–6

The Russian singer Oda Slobodskaya (1888–1970) was a believer in on-the-job training:

She sang in the Italian première of Rimsky-Korsakov's *The Invisible City of Kitesh* at the Scala, Milan; was acclaimed in Buenos Aires during a season of Russian opera there, and at length reached Covent Garden, an institution which had for some time resisted her attack. Her account of the engagement, when it came, shows her enormous professionalism. She was in Paris when the management of the Royal Opera telephoned. 'Do you sing Venus, in *Tannhäuser*?' she was asked. 'Of course I do,' she replied without a moment's hesitation. 'Do you sing the Dresden version?' the catechism continued. 'Invariably,' she answered. 'Can you be here for the first rehearsal next week?' came the question. 'Of course,' she said.

'Then,' she told me, 'I went out, bought the score and started to learn the part.'

Ivor Newton, *At the Piano*, Hamish Hamilton, 1966, pp. 110–11

After her retirement the German contralto Maria Olczewska (1892–1969) came to London to stay with her brother-in-law:

On a recent visit he told her as he was going out that the window-cleaner was expected. 'The window cleaner's always happy if he's given a cup of tea,' he told her. 'And he's rather unusual – he's very fond of opera and loves talking about music.'

Olczewska had not made herself ready for the day but was still wearing a favourite old dressing-gown and a scarf about her head when she entertained the window-cleaner to his morning tea. Before long he was advising her about the gramophone records she should buy. 'Of course,' he said, 'if you want *Der Rosenkavalier*, don't buy any of the new recordings. Get the old one – it's a bit hard to get hold of, but it's easily the best. There's Richard Mayr as Baron Ochs; the Marschallin is Lotte Lehmann and Elisabeth Schumann is Sophie, and the Octavian is . . . is . . .'

'Me,' said Olczweska.

'I can't remember her name,' said the window-cleaner. 'I know
it's Mayr and Lehmann and Schumann and . . . and . . .'

'Me,' said Olczewska.

'No, I can't remember her name,' he said, paying no attention to Olczewska's interjections. The next time he met her
brother-in-law, he mentioned the conversation. 'Who was that
funny old woman?' he asked. 'She seems to think she's an opera
singer.'

Ivor Newton, *At the Piano*, Hamish Hamilton, 1966, pp. 176–7

Kirsten Flagstad (1895–1962) comes to the Met:

[On 15 January 1935] Flagstad made her first appearance on the
Metropolitan Opera stage, dressed in costume as the *Götterdämmerung* Brünnhilde, surrounded by colleagues in street clothes.
She had never sung the role before, and was not in fact scheduled
to sing it until late February: the rehearsal was for a performance
that would be sung by Gertrude Kappel. But nobody at the Met
had ever seen Flagstad in costume or on stage. Bodanzky wanted
to get a firmer grip on the singer he and Gatti had hired to take
over what had been Frida Leider's roles for the second half of the
1934–5 season. At the end of the first act duet with Siegfried,
Bodanzky – the hard man, bored with opera and its discontents –
put down his baton and asked his assistant Karl Riedel to conduct
a reprise. A messenger was sent to Gatti, but Bodanzky himself
ran to [assistant manager] Ziegler's door: 'My God, Ned!' he
called. 'My God, come hear this woman sing!' Then he returned to
the podium and with Gatti and Ziegler in the audience – and
others of the house who had heard the rumours sweeping the
corridors – he took her and Paul Althouse through the duet one
more time. Flagstad always sang out in rehearsals, and 'at that
time', she later wrote, 'I took the high C's regularly. The orchestra
stood up and cheered me.'

Flagstad had never been a major artist in Europe. She had made
much of her early career in musical comedy (an odd thought, for

so grave and innocent an artist), and nearly all of it in Norwegian or Swedish. Kahn had heard her sing Tosca in Norwegian on a business trip in 1929, and had come back to New York raving about her; but Gatti had been unable to find anybody south of the Skaggerak who had ever heard of her at all . . .

[The Met's European agent Eric Simon] went to Bayreuth at the close of the 1934 festival at which Flagstad had made a little-remarked entry into the operatic big time, singing a Sieglinde and a Gutrune, and asked her to come to St Moritz to audition for Gatti and Bodanzky in an over-stuffed hotel room with heavy hangings and draperies. From her description it must have been quite an occasion, for there was a competitor – Elizabeth Delius, a far more experienced artist – and the judges ran both of them through a gruelling programme. After accepting Flagstad, Bodanzky said, 'Don't you go and get fat now. Learn those roles. Find yourself a good coach . . .' On further consideration, he suggested a coach: George Szell, then conducting in Prague. Flagstad went for ten days to Prague, where Szell 'was very severe with me. Not a single complimentary word until the very last day. Then he remarked, "I'm going to write to Mr Bodanzky and say that he doesn't have to worry about your not knowing the roles in time."'

At the age of thirty-nine, in other words, Flagstad was being treated as a tyro – which, in a sense, she was: she had never sung any of the Brünnhildes on any stage, or Isolde in a large house. As she worked on the heavier repertoire that fall, mysteriously the voice grew. What astonished Flagstad herself was that her back muscles seemed to swell; though she was not gaining weight as Bodanzky had feared, she was splitting her dresses at the seams. Certainly nothing in her previous career had given anyone the impression that she would produce in the cavernous Metropolitan so dark and rich and large and seamless and musical a sound, totally without strain at top or bottom.

Bodanzky had told Flagstad that they would not want her Sieglinde, but it was in that role that she made her début on 2 February 1935 (without a rehearsal), in a broadcast matinée. The voice proved not only a staggering experience in the house but also an astonishment through microphones and loudspeakers. The following Thursday, to a packed house (there was rarely thereafter an empty seat at the Met when Flagstad appeared), she sang her first Isolde, with Melchior, Olczewska, Schorr, and Ludwig Hofmann ... Ten days later she sang the *Walküre* Brünnhilde for the first time in her life, again without a rehearsal. At the end of the season, on eleven days' notice (during a period when she was already travelling on recital engagements), she sang Kundry in *Parsifal*, a role she had never so much as read through before.

Martin Mayer, *The Met: One Hundred Years of Grand Opera*, Thames & Hudson, 1983, pp. 195–6

Nobody argued about the quality of Flagstad's voice, but not everyone acclaimed her as a Wagnerian interpreter:

This regal lady had the greatest voice any of us had ever heard – greatest in volume, range, security, beauty of tone, everything a voice can have, and all of one piece, never a break in it, all rolling out with no evidence of effort or strain even in the most difficult passages. The only defect to be found in her remarkable performances was that they did not express what Wagner wrote. The immense audiences which gathered to hear her from 1935 to 1941 did not care a fig what Wagner had written: they wanted to hear this golden flood of tone over the massive orchestra ... The physiological effect of Flagstad was a thrill – a powerful one to be sure – caused by her wondrous singing. She never frightened, alarmed or repelled; she was not in the very slightest degree demonic; she enraptured her audiences, and what did it matter about Wagner? ...

I see her now in her dressing-room at the Metropolitan as I saw her once between the first and second acts of *Tristan*: calm and majestic, smiling kindly, braiding her hair with a vocal score of the opera open on the table before her, an Isolde who had never suffered humiliation of spirit or the wish to die. She had been knitting and put the work down beside the *Tristan* score while she talked to us. After we left I imagine she resumed her knitting until she was called to the stage for, of all things, Act II of *Tristan*. No more tranquil approach to unbridled passion has come under my observation.

Vincent Sheean, *First and Last Love*, Gollancz, 1957, pp. 116–17

The American soprano Emma Eames (1865–1952):

Not long after Glyndebourne became a place of pilgrimage for opera goers, the famous Emma Eames visited London. Though noted for her beauty she was not the easiest of people with whom to deal. She once sang Elsa in *Lohengrin* and looked so beautiful that she moved an admiring conductor to declare, 'I should love to do to you what Lohengrin did not do to Elsa.' She simply said, 'Change the conductor,' and the conductor was promptly changed. Of her cold, ladylike acting, *The New York Times* reported, 'Last night, Emma Eames sang Aida; we had skating on the Nile.'

During Madame Eames's visit to London, I was invited to meet her by [the music critic] Desmond Shawe-Taylor . . .

'Madame Eames,' someone said during the party, 'you simply must see *Don Giovanni* at Glyndebourne.'

The idea appalled the great prima donna. 'Are you asking me,' she demanded rhetorically, 'to undergo a journey on a British railway train, and to spend a night in the discomforts of an English provincial hotel, where they stuff the mattresses with pomegranates, to hear *Don Giovanni*? I sang Donna Anna at the Metropolitan when Gustav Mahler conducted. Victor Maurel was the Don, Chaliapin the Leporello, Caruso the Don Ottavio, Lilli Lehmann the Donna Elvira and Geraldine Farrar the Zerlina. Why should I go to Glyndebourne when I have such memories of *Don Giovanni*? The remembrance of that performance will last my lifetime.'

Ivor Newton, *At the Piano*, Hamish Hamilton, 1966, pp. 114–15

Birgit Nilsson (1918–) has a particularly sharp yet broad sense of humour. I can't document the story, but it was reported that during the Covent Garden Ring cycle in the 1960s, Wolfgang Windgassen as Siegfried came pounding up the mountain to awaken the slumbering Brünnhilde, only to find a sign reading DO NOT DISTURB pinned to her breastplate:

Her essential seriousness has been overshadowed by her much-publicized knockabout wit. There were clashes with conductors, Knappertsbusch and Karajan especially; and a long-standing and good-humoured battle with Rudolf Bing, the manager of the Met, led to various incidents, including her putting him down as a tax-deductible dependant on her Internal Revenue form – it did her no good, and in 1975 she had to abandon America for a few years when a dispute with the IRS came to a head . . . At Bing's farewell gala, she sang the closing scene from *Salome*, during which the severed head of John the Baptist, presented to her on a tray, was modelled on Bing's own.

Rupert Christiansen, *Prima Donna*, Bodley Head, 1984, p. 168

Sometimes she was on the receiving end of a prank, usually from record producer John Culshaw and his team:

Because of her broad sense of humour, and because of the intensity she puts into her work, it had become a tradition to play a joke on her during any opera we recorded. She looked forward to this, and tried to anticipate what we were up to. As soon as she arrived in Vienna for the last part of *Götterdämmerung* she began to try to find out what we had planned . . . It was a well-kept secret. There is a moment towards the end of the Immolation scene when Brünnhilde calls for her horse, Grane, on which she will shortly ride into Siegfried's funeral pyre, and we decided to produce a live Grane at that moment . . .

As Nilsson sang her cue '*Grane, mein Ross!*' the wing doors of the stage opened and our Grane trotted out, tail up, in complete command of the situation. Nilsson almost fell over with surprise, and the orchestra cheered. By the time we had got the horse off the stage and restarted the take, we had lost exactly fifty seconds on this whole incident, but we had gained enormously in a different sense: for there are times when it is necessary to lower the temperature in order to make it rise even higher. You cannot sustain the pitch of intensity required by *Götterdämmerung* without, once in a while, doing something preposterous and even childish . . . It is a form of safety-valve, which I do not expect anyone to understand except those who have been exposed to such powerful music hour after hour, day after day, and night after night.

John Culshaw, *Ring Resounding*, Secker & Warburg, 1967, pp. 204–5

The first night of Joan Sutherland (1926–) in the title role of Lucia di Lammermoor *at Covent Garden on 17 February 1959 was one of the great triumphs of post-war opera. Curiously,* Lucia *had not been performed in London since 1907, apart from a single performance in 1925. The culmination of the evening was Sutherland's Mad Scene:*

The first scene of Act III continues the celebrations in Ravenswood Castle's Great Hall but they are interrupted with the news that the bride has murdered her new husband. Lucia herself then appears and goes through an imaginary wedding ceremony with Edgardo in opera's most celebrated Mad Scene. Sutherland's appearance in her bloodstained shift and her subsequent darting and flitting across the stage as she sang the long scene, generated an atmosphere of intense excitement within the auditorium. There was something extraordinary happening on stage, a performance unlike anything that had been seen within the memory of most of the audience. The act ended with its *'Spargi d'umoro pinto'* in what David Webster described as 'a riot', and the opera's final scene in which Edgardo learns of Lucia's death and in turn kills himself, was much delayed and an anticlimax to most people without Sutherland on stage. Somehow they managed to get through, but it was obvious that everyone was just waiting to greet Sutherland and give her one of the biggest ovations for many seasons at Covent Garden.

As she took her solo curtain calls at the end of the long evening
she seemed a vastly different person from the character she had
played only a few minutes before. Now she was self-conscious, a
little unsure how to receive such an overwhelming ovation, which
she later described as more like coming from a football crowd than
an opera audience. Gradually Sutherland began to blow kisses to
the cheering throng and they responded more energetically than
ever . . .

As a result of the reception for the first night of *Lucia* the BBC
took the unprecedented step of changing its advertised schedule to
broadcast the work in full later in the week.

Brian Adams, *La Stupenda*, Hutchinson, 1981, pp. 94–7

A fair assessment of Sutherland's career:

From 1962 [Richard] Bonynge began to conduct at his wife's
performances, and the knives were drawn. The Sutherland–
Bonynge 'circus' or 'package deal' was found to be a deplorable
instance of prima donna's privilege, doubly so as Bonynge's conducting was considered noisy and amateurish (it has continued
unpopular in some quarters, but singers invariably find him extraordinarily considerate of their needs). Sutherland herself came in
for her share of criticism, as the bright, crisp, and open sound
of her early recordings gave way to a drifting, mooning way with
anything that was not perforce fast and glittering. Among the
ranks of the *bien pensant*, she could soon do nothing right. 'Spot
the consonant' became a favourite opera buff's game every time a
new Sutherland record came out, for her diction had been reduced
to a series of vowels connected by the broadest and most general-
ized of portamenti . . .

Sutherland had an immense support system, however, in the
form of her husband (who by the mid 1960s was conducting
virtually all her performances), a long-term recording contract,
excellent management, and a band of regular colleagues. Her
returns to Australia, first in Melba-style touring companies, later as

prima donna of the new Australian Opera, were invariably triumphant; in Italy the gallery dubbed her 'La Stupenda', a label which
delighted the press; and in America rumours that her fees were at
least as high as any other singer's was in itself a potent recommendation. What is more important, Sutherland proved herself a real
trouper, reliable, hard-working, and always ready to deliver the
coloratura goods that her audiences were paying for.

Rupert Christiansen, Prima Donna, Bodley Head, 1984, pp. 318–19

*The La Scala audience went berserk when in 1982 Montserrat Caballé
(1933–) cancelled a performance:*

As one of the few important events of the season, a revival of the
famous Visconti–Benois production of *Anna Bolena* was planned
for February. In 1957 Callas and Simionato had sung the leads; the
revival would have Caballé and Obraztsova. Tickets for the entire
series of performances were sold out; they were not even available
at black-market prices.

The day before the première, Caballé came down with stomatitis,
gastro-enteritis, and nausea, and she immediately informed the
management. As her condition worsened, it became obvious to her
that she would not be able to perform. According to Caballé
(every newspaper carried a different version of the story), the only
person from the management of La Scala she could find the
morning of the performance was Francesco Siciliani, the artistic
director. She advised him of her inability to perform, and her
understudy, Ruth Falcon, was notified. But instead of announcing
the change in cast on the radio and television, and changing the
advertisements posted at the opera house, no one did anything.

When, at eight o'clock on the night of the performance, an
anonymous voice announced over the theatre's loudspeaker that
Caballé would not appear, a fury unlike anything in the history of
this theatre exploded. The announcement that Ruth Falcon would
be replacing the Spanish soprano could not be heard. The conductor, Giuseppe Patané, stepped on to the podium, but instead of

starting to conduct, he walked off as the booing increased. Insults directed at the intendant, Ernesto Badini, reached such a level that he withdrew quickly from his box. The audience seemed to have gone mad. In the midst of the storm, Siciliani begged Giulietta Simionato, who was in the audience, to go on stage and try to calm the house down. But even though she is so deeply beloved, she was unable to utter a word, and all that could be heard was a shout from the audience: 'Let that clown Badini come and speak to us himself!' The imprecations – even from bejewelled ladies in the boxes – continued at such a hysterical pitch that at 8.30 the anonymous loudspeaker voice announced that the performance was cancelled and reimbursements would be made. But the pandemonium only increased; it was quite a while before the angry spectators left . . .

For the next few days there were endless stories speculating on what would happen, as Caballé's indisposition continued and several more performances were cancelled. Finally it was announced that she would sing. But what is so extraordinary is that at this performance, Caballé – who did show some signs of vocal stress, but whose *mezze voci* were as beautiful as ever – was booed, as were Obraztsova, Paul Plishka, and the other principals, by some members of the audience. Critics were divided but, on the whole, unkind.

Lanfranco Rasponi, *The Last Prima Donnas*, Gollancz, 1984, pp. 593–4

Janet Baker (1933–) goes to see Elizabeth Harwood as the Marschallin in Der Rosenkavalier *at Glyndebourne shortly before her own final operatic performances as Gluck's Orfeo:*

I was grateful for the darkened theatre; for most of the first act I sat unable to stop tears from pouring down my face. To see the Marschallin played is always a touching and nostalgic experience, especially for women, but when the character above all is sung by a colleague who is also a dearly loved friend, then the circumstances are almost unbearable. Elizabeth, with her impeccable German, perfectly phrased Strauss, her inner sweetness, her beauty, the dignity of her person and the soaring, creamy voice, was deeply moving. I felt her interpretation significant in two ways; for her, personally, at this moment in her life and career, and then for myself. In all these months since the season began, I have never felt a moment of regret for the decision I have made; I still do not, but sitting there at the back of the box, watching my friend, I felt deep grief. There is no shame at feeling grief at parting; it is a natural emotion, and it swept over me in painful waves as I listened, aware of my years as a theatre person, of my memories, my colleagues. The final nights at Covent Garden and the Coliseum were full of glory. I have every hope that the last night here at Glyndebourne will be the same; my own real 'goodbye' to the stage was being said tonight in my own heart, there in the press box, and the actual words of that 'goodbye' were being sung on the stage by my friend. It seemed planned in some remarkable way that I should feel as I did, sitting quite alone (there were strangers in the box with me, thank goodness), sharing the moment with Elizabeth, who was quite unaware of her part in the proceedings. After all these months I now fully understand what I have done. Apollo has reached out and branded me for daring to walk away from the profession instead of waiting to be cast aside, but in the pain of understanding what I have willingly given up and in my total acceptance of it, I have paid in full my debt to the theatre. The scales are even. I am handing back the power lent to me, and in so doing am burned. It is an honourable wound.

Janet Baker, *Full Circle*, Macrae, 1982, pp. 216–17

14: The Art of Singing

Singing requires so strict an Application, that one must study
with the Mind, when one cannot with the Voice.

Piero Francesco Tosi, *Observations on the Florid Song,* p. 92

VOCAL TECHNIQUE

*Rupert Christiansen on the mechanics of singing, the endless preparation
required before a singer can be said to have mastered this unstable art:*

Teachers struggle to 'equalize' the registers so that the voice
sounds seamless and homogeneous, like Ponselle's or Leider's, all
the way through its range, an achievement which involves working
hard on the passage notes which link the so-called registers. The
voice must also be 'placed'; that is, the air must be directed, at least
mentally, towards the appropriate resonating cavities which will
give the sound full and firm tone. Some singers centre it all at the
back of the mouth, others concentrate on their sinuses: most agree
that the tongue must not block or deflect the sound. Intonation, or
the maintenance of correct pitch, is another problem, particularly
in an age where vibrato is prevalent. It is impossible for a singer
accurately to hear the sound she or he is making, and within any
audience there will be surprisingly different reactions to a singer's
intonation. Very few singers sing at a perfect regularity of pitch,
and a small degree of sharpness or flatness is part of a voice's
personality. However, a singer who cannot keep steady is a sorry
thing, and a real problem with pitch, like Pasta's, is excruciating.
Diction, especially at the top of the voice, agility, and stamina are
other primary hurdles that some singers remain more successful at
surmounting than others.

There is so much that can get in the way. A sneeze can release a lot of phlegm and block paths of sound. A stomach upset can impair the breathing. Menstruation affects the abdominal muscles and can cause flatness. Ponselle could not sing near any artificial heat and would telephone the stage-door manager before entering the opera house to make sure it was suitably freezing.

Rupert Christiansen, *Prima Donna*, Bodley Head, 1984,

pp. 212–14

Sound advice on how to sing from a renowned singer and teacher of the eighteenth century:

Let the Scholar be obliged to pronounce the Vowels distinctly, that they may be heard for such as they are . . .

Let him take care, whilst he sings, that he get a graceful Posture, and make an agreeable Appearance.

Let him rigorously correct all Grimaces and Tricks of the Head, of the Body, and particularly of the Mouth; which ought to be composed in a Manner (if the Sense of the Words permit it) rather inclined to a Smile, than too much Gravity . . .

Let him learn to hold out the Notes without a Shrillness like a Trumpet, or trembling; and if at the Beginning he made him hold out every Note the length of two Bars, the Improvement would be the greater; otherwise from the natural Inclination that the Beginners have to keep the Voice in Motion, and the Trouble in holding it out, he will get a habit, and not be able to fix it, and will become subject to a Flutt'ring in the Manner of all those that sing in a very bad Taste . .

Let him accustom the Scholar to sing often in presence of Persons of Distinction, whether from Birth, Quality, or Eminence in the Profession, that by gradually losing his Fear, he may acquire an Assurance, but not a Boldness. Assurance leads to a Fortune, and in a Singer becomes a Merit.

Piero Francesco Tosi, *Observations on the Florid Song*, Wilcox, 1743,

reprinted 1926, pp. 25–7, 61–2

Stendhal on the changes in singing wrought by Rossini, who discouraged
improvisation and wrote detailed ornamentation for his singers:

Even the most devoted followers of Rossini acknowledge the
revolution he has brought to music but reproach him for having
drawn in the boundaries of fine singing, diminished the emotional
content of this great art, and denied the utility of certain forms of
singing that led to raptures of joy in the days of Pacchiarotti and
other musicians of that vanished generation, but which are rarely
experienced today. These miracles were rooted in the powers of
the human voice.

The fact is that the Rossinian revolution has killed off each
singer's originality. What is the point of taking great pains to
make evident to the audience, first, the individual and intrinsic
qualities of their voice, and second, the specific expression which
their sensibility alone can generate? In the operas of Rossini and
his imitators, the singers are fated never to find an opportunity
to demonstrate to the public the very qualities and skills they
spent so many years working to acquire. Moreover, the expectation of finding everything written down definitively in the music
they are to sing removes all their inventiveness and makes them
lazy . . .

In former times singers such as Babini, Marchesi, and Pacchiarotti invented their own very complex ornamentation; above all
they applied it as they saw fit, by drawing on the inspiration of
both their natural gifts and their qualities of soul . . . It should not
be part of the composer's role to write down all the embellishments,
because that requires the most intimate and perfect knowledge of
the singer's voice, a knowledge possessed only by the singer
himself, who has devoted twenty years of his life to training his
voice so as to give it the utmost flexibility.

Stendhal, *Life of Rossini*, chapter 32, translated by Stephen Brook

Maria Malibran, the daughter of tenor Manuel Garcia, was not born with a heaven-sent voice. Her father worked on her technique until she became the most acclaimed soprano of her times:

Her natural voice, unrefined by training, was small, uneven, and lacking in flexibility. The lower notes were rough, the middle ones unfocused, and the upper register limited in range and shrill in tone. Nor did it quickly respond to exercise ... The development of Maria's voice was the result of her father's untiring efforts. He subjected his daughter to a training as arduous as his own had been, if not more so. Maria was allowed to sing only exercises, exercises that were the product of Garcia's studies with Ansani and which were derived from those of the old Neapolitan school of singing. She repeated these again and again as her father sought to extend her range, to equalize her scale from top to bottom, to join her three registers, and to increase the flexibility of her voice until she could easily manage every conceivable embellishment ...

Once [the composer] Paer was walking with a friend near the Garcia apartment. Screams were heard through the open windows, and the friend exclaimed in alarm, 'Someone is being murdered!' 'No, no,' replied Paer calmly, 'it's only Garcia teaching his daughter to sing.'

Howard Bushnell, *Maria Malibran*, Pennsylvania State University Press, 1979, pp. 4, 5, 11

The vocal skills of Jenny Lind:

Her weakness had become her strength. At the basis of her technique was her perfect breathing control. People believed that she must have an exceptional lung capacity, but in fact it was comparatively small. She could sustain her voice so long that it was rumoured she had an ability to sing on the indrawn as well as the outgoing breath. What she could do was to replenish her lungs so skilfully that not a sign could be seen or heard. Once at Aachen she was reported to have held on to a note for sixty seconds. She could hold on until the audience believed she must be at the very end of her resources; but then, instead of breaking off, it would gradually swell out in an unbelievable crescendo of sound. Her breathing control was the secret of her wonderful pianissimo, that incomparable achievement that filled everyone with amazement and that Chopin loved so. It was a true pianissimo, scarcely more than a breath of sound, yet as full and rich as her mezzo voice and it penetrated to every corner of the largest theatre or concert hall. People spoke of it creeping up to you and touching you. Audiences held their breath as they strained to catch the moment at which the note faded away into silence ... Her shake, which was executed with fantastic speed and accuracy and unapproachable brilliance, could be toned down to a whisper that was like nothing in nature but the warbling of a bird.

Joan Bulman, *Jenny Lind*, Barrie, 1956, pp. 52–3

Tosi, in his Observations on the Florid Song *(1743), wrote disparagingly of those 'who, though they never sang, nor know how to sing, pretend not only to teach, but to perfect, and find some that are weak enough to be imposed on'. The tenor Walter Slezak also had a few half-facetious things to say about singing teachers:*

Singing teachers are a special breed of people. To become one, you only have to say: 'I am a singing teacher!' That's your diploma, these are your credentials. To supervise your four- and five-year-olds playing with blocks in the kindergarten, to teach them the A B C, to treat the corns on your feet, to cut your hair, give you a massage – all require proof of training – and a licence. But that rarest gift of God, that wonderful intangible, the human voice? Anybody can fool around with it; every broken-down, third-rate singer, every unsuccessful piano teacher, every flunked-out music student. All you need is a room with a piano, photos of a few well-known singers on the wall (the implication being that they are 'pupils'), and you are in business and automatically addressed as 'Professor'.

No mother ever looked into her newborn's crib and said with

hopeful pride: 'Someday this child will be a great singing teacher.'
(Or a great prompter in opera!) There are no schools to train the
teachers of the human voice. That profession is usually the back-
wash and last resort of failure or old age.

Walter Slezak, *What Time's the Next Swan?*, Doubleday, 1962, p. 147

*Gina Cigna shows how, with rigorous training, the range of the female voice
can be extended:*

'For seven years I studied with [Emma] Calvé. She was an exceedingly severe person, and the breathing exercises she put me through
are not to be believed. She insisted I change the air in my lungs the
way the yogis do. Calvé was sure that I was a mezzo, and in fact I
had no high notes. But I was immensely stubborn and did not
wish to be a mezzo – all the roles that attracted me belonged to the
soprano repertoire. So I tried and tried, and, miraculously, one day
my throat finally opened up and I produced an F sharp. It was like
a padlocked door that suddenly had opened. From then on I began
to consolidate what I had gained, and the other notes came until I
finally reached high C. You cannot imagine my exaltation, nor the
surprise of Madame Calvé, who simply could not believe her ears. I
advise young singers to keep trying. Somehow the stairs leading to
the top are there, but the problem is to find them. Some voices are
born perfectly placed, and the high register is there, free and easy.
But some need very strong willpower and discipline to find it.'

Lanfranco Rasponi, *The Last Prima Donnas*, Gollancz, 1984, p. 207

Zinka Milanov on the importance of technique:

'My best singing did come after my fortieth birthday, but this is
the way it should be. Today it is the other way around. Most
singers begin having their disturbances at the age of thirty-five,
because their foundations are not right. While the bloom of youth
is still in the vocal cords, the sun shines. Then the problems begin
to pile up, and very fast. Look around, please, and it's pretty much

of a disaster. Some voices are born with a vibrato; others get it by singing incorrectly. The wobble – so prevalent today – comes from forcing, and this means that the vocal cords are irritated . . .

'*Mezze voci* and pianos are a must. How can you get to the end of a Verdi aria if you don't employ them? You find that you are totally worn out. If you have developed the pianos – one must find them; they exist, believe me, in every voice – then you must learn to fence with them *vis-à-vis* the passages which, according to the score, must be loud. You will notice that when a singer can no longer handle a piano, the top is already crumbling . . .

'The colour of the sound is what made me, and it is with it that I imbued life into all my heroines. Acting is all very well, but it does not take the place of the voice. When they say "a great actress", beware. It usually means that there is not much voice there. Of course, many instruments are manufactured; but mine was not – it was all there from the very beginning. It needed to be fortified and disciplined. Today the confusion is utterly bewildering, for there are so many singers who cross over, like in a ferry, between soprano and mezzo roles. They simply don't seem to know what they are. If they have a limited top, they become inclined to sing mezzo roles; and if mezzos have a top, instead they take on soprano parts. But a mezzo with a dazzling top is one thing, and carrying on throughout the opera the tessitura of a soprano is another. Most lyrics today take on dramatic parts, and either you cannot hear them or they shout. A dog is a dog and remains a dog even if he wishes he were a cat. The laws of nature cannot be changed. You are what you are.'

Lanfranco Rasponi, *The Last Prima Donnas*, Gollancz, 1984, pp. 221–2

The ultimate test of technical training as far as most opera fans are concerned is the mastery of coloratura singing. Amelita Galli-Curci sums up the fate of the coloratura:

'It is the destiny of the coloratura to be like an acrobat on a steel wire. The public waits anxiously to see if you are going to crack on a certain note or be unable to finish a certain difficult *filatura*, just like the public in a circus follows attentively to see if the poor wretch is going to miss a jump and fall below.

'A coloratura must possess, at all times, a total serenity not to fall into the traps the music offers her, and I have always preferred to sacrifice some of the purity of tone to find a more human expression. And the result has been, undoubtedly, that a more metallic type of production has come into being.'

Lanfranco Rasponi, *The Last Prima Donnas*, Gollancz, 1984, p. 157

Iris Adami Corradetti on the technique of verismo singing:

'It is a mistake to think that for verismo it is not necessary to have a solid base of bel canto. It is rather a question of learning how to express with more sensibility and dramatic power. Diction plays an essential part. One simply cannot put over a role without excellent diction. Toscanini taught me that one must respect what is written, within one's own possibilities.

'I will give you an example. In *La Bohème* there is an effect in "*Mi chiamano Mimi*" in the passage between the F sharp and the A natural on the word "*primavera*", Puccini places a graphic mark to indicate that the note must be taken softly and with little voice, then amplified until it arrives at a fortissimo to conclude the word, which must express the joy of the coming of spring. No one does it any more. Why? Does it mean nothing that it is written in the score? Certainly it's difficult; it means a lot of extra work. Today these sopranos sing Mimi as if it were Toselli's "Serenata". This little seamstress is not a character that dominates the stage, like Butterfly, and so the colouring of the voice must do a great deal. Some voices are born with a far wider palette of shades; the others must develop this ability. In some verismo operas, however, there are passages of pure bel canto. Take the love duet at the end of the first act of *Butterfly*, with the final high C. This is pure singing and demands a fine technique.

'But, alas, verismo today has become a joke. They think they can obtain the effects with sobs and ranting around. I heard all the fabulous divas of verismo and I believe I know what I am talking about.'

Lanfranco Rasponi, *The Last Prima Donnas*, Gollancz, 1984,

p. 367

Vocal training is often completed at the expense of diction. For opera goers who seek drama as well as sound, this relegation of diction to an also-ran is infuriating. Joan Sutherland was notorious for her poor enunciation:

[Her husband Richard] Bonynge stated his views on the matter: 'The emotion must come from the musical score – the sounds of the voice. If one over-enunciates the words, as in the big ensembles, they can only get in the way of the music. They frequently get right in the way of the music and spoil the line. In fact, I frequently ask the chorus not to enunciate so much because I do not want to hear the words. When we go to the theatre we must hear every word that is spoken throughout the piece, but not in opera. I think when one goes to certain performances in English one hears the singers spitting out the words in a most ghastly manner; it has nothing to do with the music. They destroy opera and I'm very anti spitting out words except in recitatives where they should be heard. The recitative is to tell the story. The music is to carry on the emotion, not the words.'

Brian Adams, *La Stupenda*, Hutchinson, 1981, p. 213

THE RISE OF THE TENOR

The tenor is a relative newcomer to the operatic stage:

In baroque days it had been the castratos who stalked the scene . . . With the advent of the romantic style and the invasion of the theatres by a bourgeois audience, these male sopranos were inevitably succeeded by prima donnas, whose voices could contrive similar effects. It was not until Napoleon's day that a revolution in

the production of the tenor voice came about. The problem lay in
the management of the falsetto register which would bring into
play more than a fifth of an octave in range and enable the tenor to
vie with the soprano. The history of singing throughout the
nineteenth century deals with the fashion in which these notes were
produced so as to sound out over the increasingly strenuous
accompaniments and appeal to the singer's masculine ego. Initially,
the tenor's upper range did not extend far; by Rossini's day,
however, it encompassed the high C, sometimes C sharp and even
D. These notes were still produced in falsetto, not the coarse, white
and open tone that the term may suggest today, but in a blending
of the registers – the *voce mista* – in which the head voice predom-
inated. In the next generation came Giovanni Battista Rubini, one
of the legendary names from the age of bel canto. His influence was
to have a profound effect on singing even up to the time of Caruso.
His was a vaunting virtuosity; the tale of his singing an F instead of
a D flat during a run-through of Bellini's *I puritani* in 1835, and of
the composer's decision thereupon to mark it in the score, much to
the embarrassment of every Arturo since, has become a legend. But
for certain the F would have been completely in falsetto; physio-
logically it could not have been otherwise . . .

In the third quarter of the nineteenth century there gradually
came about a definite separation between the lighter and heavier
types of tenor voice . . .

It was not until 1890 that all the ingredients of verismo were
finally brought together under one act in Mascagni's *Cavalleria
rusticana* . . . There was the inevitable delay while singers hastened
to adapt their techniques, for the high degree of realism demanded
an appropriate singing style. In the course of the next few years
this would become apparent in a shift away from those elegant,
albeit tremulous tenors of the post-Rubini tradition, to tenors with
less charm and more decibels. It was their concern to contrive a
more manly sounding timbre, so as to match the heroes of verismo
opera. Producing an altitudinous range was no longer regarded as
so important, especially when this depended upon the use of a
marked vibrato which became, with the increasing power of the

orchestra, more bleat-like. It seems likely that Masini, although he never made any records, had a smooth round tone without the 'goat bleat', and Francesco Marconi too; his records confirm this. So Caruso was not the first tenor to abandon it, yet he was the first to achieve a complete success in so doing . . .

Until 1902 there were many different singing styles but in the course of the next generation almost all Italian-type tenors began obviously to ape Caruso . . . Although certain aspects of his style have been ignored or become modified . . . he has remained, thanks to the phonograph's influence, the archetypal tenor.

Michael Scott, *The Great Caruso*, Hamish Hamilton, 1988,

pp. 10–14, 57

John Rosselli examines this same evolution in terms of the roles tenors were assigned:

By the 1830s [tenors] were the lovers; the contralto in breeches began to seem old-fashioned. The mature works of Bellini and Donizetti established other normal male singers as the pillars of romantic opera: the baritone . . . in the parts of villains or men of power; the true bass, already familiar from some of Rossini's works, as priest or noble father . . .

By 1877 the *tenore di forza* was so much the norm that an agent was asked to supply one 'who can shout well' to sing all the tenor parts in a season at Bilbao; the repertory was to include *La sonnambula* and *I puritani*, works that demand refined lyrical singing. The 'shrieking manner' had carried everything before it.

In that same year, 1877, the Spanish tenor Julian Gayarre first displayed at Covent Garden his 'quasi-nasal' emission – what Bernard Shaw was to call his 'goat bleat'. There was a flock of such goats; Gayarre had been preceded by Francesco Tamagno, who would later create Verdi's Otello. Both were marvels even if their sound was unpleasing by the lights of the pre-Verdi period. Tamagno, the poor *trattoria* keeper's son, had first made a mark by interpolating a sensational high B in a Donizetti part he had been called upon to sing at short notice. The key to 'superhuman' applause was now the high note shot fortissimo from the chest.

John Rosselli, *Singers of Italian Opera*, Cambridge University Press, 1992, pp. 176–8

It comes as something of surprise that Luciano Pavarotti, the King of High Cs, should play down the importance of ringing top notes and ardently advocate the bel canto style:

'Top notes are like the goals in football. If you can do them, fine. If not, no matter. You can still be a great tenor without the high C. Caruso didn't have it. Neither did Tito Schipa, Schipa didn't even have a particularly beautiful voice. But he was a great singer. His musicality was so great that it enabled him to override every handicap. Listening to his records, you can hear him guiding his voice along, like a skipper steering his ship through all kinds of treacherous waters in an exemplary way that should be a lesson to us all. He had something far more important, twenty times more important, than high notes: a great line' . . .

He considers bel canto 'the best medicine for the voice, because of the discipline and the combination of qualities it requires: agility, elasticity, a smooth, even flow of liquid, well-focused sound, uniformity of colour, the ability to spin long, expressive legato lines without recourse to portamenti and, most important, without ever overdoing anything or giving the impression that you are over-exerting yourself, something you can do in verismo. Every singer needs *all* of those qualities as part of their technical equipment. And if they are interested in having a long career, they should impose on themselves the task of mastering the bel canto style like a religious duty! Because they could never acquire those qualities by singing Rodolfo or Cavaradossi or any other verismo roles, which, from the technical point of view, are not all that difficult. But, alas, nowadays very few singers are prepared to try this solution and most prefer to plunge into the meatier repertoire

right away – a guarantee for their never fulfilling any early
promise they might show.'

Helena Matheopoulos, *Bravo*, Weidenfeld & Nicolson, 1986,

pp. 124–5, 132–3

TRANSPOSING

*It is common practice for singers to transpose high-lying roles downwards to
make them easier to sing. Here Pauline Viardot, on 15 March 1859, writes
to the conductor Luigi Arditi with her instructions:*

Caro Maestro,
Here are the transpositions which I am making in the part of Lady
Macbeth. The most difficult of all, which will necessitate certain
changes in the instrumentation, will be that of the Cavatina. The
recitative in D flat, the Andante, '*Vieni, t'affretta*' in B flat, and the
Allegro '*Or tutti sorgete*' in D flat, consequently the whole scene
must be a minor third lower. Not bad! All the rest of the act may
be given as written . . .

The sleep-walking scene must be a tone lower; that is, the
melody and recitative in E flat minor, and the Andante in B major.
I fancy I see our orchestra making faces at the horrible aspect of
the six double flats and five double sharps! Dear maestro, you
must have the parts of these numbers copied, because the orchestra
we shall have only likes to transpose (transport) the public.

Quoted in Luigi Arditi, *My Reminiscences*, Skeffington, 1896, pp. 61–2

The tenor Alfredo Kraus disapproves of the practice:

He was appalled when he sang Edgardo in *Lucia di Lammermoor* in
Florence in 1983, alternating with two colleagues who both trans-
posed the tessitura down a semitone. The fact was never even
mentioned in the reviews, 'as if it made no difference! But singing
the last act of *Lucia* the way Donizetti wrote it, rather than a
semitone lower, *does* make all the difference and failing to notice

this seems to me a very serious and important matter. Because I feel that critics and public alike are in the process of *un*learning what singing really is. They think that what they are used to hearing today is what the art of singing is about. But it's not true! This is *not* what the art of singing is about! This is *not* the way to sing, or, at least, not the way one *should* sing! But neither the public nor today's generation of singers know this, because the dearth of good teachers has deprived the latter (and the lack of good singers deprives the former) of a living link with the true tradition of our art.'

Helena Matheopoulos, *Bravo*, Weidenfeld & Nicolson, 1986, p. 121

TAKING CARE OF THE VOICE

In 1597 Battista Codronchi, a Paduan, published De vitiis vocis, *a work on the cultivation and preservation of the voice:*

[Codronchi's treatise was based] on the authority of the ancients ... Weakness of the voice is caused by general bodily weakness, fatigue, too much sleep especially after eating, and from weakness of muscles which move the throat. Quintilian is quoted on the importance of bodily health for the conservation and preservation of the voice, by taking walks, temperance, abstinence from love, and the use of ointments; all of which promote digestion, stronger breathing, open passages and good elimination. It is bad to exercise the voice after eating, for the spirit is made hot by food and is disturbed by indigestion. Codronchi is especially careful to warn against over-indulgence of cohabitation. He mentions the practice of infibulation among ancient actors in order to prevent sexual indulgence and thus save the voice, and comments that in his time the custom of castration prevails for the same purpose. As an anaphrodisiac he suggests the root of the 'Bride of Hercules', which causes cessation of sexual functions, thus conquering the flesh. Besides one should avoid evil thoughts, the sight or company of women, and the reading of evil books.

Food and drink come in for considerable attention. So as not to harm the voice one should refrain from eating caterpillars, chives, headed vine, asparagus, basil, fennel, *cunila*, parsnips, artichokes, ragwort, *Nux myristica*, galangal, pine nuts, *Nux avellana*, pistachios, *Mala insana*, and many more of such. Abstain also from wine, meat and eggs while there is an excess of sexual activity; also, cold drinks are bad and Galen is quoted as saying that it is bad to take wine without food after exercise.

One should sleep on a hard bed but not on the back nor in a reclining position.

Philip A. Duey, *Bel Canto in Its Golden Age*, Columbia University Press,

1951, pp. 22–3

Novel ways to refresh the voice were devised by thirsty singers:

All singers, from the prima donna down to the merest tyro, are agreed upon one point, that is, that to preserve the voice it must from time to time – especially when performing – be nourished and refreshed. But when it comes to the question of what this restorative should be, the opinions of singers are anything but unanimous, and most forcibly prove the truth of the adage that 'what is one man's food is another man's poison'. From the eagerness with which the writer has frequently seen it imbibed by some great singers, and from all reports, stout stands *facile princeps*. Malibran, it will be remembered, believed in its efficacy ... Formes swore by a pot of good porter, and Wachtel is said to trust to the yolk of an egg beaten up with sugar for his chest Cs. Some continental artists are more fastidious. Thus we gather from a Vienna paper ... that the Swedish tenor Labatt takes two salted cucumbers, and declares that this is the best thing in the world for strengthening the voice and giving it the true metallic ring. Walter's drink is cold black coffee; another makes a perfect little cistern of his stomach, and takes in spring water till he can drink no more. Southeim is an advocate of snuff and cold lemonade; Steger, 'the corpulent', as he is surnamed, drinks the brown juice of the gambrinus; Niemann, champagne slightly warmed; Tichatschek, mulled claret. Ferenczy, the tenor, smokes, and strongly recommends a cigar to his colleagues; but others regard such a recipe as fatal, save perhaps Draxler, who smokes Turkish tobacco and cigarettes, cooling his throat betimes with a glass of good beer. But these are not all. Rübgam, the baritone, drinks mead; another drinks soda water; another sucks dried plums; Nachbaur eats bonbons; Beck, the baritone, takes nothing at all, and refuses to speak . . . Mlle Brann-Brini takes beer and *café au lait*, but she also firmly believes in champagne, and would never dare venture the great duet in the fourth act of the *Huguenots* without a bottle of Moët Crémant Rosé.

Frederick Crowest, *A Book of Musical Anecdotes*, Bentley, 1878, II, pp. 8–10

The growing internationalism of operatic performance has encouraged singers to take on roles for which their voices are not well suited. Iris Adami Corradetti takes a forthright view of the matter:

'All my colleagues are down on [Mirella] Freni and [Renata] Scotto . . . I deplore what they are doing, but I do not blame them individually. They are the victims of a system that has gone totally off balance. Freni has arrived because of all the concessions that she has made – totally wrong in my way of thinking, but they have made her a big name and, above all, a big recording artist. Karajan asked her to do *Aida* and she accepted . . . Scotto's is no *Norma*; it is a *Normina*. My pupil Margherita Rinaldi, a lyric coloratura, sang Adalgisa with her in Florence. The fact is that this is an affront to tradition, and tradition is what they want to destroy today. It is very hard to follow, believe me, even for someone who is, like myself, in the operatic kitchen seven days a week and twenty-four hours per day. I was very pleased with the way [Katia] Ricciarelli has progressed and matured, but now she is beginning to make some of the compromises that are constantly demanded of her. She has become a better actress, however; she moves with more assurance on the stage and is now very pretty indeed. Those who want to work in the lyric theatre today must learn to say yes, for none of the conductors seems to know that composers wrote for different types of voices. Now any voice will do.'

Lanfranco Rasponi, *The Last Prima Donnas*, Gollancz, 1984, p. 370–71

Gigli, too, argues that singers must resist attempts by impresarios to force them to sing unsuitable roles:

Singers must sometimes be on their guard against the imprudent proposals of managers and impresarios. The latter are interested in immediate results, while the singer has to think far ahead. Unsuitable roles can cause permanent damage to both voice and career. Toti Dal Monte is a case in point. In 1918, when I sang with her in [Mascagni's] *Lodoletta*, she had a beautiful lyric soprano voice, perfect for the romantic heroines of *La traviata* and *La Bohème*. Her impresarios, however, persuaded her that her imposing physique would be somewhat incongruous in these fragile roles, and they urged her to turn to other operas – *Il barbiere di Siviglia*, *Rigoletto*, *Lakmé*, *La sonnambula* – where the heroine is not supposed to be a consumptive.

This meant that she had to force her voice into the mould of a coloratura soprano, and as such she achieved world fame; her greatest role of all was Lucia di Lammermoor. Then, after enduring the strain for years, her vocal cords finally slackened, and she found herself unable to sing coloratura any longer. Her natural, lyrical soprano voice was still intact, but her impresarios clamoured only for *Lucia*, and to the consternation of the public, she suddenly vanished into premature retirement.

Beniamino Gigli, *Memoirs*, translated by Darina Silone, Cassell, 1957,

pp. 211–12

SINGING AND ACTING

The East German opera director Walter Felsenstein on the role of singing within music theatre:

Singing on-stage is nothing other than acting. If the physical action impedes the singing, then this action is faulty in its primary intention and in its expression. For even singing is merely a part of making music; it is no different from an instrumental part in the orchestra, which belongs to the actor no less than the singing. After all, singing is not first and foremost the technical production of vocal sounds. It is chiefly a human statement that has been evoked by an inner process and is thus insuppressible and cannot be dispensed with; it goes far beyond speaking, because it gives expression to what can no longer be conveyed by words alone. It is therefore important for the music theatre to create situations that call forth music. As far as singing is concerned, it must of course be technically controlled, but we must not characterize as excessive the basic requirements of the music theatre simply because certain people do not have an adequate vocal technique.

The Music Theatre of Walter Felsenstein, translated by Peter Paul Fuchs,
Quartet Books, 1991, p. 140

Sherrill Milnes on the differences between acting and singing:

'Straight actors almost never play roles that stretch their actual physical skills right to the limits whereas in the big operatic roles singers are *constantly* being pushed to the limits of physical stamina. In addition, singing is made even more precarious by the fact that the voice is such a fragile thing and can be affected by factors such as pollen, phlegm, dust in the theatre, the slightest health upset. You might be in great voice when suddenly a piece of phlegm just flicks into the sound and sometimes the audience hear it and sometimes they don't. But *we* hear it and we feel it and it is one of the factors contributing to the unpredictability of the instrument we have to work with.'

He explains that this is one of the reasons why singing is such a high-tension profession, especially when one is talking about the top twenty-five or so singers from whom audiences expect wonders all the time ... There have been mornings when he got up thinking he might have to cancel that night's performance only to find that, after two hours, the body warmed up and the voice began to feel normal. The opposite has also happened on occasion and he considers this independence and unpredictability of an instrument that resides in his own body 'inexplicable and something akin to magic: for although you can tell whether the voice will be somewhere within the area of normal, you can't be sure of *exactly* how the sound will come out, until after it happens. It is an entity within ourselves, dependent yet also independent, and never wholly controllable. In fact it feels almost like a third person and I suppose this is why Caruso never referred to it as "my" voice but as "the" voice.'

Helena Matheopoulos, *Bravo*, Weidenfeld & Nicolson, 1986, pp. 192–3

THE TERRORS OF SINGING

Franco Corelli told Newsweek:

'I have always been afraid. I wasn't born to be a singer. In the beginning I didn't have the high C so I was afraid. Then I did have the B and the C but was afraid I would lose them. Sometimes I get up in the morning and the voice doesn't answer. If I'm on holiday and not singing I worry if it's still there. I tape every performance. I then spend three hours listening to the tapes. I am exhausted. I need rest but I can't sleep. If the performance was good I can't sleep for joy. If not, I cannot sleep for despair. What is this life? It is the life of a prisoner, in a hotel room, in front of the television or playing solitaire.'

Newsweek, 15 March 1976

The baritone Piero Cappuccilli on stage fright:

He believes singers should lead normal, sane lives and not 'over-protect' themselves. He professes himself 'puzzled by the paradox of colleagues who during the rehearsal period eat, drink, and live normally in every respect, and sing extremely well, but who, come the performances, are transformed into nervous wrecks, lock themselves in, abstain from drinking and so on, and sing less well!

'This is a psychological problem I have never been able to explain. The only protection we singers should resort to is to acquire a sound technique at the beginning of our careers and then proceed a step at a time, never exceeding our vocal means. This is the only way to be free of insecurity, stage fright and suchlike, because we are then masters of our voice instead of the reverse. Then we can afford to relax because we *know* the voice is ready to respond to every exigency.'

Helena Matheopoulos, *Bravo*, Weidenfeld & Nicolson, 1986, p. 183

Sheer emotion, and not only stage fright, can hamper and unnerve singers, who, paradoxically, must learn to express great depths of feeling without succumbing to them. Ruggiero Raimondi recalls the demands made by the role of Boris Godunov:

He has a hallucination in which he sees a bloodstained child. 'This obsession weighs on him more and more and almost brings him to the brink of madness. Gradually you must work yourself into this state of mind and build up this load of anguish inside you, so the audience can feel it too. Yet at the same time you must strive to keep your involvement under control so you don't lose contact with reality. Otherwise you'd be finished, because this scene is also very difficult from the vocal point of view: it is rhythmically imprecise, and while going through the excruciating emotions I've described you have to keep counting in order to stay within the measures.'

The most difficult technical demand of this role is the variety of vocal effects it requires: groans, gasps, sighs and choking sounds which every interpreter must invent according to his abilities. The tessitura itself is not uncomfortable and the most difficult moment from this point of view is that passage in the death of Boris which contains an E above the stave that has to be sung pianissimo. 'This is an agonizing moment, both vocally and dramatically, because Boris is dying of a broken, destroyed heart. A bell tolls and the chorus of monks enter, according to tradition, to dress him in a monk's habit and carry him to the altar for his death. At that precise moment the words change and he says he sees a child again, then, bang, comes the cerebral haemorrhage that kills him. All this is so harrowingly, so overwhelmingly intense that at the end you yourself feel dead, totally spent.'

Piero Faggioni remembers that the first time Raimondi sang this scene he fainted and had to be carried off the stage. 'He cried real tears, experienced Boris's agony and gave so much of himself that he was in a state of trance.'

Helena Matheopoulos, *Bravo*, Weidenfeld & Nicolson, 1986, pp. 254–5

Thomas Allen also ponders the need to control emotion while singing on stage:

It is easy as an opera singer to become very involved in the emotions of whatever scene is being played. At Covent Garden some years ago, during the performances we gave of *Butterfly*, I watched Anne Mason, who was singing Suzuki, begin to weep at the tragedy unfolding before her. I wasn't surprised. Yoko Watanabe, singing the title role, was remarkably touching and I was affected myself in exactly the same way as Anne. But we had to steel ourselves against these feelings, otherwise the illusion would be lost and we would no longer be able to sing . . .

Anger is another of the dangerous qualities to interpret. Too much involvement, ranting and raving, and the voice is lost. The facial grimaces and tensions of body that one genuinely feels at such times must be reproduced for the stage, but without including any destructive over-emotional element, otherwise the game is over. Producing the necessary voice to be angry, cold or sexy is largely a question of experience and technique. But, in truth, if I am in the frame of mind which is right for the character and if I am absolutely clear in my head about the intention of the scene, then my voice will come out with all the colours on it proper for that mood.

Thomas Allen, *Foreign Parts*, Sinclair-Stevenson, 1993, p. 127

René Kollo on the dangers of burn-out:

'[There are] directors who know and care little about singers and symphonic conductors who know nothing about opera or the intricacies of voice production. This is the real problem. It's not true to say there are no voices around. There are, and there always will be, voices. But they will never come to fruition because, instead of being built up, nowadays singers are simply used up! As long as they can hit the notes, they are offered huge parts right away, sing them for a couple of years, and then burn themselves out. This is simply catastrophic for the future of opera. One cannot pull Tristans, Brünnhildes and Turandots out of a drawer. One has to build them up, gradually, carefully and, dare I say it, lovingly, for the future. Unless we make this kind of concerted effort at long-term planning, opera will soon disappear as an art form.'

Helena Matheopoulos, *Bravo*, Weidenfeld & Nicolson, 1986, pp. 103–4

The notable French tenor Duprez did burn out. Born in 1806, he lived to the age of ninety, but his career was brief:

Duprez was celebrated for the exquisite way in which he sang recitative. But he did not know how to control or husband his voice, and after he developed its full strength he strained it each time he sang. When Rossini heard him in *William Tell* he rushed round to the stage and embraced the singer, weeping meanwhile. 'But why these tears?' asked Duprez. 'I weep for those who heard Duprez tonight in *William Tell*, for they will never hear anyone sing it as he has sung, and alas! alas! Duprez's voice cannot last much longer.' Rossini's prophecy came true and with startling suddenness. 'I have lost my voice,' wrote Duprez, in despair, to Rubini. 'How have you kept yours?' 'My dear Duprez,' Rubini answered, 'you have lost your voice because you have sung with all your capital; I have kept mine because I sing only with the interest.'

Mrs Godfrey Pearse and Frank Hird, *The Romance of a Great Singer:*
A Memoir of Mario, Smith, Elder, 1910, p. 84

The Austrian baritone Bernd Weikl reflects on the damage done by forcing the voice:

'There *is* no such thing as a twenty-five-year-old Tristan. There cannot be. You have to be at least forty for Tristan and for Tannhäuser, which is even more demanding because of its even higher tessitura, but especially for Siegmund which, as all singers realize only after they have sung it, is *the* hardest of all *Heldentenor* roles' . . .

When asked to explain why forcing the voice damages the higher range, Weikl replied that this was a physical thing, like an elastic band snapping. 'When you force the middle range up you lose the top, which should sound smooth and light; because at a certain age the physical possibilities for the voice to stretch naturally don't exist, so the voice simply snaps. When the middle range becomes *naturally* more solid and massive with age, like Gigli's and Beirer's did, then one can produce those big sounds fearlessly, without danger of the voice snapping. It's a question of patience and natural, gradual vocal maturity. There is no substitute for time and no way one could speed this process up and jump from light-lyric to heavy Wagnerian parts.'

Helena Matheopoulos, *Bravo*, Weidenfeld & Nicolson, 1986, pp. 228–9

Frida Leider suffered the ultimate humiliation when she lost her voice during the last act of Die Walküre *at the Metropolitan Opera:*

I was sitting in the middle of the sixth row, so close that every detail was impressed on my retina as well as my ears. I have never had such an instantaneous and overwhelming horror in my experience in the theatre . . .

She was on her knees before Wotan (Friedrich Schorr) with her noble head humbly bent and her left hand at her throat. She wore a flowing white dress and a red cloak over it – traditional; but I am telling it exactly as I see and hear it even now, more than twenty years later. She had reached the point where she had to sing the phrase '*War es so schmählich?*' She sang the first two words and notes – that is, '*War es*' – after which a strange, very small sound came out of her throat and no note followed. That weird small sound is quite impossible to describe and if I had not been sitting so close I could not have heard it; I suppose most of the three thousand people there present did not. The click (if it was a click) seemed like the electrocution, the murder, of the great voice. A sound then came from the wings on the word '*schmählich*' and continued the development for five notes more.

(We all learned afterwards that Dorothee Manski from the Berlin Opera, who was one of the Walküre and had been standing in the wings anxiously watching Leider, had thus saved the day by singing her notes.)

Leider kept her head down and I saw her shake it in a kind of fury ... She had been singing the whole performance over a bad cold, so bad that she could not even speak. Now the voice itself, the very sense of her existence, refused its divine grace and there she was, on her knees, with the ruin of a great career in plain view before her. Such a concentrated ordeal seldom befalls an artist.

I felt, or imagined I felt, the struggle of her will to conquer her body. Then she threw back her really grand head and looked out beyond all the three thousand of us to some utter truth beyond us, opened her mouth with confidence, it seemed to me, and by some power (I could see her throat quivering) the voice was given again.

From then on to the end of the act Leider sang with everything an artist has to give, although the sacrifice of her voice must have been tragic.

Vincent Sheean, *First and Last Love*, Gollancz, 1957, pp. 100–102

Wayne Koestenbaum points out that the sense of danger intrinsic to operatic singing forms part of the listener's pleasure and appreciation:

The diva is allowed to sing but not for too long; she is granted the power to soar in a phrase, but only under certain conditions; and when the voice breaks down, she shows us how beggared and partial the terms of her triumph have been. Vocal crisis is a form of communication. It tells us that opera is an art of interruption, rupture, and bodily danger. The singer in vocal crisis has been punished for sublimity. But vocal crisis is also the moment when the queer meanings of opera begin to speak – because at the moment of vulnerability and breakdown, the diva proves that seamless singing had been masquerade, and now her cracked, decayed, raucous, and undisguised self is coming out . . .

The audience is excited by the danger that hysterical or extreme parts pose to the voice: opera requires the preservation of a singing instrument, and yet opera also explodes the boundaried, obedient self, moving listeners and performers away from respectability and towards rage, even if the throat is silenced by the travail of speaking out.

Wayne Koestenbaum, *The Queen's Throat: Opera and Homosexuality and the Mystery of Desire*, Gay Men's Press, 1993, p. 127

COMPOSERS

15: Operatic Composers

A good composer does not imitate: he steals

Igor Stravinsky, quoted in Peter Yates, *Twentieth Century Music*,
Chapter 8

Lully's Armide, *first produced in 1686, was not an immediate hit:*

[*Armide*] was at first coldly received, the music not having pleased
so much as usual. Lully, who was so passionately fond of his own
compositions that (as he himself confessed) he would have killed
anyone who said they were bad, had it performed for his own
gratification, he himself forming the whole audience. This odd
circumstance having been reported to the King, he thought that
the opera could not be bad if Lully himself had so good an opinion
of it. Having, therefore, ordered it to be performed before him, he
was charmed with it; and then both the court and the public
changed their opinion of its merits.

George Hogarth, *Memoirs of the Musical Drama*, Bentley, 1838, I, p. 43

Handel's Rinaldo *was a tremendous success, but it was not the composer
who profited most:*

It was given in February of 1711, mounted sumptuously, performed
splendidly with a cast of Italian singers, and it had an immediate
and spectacular success . . . Because of the opera's popularity, the
'song hits' of *Rinaldo* were published by a London music publisher,
John Walsh. The sheet music sold so well that Walsh made £1500
from the publication, obviously an enormous sum for the time.

Handel, however, received very little for his labours. It was only later, when he ran his own theatre in London, that he was able to make money. Naturally this inequality rankled in the composer's mind, so much so that Handel is supposed to have addressed a letter to Walsh which read, 'My Dear Sir: As it is only right that we should be on an equal footing, you will compose the next opera, and I shall sell it.'

George R. Marek, *A Front Seat at the Opera*, Harrap, 1951, p. 42

François Philidor, an obscure French composer and chess fanatic, sometimes employed short cuts to put his operas together:

Philidor's skill at chess earned him a pension from the London Chess Club; his opera, *Le Sorcier*, the reputation of one of the most blatant (and apparently unapprehended) plagiarists in musical history. He calmly took a whole aria, note for note, from Gluck's *Orfeo* and had his librettist put new words to it – a concession to morality which in the circumstances appears almost ostentatious. To the Turin audience, of course, the whole question was unimportant when they heard *Le Sorcier*, for *Orfeo* was not heard in the city at all until more than a century later, in 1889, so Philidor could have filched the lot without anybody being much wiser.

The other Philidor curiosity to reach Turin was an opera called *Tom Jones*. It had a fair cosmopolitan success, being performed in German, Russian, Swedish and Dutch, but significantly it was never heard in English or in England although in the age of free-for-all libretto-grabbing Dr Samuel Arnold, of London, wrote a Tom Jones opera for Covent Garden, using a great deal of the original French libretto used by Philidor – which is surely an unusually tortuous way round of adapting an English novel for the English stage.

Spike Hughes, *Great Opera Houses*, Weidenfeld & Nicholson, 1956,
pp. 281–2

Beethoven's Fidelio *received its première in Vienna in 1805, but was not a success. It was revived in 1814, and Beethoven was urged to revise it:*

He felt that the opera needed considerable revision and tightening, particularly the libretto, and that the one man who could accomplish this was Georg Friedrich Treitschke. Would Treitschke be willing? He would, indeed. Treitschke was delighted and, having obtained permission from the original librettist, Sonnleithner, set to work. So did Beethoven . . .

His principal changes were two: the first at the beginning of the second act, with Florestan alone in the prison. Florestan had to be introduced, and he needed an aria. Yet, said Treitschke, it could not be a bravura aria, because a man dying of starvation could hardly give forth a lot of florid music. They tried one idea, they tried another. Nothing seemed right. Then one night Treitschke wrote the words 'which describe the last blazing up of life before its extinguishment'. Treitschke tells what happened:

'What I am now relating will live for ever in my memory. Beethoven came to me about seven o'clock in the evening. After we had discussed other things, he asked how matters stood with the aria. It was just finished, I handed it to him. He read, ran up and down the room, muttered, growled, as was his habit instead of singing – and tore open the pianoforte. My wife had often vainly begged him to play; today he placed the text in front of him and began to improvise marvellously – music which no magic could hold fast. Out of it he seemed to conjure the motive of the aria. The hours went by, but Beethoven improvised on. Supper, which he had purposed to eat with us, was served, but – he would not permit himself to be disturbed. It was late when he embraced me, and declining the meal, he hurried home. The next day the admirable composition was finished.'

George R. Marek, *Beethoven: Biography of a Genius*, Kimber, 1970, pp. 470–71

Cherubini meets an unusually hostile critic in the form of Berlioz:

Cherubini never spared the rod of musical criticism. Friends and foes alike all suffered in their turn from his blunt and unsparing judgement. When therefore Cherubini fell into the hands of critics, it may easily be imagined that any weak point was met in a spirit that quite reciprocated the old contrapuntist's unseasoned justice. Fortunately Cherubini offered his enemies few loopholes for attack, but like all of us he had his weak moments, and according to the Parisian critics of his day, it was at one of these that he 'let go' his last opera – *Ali Baba*, concerning which even his friends, and he himself, had great misgivings. At length the day of its first performance came round. Cherubini, more anxious for his reputation in his old age than he had ever been in his young days, had not forgotten to paper the pit of the 'Grand Opera', which on this occasion was unusually well attended by Conservatoire scholars.

Berlioz by some means obtained a ticket for the début of *Ali Baba*, but he soon found it tedious pleasure, and, what is more, gave evidence of his uneasiness by creating a disturbance.

'Towards the end of the first act' (these are Berlioz's own words), 'I was so disappointed at not having heard something new, that I could not restrain myself from muttering loud enough to be heard by those around, "Twenty francs for an idea!" In the second act I increased my bid – "Forty francs for an idea!" The finale began, and the same tame music continued. "There!" I exclaimed, "eighty francs for an idea!" The finale over, I rose up exclaiming, "Ah! my faith, I am not rich enough – I give it up." On the same bench with me were some young folks – Conservatoire scholars who had places there, in order to admire usefully their director. They looked at me fiercely, and on the following day they did not omit to acquaint Cherubini of my insolence. Cherubini was much outraged and annoyed at finding me so horribly ungrateful; and he ever afterwards avoided me.'

Frederick Crowest, *A Book of Musical Anecdotes*, Bentley, 1878, I, pp. 208–9

*In a letter to his father from Paris on 19 December 1831 Felix Mendelssohn
primly expresses distaste for the idea of composing an opera:*

None of the new libretti here would, in my opinion, be attended
with any success if brought out for the first time on a German
stage. One of the distinctive characteristics of all of them is
precisely of a nature that I should resolutely oppose, although the
taste of the present day may demand it, and I truly admit that it
may, in general, be more prudent to go with the current than to
struggle against it. I allude to that of immorality. In [Meyerbeer's]
Robert le Diable the nuns come one after the other to seduce the
hero, till at last the abbess succeeds. The same hero is conveyed by
magic into the apartment of the one he loves and casts her from
him in an attitude which the public here applauds, and probably all
Germany will do the same; she then implores his mercy in a grand
aria. In another opera a young girl divests herself of her garments,
and sings a song to the effect that next day at this time she will be
married; all this produces effect, but I have no music for it. I
consider it ignoble, and if the present epoch demands this style and
considers it indispensable, then I will write oratorios.

Felix Mendelssohn, *Letters*, Pantheon, 1945, pp. 180–81

Meyerbeer was famous for his intrigues:

In the course of a long walk with Madame Viardot she told me many
interesting stories of Meyerbeer, and of the extraordinary precautions he took to insure a success for his operas. He always sat at the
final rehearsal next to Père David, the 'Chef de Claque', and arranged
with him the places where the applause was to come in. He even altered passages which David did not think quite effective enough to
give him his cue. He used to wander about the back of the stage to
hear if the scene-shifters had any criticisms to make amongst themselves, and to note if they whistled or hummed any of his tunes.

Charles Villiers Stanford, *Pages from an Unwritten Diary*, Edward Arnold,
1914, p. 286

*Wagner had a fierce contempt for Meyerbeer, typically expressed in a letter
of 1 January 1847 to the music critic Eduard Hanslick:*

That a world of difference separates us is revealed by your high
opinion of Meyerbeer; I say this without the least embarrassment,
since Meyerbeer is a very close personal friend of mine, & I have
every reason to value him as a kind & sympathetic man. But if I
were to try to sum up precisely what it is that I find so offensive
about the lack of inner concentration & the outer effortfulness of
the opera industry today, I would lump it all together under the
heading 'Meyerbeer', & I should be all the keener to do so because
I see in Meyerbeer's music a great skill at achieving superficial
effects which prevents his art from attaining a noble maturity, &
the reason for this is that it denies the essential inwardness of art
& strives instead to gratify the listener in every way possible: – the
man who strays into the realm of triviality must pay for his
transgression at the cost of his own more noble nature; – but he
who seeks it deliberately, that man is – fortunate, for he has nothing
worth losing.

Richard Wagner, *Selected Letters*, translated by Stewart Spencer and
Barry Millington, Dent, 1987, p. 135

*Bellini reports breathlessly to his friend Francesco Florimo on the première
of* Norma *in December 1831:*

'I am writing to you under the shock of sorrow; of a sorrow that I
cannot put into words for you, but that only you can understand. I
have come from La Scala; first performance of *Norma*. Would you
believe it? . . . Fiasco!!! fiasco!!! solemn fiasco!!! To tell the truth,
the audience was harsh, seemed to have come to pass sentence
upon me; and in its haste wanted (I believe) my poor *Norma* to
suffer the same fate as the Druidess. I no longer recognized those
dear Milanese, who greeted *Il pirata*, *La straniera*, and *La sonnambula*
with happy faces and exulting hearts; and yet, I thought that in
Norma I was presenting them with a worthy sister [of the other
three operas]. But unhappily that was not so; I was wrong; my

protagonists failed and my hopes were deluded. Despite all that, with my heart on my lips I tell you (if passion doesn't deceive me) that the Introduction, Norma's entrance and cavatina, the duet between the two donnas, with the trio that follows, the finale of the first act, then the other duet of the two donnas and the whole finale of the second act, which begins with the Hymn of War and proceeds, are pieces of music of a kind – and please me so much (modesty) – that I confess I should be happy to create their likes for the rest of my artistic life. Enough!!! I hope to appeal against the sentence it [the audience] pronounced against me, and if I succeed in changing its mind, I shall have won my case, and then I'll proclaim *Norma* the best of my operas'. . . .

Norma went on to be sung thirty-nine times at La Scala during that 1831–2 season. It therefore was almost certain to become a popular opera elsewhere. How widespread its popularity became in less than fifteen years is demonstrated by an astonishing passage in Glinka's *Memoirs*. Writing of a visit to Murcia in Spain in the autumn of 1845, Glinka said: 'The children's theatre consisted of a presentation of Bellini's *Norma* – which had indeed been written to be performed by children – for the diversion of their parents. We went to a rehearsal and thought the children sang pretty well. The eleven-year-old in the part of Norma sang with enthusiasm – though not really adequately, of course – and was an excellent little actress, besides.'

Herbert Weinstock, *Vincenzo Bellini*, Knopf, 1971, pp. 105, 107–8

The fate of operatic premières is sometimes determined by factors outside the composer's control, as Donizetti discovered in 1834:

Preparations for the presentation of *Maria Stuarda* continued under great strain. The worst blow came at the dress rehearsal, to which Maria Cristina, Queen of Naples and the Two Sicilies, was invited. In such politically troubled times it was unthinkable for royalty to be portrayed in distress before countless impressionable citizens, and as Mary was led to the block to be beheaded,

Maria Cristina was carried fainting from the theatre. Within hours Donizetti received orders to cancel the première of his opera.

On 7 October 1834, the composer wrote naïvely: 'Stuarda has been forbidden, heaven knows why! but better not to ask, as the King himself has forbidden it.' Donizetti then hastily revised the work, setting the music to another libretto. This was presented at the San Carlo on 18 October as something called *Buondelmonte*. *Buondelmonte* sank without a ripple to the bottom of the operatic stream, and there, for the time being, it lay.

Howard Bushnell, *Maria Malibran*, Pennsylvania State University Press,

1979, p. 203

Berlioz is grudgingly given a production of Benvenuto Cellini *at the Paris Opéra in September 1838:*

The then director of the Opéra, Duponchel, regarded me as a kind of lunatic whose music was a conglomeration of absurdities, beyond human redemption; but in order to keep in with the *Journal des débats* he consented to listen to a reading of the libretto of *Benvenuto*, and appeared to like it, for he went about saying that he was putting on the opera not because of the music, which he knew would be preposterous, but because of the book, which he found charming.

Accordingly he had it put into rehearsal. I shall never forget the horror of those three months. The indifference, the distaste manifested by most of the singers (who were already convinced that it would be a flop); [conductor] Habeneck's ill humour, and the vague rumours that were constantly going round the theatre; the crass criticisms provoked among that crowd of illiterates by certain turns of phrase in a libretto so different in style from the empty, mechanical rhyming prose of the Scribe school – all this was eloquent of an atmosphere of general hostility against which I was powerless, but which I had to pretend not to notice . . .

When we came to the orchestral rehearsals, the players, influenced by Habeneck's surly manner, held aloof and treated me with reserve. They did their duty, however, which can hardly be said of Habeneck ... But by the time the final rehearsals were reached, they were openly enthusiastic about several numbers. One or two pronounced my score one of the most original they had ever heard. This reached the ears of Duponchel. I heard him one evening deriding the 'curious change of front': 'We're now told that Berlioz's music is charming. It seems our ridiculous orchestra is lauding it to the skies.' Some of them had, however, preserved their independence, like the two who were discovered during the finale of the second act playing that well-known air '*J'ai du bon tabac*' instead of their own parts; they hoped it would ingratiate them with the conductor. I met the equal of this skulduggery on the stage. In the same finale, where the stage is darkened and represents the Piazza Colonna at night with an immense crowd in masks, the male dancers amused themselves by pinching the female dancers and, when they screamed, screaming too, to the discomfiture of the chorus, who were attempting to sing. When I indignantly appealed to the director to put an end to this insolent and undisciplined behaviour, Duponchel was nowhere to be found: he did not deign to attend rehearsals.

Briefly, the performance took place. The overture was extravagantly applauded; the rest was hissed with exemplary precision and energy. It was performed three times, however, after which Duprez saw fit to abandon the role of Benvenuto and the work disappeared from the bills, not to reappear until much later.

Hector Berlioz, *Memoirs*, translated by David Cairns, Gollancz, 1969,

pp. 243-5

Rimsky-Korsakov recalls Modest Mussorgsky, whose Boris Godunov *he was subsequently to rewrite:*

During this very season (1869–70) Mussorgsky submitted his completed *Boris Godunov* to the board of directors of the imperial theatres ... It was rejected. The freshness and originality of the music nonplussed the honourable members of the committee, who reproved the composer, among other things, for the absence of a decently important female role. Indeed, there was no Polish act in the original score; consequently Marina's part was lacking. Much of the fault-finding was simply ridiculous. Thus the double-basses *divisi* playing chromatic thirds in the accompaniment of Varlaam's song were entirely too much for Ferrero, the double-bass player, who could not forgive the composer this device. Mussorgsky, hurt and offended, withdrew his score, but later thought the matter over and decided to make radical changes and additions. The Polish act in two tableaux and the scene near Kromy were new conceptions ... Mussorgsky set zealously to work on the above changes, in order to re-submit his revised *Boris Godunov* to the board of directors ...

On 24 January 1874, *Boris Godunov* was produced with great success at the Mariinski Theatre. We all were jubilant. Mussorgsky was already at work on *Khovanshchina* ... None of us knew the real subject and plan of *Khovanshchina*, and from Mussorgsky's accounts, flowery, affected and involved (as was his style of expression then) it was hard to grasp its subject as something whole and consecutive. In general, since the production of *Boris Godunov*, Mussorgsky appeared in our midst less frequently, and a marked change was to be observed in him: a certain mysteriousness, nay even haughtiness, if you like, became apparent. His self-conceit grew enormously, and his obscure, involved manner of expressing himself (which had been characteristic even before) now increased enormously. It was often impossible to understand those of his stories, discussions, and sallies which laid claim to wit. This is approximately the period when he fell to loitering at the Maly Yaroslavyets and other restaurants until early morning over cognac, alone or with companions then unknown to us. When he dined with us or with other mutual friends, Mussorgsky usually definitely refused wine, but hardly had night come, when something at once drew him to the Maly Yaroslavyets. Subsequently, one of his boon companions of this period, a certain V—ki, whom I had known from Tervajoki, told us that in the lingo of their set there existed a special term 'to trans-cognac oneself', and this they applied in practice. With the production of *Boris* the gradual decadence of its highly gifted author had begun.

N.A. Rimsky-Korsakoff, *My Musical Life*, Martin Secker, 1924,
pp. 96, 121, 123

In 1878 Tchaikovsky expresses his aims in composing Eugene Onegin:

Very probably you are quite right in saying that my opera is not effective for the stage. I must tell you, however, I do not care a rap for such effectiveness. It has long been an established fact that I have no dramatic vein, and now I do not trouble about it. If it is really not fit for the stage, then it had better not be performed! I composed this opera because I was moved to express in music all that seems to cry out for such expression in *Eugene Onegin*. I did my best, working with indescribable pleasure and enthusiasm, and thought very little of the treatment, the effectiveness, and all the rest. I spit upon 'effects'! Besides, what are effects? For instance, if *Aida* is effective, I can assure you I would not compose an opera on a similar subject for all the wealth of the world; for I want to handle human beings, not puppets. I would gladly compose an opera which was completely lacking in startling effects, but which offered characters resembling my own, whose feelings and experiences I shared and understood. The feelings of an Egyptian princess, a Pharaoh, or some mad Nubian, I cannot enter into, or comprehend . . .

P.I. Tchaikovsky, letter to S.I. Tanelev, in *Life and Letters of
Peter Illich Tchaikovsky*, Lane, 1906

Rimsky-Korsakov ran into problems with the Russian censors:

During the season of 1894–5 the instrumentation and printing of *Christmas Eve* was making forced headway, and I apprised Director of the Theatres Vsyevolozhski of the existence of my new opera.

He demanded that I submit the libretto to the dramatic censor, at the same time expressing serious doubts about its being approved by the censor, owing to the presence of the Empress Catherine II (The Great) among the dramatis personae. As I was somewhat familiar with censorship requirements, I had not introduced that name into the opera from the very outset, having called the character merely *tsaritsa*, and invariably calling St Petersburg merely *grad-stolitsa* (capital city). It would seem that the censor might be satisfied: how many are the varieties of *tsaritsas* that appear in operas? On the whole, *Christmas Eve* is a fairy-tale, and the *tsaritsa* merely a fairy-tale personage. I submitted the libretto in this form to the dramatic censor, being positive it would be approved . . . But nothing of that sort! At the censorship bureau I was flatly refused permission to put on Tableau VII of the opera (scene before the Queen's palace), as, under an Imperial Order of 1837 to the censorship bureau, under no circumstances might Russian monarchs be introduced in operas. I argued that there was no personage of the Romanoff house in my opera, that only some fantastic queen appears in it, that the theme of *Christmas Eve* deals with a mere fairy-tale, an invention of Gogol's, in which I have a right to change any one of the dramatis personae, that even the word 'St Petersburg' is mentioned nowhere, that consequently all allusions to actual history have been steered clear of, etc. At the censor's I was told that Gogol's story was familiar to everybody and that nobody could have any doubts about my queen being none other than Empress Catherine and that the censorship bureau had no right to sanction the opera! I made up my mind, if possible, to petition in the higher spheres for permission to produce the opera . . .

During the Christmas holidays a courier came to me and brought from the director of the administrative section of the Ministry of the Court an announcement to this effect: 'In accordance with the most devoted report on the petition submitted by you to the Minister of the Imperial Court, His Majesty the Emperor's permission has been granted for admitting the opera *Christmas Eve* composed by you to be produced on the imperial stage without change in the libretto' . . .

The première of *Christmas Eve* was set for 21 November . . .
The Grand Dukes Vladimir Alyeksandrovich and Mikhayil
Nikolayevich came to the dress rehearsal and both of them
showed indignation at the presence (on the stage) of the queen,
in whom they insisted on recognizing the Empress Catherine II.
Vladimir Alyeksandrovich was roused to particular exasperation
by it.

After the end of the dress rehearsal, all the performers, the
stage-managers and the theatre administration lost heart and
changed their tune, saying that the Grand Duke had gone from
the opera directly to the Emperor to ask that my opera be
forbidden a public performance. For his part, the Grand Duke
Mikhayil Nikolayevich ordered the cathedral to be daubed over
on the drop representing St Petersburg and the . . . Fortress of St
Peter and St Paul visible in the distance: in this fortress, he cried,
his ancestors lay buried, and he could not permit it to be represented on the stage of a theatre. Vsyevolozhski felt utterly taken
aback. Palyechek's benefit performance had been announced, the
tickets were on sale; everybody was nonplussed and quite at a loss
what to do . . . Vsyevolozhski, who was eager to save Palyechek's
benefit performance and his own production, suggested that I
substitute a Most Serene Highness (baritone) for the *tsaritsa*
(mezzo-soprano). From a musical point of view this change presented no difficulties. a baritone could easily sing the part of
mezzo-soprano an octave lower, the part consisting of recitatives
throughout, without a single ensemble. To be sure the result was
not what I had had in mind, the result was foolish, it amounted to
an absurdity, as the master of the queen's wardrobe turned out to
be a Most Serene. Further explanations on the subject are superfluous on my part. True, it caused me both sorrow and amusement,
but a human head is of no avail against a stone wall, after all – so
I consented.

N.A. Rimsky-Korsakoff, *My Musical Life*, Martin Secker, 1924,
pp. 296–8, 302–3

*The eccentric Hugo Wolf, renowned for his songs, was also the composer of
the opera* Corregidor, *which Gustav Mahler conducted in 1904:*

Soon after Mahler had been made director of the Vienna Opera,
Wolf was announced; and there he stood, lean as a skeleton, with
burning eyes, and imperiously demanded the instant production of
Corregidor. Mahler, knowing the work and its defects, made the
usual evasions: no singers suited to it, etc. Wolf grew obstreperous
and Mahler did not like the look of him. He had a special bell
within reach for such occasions. He pressed it and his man came in
with the prearranged message: 'The superintendent wishes to see
you at once, sir.'

Wolf found himself alone. He rushed downstairs and along the
Ring. His mind gave way; he thought he was the director and on
his way home. When he arrived at Mahler's flat . . . he rang the
bell; and when the servant opened the door, he shouted at her to
let him pass – he was the director. She slammed the door in his
face in terror. Shortly afterwards he was shut up in a lunatic
asylum.

Alma Mahler, *Gustav Mahler: Memories and Letters*, translated by
Basil Creighton, Murray, 1946, pp. 53–4

Debussy writes about his approach to opera in Le Figaro *on 16 May 1902:*

On hearing opera, the spectator is accustomed to experiencing two
distinct sorts of emotion: on the one hand the *musical emotion*, and
on the other the emotion of the characters – usually he experiences
them in succession. I tried to ensure that the two were perfectly
merged and simultaneous. Melody, if I dare say so, is anti-lyrical.
It cannot express the varying states of the soul, and of life.
Essentially it is suited only to the song that expresses a simple
feeling.

I have never allowed my music to precipitate or retard the
changing feelings or passions of my characters for technical convenience. It stands aside as soon as it can, leaving them the freedom of
their gestures, their utterances – their joy or their sorrow . . .

Certainly my method of composing – which consists above all of dispensing with 'methods of composing' – owes nothing to Wagner. In his work each character has, one might say, his own 'calling card', his image – his leitmotiv – which must always precede him. I must confess that I find this procedure somewhat gross. Also, the symphonic development that he introduced into opera appears to me to conflict continually with the moral argument in which the characters are involved and with the play of passions, which alone is important.

Claude Debussy, *Debussy on Music*, translated by Richard Langham
Smith, Secker & Warburg, 1977, pp. 80–81

Debussy's uncompleted opera:

Paradoxically, Debussy, who hated Wagner, considered an opera on the Tristan legend ... The Tristan opera never went beyond the idea stage; Debussy's most serious uncompleted project was an opera called *La Chute de la Maison Usher*, in which title you will recognize the Edgar Allan Poe tale. [Impresario] Gatti-Casazza paid Debussy an advance of two thousand francs for the production rights of this opera, for Gatti knew the worth and the success of *Pelléas*. Debussy did not want to take the money, nor did he promise to deliver the opera, as he was 'such a lazy composer'. But Gatti insisted, and in the course of several visits assured the composer that the Metropolitan would do everything to give the new work a worthy production. Debussy had the opportunity to convince himself of what the Metropolitan was capable, for in 1910, when the company made a guest appearance in Paris, Debussy attended a performance of *Aida* in which Caruso sang and which Toscanini conducted.

Debussy worked hard and long on *The Fall of the House of Usher*. He steeped himself in the atmosphere of the Poe story, and we know that he invented for the music a strange orchestral effect involving the low tones of the oboe contrasted with violin chords.

Nothing remains of this music. Like Brahms, Debussy was a critical destroyer of unfinished or unsatisfactory manuscripts.

George R. Marek, *A Front Seat at the Opera*, Harrap, 1951, pp. 37–8

Chaliapin reveals that Raoul Gunsbourg (whom he calls Ginsburg), the director of the Monte Carlo Opera, was also a composer:

Ginsburg, 'with God's help', as he used to say, even wrote an opera entitled *Ivan the Terrible*, and into it he piled everything, including the gas-stove. We had in it a fire, a hunt, a bacchanalia in a church, the most mad dances and frenzied battles. Ivan himself rang the bells, played chess, danced and died. He crammed in all the better-known Russian words, like Izba, Boyarin, Zakuska, Steppe, Vodka. A work of monumental ignorance and daring, but Ginsburg was firmly convinced that he had written a masterpiece, and kept on repeating: 'This is a remarkable piece. There isn't a better opera anywhere. All will fade and be forgotten, and only Mozart and I, who stand before you now, will remain. Even if the public doesn't understand this opera now, it will be understood in a thousand years.'

I really lost my temper with him, and told this aspiring genius he was a cocksure little fool. How angry he got, with a face as red as the turkey cock, as he declared: 'Chaliapin, for words like that, in France swords are called for.'

I willingly agreed, and suggested that his weapon should be more lethal than my own. I also suggested that the duel be postponed until after the first performance of the work, as should I be killed, there would be nobody to play Ivan.

Maddened even further by my jokes, he rushed off at once to arrange about seconds. I waited, but they never came. The quarrel fizzled out. We kept clear of each other's company for a fortnight, but after the production, the *Terrible* production, we made it up.

Feodor Chaliapin, *Chaliapin: An Autobiography as Told to Maxim Gorky*, ed. Nina Froud and James Hanley, Macdonald, 1968, pp. 162–3

Benjamin Britten on transforming A Midsummer Night's Dream *into an opera:*

I do not feel in the least guilty at having cut the play in half. The original Shakespeare will survive. Nor did I find it daunting to be tackling a masterpiece which already has a strong verbal music of its own. Its music and the music I have written for it are at two quite different levels. I haven't tried to put across any particular idea of the play that I could equally well express in words, but although one doesn't intend to make any special interpretation, one cannot avoid it . . .

Writing an opera is very different from writing individual songs: opera, of course, includes songs, but has many other music forms and a whole dramatic shape as well. In my experience, the shape comes first. With *A Midsummer Night's Dream*, as with other operas, I first had a general musical conception of the whole work in my mind. I conceived the work without any one note being defined. I could have described the music, but not played a note.

Benjamin Britten, 'The Composer's *Dream*', *Observer*, 5 June 1960

In 1951 W.H. Auden entertained Igor Stravinsky with Britten's views of his opera The Rake's Progress:

Conversation turning to *The Rake*, Wystan repeats his story about Benjamin Britten liking the opera very much, 'Everything but the music' (a story I.S. did not find very amusing).

[*Stravinsky retaliated in 1964:*]

Speaking of Britten's *A Midsummer Night's Dream*, [Stravinsky] suggests that 'it is a mistake to conclude each act with people going to sleep'.

Robert Craft, *Stravinsky: Chronicle of a Friendship*, Vanderbilt University Press, 1994, pp. 58, 393

16: Mozart

There is no hope for *Così fan tutte* on the stage as the work stands.

Henry Chorley, *Thirty Years' Musical Recollections* (1862), p.138

In his garrulous letters, the young Mozart traces the progress of Die Entführung aus dem Serail:

The day before yesterday Stephanie junior gave me a libretto to compose. I must confess that, however badly he may treat other people, about which I know nothing, he is an excellent friend to me. The libretto is quite good. The subject is Turkish and the title is: *Belmonte und Konstanze*, or *Die Verführung aus dem Serail*. I intend to write the overture, the chorus in Act I and the final chorus in the style of Turkish music. Mlle Cavalieri, Mlle Teiber, M. Fischer, M. Adamberger, M. Dauer and M. Walter are to sing in it. I am so delighted at having to compose this opera that I have already finished Cavalieri's first aria, Adamberger's aria and the trio which closes Act I. The time is short, it is true, for it is to be performed in the middle of September; but the circumstances connected with the date of performance and, in general, all my other prospects stimulate me to such a degree that I rush to my desk with the greatest eagerness and remain seated there with the greatest delight . . .

As Osmin's rage gradually increases, there comes (just when the aria seems to be at an end) the *allegro assai*, which is in a totally different tempo and in a different key; this is bound to be very effective. For just as a man in such a towering rage oversteps all the bounds of order, moderation and propriety and completely forgets himself, so must the music too forget itself. But since passions, whether violent or not, must never be expressed to the point of exciting disgust, and as music, even in the most terrible situations, must never offend the ear, but must please the listener, or in other words must never cease to be *music*, so I have not chosen a key remote from F (in which the aria is written) but one related to it – not the nearest, D minor, but the more remote A minor. Let me now turn to Belmonte's aria in A major, '*O wie ängstlich, o wie feurig*'. Would you like to know how I have expressed it – and even indicated his throbbing heart? By the two violins playing octaves. This is the favourite aria of all those who have heard it, and it is mine also. I wrote it expressly to suit Adamberger's voice. You feel the trembling – the faltering – you see how his throbbing breast begins to swell; this I have expressed by a crescendo. You hear the whispering and the sighing – which I have indicated by the first violins with mutes and a flute playing in unison . . .

The first act was finished more than three weeks ago, as was also one aria in Act II and the drunken duet ['*Vivat Bacchus*'] which consists entirely of *my Turkish tattoo*. But I cannot compose any more, because the whole story is being altered – and, to tell the truth, at my own request. At the beginning of Act III there is a charming quintet or rather finale, but I should prefer to have it at the end of Act II. In order to make this practicable, great changes must be made, in fact an entirely new plot must be introduced – and Stephanie is up to the eyes in other work. So we must have a little patience. Everyone abuses Stephanie. It may be that in my case he is only very friendly to my face. But after all he is arranging the libretto for me – and, what is more, as I want it – exactly – and, by Heaven, I do not ask anything more of him.

W.A. Mozart, letters to his father, 1 August 1781 and 26 September 1781, translated by Emily Anderson, in *The Letters of Mozart and His Family*, Macmillan, 1966, pp. 754–5, 769–70

As a young tenor, Michael Kelly sang at the imperial opera in Vienna in the 1780s. He gave a (deeply unreliable) account of the première of Le nozze di Figaro *in which he gave Mozart a helping hand:*

There were three operas now on the tapis, one by Regini, another by Salieri (*The Grotto of Trophonius*), and one by Mozart, by special command of the Emperor. Mozart chose to have Beaumarchais' French comedy *Le Mariage de Figaro* made into an Italian opera, which was done with great ability, by Da Ponte. These three pieces were nearly ready for representation at the same time, and each composer claimed the right of producing his opera for the first. The contest raised much discord, and parties were formed. The characters of the three men were all very different. Mozart was as touchy as gunpowder, and swore he would put the score of his opera into the fire if it was not produced first; his claim was backed by a strong party: on the contrary, Regini was working like a mole in the dark to get precedence.

The third candidate was Maestro di Cappella to the court, a clever shrewd man . . . and his claims were backed by three of the principal performers . . . I alone was a stickler for Mozart, and naturally enough, for he had a claim on my warmest wishes, from my adoration of his powerful genius, and the debt of gratitude I owed him, for many personal favours.

The mighty contest was put an end to by his majesty issuing a mandate for Mozart's *Nozze di Figaro*, to be instantly put into rehearsal; and none more than Michael O'Kelly enjoyed the little great man's triumph over his rivals . . .

I called on him one evening; he said to me, 'I have just finished a little duet for my opera, you shall hear it.' He sat down to the piano, and we sang it. I was delighted with it, and the musical world will give me credit for being so, when I mention the duet, sung by Count Almaviva and Susan, '*Crudel perchè finora farmi languir così*'. A more delicious *morceau* never was penned by man, and it has often been a source of pleasure to me, to have been the first who heard it, and to have sung it with its greatly gifted composer. I remember at the first rehearsal of the full band,

Mozart was on the stage with his crimson pelisse and gold-laced cocked hat, giving the time of the music to the orchestra. Figaro's song, '*Non più andrai, farfallone amoroso*', Bennuci gave, with the greatest animation, and power of voice.

I was standing close to Mozart, who, *sotto voce*, was repeating, 'Bravo! Bravo! Bennuci'; and when Bennuci came to the fine passage, '*Cherubino, alla vittoria, alla gloria militar,*' which he gave out with stentorian lungs, the effect was electricity itself, for the whole of the performers on the stage, and those in the orchestra, as if actuated by one feeling of delight, vociferated, '*Bravo! Bravo, Maestro! Viva, viva, grande Mozart.*' Those in the orchestra I thought would never have ceased applauding, by beating the bows of their violins against the music desks. The little man acknowledged, by repeated obeisances, his thanks for the distinguished mark of enthusiastic applause bestowed upon him.

The same meed of approbation was given to the finale at the end of the first act; that piece of music alone, in my humble opinion, if he had never composed anything else good, would have stamped him as the greatest master of his art. In the *sestetto*, in the second act (which was Mozart's favourite piece of the whole opera), I had a very conspicuous part, as the Stuttering Judge. All through the piece I was to stutter; but in the *sestetto*, Mozart requested I would not, for if I did, I should spoil his music. I told him, that although it might appear very presumptuous in a lad like me to differ with him on this point, I did, and was sure the way in which I intended to introduce the stuttering would not interfere with the other parts, but produce an effect; besides, it certainly was not in nature, that I should stutter all through the part, and when I came to the *sestetto* speak plain; and after that piece of music was over, return to stuttering; and, I added (apologizing at the same time, for my apparent want of deference and respect in placing my opinion in opposition to that of the great Mozart), that unless I was allowed to perform the part as I wished, I would not perform it at all.

Mozart at last consented that I should have my own way, but doubted the success of the experiment. Crowded houses proved that nothing ever on the stage produced a more powerful effect;

the audience were convulsed with laughter, in which Mozart himself joined. The Emperor repeatedly cried out 'Bravo!' and the piece was loudly applauded and encored. When the opera was over, Mozart came on the stage to me, and shaking me by both hands, said, 'Bravo! young man, I feel obliged to you; and acknowledge you to have been in the right, and myself in the wrong.' There was certainly a risk run, but I felt within myself I could give the effect I wished, and the event proved that I was not mistaken.

Michael Kelly, Reminiscences, 1826, I, pp. 257–61

In Rococo-Bilder *the Czech academic Alfred Meissner records his grandfather's memories of working with Mozart and Lorenzo Da Ponte. They include a vivid account of how Mozart was tricked into composing the overdue overture to* Don Giovanni *while visiting his friends the Duscheks in Prague:*

[The singer Bondini] opened the harpsichord and pleaded: 'Mozart! Just a few chords from the overture, only one or two!'

Mozart sat down and played a loud, reverberating chord. He had no idea that a conspiracy was in train. Everyone tiptoed silently backwards, opened the door without a sound, and one after another crept out of the room.

When the key turned in the lock Mozart realized what was happening. He sprang up. 'What are you doing? What on earth does this mean?'

'It means that you're caught, and instead of spending the evening in the Tempelgässchen you'll spend it here in your room.'

'But what have I done?'

'Hear the sentence of the court!' cried Saporiti, laughing. 'Wolfgang Amadeus Mozart, who has been criminally in debt for such a long time for the overture to his opera, thereby jeopardizing both his own interests and ours, is condemned to several hours' imprisonment, during which time he will be obliged to redeem his debt.'

'But, ladies,' said Mozart, appearing at the window as everyone gathered below, 'you won't deprive me of your company? How can I write without light or anything to eat or drink?'

'There's nothing you can do about it — you're a prisoner! If you want to be set free quickly, then get to work straight away. You shall have light, and wine, and a big cake — you shan't lack for anything.'

'You're a lot of traitors!' Mozart cried. 'I can't bear being alone. Supposing I was so miserable that I decided to end my life, and jumped out of the window?'

'No need to worry about that! You enjoy life far too much, little Amadeo!' Micelli cried.

'And what about you, Duschek, are you going to allow this?' Mozart said to his friend, who was almost invisible at the back of the group.

'We mean well, we really do!' Duschek said.

'It seems that good intentions excuse anything, even treachery,' Mozart cried, now really concerned that they would leave him locked up, but his face, which had grown serious, broke into laughter, despite himself, as he saw the three women singers march up in line. They had shared out the long poles from the vines, which lay in a corner of the courtyard, and to each of them had tied the various requisites that the prisoner would need for the night.

'Here are two lamps — and a couple of bottles of wine — and cakes and sweets!' they called out as the various objects were balanced on the edge of the window-sill. But Da Ponte, more down-to-earth than the others, appeared with a rake to which an article was attached which was as necessary as it was unaesthetic, and cried, 'You'll need this too. Take it, divine *maestro*.'

'A pity, it's empty,' Mozart retorted, 'otherwise it would be the worse for you,' and he stood there half-annoyed, half-amused, among the objects which had been hoisted up to him . . .

'The end justifies the means,' called Guardasoni. 'Goodnight, Mozart. Tomorrow morning early we'll come and see if the overture is ready.'

'Yes, yes, all of us!' the ladies echoed. 'Goodnight, dearest Mozart, goodnight! Set to work!'

Quoted in Sheila Hodges, *Lorenzo Da Ponte*, Granada, 1985, pp. 90–91

The baritone Thomas Allen on the role of Don Giovanni:

This role becomes more and more fascinating. Several key points spring to mind. Stillness – I now lay great store on the power of stillness. An almost hypnotic concentration – such as those moments when Giovanni, at his own party, sizes up Zerlina as his next prey. In this scene I try to make Zerlina feel as uncomfortable as possible on the stage, as though Giovanni had stripped her naked in front of everyone. Giovanni is, I think, like a cheetah. It's fascinating to watch a slow-motion film of this animal as it first selects its target, then stalks it, and finally begins the run that will demonstrate how it moves in complete harmony with all its constituent forces. And, all this time, and with all that energy to unleash to its service, the head of the cheetah remains in one position at one level. Its concentration is of white-hot intensity. Stalking Zerlina, I try to emulate the cheetah.

Thomas Allen, *Foreign Parts*, Sinclair-Stevenson, 1993, p. 54

At the Paris Opéra The Magic Flute *underwent an interesting transformation:*

It was to ensure the success of *The Magic Flute* that the director of the Opéra, some twenty years earlier, commissioned the remarkable potpourri which under the title of *The Mysteries of Isis* has become part of our cultural heritage (the libretto is itself a mystery that no one to this day has ever fathomed). When the text had been suitably 'fixed', the director had the sagacity to send for a *German* musician to fix the music. The German musician did not flinch from his task. He tacked a few bars on to the end of the overture, made a bass aria out of the soprano line of one of the choruses, likewise adding a few bars of his own composition; removed the wind instruments from one scene and put them into another; altered the vocal line and the whole character of the accompaniment in Sarastro's sublime aria; manufactured a song out of the Slaves' Chorus 'O cara armonia'; converted a duet into a trio; and, as if The Magic Flute were not enough to sate his rage, gorged himself on Titus and Don Giovanni: for the aria 'Quel charme à mes esprits rappelle' is taken from Titus, the andante at least; the allegro with which it ends not apparently satisfying our uomo capace, he ripped it out and stuck in another of his own fabrication, in which one may perceive only the frayed ends of Mozart's. After this, need one add that in the hands of this master the famous 'Fin ch'han del vino' – that explosion of licentious energy in which the whole essence of the Don is summed up – duly reappeared as a trio for two sopranos and bass . . .

When the whole lamentable concoction was complete, it was christened 'The Mysteries of Isis, opera' and the said opera in that state performed, printed and published in full score, in which, alongside Mozart's name, the arranger had condescended to place his own, the name of a fool and a vandal, the name of Lachnith.

Hector Berlioz, Memoirs, translated by David Cairns, Gollancz, 1969,

pp. 89–90

17: Rossini

When Donizetti was told that Rossini had written the *Barber of Seville* in a fortnight, he replied: 'That does not surprise me; he is so lazy.'

Mrs Godfrey Pearse and Frank Hird, *The Romance of a Great Singer: A Memoir of Mario*, p. 113

Stendhal visits Rossini in February 1817:

I have met with no man of more brilliant intellect within the furthest frontiers of Italy – yet assuredly he has not the least notion of his own quality, for Italy still lies and suffers beneath the grinding heel of *pedantry* ... Why (I pressed him) should he not collect royalties from the divers companies which perform his twenty-odd operas? He showed me plainly, however, that, in the unsettled turmoil of present disorders, the very proposal was absurd.

We sat on, drinking tea, until well beyond the hour of midnight; this was the merriest evening I have yet spent in Italy; all seemed steeped in the boyish high spirits of a man who is happy at heart. Yet when, at long last, I took my leave of this great composer, I was possessed by melancholy. Canova and Rossini – none but these two (so intolerable is grown the government of Italy) are preserved to flower, alone and solitary, in the final devastation of this *Land of Genius*.

Stendhal, *Rome, Naples, and Florence*, translated by Richard N. Coe, Calder, 1959, pp. 348–9

Rossini's methods of composition were engagingly casual, although his later biographer Francis Toye insists this story about Totola is not true:

The following season *Moses in Egypt* was revived with, I've heard, the same enthusiasm for the first act, and the same outbursts of laughter during the scene of the crossing of the Red Sea. I wasn't in Naples at the time, but was present for the third revival of the opera. The evening before the first performance, one of my friends looked in on Rossini at midday, and found him as usual still in bed, holding court among a score of friends. Then suddenly, to the great delight of everybody present, the poet Totola came bursting in, and without greeting anybody began shouting: '*Maestro! maestro! ho salvato l'atto terzo* [I have saved the third act!] . . . I have written a prayer for the Hebrews before the crossing of the Red Sea.' At that point the poor mud-spattered librettist pulled from his pocket a wad of papers docketed like a lawyer's brief. He passed them to Rossini who began to read the scribblings scrawled in the margins of the main document. While Rossini was reading, the wretched poet greeted the others present and kept whispering, '*Maestro, è lavoro d'un'ora* [I wrote this in an hour] . . .'

'Very well,' said Rossini, 'if it took you an hour to write this prayer, it'll only take me fifteen minutes to write the music for it.' So saying, Rossini jumped out of bed wearing only his nightshirt, sat himself at his desk and wrote the music for Moses' prayer in eight or ten minutes at most, without using the piano and unmindful of his friends, who were chattering away at the tops of their voices, as people always do in Italy.

'Here's the score. Take it!' Rossini told the poet, who ran off. Rossini leapt back into bed, laughing along with the rest of us at Totola's startled behaviour.

The next day I took myself off to San Carlo opera house. As at previous performances, everybody was ravished by the first act. As the third act began, when we reached the famous passage of the crossing of the Red Sea, the joking and sniggering began as before. Indeed, down in the pit there were already some bursts of laughter, when all of a sudden we heard Moses beginning a new and unfamiliar aria: '*Dal tuo stellato soglio*', this being the prayer which the people repeat in chorus after Moses has sung it. Taken aback by this novelty, the pit pricked up its ears and the laughter soon stopped . . . It's impossible to describe the thunderous applause that brought down the house. Those in the boxes stood up and leaned out over the edge as they applauded, screaming, '*Bello! bello! o che bello!*' I have never witnessed such excitement, such a triumph, which was all the sweeter because everyone had come here to laugh and poke fun.

Stendhal, *Life of Rossini*, chapter 26, translated by Stephen Brook

Rossini and the Venetians:

At the Fenice Rossini inaugurated the traditional Carnival season on 26 December 1814, with *Sigismondo*, a work which bored the Venetian audience into a stupor, for they found the music as unprepossessing as the libretto and only the orchestra had a good word to say for it . . .

Rossini returned to Venice in 1819 for a brief visit bringing with him the score of *Edoardo e Cristina* consisting of twenty-six numbers, only seven of which had not been taken from other Rossini operas. The audience at the San Benedetto were remarkably good humoured and patient and asked slyly why the libretto had been changed since the previous performance.

When Rossini finally came back with a brand new work it was *Semiramide*, produced at the Fenice in 1823. This was a tremendous success owing, as much as anything, to the introduction of a military band on to the stage, a characteristic Rossinian innovation which delighted the Venetians and at night inspired them to accompany the composer back to his house in illuminated gondolas with waterborne Austrian military bands playing selections of favourite airs from his works.

Spike Hughes, *Great Opera Houses*, Weidenfeld & Nicolson, 1956,

pp. 73-4

Byron, writing to Samuel Rogers on 3 March 1818, describes a Venetian performance of Otello*:*

They have been crucifying Othello into an opera (*Otello* by Rossini) – Music good but lugubrious – but as for the words! – all the real scenes with Iago cut out – & the greatest nonsense instead – the handkerchief turned into a billet-doux, and the first Singer would not *black* his face – for some exquisite reasons assigned in the preface. – Scenery – dresses – & Music very good.

Lord Byron, Letters and Journals, Murray, 1976, p. 18

At the Paris première of Rossini's Semiramide *at the Théâtre Italien on 9 December 1825 the French singer Josephine Fodor lost her voice:*

The audience greeted Madame Fodor with the most flattering enthusiasm. The voice of *la prima delle prime donne*, as the Italians called her, was in excellent order, though she was suffering from almost overpowering timidity, unaccountable in so practised a performer; and she went through the first scene of the opera in a style which excited the audience to a pitch of almost delirious delight. On her reappearance in the next scene, she had not proceeded beyond the fifth or sixth bar of the first air, when her voice suddenly failed her: not a note could be heard. The orchestra ceased playing; and the *cantatrice*, nearly fainting from agitation, made the most violent exertions to recover herself: her chest heaved, her blanched lips quivered, cold drops of perspiration bedewed her brow, but not even a cry of agony escaped her. Her voice was gone!

The curtain was dropped, and the whole house was in consternation. The manager (Mr Ayrton) appeared, and explained that the sudden indisposition of Madame Fodor must cause the performance to be suspended for a few minutes, and the audience, indulgent as usual on such an occasion, promised to wait patiently. The dressing-room of the unhappy vocalist was a scene of indescribable confusion. Lying on a sofa, in a frenzy of grief, she was flinging her arms about in the wildest despair, striking her face, tearing her hair, and giving way to her anguish in mute agony: she uttered no audible cries. Rossini fairly wept; and Choron fell on his knees, entreating her to calm her agitation. Half an hour had elapsed, and the house was becoming violent in its impatience. Poor Ayrton then came and informed Madame Fodor that the audience would no longer wait, and that he was about to announce to them that the performance could not proceed. The colour rushed to the face of the *cantatrice*; her eyes flashed fire, her lips moved convulsively, and springing to her feet, she exclaimed, in a loud, full, and resonant voice, 'Draw up the curtain, I will sing!'

'Saved! saved!' cried Rossini, embracing her.

The curtain was again raised; and the prima donna entered, and was welcomed by shouts of applause. A profound silence succeeded, and then the audience remained in expectancy. Madame Fodor went through the remainder of the opera; but at the conclusion of the last scene, she fell to the ground in a swoon. On her recovery, she found that her voice was completely gone.

[*She never fully recovered her vocal powers.*]

Ellen Creathorne Clayton, *Queens of Song*, Smith, Elder, 1863, pp. 338–9

Stendhal describes a typical Rossini première at a minor Italian opera house in the early nineteenth century:

The maestro takes his seat at the piano. The house is packed with people who have poured in from twenty miles around. Some folk are so fascinated they are more or less camping in their coaches in the middle of the streets; all the inns have been full since the day before . . .

The overture begins, and you could hear a pin drop. When it's over, the auditorium explodes with excitement, with shouts of praise up to the very heavens, with incessant whistling and roaring . . .

Each aria of the new opera is listened to in complete silence, and then received with the same astonishing uproar. Not even the howling of a wrathful sea can give you an idea of the racket. You can hear the audience appraising both the singers and the composer. They shout *'Bravo Davide, bravo Pisaroni'*; or else the whole house will resound to the cries of *'Bravo maestro!'* Rossini rises from his place at the piano, his handsome face looking grave, which is not at all characteristic. He bows three times as the applause washes over him, deafening him with adulation. Then the performance continues with the next item.

Rossini himself is at the piano for the first three performances of a new opera, after which he receives his fee of seventy sequins (800 francs), participates in a splendid farewell feast hosted by his new friends — the whole town, in other words — and then sets off in his carriage . . . ready to go through the same rigmarole forty miles from here in a neighbouring town.

Stendhal, *Life of Rossini*, chapter 6, translated by Stephen Brook

Meyerbeer and Rossini enjoyed a lengthy feud:

Meyerbeer . . . used to send two elegantly dressed gentlemen to every performance of Rossini's operas. It was the duty of these two gentlemen to sit in well-exposed box seats and fall fast asleep fifteen minutes after the curtain rose. At the end of the opera they had to be wakened by the usher. Regular opera subscribers were familiar with these *'sommeilleurs de Meyerbeer'*. For a performance of *Semiramis*, Rossini sent two tickets to Meyerbeer himself. 'Please do me the favour,' he wrote, 'of using these tickets yourself. The box is visible from all parts of the house. The chairs are comfortable. Shortly before the end of the performance I shall have you waked. Your true admirer, G. Rossini.'

George R. Marek, *A Front Seat at the Opera*, Harrap, 1951, pp. 216–17

It is hard to imagine operatic composers more different than Rossini and Wagner. One would have given much to have been a fly on the wall when the two men met in Paris in March 1860:

Wagner had come to Paris to try to arrange for the production of

Tannhäuser at the Opéra, and, as was the custom in those days, paid visits of courtesy to every musical personality of importance. He felt especially nervous in the case of Rossini, for a story had gone the round of the drawing-rooms and the press that Rossini had shown his opinion of Wagner's music by asking an admirer of it to lunch, and then serving him with a dish called '*Turbot à l'allemande*', which consisted of sauce and no fish, the lack of the principal ingredient being intended to suggest that Wagner's music lacked the most vital thing of all: melody. But this wholly apocryphal story much annoyed Rossini, who had grown very tired of every cynical witticism in Paris being fathered on himself. He took the trouble to deny it publicly, and caused Wagner to be informed by Michotte that he would be more than delighted to receive him . . .

Rossini's first care was to put his visitor at ease, saying that, though he knew he was neither a Mozart nor a Beethoven and made no pretence to be a very learned person, he did claim to have some manners. The last thing in the world he would do was to say rude things about a musician who, as he had been told, was trying to extend the limits of their common art . . .

Rossini turned the conversation on to Wagner and the Music of the Future. Why did not Wagner write a French opera? Wagner replied that this was impossible owing to the development of his literary and musical style. He would now have to write, not a French *Tannhäuser*, but a French *Tristan*, which would inevitably fail to please the taste of the Parisian public. He then began to expose his theories, enlarging on his objection to the conventional operatic forms, especially the ensembles 'indispensable in every self-respecting opera'. Rossini agreed that sometimes these ensembles were ridiculous, and that the singers lined up in front of the footlights reminded him of a lot of porters come to sing for a tip . . . Then, returning to Wagner's theories, he said that they were unanswerable so far as the literary side was concerned; the difficulty began when words had to be allied with some musical form, which must, in any event, always remain a convention. After all, in real life, with the possible exception of lovers who might be said to coo, nobody either lived or died in terms of song. Even in the most turbulent orchestral passages who could distinguish between a storm, a riot or a fire? All this was convention. Wagner admitted the necessary existence of convention but protested that he was opposing only its abuse. For this reason his enemies had maliciously invented the fable that, with the exception of Gluck and Weber, he was hostile to all previous operas, even those of Mozart. Rossini interposed with horror that that would indeed be sacrilege: '*Mozart, l'angelo della musica!*'

With considerable ingenuity Wagner proceeded to cite Rossini's share in the fashioning of the libretto of *William Tell* as a justifica tion of his own theories about the necessity of a composer being his own librettist. An extension of this principle would give him his point; just as Rossini's influence in Italy proved the possibility of the complete revolution in the conceptions of composers, singers and public that he had in mind. Rossini, while admitting that in the abstract Wagner's theories seemed attractive, objected that, as regards musical form and practice, they must lead exclus- ively to declamatory recitative ...

Wagner agreed that, pushed to a logical extreme, this might be so. He, too, wanted melody in a generous measure, but his conception of it was something far more plastic, more independent than what was generally understood by the term. And once again he instanced the '*Sois immobile*' scene in *William Tell* as a perfect example of musical expression, both as regards the accentuation of the words and the use of the cellos that accompanied them. Rossini answered that he seemed to have been writing the Music of the Future without knowing it. To which Wagner replied that, in this instance, Rossini had written music for all time, and that was the best kind of music of all.

Francis Toye, *Rossini*, Heinemann, 1934, pp. 216 20

18: Wagner

Wagner never lacked self-confidence. Indeed, without it his immensely ambitious projects could never have been realized. Even in retrospect, the notion of composing a twenty-hour tetralogy and of building an opera house exclusively devoted to Wagnerian production seems mad. But he did it, with the aid of lies and manipulation and, of course, overwhelming genius. If Wagner and his operas take up a good deal of space here, it is because his achievement was so astonishing and so minutely documented.

Yet it would have been hard to predict from the 1836 première of his first opera, Das Liebesverbot, *that this was the beginning of the most remarkable career in operatic history:*

The first performance, on 29 March, must have stood out for heartbreaking ineptitude even in the annals of the German provincial theatre of the time. In spite of the zeal with which Wagner so kindly credits them, none of the singers knew their parts. The tenor who played Luzio fell back, when his memory failed him, on what he could remember of *Fra Diavolo* and *Zampa*. As the cynical Bethmann had neglected, for financial reasons, to have the libretto printed in time, the audience could get no more than the vaguest idea of the action and the psychology of the work, the subject of which was new to them. The orchestra was as incompetent as the singers. The word must have gone round the town that the thing

had been a fiasco, for at the second performance – which was also
to be the final night of the theatre – the house was empty . . . But
before a note of the overture was sounded, bedlam broke loose
behind the scenes. The husband of the leading lady, the charming
Frau Pollert, made for her lover (the second tenor, who played
Claudio), and smote him on the nose, concentrating a whole
season's marital rancour in the blow; and poor Claudio had to
retire to his dressing-room to wash off the blood that was pouring
down his face. Frau Pollert, who was to have played Isabella, tried
to appease her enraged husband, received a castigation that was no
doubt well deserved, and went off into hysterics. The rest of the
company took sides according to their sympathies in the case, the
occasion being warmly welcomed, without any superfluous inquiry
into first causes, as a heaven-sent one for working off all the
professional animosities and jealousies that had been accumulating
since the commencement of the season.

   . . . There was nothing for it but for the manager to appear
before the curtain and inform the infinitesimal audience that owing
to unforeseen circumstances there would be no performance that
evening. Nor was Wagner to be any more successful with the
opera elsewhere . . . Wagner never heard his *Liebesverbot*.

Ernest Newman, *The Life of Richard Wagner*, Knopf, 1933 I, pp. 207–8

Wagner wrote to his relatives, Eduard and Cäcilie Avenarius, on 1 October
1842 about the Dresden première of Rienzi:

Let me – in all haste & in utter exhaustion – at the very least drop
you a line to report what happened yesterday. I'd prefer you to
learn it from someone else – for I'm bound to tell you – that, as
everyone assures me, *never* has an opera been given its first performance in Dresden & been received with such enthusiastic acclaim as
was the case with my *Rienzi*. The whole town was caught up in the
excitement, it was a veritable *revolution*; – I was called on stage *four*
times by the tumultuous applause. I am assured that not even the
success of Meyerbeer's *Huguenots*, when it was performed here,

was comparable with that of my *Rienzi*. The second performance is the day after tomorrow: – & for the third one, too, all the seats have already been sold.

Richard Wagner, *Selected Letters*, translated by Stewart Spencer and
Barry Millington, Dent, 1987, p. 97

Wagner, writing to Mathilde Wesendonck, celebrated his own genius:

[29 October 1859:] I recognize now that the characteristic fabric of my music (always of course in the closest association with the poetic design), which my friends now regard as so new and so significant, owes its construction above all to the extreme sensitivity which guides me in the direction of mediating and providing an intimate bond between all the different moments of transition that separate the extremes of mood. I should now like to call my most delicate and profound art the art of transition, for the whole fabric of my art is made up of such transitions: all that is abrupt and sudden is now repugnant to me; it is often unavoidable and necessary, but even then it may not occur unless the mood has been clearly prepared in advance, so that the suddenness of the transition appears to come as a matter of course. My greatest masterpiece in the art of the most delicate and gradual transition is without doubt the great scene in the second act of *Tristan und Isolde*. The opening of this scene presents a life overflowing with all the most violent emotions – its ending the most solemn and heartfelt longing for death . . . This, after all, is the secret of my musical form, which, in its unity and clarity over an expanse that encompasses every detail, I may be bold enough to claim has never before been dreamt of . . .

[August 1860:] *Tristan* is and remains a miracle to me! I find it more and more difficult to understand how I could have done such a thing: when I read through it again, my eyes and ears fell open with amazement! How terribly I shall have to atone for this work one day, if ever I plan to perform it complete: I can see quite clearly the most unspeakable sufferings ahead of me; for if I am honest with myself, I have far overstepped the limits of what we are capable of achieving in this field; uniquely gifted performers, who alone would be equal to the task, are incredibly rare in the world. And yet I cannot resist the temptation if only I could hear the orchestra!!

Richard Wagner, *Selected Letters*, translated by Stewart Spencer and
Barry Millington, Dent, 1987, pp. 474–5, 499–500

Wagner, a political exile, sought to revive his career by organizing a revised version of Tannhäuser in Paris in 1861. Hounded by aristocratic cabals in the French capital, and by the incompetence of the lead tenor, the performances were a disaster:

There were seventy-three piano rehearsals, forty-five choral rehearsals, twenty-seven rehearsals for stage details (without orchestra), four for the décors, and fourteen of various kinds for the orchestra . . . Wagner was at every rehearsal except nine of those with piano (during his illness in October and November), and those of 5, 7 and 8 February on the stage without the orchestra.

The *special* expenses of the production ran to 100,000 francs, the décors and accessories accounting for 35,000 francs, the costumes and arms for 52,000, copying the music for 7,000. Extra choralists, and instruments on or under the stage, meant a further expense of 860 francs a performance . . .

As against the 54,000 francs . . . drawn by the vain young lout of a tenor [Albert Niemann] who had so basely betrayed Wagner in his hour of need, the mere creator of *Tannhäuser* received in respect of the three performances given, only 750 francs.

Ernest Newman, *The Life of Richard Wagner*, Knopf, 1941, III,
pp. 107, 120

Writing to the novelist Eliza Wille on 26 May 1864, Wagner describes his bizarre relationship with his patron King Ludwig II of Bavaria:

He is fully conscious of who I am and of what I need: I did not have to waste a word in describing my position to him. He feels a king's power ought to suffice to protect me from all that is base, to leave me wholly free for my Muse, and to provide me with all the resources I need to perform my works, when and as I wish. He spends most of his time at present in a small castle near here; his carriage takes me there in ten minutes. He sends for me once or twice a day. I then fly to him as to a lover. He is delightful company. This urge for instruction, this gift of understanding, this trembling and warming to each new subject is something that it has never before been my lot to experience so utterly unreservedly. And then his tender solicitude for me, his enchanting chastity of heart, of his every expression as he assures me how happy he is to possess me; thus we sit for hours on end, lost in each other's gaze. Everyone will come to love me in time; even now the young King's immediate entourage is happy to discover and know the sort of man I am, for they can all see that my immense influence upon the prince's mind can lead only to the common good, and can be to no one's disadvantage. And so everything within us and around us grows better and more beautiful by the day!

[*Despite his glowing expectation of being universally admired, Wagner would subsequently be driven out of Munich.*]

Richard Wagner, *Selected Letters*, translated by Stewart Spencer and
Barry Millington, Dent, 1987, pp. 602–3

Wagner slavishly buttered up his royal patron. This typical letter was written on 6 November 1864:

My glorious and dearly beloved King,
There is a secret which can be revealed to my august and gracious friend only in the hour of my death: but then it will become clear to him what today must seem obscure – that *he* alone is the creator and author of all that the world will attribute to my name from this day on. My sole reason for living is the wondrous love which descends upon me like drops of dew from the heart of my royal

friend – as though from the lap of God – fructifying new seeds of life within me! . . .

It is to my royal friend that I dedicate the convalescent's new-found strength in these feeble lines herewith . . . Soon, indeed very shortly, I shall be back at my work again, like a man reborn, and I shall not forsake it again until it is completely finished. It is a marvellous passage where I now have to resume composition [of Act III, Scene i, of *Siegfried*], having put the finishing touches to a number of earlier passages! It is the most sublime of all scenes for the most tragic of all my heroes, Wotan, who is the all powerful will-to-exist and who is resolved upon his own self-sacrifice . . . Wotan lives on in Siegfried as the artist lives on in his work of art: the freer and the more autonomous the latter's spontaneous exist-ence and the less trace it bears of the creative artist – so that through it (the work of art), the artist himself is forgotten, – the more perfectly satisfied does the artist himself feel: and so, in a certain higher sense, *his* being forgotten, his disappearance, his death is – the life of the work of art. – This is the frame of mind in which I am now turning once again to the completion of my work: I want to be destroyed by my Siegfried – in order to live for ever! O beauteous death!

With what awesome solemnity shall I now awaken Brünnhilde from her long sleep! She slept while Siegfried grew to young manhood . . . But, if I am Wotan, I have now succeeded through Siegfried: it is *he* who awakens the maid, the most precious thing in the world. My work of art will live, – it lives!

Richard Wagner, Selected Letters, translated by Stewart Spencer and
Barry Millington, Dent, 1987, pp. 626–7

Evenings among the Wagner household, especially at Wahnfried, their villa at Bayreuth, were as restful as a series of college tutorials. The great composer seemed to enjoy nothing more than entertaining the household with piano reductions of his operas:

[28 February 1869.] Spend my time with the children. It is Sunday, which belongs to them, and they also eat with us. Unfortunately R[ichard] decides after the meal to play something from *Siegfried*. Loldi [daughter Isolde] became restless during it, R. got impatient; to prevent an explosion I took her up to my room and let Eva come, too; R. became very angry, and unfortunately in the presence of the children, which distressed me deeply.

[5 January 1873.] R[ichard] goes through parts of Act III of *Götterdämmerung*, then *Tristan*, and finally the *Idyll*, which charms us all. 'Yes,' says R., 'that was our poetic period, the dawn of our life, now we are in the full glare of the midday sun, my dear wife, and climbing the mountain.' The memory moves me to tears, but much more the work itself. Alas, what gifts have here been deposited in an earthly frame, how well I understand what he must suffer when life eternally keeps him from pouring out these gifts!

[10 September 1873.] In the afternoon music − from *Götterdämmerung* 'Hagen's Watch', 'Hagen's Call', The 'End of the World' − and after supper R. reads us his *Parsival*. Ever-increasing astonishment at this divine power of his.

[23 August 1878.] R. did not have a good night, he spends the morning writing to the King for his birthday. In the afternoon he plays '*Komm', holder Knabe*' from *Parsifal*, this captivates my father [Franz Liszt] at once, R. fetches the manuscript, and then the whole second act up to the kiss is gone through, R. thrilled by the fascination the divine work exerts on my father and radiating genius, greatness, kindness!

Sunday, 22 September [1878] ... In the evening R. is in the most splendid high spirits, even his most dismal of experiences he describes gaily. Of an opera called *Nero* he inquires, 'Is that a watchdog?', and of *Messalina* he wants to know whether many *mésalliances* occur in it! He complains with indescribable humour that now, when he has to compose Kundry, nothing comes into his head but cheerful themes for symphonies . . .

Cosima Wagner, *Diaries*, translated by Geoffrey Skelton, Harcourt Brace Jovanovich, 1978, I, pp. 66–7, 580, 673; II, pp. 139, 154

Engelbert Humperdinck visits Wagner in Italy in 1880:

All were avidly engaged in preparations to celebrate the Master's birthday – the not inconsiderable plan of the little group was a performance – the first – of the Communion Scene from *Parsifal*. Rubinstein and Plüddermann had taken upon themselves the task of rehearsing a children's choir in the far-from-easy Grail Scene which, at that moment, had just been written out . . .

To the right of the piano, at which sat Rubinstein, were the gaily jewelled girls, arranged like a row of pearls, their youthful faces radiant with anticipation and excitement. Opposite them I stood with Plüddermann, each of us with a Knights' score in our hand, while, in the background, Frau Cosima Wagner and her son Siegfried were listening, Joukowsky and Hartmann by their side. In the middle of the circle sat Wagner, behind a desk on which was the outline sketch of *Parsifal*, from which he sang as well as directed – he was soloist, conductor and producer, all in one. With his not large, but tuneful and well-produced voice, capable of all registers, he took all the parts in a most expressive manner – admonitions from Gurnemanz, Amfortas's cry to the deserted sanctuary and the woeful, sepulchral tones of Titurel. In between, the singers from above sounded like angels – their voices ringing the changes on the rugged tones of the Knights and Esquires. And, if a soprano came to grief, or a tenor was conspicuous by his absence, then the Master helped out and brought the piece to a successful conclusion.

Dusk was already about us as the final sounds hung in the air – '*Selig in Glauben*' – everyone was left in silent rapture, in another world, until the spell spontaneously dissolved – but nevertheless, the rapture remained. 'Now my children, may I not be well satisfied with myself?' laughed the Master.

Quoted in Robert Hartford, ed., *Bayreuth: The Early Years*, Gollancz, 1980, pp. 114–15

Wagner entrusted touring productions of the Ring *cycle to the impresario Angelo Neumann, the former director of the Leipzig Opera:*

It was in London that he had planned to open his campaign; and thither he had gone with his Leipzig machinist in October 1881 to inspect the stage of His Majesty's Theatre. Convinced that the work would be practicable there he made the necessary advance arrangements, and in April of the following year went once more to London with the whole of his technical staff to install the Bayreuth appliances, the opening performance being fixed for 5 May ... 'Under my contract with the director Mapleson,' says Neumann, 'the theatre was to be in complete working order for me, including the whole of the necessary technical and administrative personnel, heating and lighting during the rehearsals and performances, an orchestra of the numbers I had specified, a male voice chorus of about twenty-eight for the *Götterdämmerung*, and the "supers", placards and announcements – the last two being a very important and expensive factor in London. When I arrived I asked for Mapleson; I was informed that he was on an opera tour in America. I had hardly inspected the theatre and started on the preliminary arrangements when I received from the owners of the theatre, a London bank of high standing, a letter containing the surprising information that Mr Mapleson was still in debt to the bank for his rent and consequently had no right to dispose of the theatre: if I wished to give the performances in May I must first come to an agreement with the bank as to conditions.'

He sought out Mapleson's representative, who told him that the impresario was still in America, or it might be Africa, or it might be anywhere. Were the chorus and orchestra ready for him, asked Neumann. 'It's doubtful.' The technical and administrative staffs? 'These you will have to engage yourself.' So there he was in London, with the whole of the Bayreuth apparatus, all the contracts with his singers signed, but no theatre, no orchestra, no chorus, no local technical personnel; and he was due to open in a month with the *Ring*. But Neumann was a great general, for whom difficulties existed only to be overcome. He made a financial arrangement

with the bank as to the theatre. He engaged the necessary staffs.
He put the placarding and advertising in hand. He telegraphed to
Seidl to bring over the Laube Orchestra from Hamburg after a
month's rehearsal with it there. He engaged the chorus of the
Cologne Town Theatre. And now, he fondly imagined, he had
provided for everything. The poor man did not know his London.
There was still something he had not reckoned with – the carpets.

'It is well known that in the London theatres the foyers, boxes,
stairs and so forth are furnished with splendid carpets and tasteful
hangings. When I entered the theatre one day just before the
general rehearsal I received a shock. the carpets and draperies had
disappeared. When I asked what had happened I was informed
that these valuable articles belonged to the furnishers and would
be supplied to the theatre only for a certain payment. More
negotiations, more agreements, more money to be paid out!'

But the curtains and hangings were there for the final rehearsal,
and to the amazement of everyone the curtain went up on the
Rhinegold on the day and at the hour fixed by Neumann months
before – eight o'clock on the evening of 5 May.

Ernest Newman, *The Life of Richard Wagner*, Cassell, 1947, IV, pp. 643–5

Parsifal *came to New York in 1903 at the instigation of Metropolitan
Opera manager Heinrich Conried:*

The Wagner family made, without success, every possible effort to
prohibit the planned performance. When an informal appeal to the
Kaiser yielded nothing worth while, a civil suit was instituted in
the New York courts. No copyright agreements were in effect
between Germany and the United States; hence none were being
violated. Thus an appeal for an injunction could not be acted upon
favourably. For that matter, Conried offered to pay a performance
fee, which was curtly rejected by the Wagner heirs. In non-musical
circles the desirability of *Parsifal* was hotly argued, with most heat
by those most ignorant of its content. One Protestant worthy
stated his objection, in the *Sun* of 15 November, to a work in

which 'not only is Christ's person represented, but the blood' . . .

Meanwhile, plans went forward for a December première, with intensifying objections from the clergy and even a petition to Mayor Seth Low that he suspend the Metropolitan's licence. Some part of the objection was incurred by Conried because he had scheduled his first performance for Christmas Eve. He had, doubtless, no intention of further offending those who thought of Christmas as a religious ceremonial as well as a season of good cheer; he was merely looking for an attraction for the worst theatrical night of the season. In terms of what would now be called 'public relations', it was an inspired piece of bad judgement . . .

Whatever the fine points of the performance – the conducting of [Alfred] Hertz did not please all tastes, some of his tempos, for an oddity, being considered over-fast – the interest of thousands had been stimulated. Ten repetitions were completely sold out, for total receipts of $183,608. Allowing for production costs and the expenses of the cast, it was guessed that close to $100,000 could be reckoned as profit.

Irving Kolodin, *The Story of the Metropolitan Opera*, New York, 1953,
pp. 182–4

At the Hamburg Opera the young Bruno Walter conducted Wagner for the first time:

A *Siegfried* stage rehearsal with orchestra was scheduled, and Mahler had not shown up. Everybody was waiting, and Pollini [director of the Hamburg Stadttheater] finally turned impatiently to me, asking me if I trusted myself to conduct the rehearsal. Of course I trusted myself, and a minute later the supreme desire which had agitated my heart for years was fulfilled – I was conducting Wagner. It was the stormy beginning of the third act, the awakening of Erda, whose mythical primordial strains I was privileged to conjure up. My luck lasted until far into the scene between the Wanderer and Siegfried – until the passing through the fire, I believe. A misunderstanding had caused Mahler to be half an hour late, and, instead of relieving me at once, he had good-naturedly proposed to Pollini to let me keep on conducting.

Bruno Walter, *Theme and Variations*, translated by James A. Galston, Hamish Hamilton, 1947, pp. 42, 90–91

In about 1900 Bruno Walter was asked to call on Cosima Wagner after he conducted a performance of an opera by her son Siegfried:

Clad in black and carrying herself regally, Cosima came to meet me, saying that she wished to thank me for the beautiful performance ... [I] said that I was impressed by the natural simplicity of the work. That, however, was not enough for Cosima's motherly pride. She replied, and her words have remained unforgettable to me: 'It has rather more than natural simplicity. My son has succeeded, in his *Bärenhäuter*, in writing the finest non-tragic opera since the *Meistersinger*.' After that unbelievably daring, yes, blasphemous utterance of Richard Wagner's widow, there was nothing I could do but change the subject. Our conversation soon assumed the character of a lecture delivered by the regal woman. Only now and then did I manage to make a modest remark. She touched upon any number of topics, the nature of which I do not recall, until I blundered once more. This time I acted in total disregard of a strict Bayreuth rule by mentioning the name of Verdi. Frau Wagner's face became icily rigid, and when, in my unsuspecting guilelessness, I dared to speak of the astonishing change and development in Verdi's work, from *Ernani* to *Aida* and finally to *Falstaff*, she merely remarked: 'Development? I can see no difference between *Ernani* and *Falstaff*.' I never saw Cosima Wagner again, and I am under the impression that my remark about Verdi had served thoroughly to dispel her initially favourable opinion of me.

Bruno Walter, *Theme and Variations*, translated by James A. Galston, Hamish Hamilton, 1947, p. 139

Verdi's views on Wagner were considerably more generous than the Wagner household's opinion of Verdi. On the centenary of Verdi's birth in 1913, Felix Philippi wrote an article for the Berliner Tageblatt *about his conversation with the composer shortly before his death:*

'You are German and therefore, of course, a follower of the Bayreuth master?'

'I am more than a follower,' I replied, 'for as long as I can remember I have been one of Wagner's most ardent and passionate admirers; I believe I am one of his oldest and most loyal vassals.'

'You do well to honour your Maestro. He is one of the greatest geniuses. He has made people happy and presented them with treasures of immeasurable and immortal worth. You will understand that I, as an Italian, do not yet understand everything. That is due to our ignorance of German legend, the strangeness of Wagner's subject-matter, its prevailing mysticism and the pagan world with its gods and Norns, its giants and dwarfs. But I'm still young,' the eighty-six-year-old smiled with genuine childlike goodness, 'I never cease exploring Wagner's sublime world of ideas. I owe him an enormous amount – hours of most wonderful exaltation . . .

'The work which always arouses my greatest admiration is *Tristan*. This gigantic structure fills me time and time again with astonishment and awe, and I still cannot quite comprehend that it was conceived and written by a human being. I consider the second act, in its wealth of musical invention, its tenderness and sensuality of musical expression and its inspired orchestration, to be one of the finest creations that has ever issued from a human mind. This second act is wonderful,' and utterly immersed in his thoughts, he kept repeating: 'Wonderful . . . quite wonderful!'

Translated by Richard Stokes and reprinted in Marcello Conati, ed.,
Interviews and Encounters with Verdi, Gollancz, 1984, pp. 328–9

Wagner's musical influence was often pernicious. The French composer Vincent d'Indy caught the bug badly:

His *Fervaal* appeared in 1897. The setting of the story, the struggle between the Saracen south and the vague Celtic Cravann, was familiar ... *Fervaal* is the French *Parsifal* ... The wound of Fervaal cured in the magic gardens of Guilhen, the oath of chastity which binds him until he sees that 'purity is more than chastity', and the vague apotheosis, in which the hero disappears on the mountainside to the theme of the *'Pange lingua'*, announcing the new religion of love – the whole story suggests numerous parallels with *Parsifal*. Arfagard's initiation of his pupil into the mythology of the old Celtic religion (Act I) recalls Wotan. Even the key signatures are made to serve as symbols. Thus F sharp major is the key of divine love ... the enharmonically identical G flat major that of human love; A flat major represents false love; G minor the obsolete religion of the Druids; and so forth. But the pace of the work is slow and the orchestra again and again interrupts the simplest conversation or narration with a pointed comment or reference, to drive home the full significance to the listener. In the last act the action puts a great strain on any but the most sympathetic audience. Guilhen rejoins Fervaal but dies as the moon goes behind a cloud. He picks her up in a thunderstorm and starts to climb the mystical mountain, intoning a metrical version of the *'Pange lingua'*, which is taken up by the invisible chorus, while Fervaal executes what can only be described as a form of yodelling to punctuate their phrases. It is only too easy to make fun of this intensely serious work

Martin Cooper, *French Music from the Death of Berlioz to the Death of Fauré*, Oxford University Press, 1951, p. 113

Claude Debussy on Parsifal:

In *Parsifal*, the final accomplishment of a genius before whom we must bow our heads, Wagner tried to be less rigidly authoritarian towards the music; he lets it breathe more easily. You no longer find that enervated breathlessness in pursuit of a dark obsession that characterizes a Tristan, nor the animal cries of an Isolde, nor the grandiloquent commentary on the inhumanity of a Wotan.

Nothing in Wagner's music attains a more serene beauty than the Prelude to the third act of *Parsifal* and the 'Good Friday' music – although in truth Wagner's deepest insights into humanity are manifested in the portrayal of several characters in this drama: look at Amfortas, the sorrowful Knight of the Grail who grumbles like a milliner and moans like a baby. *Sapristi!* When one is a Knight of the Grail and the son of a king, one should sooner plunge a spear through one's own body than wander about with a guilty wound singing melancholy arias for three whole acts. As for Kundry, the old rose of hell, she has been an abundant source for Wagnerian commentary, though I must confess to a soft spot for the emotional old dragon. The finest character in *Parsifal* is Klingsor (former Knight of the Grail, ousted from the Holy Place for his idiosyncratic views on chastity). How wonderful is his rancorous hatred; he knows what men are really worth, and weighs the strength of their vows to chastity on his contemptuous scales. It's easy to argue that this wily sorcerer and old miscreant is not only the one 'human' character but also the only 'moral' one in this drama of misguided moral and religious ideas – ideas of which the young Parsifal, heroic but dim-witted, is the knightly proponent . . .

All I've written applies only to Wagner the poet, since the musical side of *Parsifal* is of superlative beauty, expressed in orchestral sonorities that are unique and unprecedented, noble and powerful. It adds up to one of the most beautiful monuments in sound ever raised to the immutable glory of music.

Claude Debussy, article in *Gil Blas*, 6 April 1903, translated by
Stephen Brook

Taking a touring production of the Ring *to the provinces of England, Sir Thomas Beecham encountered a hitch:*

We had ploughed our way through a tolerable representation of the *Ring* cycle, and everything had gone without a hitch until the final scene, which as all the world knows is one of the grandest and most moving in opera. Brünnhilde was getting along in capital

style with her farewell song, when to my dismay and astonishment
the curtain came down. There was general consternation both on
and off the stage; but continuing to conduct I pressed repeatedly
the bell-button at my desk, and presently to my great relief the
curtain rose and we went on as if nothing untoward had happened.
But only for a minute or so: once more it descended. Again I
renewed my attack on the button and again it went up, this time
staying there until the end.

I hurried behind to discover the cause of this nerve-racking
experience, and a sheepish and tired-looking individual was
brought forward and introduced to me as the manipulator of the
volatile piece of machinery. It appeared that, wearied by the length
of the piece, he had gone off to sleep, and upon waking had found
that it was well past eleven. As never before in the history of the
theatre had any performance been known to continue beyond that
hour, he had hastily concluded that it must be over and had rung
down the curtain. On hearing my signal, he had hoisted it up, but,
after a few moments of dazed reflection during which he remembered that his wife was expecting him for supper (also at eleven
o'clock), and would be seriously put out if he were late, he could
not help thinking there must be a mistake somewhere. So what
with one thing and another he had thought it best to drop it again
... I do not remember if we expected some little expression of
regret from him for this unwelcome contribution to the evening's
entertainment, but if so we were most certainly disappointed. Far
from admitting that he could be in any way at fault, he declared
emphatically that if people did not know enough to bring any
piece, opera or play, to its termination by eleven o'clock at night,
they had no right to be in the theatre business at all.

Sir Thomas Beecham, *A Mingled Chime*, Hutchinson, 1944, pp. 173-4

Sir Adrian Boult's devotion to the Master was less than whole-hearted:

I ran into Dame Ethel [Smyth] in the street during a Munich
Festival: 'You are the man I'm looking for; you've got to come

and dine with me at the theatre restaurant tonight during the
second act of *Walküre*; all the Walters are coming.'

It happened that I had come a very long way to hear and see the
second act of *Walküre*, among other things, but my hesitation was
promptly sat on, and I joined a most hilarious and happy party.
[Karl] Muck was conducting, and Bruno [Walter] having a night
off, enjoying himself. We felt particularly superior when the audience all rushed frantically out for beer and sandwiches in the
second interval, while we had dined comfortably and could go
leisurely back for the third act.

Then I learnt a lesson; I thought I knew that act well, but I
heard much in it that I had never heard before, and I decided then
and there that to concentrate on two acts of Wagner was enough
for any one evening, and I have always tried to escape one act,
whatever the cost, ever since.

Sir Adrian Boult, *My Own Trumpet*, Hamish Hamilton, 1973, pp. 75–6

*In the days when recordings had to be played at 78 r.p.m., putting complete
operas on record proved exceptionally problematic:*

Not long ago a colleague of mine came across an old 78 r.p.m. set
of *Walküre* on the HMV label. It contained fourteen records,
twenty-eight sides, and played for roughly two hours – which is
just over half the average timing for the whole work. It was,
therefore, a 'condensed' *Walküre*, although the process of condensa-
tion seems, from today's standpoint, to be the least of its surprises.
Seven sides, or about thirty-two minutes, are devoted to Act I,
with Walter Widdop as Siegmund and Göta Ljungberg as Sieglinde. Over the first four of these seven sides the London Symphony Orchestra is conducted by Albert Coates, but when we
come to sides five and six an anonymous orchestra has taken over;
and Lawrance Collingwood is the conductor. (The singers remain
the same.) By side seven, which contains the end of Act I, Mr
Coates has reappeared with the London Symphony.

The interjection of another orchestra and conductor in the

middle of Act I may seem startling enough today, but it is as nothing when compared with the comings and goings in Act II. For the opening of the second act the orchestra has changed to that of the Berlin State Opera, and the conductor is Leo Blech. There is a fine cast, with Frida Leider as Brünnhilde and Friedrich Schorr as Wotan, and these forces manage to remain constant for three sides, or about thirteen minutes. But when, on sides eleven and twelve, it is necessary for Siegmund and Sieglinde to reappear, the orchestra becomes the London Symphony once again and Mr Coates is back on the podium. From that point onwards a state of anarchy may be proclaimed. In the *Todesverkündigung* scene the orchestra and conductor (Coates) remain the same, and Widdop is still the Siegmund; but the part of Brünnhilde has been taken over by Florence Austral. By side sixteen, where Siegmund challenges Hunding, we are back in Berlin again. The Siegmund is still Walter Widdop, who presumably went to Berlin in the hope of meeting his former Sieglinde, Miss Ljungberg – but no such luck, for another singer has taken over the part. However, Miss Ljungberg manages to reappear on the very next side to witness the death of her brother, along with Mr Coates and the London Symphony Orchestra. Miss Austral is still the Brünnhilde, but for the end of Act II we find a new Wotan, Mr Fry. Miss Leider is back as Brünnhilde for Act III; Mr Fry has been replaced as Wotan by Mr Schorr; and the Berlin forces are again conducted by Leo Blech. Altogether, this is a very confusing set of records . . .

It is a sobering thought that if anyone had tried to put the *Ring* on 78 r.p.m. discs, the complete work would have required something like two hundred and twenty-four sides, or one hundred and twelve records. You would have been interrupted thirty-five times in *Rheingold* and over seventy times in *Götterdämmerung*; and most of the breaks would have made musical nonsense.

John Culshaw, *Ring Resounding*, Secker & Warburg, 1967, pp. 18–21

John Culshaw, who produced the first complete recording of the Ring, *on the difficulties of finding anvils for* Rheingold, *conducted by Georg Solti:*

We needed anvils – eighteen of them in various sizes, and eighteen percussionists to play them. The rhythmic hammering of Nibelheim slaves is heard twice in *Rheingold*: first in the interlude when Wotan and Loge descend to Nibelheim, and again when they depart with Alberich as their captive. The rhythms are precisely notated by Wagner, and you would think that anyone with the slightest dramatic or musical perception would grasp, simply by looking at the score, what he was after. Yet I have never seen a theatre production which attempted to meet his wishes. Sometimes you get fobbed off with a sort of electronic compromise; sometimes you get a tinkling sound made by a few people beating metal bars together: but you never get the firm, frightening sound of eighteen anvils hit with rhythmical precision and building into a deafening assault on the nerves which, to quote [Ernest] Newman from a different context, should 'approach the threshold of pain'. Of course it *could* be done in the theatre; I imagine the reason for its absence is that although Wagner made it quite clear that he wanted a primitive *noise* for dramatic reasons, most conductors cannot abide noise of any sort. Their instincts tell them that it is unmusical, and so they skirt the problem by making it as inconspicuous, and as inoffensive, as possible . . .

We called upon our friend Adolf Krypl for help. We required eighteen anvils and a few spares, and lots of different hammers to bang them with . . . Krypl announced that he had discovered something called an anvil school from which we could obtain any number of anvils in all sorts of shapes and sizes. To this day I have failed to discover what goes on at the anvil school, or what career you adopt once you have graduated there, but we were grateful for its existence . . .

The anvil sound on the first rehearsal was a sensation, but there were problems. Solti rightly had to convince the players that the effectiveness of the passage depended entirely on absolute rhythmical precision, but the noise was so enormous that the players could not hear themselves, and could therefore not tell when they got out of rhythm.

[*In Act II of* Siegfried, *Siegfried awakens Fafner with a long solo on the horn. This provided the recording team with an opportunity to play a joke on the Vienna Philharmonic Orchestra's leading horn player Roland Berger:*]

[Berger] was scheduled to come and play, but he did not know that a few months before, when we were recording in Israel, we had met a young horn player of French origin who specialized in playing a ghastly parody of the sort of watery, wobbly horn sound which the French seem to adore and which is anathema to the Austrians. We persuaded our friend in Israel to give the weakest and most toneless performance of *Siegfried*'s horn call imaginable, which we carefully preserved on tape and brought to Vienna. Most horn players try to act the prima donna, and Roland Berger is no exception. He arrived at the Sofiensaal complaining that he was tired and needed beer before he could play a note. This was provided, and he finally consented to play the long horn call as a test. When he came back to hear it, we played him the version we had made in Israel. His face was a picture. It was, he said, our lousy machinery. He became apoplectic. For any witness who did not know that we were good friends, it must have been an alarming scene. Finally, we told him the truth: and at that very moment the machinery *did* blow up, and quite seriously. Roland, mumbling about our utter incompetency, took himself off to the flat, drank several more beers and was found fast asleep in bed two hours later, after we had made the repairs. Then he gave the magnificent performance of the horn call which appears on the records.

John Culshaw, *Ring Resounding*, Secker & Warburg, 1967, pp. 94-5, 158

The director Peter Hall, a practical man of the theatre who produced a
Ring cycle at Bayreuth with Georg Solti, reflects:

Everything in Wagner's world takes longer because it is more
intense. His music exists in a hallucinatory, slowed-up tempo – the
kind that comes upon us when we are in acute crisis, as when the
car moves with dreadful inevitability towards the crash. In *The*
Ring there are long, long scenes in slow motion; then, in two
minutes flat, the world turns upside down. The feelings are
eternal; but the action when it comes is quick and apocalyptic.

Peter Hall, *Making an Exhibition of Myself*, Sinclair-Stevenson, 1993,

p. 223

19: Wagner at Bayreuth

Sad. Sad. Sad!
    Wagner is dead!
    When I read the news yesterday I was, so to speak, horrified! Let us not discuss it. It is a great individual who has disappeared! A name that leaves the most powerful imprint on the history of art!

        Giuseppe Verdi, letter of 14 February 1883, *Letters*, p. 219

Wagner, overseeing the first Bayreuth Festival of 1876, encountered practical difficulties in staging Das Rheingold *that have also dogged subsequent producers:*

All sorts of unexpected difficulties, trifling in themselves and most of them ultimately capable of being overcome or bypassed, but time-wasting and temper-trying when they first reared their heads, sprang up when his inner vision came to be translated into theatrical reality. It was easy enough to see, in imagination, Alberich disappearing in a magic cloud of vapour; but when the vapour became a physical fact the steam penetrated to the recesses of the orchestral pit, so that the harpists could not keep their instruments in tune . . .

The Rhine Maidens' swimming machines were thoroughly tried out for the first time on 30 May, with three local gymnasts to impersonate the swimmers. Each of them had to recline in a sort of long cradle, the supporting undershaft of which ran down below the scenes to a trolley on three wheels. The cradle could be lowered or raised and propelled backwards and forwards; a 'steersman' ran the trolley to and fro across the ground, while three conductors . . . controlled the evolutions of the Rhine Maidens in accordance with the music for each part.

Four days later, the sisters Lehmann and Fräulein Lammert
having meanwhile arrived, the time for the supreme test had come.
The three ladies watched the perilous machines going up and
down with their passengers in them, and were horrified. Lilli at
once declared that for no man, for nothing on earth, would she
deliver herself up to such a device of the devil: she had just risen
from a sick-bed and still suffered from dizziness. The other two
daughters of the waves remained mute. Fricke tried to cajole them.
'Courage, Fräulein Marie,' he said, 'just try it, and I wager that
your fears will vanish and you will feel nothing but the joy of
swimming.' A ladder was hoisted, and Marie Lehmann, with many
an 'Ach' and 'Oh' and squeals and squeaks was assisted into it by
Brandt and Fricke. They buckled her in fast and the maiden
voyage began. Soon the terror vanished from her face; she began
to find the gyrations quite delightful. Lilli next tried it, then
Fräulein Lammert; and soon all three were not only careering in
the depth of the Rhine like happy children born to the sport but
singing divinely.

Ernest Newman, *The Life of Richard Wagner*, Cassell, 1947, IV,

pp. 454–5

*Cosima Wagner records the daily traumas of the rehearsals for the opening
festival:*

Saturday, 15 July. Herr Siehr at rehearsal; R[ichard] satisfied with
him, engages him for Hagen! In the evening final rehearsal of *Das
Rheingold*; many vexations for R. in the course of it, the rainbow
bridge wrong (so far), the steam fails to work, because Herr
Brandt, warned by the management committee about the need for
economy, could not produce the proper vapours! . . .

Monday, 17 July. First act of *Walküre*, Frl. Scheffsky [as Sieg-
linde] terrible! . . .

Tuesday, 18 July. Second act of *Walküre*, Frl. Scheffsky even
more horrible; she previously at lunch, an excess of ungainliness
and gracelessness! Conference over whether to get rid of her at all

costs. Fears that another singer would no longer have time to learn it . . .

Thursday, 20 July. First act of *Siegfried*, Herr Unger quite good, in spite of the players' not giving him enough support. Unfortunately Herr Schlosser has forgotten a lot of Mime through having had to sing all sorts of different things in Munich . . .

Sunday, 13 August. First performance of *Rheingold*, under a completely unlucky star: Betz loses the ring, runs into the wings twice during the curse, a stage-hand raises the backdrop too soon during the first scene change and one sees people standing around in shirtsleeves and the back wall of the theatre, all the singers embarrassed, etc., etc . . .

Monday, 14 August. *Walküre*, this time without trouble . . .

Tuesday, 15 August. Herr Betz has *Siegfried* postponed! He says he is hoarse. Much ill feeling; the newspapers, already extremely malicious, will draw inferences from it . . .

Wednesday, 16 August. *Siegfried* also goes well, people are saying that Herr Betz was never hoarse at all! Let others attempt to explain such characters, we do not understand them.

Cosima Wagner, *Diaries*, translated by Geoffrey Skelton, Harcourt
Brace Jovanovich, I, pp. 915–16, 918–19

Various American correspondents reported on the opening of the first Bayreuth Festival in 1876:

On the day of the opening, around 4 p.m., the streets were alive with people taking the road to the theatre. There were no cabs to be had. Altogether Bayreuth had only seven hacks, and almost none could be produced in the neighbouring towns . . . The performance began at 7 p.m. The trumpets sounded a fanfare (the sword motif), the Emperor William stepped into his box, there were plenty of cheers – and then attentive silence!

Of the thirteen hundred seats in the theatre, a thousand were reserved for the patrons and three hundred for visitors. In addition, every inhabitant of Bayreuth who provided a member of the

orchestra with free lodging was entitled to a seat in the far rows
for one series of rehearsals. Most of them did a thriving business
selling these seats. In fact, in spite of all precautions, the ticket
speculators had plenty of seats to offer . . .

Naturally, the town was full of Wagnerian souvenirs, Wagner's
picture was to be had on pipe bowls, tobacco boxes, toilet ornaments, album covers; it was displayed in every shop window and
restaurant. Wagner's music filled the streets. Here some soprano
declaimed at the top of her voice, there a tenor's voice floated
down from his room, across the street a bass practised. 'As I sit
here, I hear Wagner motifs being hummed, sung, yodelled, and
bellowed from the garden,' wrote Grieg. But there were other
sounds, too. One night a brawl broke out in a restaurant when a
Berlin critic said something derogatory about the *Ring*, whereupon
a Wagner defender hit him with a beer mug and broke his nose.
The Wagner champion was taken to gaol . . .

George R. Marek, *A Front Seat at the Opera*, Harrap, 1951, pp. 142–4

*Tchaikovsky attended the opening of the festival in 1876 and sent puzzled
articles back to a Russian newspaper:*

Wagner shows an astonishing wealth of harmonic and polyphonic
technique. This wealth is too great. Constantly forcing your attention. Wagner finally tries it so that at the end of the opera,
particularly in *Götterdämmerung*, your fatigue becomes such that the
music ceases to be a harmonious combination of sounds and gets
to be some kind of tiring noise. Is this what art is supposed to
achieve? Since I, a professional musician, was nearing a complete
moral and physical exhaustion, then what must have been the
fatigue of the unprofessional listener? . . .

I am ready to admit that through my own fault, I have not yet
reached the point of completely understanding this music, and that
if I study it carefully, I too shall some day belong to the large
circle of admirers. For the present, however, speaking quite frankly,
the *Ring* impressed me not so much by its musical beauties, of

which there may be too generous an amount, as by its lengthiness, its gigantic size. And now I'd like to say what I finally got out of the *Ring*. I have a vague remembrance of much extraordinary beauty, especially symphonic beauty, which is very odd, since Wagner meant least of all to write an opera in a symphonic style; I have an astonished admiration for the enormous talent of the author and his incredibly rich technique; I have my doubts as to the justice of Wagner's view on opera; I have a feeling of great fatigue, but along with it I have a desire for further study of this most complicated of all music ever written.

P. I. Tchaikovsky, *Life and Letters*, Lane, 1906

When the Irish composer Charles Villiers Stanford attended the 1876 festival, he did not find the event uplifting:

The atmosphere was not sympathetic, and gave a feeling of polemic prejudice which militated against wholehearted appreciation or valuable discrimination. 'He that is not with me is against me' was the motto of the whole festival. The theatre was not finished as far as the exterior went; the road up the hill from the station was very much in the rough, and after rain was a sea of mud. The town was hopelessly unprepared for the incursion of so many strangers . . .

Steam was used, I believe for the first time, for stage purposes; but the noise of its escape was so great that it often nearly drowned the music. The close of the *Rheingold* and the *Walkürenritt* [Ride of the Valkyries] were, scenically speaking, failures, as was also the end of the *Götterdämmerung* . . .

Mr Hercules McDonnell, who came from Dublin for the festival, put his clever finger on the weak spot of the work, when he said that the underlying mischief was the composer being his own librettist: the librettist having no composer to keep him within bounds, and the composer having no librettist to warn him of undue length. No one can deny the prevalence of the failing known as 'stage waits'. A fad, which first obtruded itself in *The Flying Dutchman*, of making the hero and heroine stand motionless and stare at each other for the best part of five minutes, grew upon the composer as he developed, and to such an extent, that in *Parsifal* his chief figure has to stand rooted to the ground for nearly an hour. This may be all very well in theory and on paper, but just as the long sitting tells on the audience, so the long standing is a torture to the actor . . .

Wagner appeared on the stage at the close of the cycle, but happily did not make one of his unfortunate speeches. I regretted seeing him in the flesh . . . Whatever magnetism there was in the man, his physiognomy did its best to counteract. The brow and head was most impressive, the mouth and chin equally repulsive. Together they made a most curious combination of genius and meanness.

C.V. Stanford, *Pages from an Unwritten Diary*, Edward Arnold, 1914,

pp. 168–71

Shaw, of course, gives the most astute description of the early Bayreuth festivals:

When the Bayreuth Festival Playhouse was at last completed, and opened in 1876 with the first performance of *The Ring*, European society was compelled to admit that Wagner was 'a success'. Royal personages, detesting his music, sat out the performances in the row of boxes set apart for princes. They all complimented him on the astonishing 'push' with which, in the teeth of all obstacles, he had turned a fabulous and visionary project into a concrete commercial reality, patronized by the public at a pound a head. It is as well to know that these congratulations had no other effect upon Wagner than to open his eyes to the fact that the Bayreuth experiment, as an attempt to evade the ordinary social and commercial conditions of theatrical enterprise, was a failure. His own account of it contrasts the reality with his intentions in a vein which would be bitter if it were not so humorous. The precautions taken to keep the seats out of the hands of the frivolous public and in the hands of earnest disciples, banded together in little Wagner

Societies throughout Europe, had ended in their forestalling by
ticket speculators and their sale to just the sort of idle globe-
trotting tourists against whom the temple was to have been strictly
closed . . .

Since then, subscriptions are no longer needed; for the Festival
Playhouse pays its own way now, and is commercially on the same
footing as any other theatre . . .

Unlike the old opera houses, which are constructed so that the
audience may present a splendid pageant to the delighted manager,
it was designed to secure an uninterrupted view of the stage, and
an undisturbed hearing of the music, to the audience. The dramatic
purpose of the performances was taken with entire and elaborate
seriousness as the sole purpose of them; and the management was
jealous for the reputation of Wagner. The sightseeing globe-trotter
no longer crowds out the genuine disciple: the audiences are now
as genuinely devoted as Wagner could have desired: the discon-
certed, bewildered, bored followers of fashion have vanished with
the sportsman on a holiday . . .

Besides, the early Bayreuth performances were far from delect-
able. The singing was sometimes tolerable, and sometimes abominable. Some of the singers were mere animated beer casks, too lazy
and conceited to practise the self-control and physical training that
is expected as a matter of course from an acrobat, a jockey or a
pugilist. The women's dresses were prudish and absurd. It is true
that after some years Kundry no longer wore an early Victorian
ball dress with 'ruchings', and that Freia was provided with a
quaintly modish copy of the flowered gown of Spring in Botticelli's
famous picture; but the mail-clad Brynhild still climbed the
mountains with her legs carefully hidden in along white skirt, and
looked so exactly like Mrs Leo Hunter as Minerva that it was quite
impossible to feel a ray of illusion whilst looking at her. The ideal
of womanly beauty aimed at reminded Englishmen of the barmaids
of the seventies, when the craze for golden hair was at its worst.
Further, whilst Wagner's stage directions were sometimes
disregarded as unintelligently as at the old opera houses, Wagner's
quaintly old-fashioned tradition of half rhetorical, half historical-

pictorial attitude and gesture prevailed. The most striking moments of the drama were conceived as *tableaux vivants* with posed models, instead of as passages of action, motion, and life.

. . . Prima donnas and tenors were as unmanageable at Bayreuth as anywhere else. Casts were capriciously changed; stage business was insufficiently rehearsed; the audience was compelled to listen to a Brynhild or Siegfried of fifty when they had carefully arranged to see one of twenty-five, much as in any ordinary opera house. Even the conductors upset the arrangements occasionally. On the other hand, we could always feel assured that in thoroughness of preparation of the chief work of the season, in strenuous artistic pretentiousness, in pious conviction that the work was of such enormous importance as to be worth doing well at all costs, the Bayreuth performances would deserve their reputation. Their example raised the quality of operatic performances throughout the world, even in apparently incorrigible centres of fashion and frivolity.

George Bernard Shaw, from *The Perfect Wagnerite*, reprinted in
Shaw's Music, Bodley Head, 1989, III, pp. 535–8

But it was Eduard Hanslick, the celebrated music critic, who put the boot in. Here he is at Die Walküre *at Bayreuth in 1876:*

The second act is an abyss of boredom. Wotan appears, holds a long conversation with his wife, and then, turning to Brünnhilde, gives an autobiographical lecture covering eight full pages of text. This utterly tuneless, plodding narrative, in a slow tempo, engulfs us like an inconsolable broad sea from which only the meagre crumbs of a few leitmotivs come floating towards us out of the orchestra. Scenes like this recall the medieval torture of waking a sleeping prisoner by stabbing him with a needle at every nod. We have heard even Wagnerites characterize this second act as a disaster. It is entirely unnecessary, since with two cuts both episodes could be done away with, painlessly. *Die Walküre* has, indeed, a very loose relationship with the action of the whole; it tells nothing of the fateful ring which we have not already learned in *Rheingold*, and only Brunnhilde's punishment is important for the purpose of the drama . . .

Wagner is mannered; an inspired genius, but still a mannerist. His eccentricities of declamation, modulation and harmonization are imposed on every kind of material. In this style he could probably write ten more operas without undue effort or inspiration. Although the element of passionate exaltation never seems to achieve satiety, it is often difficult to believe in its truth and necessity. It is reminiscent of many of Victor Hugo's poems, products of inner coldness which imagine themselves glowing and inspired. The music to *Götterdämmerung* characterizes its author anew as a brilliant specialist, rather adjacent to music than of it. It is unthinkable that his method shall be, as he contends, the only valid opera style from now on, the absolute 'art-work of the future'. When an art arrives at a period of utmost luxury, it is already on the decline. Wagner's opera style recognizes only superlatives; but a superlative has no future. It is the end, not the beginning.

Eduard Hanslick, *Musical Criticisms 1846–99*, translated by
Henry Pleasants, London, 1951

Mark Twain, a Wagner enthusiast, visited Bayreuth in 1891 and heard Parsifal:

The entire overture, long as it was, was played to a dark house with the curtain down. It was exquisite; it was delicious. But straightway thereafter, of course, came the singing, and it does seem to me that nothing can make a Wagner opera absolutely perfect and satisfactory to the untutored but to leave out the vocal parts. I wish I could see a Wagner opera done in pantomime once. Then one would have the lovely orchestration unvexed to listen to and bathe his spirit in, and the bewildering beautiful scenery to intoxicate his eyes with, and the dumb acting could not mar these pleasures, because there is not often anything in the Wagner opera that one would call by such a violent name as acting; as a rule all you would see would be a couple of silent people, one of them standing still, the other catching flies. Of course I do not really mean that he would be catching flies; I only mean that the usual operatic gestures which consist in reaching first one hand out into the air and then the other might suggest the sport I speak of if the operator attended strictly to business and uttered no sound . . .

I trust that I know as well as anybody that singing is one of the most entrancing and bewitching and moving and eloquent of all vehicles invented by man for the conveying of feeling; but it seems to me that the chief virtue in song is melody, air, tune, rhythm, or what you please to call it, and that when this feature is absent what remains is a picture with the colour left out. I was not able to detect in the vocal parts of *Parsifal* anything that might with confidence be called rhythm or tune or melody; one person performed at a time – and a long time, too – often in a noble, and always in a high-toned, voice; but he only pulled out long notes, then some short ones, then another long one, then a sharp, quick, peremptory bark or two – and so on and so on; and when he was done you saw that the information which he had conveyed had not compensated for the disturbance. Not always, but pretty often. If two of them would but put in a duet occasionally and blend the voices; but no, they do not do that . . .

Singing! It does seem the wrong name to apply to it. Strictly described, it is a practising of difficult and unpleasant intervals, mainly. An ignorant person gets tired of listening to gymnastic intervals in the long run, no matter how pleasant they may be. In *Parsifal* there is a hermit named Gurnemanz who stands on the stage in one spot and practises by the hour, while first one and then another character of the cast endures what he can of it and then retires to die . . .

Yesterday the opera was *Tristan und Isolde*. I have seen all sorts of audiences – at theatres, operas, concerts, lectures, sermons, funerals – but none which was twin to the Wagner audience of Bayreuth for fixed and reverential attention. Absolute attention

and petrified retention to the end of an act of the attitude assumed
at the beginning of it. You detect no movement in the solid mass
of heads and shoulders. You seem to sit with the dead in the gloom
of a tomb . . . You hear not one utterance till the curtain swings
together and the closing strains have slowly faded out and died;
then the dead rise with one impulse and shake the building with
their applause. Every seat is full in the first act; there is not one
vacant one in the last. If a man would be conspicuous, let him
come here and retire from the house in the midst of an act. It
would make him celebrated.

> Mark Twain, 'At the Shrine of St Wagner', *New York Sun*,
> 6 December 1891

*Shaw reports performance by performance on the progress of the 1896
Bayreuth Festival:*

The first act of *Die Walküre* has just been rescued from a *succès de
sommeil* by the perennial and passionate Sucher, who suddenly
broke into one of her triumphs as Sieglinde. Gerhäuser, as Siegmund, made up as a stout middle-aged gentleman in sheepskins
and a red beard, has been as null and wooden as anybody could
desire. With the assistance of Wachter as Hunding, he all but put
us asleep in the first half of the scene. In pulling the sword from
the tree he was much less exciting than an English vestryman
taking his hat from a peg . . .

The first act of *Siegfried* has been the worst disappointment so
far. Grüning, as Siegfried, is hardly to be described without
malice. Imagine an eighteenth-century bank clerk living in a cave,
with fashionable sandals and cross garters, an elegant modern
classic tunic, a Regent Street bearskin, and a deportment only to
be learnt in quadrilles . . . If the performance had been given at an
ordinary German theatre, with ordinary German prices, I should
have been delighted with the orchestra and the mounting; but I
should have roundly denounced the choice of the principal artist.
And since *Siegfried* is a drama which depends as much on the actor

who plays the title part as *Hamlet* does, my condemnation of Herr Grüning practically gives away the whole performance . . . Consequently the people who have made tedious and costly pilgrimages from the ends of the earth to Bayreuth, as the one place in the world where Wagner music-dramas can be witnessed in their utmost attainable excellence and fidelity of representation, have every right to remonstrate indignantly at being deliberately put off with a third-rate Siegfried . . . Lilli Lehmann-Kalisch is famous for her Brynhild – famous in America. She has a bright soprano voice, brilliant at the top, but not particularly interesting in the middle – just the wrong sort of voice for Wagner. When dressed as the war maiden, she is plump, pretty, very feminine, and not at all unlike our clever comedienne, Miss Kate Phillips – therefore just the wrong sort of person for Brynhild.

George Bernard Shaw, article in *The Star*, 22–5 July 1896, reprinted in
Shaw's Music, Bodley Head, 1989, III, pp. 367, 371–4

Alban Berg writes to his wife about his experiences at Bayreuth:

12 August 1909: . . . Altogether, Bayreuth is an empty delusion. I'd never want to set foot in it again, but for the unforgettable *Parsifal*. If Wagner had not long ago turned in his grave, I am sure, he would rise and take flight in disgust at what goes on in and around Wahnfried . . .

Picture the scene. Left and right of the Festspielhaus a Festspiel beer-house and a Festspiel restaurant. I arrived at the theatre in devout mood to find the entire audience (mostly Bavarians and Americans) disporting themselves in those places – led by Siegfried Wagner and his friends. After the first act the same business started again, and I could have run off into the fields nearby and wept. People strolled around laughing and chattering, feeling they simply must have a drink, or else ordering supper for the next interval . . .

Then we were called back to the theatre for the second act. I had some Munich folk behind me, looking like caricatures out of

Simplicissimus [a humorous periodical published in Munich], and heard one of them say: 'Now for the flower scene, nice and sentimental.' *Parsifal* sentimental! And Wagner wrote his music for people like this! Then Cosima appeared, and of course everybody had to turn round in great curiosity to look at Bayreuth's talented business manageress.

After the second act we had a repetition of the first interval, only guzzling was now more or less *de rigueur*. The Bavarians drank beer, and Americans champagne. Siegfried Wagner had changed from his immaculate white tennis kit into a dark suit, and with all the autograph hunters hardly had time to enjoy his 'Parsifal steak' with rice and stewed fruit, before it was time to go back for Act III . . .

As to the performance itself, it might have been up to the highest standards of those when Wagner was alive, but hasn't quite caught up with the advances made since then. You could compare it to a first-class production in pre-Mahler Vienna.

Alban Berg, *Letters to His Wife*, translated by Bernard Grun, Faber,

1971, pp. 85–6

Stravinsky also failed to succumb to Bayreuth's magic:

I [received] an invitation from Diaghilev to join him at Bayreuth to hear *Parsifal* in its hallowed setting. I had never seen *Parsifal* on the stage, the proposal was tempting, and I accepted it with pleasure . . . The performance which I saw there would not tempt me today even if I were offered a room gratis. The very atmosphere of the theatre, its design and its setting, seemed lugubrious. It was like a crematorium, and a very old-fashioned one at that, and one expected to see the gentleman in black who had been entrusted with the task of singing the praises of the departed. The order to devote oneself to contemplation was given by a blast of trumpets. I sat humble and motionless, but at the end of a quarter of an hour I could not bear any more. My limbs were numb and I had to change my position. Crack! Now I had done it! My chair had made a noise which drew down on me the furious scowls of a hundred pairs of eyes. Once more I withdrew into myself, but I could think of only one thing, and that was the end of the act which would put an end to my martyrdom. At last the 'Pause' arrived, and I was rewarded by two sausages and a glass of beer. But hardly had I had time to light a cigarette when the trumpet-blast sounded again, demanding another period of contemplation. Another act to be got through, when all my thoughts were concentrated on my cigarette, of which I had had barely a whiff. I managed to bear the second act. Then there were more sausages, more beer, another trumpet-blast, another period of contemplation, another act – Finis!

I do not want to discuss the music of *Parsifal* nor the music of Wagner in general. At this date it is too remote from me. What I find revolting in the whole affair is the underlying conception which dictated it – the principle of putting a work of art on the same level as the sacred and symbolic ritual which constitutes a religious service. And, indeed, is not all this comedy of Bayreuth, with its ridiculous formalities, simply an unconscious aping of a religious rite?

Igor Stravinsky, *Chronicle of My Life*, Gollancz, 1936, pp. 66–8

Toscanini, an Italian, conducted at Bayreuth in 1930:

The festival orchestra was made up of players assembled from a number of German orchestras, and there was necessarily a larger year-to-year turnover of personnel than in a permanent orchestra. Even if the members were individually of high calibre, this did not mean that a first horn from the Munich Opera and a second horn from the Berlin Philharmonic would be well-matched, or that the principal flute and principal oboe would have learned to adapt perfectly to each other after only a few weeks. Besides, the Bayreuth pit is exceptionally deep and almost entirely covered by the stage, and players therefore have the additional problem of becoming accustomed to very unusual acoustical conditions.

Before the first orchestral rehearsal Siegfried [Wagner] had presented Toscanini to the orchestra, and Toscanini had told the members of his deep and long-standing desire to be able to conduct at Bayreuth; but when he heard the orchestra he was dumbfounded and furious. By the time that session had ended he had decided not to conduct, and it was only when Siegfried assured him that replacements could easily be found for the weaker players that the situation was brought under control. Perhaps control is not the right word, however, because the orchestra soon found themselves subjected to Toscanini's worst sort of shock therapy. They had never experienced anything quite like it; nor were they less astonished when *der Italiener* – rehearsing from memory, as always – began to hear and correct mistakes in the parts which had gone unnoticed for decades by Bayreuth's famous conductors.

Harvey Sachs, *Toscanini*, Weidenfeld & Nicolson, 1978, p. 204

How Toscanini revitalized the Bayreuth orchestra:

Rudolf Bockelmann, the excellent baritone who sang Kurwenal [in *Tristan und Isolde*], recalled, 'The piano rehearsals were terribly fatiguing because he insisted on our singing in full voice. I have known many conductors of international reputation. Remembering them I now think that Toscanini was the most objective of them all; faithfulness to the work under consideration was for him the basis of performance. While wiping away all pedantry he did not tolerate the slightest rhythmic imperfection. Hitting the score with his baton or his hand, he used to say in German, *"Hier steht, hier steht"* ("It is written here"). He did not speak German, but those two words he knew. The singer who did not remember all his instructions was roughly treated. But when everything went well, when he was pleased with us, he used to chat amicably, tell us stories about Verdi, talk of Wagner. *"C'est mon grand maître,"* he

would say, "*è il mio grande maestro*" ... We heard that he had
returned his entire fee to Bayreuth. He said Bayreuth was the
greatest experience of his life ...'

When he was rehearsing the orchestra at the end of Act I of
Tristan, he suddenly stopped and asked, 'Where is the cymbal?'
There was no cymbal crash marked in the score, there never had
been. They showed him the part, but he could not be convinced.
Finally they got out Wagner's manuscript: there was the cymbal
crash. It had dropped out over the years.

George R. Marek, Toscanini, Vision Press, 1975, p. 5

Walter Legge recalls the Bayreuth Festival of August 1933:

It would have been a pardonable error on the part of any casual
visitor to Bayreuth to have mistaken this year's Wagner festival for
a Hitler festival. For previous festivals every shop, no matter what
its wares, managed by hook or by crook to display a photograph
of at least some reproduction of Wagner's face. From the windows
of china shops dozens of ceramic Wagners used to gaze into space.
Booksellers displayed Wagner's autobiography. This year the china
shops are full of Hitler plaques, and *Mein Kampf* has displaced *Mein
Leben*. From every flagstaff and nearly every window a swastika
flag is flying. Brown shirts are almost *de rigueur*, and passing Café
Tannhäuser and Gasthof Rheingold one hears nothing but the
'*Horst Wessel Lied*'.

Herr Hitler attended the first six performances of the festival,
and the behaviour of the audience gave one the impression that for
them 'this is a Hitler festival, and, since Hitler likes Wagner's
music, we are here, too'. Thousands of people lined the streets
from his house to the Festspielhaus, and, with the exception of the
foreign visitors, the audience waited outside the theatre to cheer
him as he arrived, and then rushed into their seats to gaze
admiringly, almost reverently, at his box until the lights were
lowered. At the end of each act the centre of attraction changed
immediately from the stage to the Chancellor's box. And when

business detained Herr Hitler in Berlin, two thousand people were made to wait an hour and a half for their opera until he should take his seat in the theatre.

It would be idle to pretend that this outward display of national politics increased the pleasure of the international music-lover whose only interests were artistic. But, unfortunately, Hitler's influence over Bayreuth was not confined to outward show. Through his policy we were deprived of the presence of Toscanini and consequently the performances of *Die Meistersinger* and *Parsifal* were considerably inferior to those that most of us expected when, five or six months ago, we bought our tickets.

Elisabeth Schwarzkopf, *On and Off the Record: A Memoir of*
Walter Legge, Faber, 1982, p. 21

After the Second World War, Wagner's grandson Wieland Wagner
radically overhauled the Bayreuth productions:

It is now fashionable in opera to let theatrical considerations dominate musical ones, and Wieland Wagner was the first producer aggressively radical enough to revolutionize the old orthodoxies of staging. A new Germany had to look at its old heroes in a new light, and the Wagner stable had to be cleaned out. Wieland's singers not only had to act, they had to act in a style which fitted his approach. Flagstad's small repertoire of attitudes and poses would have been no good to him. Cosima had aimed at once-and-for-all definition, but Wieland constantly explored possibilities: his later productions often contradicted the implications of his earlier ones. In 1951 Bayreuth had little money and Wieland made a virtue of necessity by sweeping away spears, helmets, forests, and the detritus of realistic presentation, replacing them with austere 'timeless' settings and sophisticated lighting – with the effect of emphasizing the universal mythic content of his grandfather's works, rather than their roots in Germanic folklore. None of Wieland's first prima donnas were singers of Flagstad's or Leider's stature, but they performed with unfailing commitment and intelligence. Astrid Varnay and Martha Mödl were early and distinguished exponents of the 'singing actress' type, that favourite companion of producer's opera whose sometimes chronic vocal inadequacies we are asked to excuse on account of an overriding dramatic credibility. Schröder-Devrient and Pauline Viardot are earlier names which might come to mind here, but they were blazing exceptions: in the post-war period, the good actress whose singing wobbles, screams, or dries up has become a regrettable norm.

Rupert Christiansen, *Prima Donna*, Bodley Head, 1984, pp. 166–7

Otto Klemperer found Wieland Wagner less reverential than expected when directing the works of his grandfather:

I found Wieland Wagner really agreeable and refreshing. But he was very ready to make concessions. I said to him, 'Why have you cut some of the choruses in the second act in your production of *Lohengrin*?' 'Because I don't like them.'

Peter Heyworth, *Conversations with Klemperer*, Gollancz, 1973, p. 84

How Wagner's desire to control encompasses his audiences too:

Wagnerian providence leaves his characters with the afflicted sense of being immured in a forbiddingly unified work of art. The years between Brünnhilde's transgression and her awakening have been elided, just as the circularity of the *Ring* and its thematic repetitiveness ensure that no time seems to have elapsed between the theft of the ring and its recovery, except the four days which the audience has spent listening to the music. And even this free time Wagner begrudges to his audience and wishes to appropriate. One of the reasons for drawing listeners to Bayreuth was to remove them from the private lives they would otherwise resume during bouts of abandonment to Wagner. The circumstances of Bayreuth made these interstices a limbo, passed in a tedious suspension, waiting for life itself to resume with the next evening's music. Wagner treats his audience as he treats his characters, who are permitted no liberty to shape events for themselves.

Peter Conrad, *Romantic Opera and Literary Form*, California University Press, 1977, p. 23

20: Verdi

*Born in 1813, Giuseppe Verdi's career spanned the remainder of the
nineteenth century. His art evolved from the formal conventions of bel canto
to the innovations of his final opera* Falstaff. *Identified with the cause of
national liberation, Verdi became a symbol of Italy, earning an affection
and profound respect far removed from the awe inspired by the self-
aggrandizing Wagner. Here, in an interview conducted in his old age, Verdi
reminisces about his early years as an operatic composer:*

The conversation turned once more upon music. The inevitable
organ-grinder had struck up the equally inevitable selection from
Il trovatore on the roadway some distance off. I asked the composer
whether he did not find this method of rendering his music
peculiarly irritating.

'No,' he replied, 'on the contrary. It pleases me . . . The people
have always been my best friends – from the very beginning. It
was a handful of carpenters who gave me my first real assurance of
success . . . It was after I had dragged on in poverty and disappointment for a long time at Busseto, and had been laughed at by all the
publishers, and shown to the door by all the impresarios. I had lost
all real confidence and courage, but through sheer obstinacy, I
succeeded in getting *Nabucco* rehearsed at the Scala, in Milan. The
artists were singing as badly as they knew how, and the orchestra
seemed to be bent only upon drowning the noise of the workmen
who were busy making alterations in the building. Presently the

chorus began to sing, as carelessly as before, the "*Va, pensiero*", but before they had got through half-a-dozen bars the theatre was as still as a church. The men had left off their work, one by one, and there they were, sitting about on the ladders and scaffolding, listening! When the number was finished they broke out into the noisiest applause I have ever heard, crying "*Bravo, bravo, viva il maestro!*", and beating on the woodwork with their tools. Then I knew what the future had in store for me.'

Annie Vivanti, 'Verdi's *Falstaff*', in the *Daily Graphic*, London,
14 January 1893

Verdi always longed to write an opera based on King Lear *but never did so. In a letter of 28 February 1850 to the librettist Salvatore Cammarano, he set out how Shakespearian drama would have been transformed into Verdian opera:*

King Lear at first sight is so vast and intricate that it seems impossible one could make an opera out of it. However, on examining it closely, it seems to me that the difficulties, though no doubt immense, are not insuperable . . .

Would you agree that the reason for disinheriting Cordelia is rather infantile for the present day? Certain scenes would definitely have to be cut, for instance the one in which Gloucester is blinded, the one in which the two sisters are carried on to the stage etc., etc., and many others which you know better than I do . . .

Act I, Scene i

Great Stateroom in Lear's palace. Lear on his throne. Division of the kingdom. Demonstration by the Earl of Kent. Rage of the King who banishes the Earl. Cordelia's farewell.

Scene ii

Edmund's soliloquy. Gloucester enters (without seeing Edmund) and deplores the banishment of Kent. Edmund, encountering

Gloucester, tries to hide a letter. Gloucester forces him to reveal it. He believes that Edgar is plotting. Edgar enters; and his father, blind with fury, draws a sword against him. Edgar flees, after trying to assuage his father's anger with soothing words.

Scene iii

Hall (or vicinity) of Goneril's castle. Kent is seen dressed as a beggar. Lear arrives and takes him into his service. Meanwhile, the Fool with his bizarre songs mocks Lear for having trusted his daughters. Goneril enters, complaining of the insolence of her father's knights, whom she refuses to allow to stay in the castle. The king erupts with anger when he realizes his daughter's ingratitude. He fears he will go mad ... but remembering Regan, he calms himself and hopes to be treated better by her. The arrival is announced of Regan, who has been invited by her sister. Lear approaches her and tells how Goneril has wronged him. Regan cannot believe this and says he must have offended her. The sisters unite to persuade Lear to disperse his followers. Then Lear, realizing his daughters' heartlessness, cries: 'You think I'll weep; no, I'll not weep.' He swears vengeance, exclaiming that he will do terrible things, 'what they are yet,' he knows not, 'but they shall be the terrors of the earth.' (The noise of a tempest begins to be heard.) The curtain falls.

Act II, Scene i

Country. The tempest continues. Edgar, a fugitive, banished and accused of an attempt on his father's life, laments the injustice of his fate. Hearing a noise he takes refuge in a hut. – Lear, Fool and Kent. – 'Blow, winds, and crack your cheeks . . .' The Fool (still joking): 'O, nuncle, court holy-water in a dry house is better than this rainwater out o' door.' He enters the hut and is frightened when he sees Edgar, who feigns madness and utters cries of woe. Lear exclaims: 'What, have his daughters brought him to this pass?' . . . (magnificent quartet). Someone bearing a torch approaches. It is Gloucester who, in defiance of the decree of the daughters, has come in search of the King.

Scene ii

Hall in Goneril's castle. Huge chorus (in various verse metres): 'Do you not know? Gloucester transgressed the command! ... Well then? A terrible punishment awaits him!! ...' The events relating to Lear, Cordelia, Kent, Gloucester, etc., are recounted, and finally all fear a horrifying war which France will wage against England to avenge Lear.

Scene iii

Edmund: 'To both these sisters have I sworn my love; each jealous of the other, as the stung are of the adder. Which of them shall I take?' ... Goneril enters and, after brief dialogue, offers him command of the army, and gives him a token of her love.

Scene iv

A poor room in a cottage. Lear, Kent, Edgar, the Fool, and peasants. The Fool asks Lear, 'Whether a madman be a gentleman or a yeoman.' Lear replies: 'A King, a King!!' – Song – Lear, in a state of delirium, continually obsessed with the idea of the ingratitude of his daughters, wishes to set up a court of justice ... Extremely bizarre and moving scene. Finally, Lear tires and gradually falls asleep. All weep for the unhappy King. End of second act.

Act III, Scene i

The French camp near Dover. Cordelia has heard from Kent of her father's misfortune. Great sorrow on Cordelia's part. She sends messenger after messenger to see if he has been found. She is ready to give all her possessions to whoever can restore his reason; she invokes the pity of nature, etc., etc. The doctor announces that the King has been found and that he hopes to cure him of his madness. Cordelia, intoxicated with joy, thanks heaven and longs for the moment of vengeance.

Scene ii

Tent in the French camp. Lear asleep on a bed. The doctor and Cordelia enter very quietly. '[He] sleeps still . . .' After a brief dialogue very sweet sounds of music are heard behind the scenes, Lear awakes. Magnificent duet, as in the Shakespeare scene. The curtain falls.

Act IV, Scene i

Open country near Dover. The sound of a trumpet from afar.

Edgar appears, leading Gloucester: moving little duet in which Gloucester recognizes that he has been unjust to his son. Finally, Edgar says: 'Here, father, take the shadow of this tree for your good host; pray that the right may thrive.' (Exit) Sound of trumpet nearer, noises, alarm; finally the signal to assemble is given. Edgar returns: 'Away, old man; give me thy hand; away! King Lear hath lost, he and his daughter ta'en.' (March) Edmund, Albany, Regan, Goneril, officers, soldiers, etc., enter in triumph. Edmund gives an officer a letter: 'If thou dost as this instructs thee, thou dost make thy way to noble fortunes.' An armed warrior with lowered vizor (Edgar) enters unexpectedly and accuses Edmund of high treason: in proof, he offers a letter to Albany. A duel takes place. Edmund is mortally wounded: before he dies he confesses all his crimes, and tells them to hurry to save Lear and Cordelia . . .

Final scene

Prison. Moving scene between Lear and Cordelia, Cordelia begins to feel the effects of the poison: her agony and death. Albany, Kent and Edgar rush in to save her, but too late. Lear, unconscious of their arrival, takes Cordelia's corpse in his arms, and exclaims: 'She's dead as earth. Howl! Howl!' etc. Ensemble in which Lear must have the leading part. End.

Giuseppe Verdi, *Letters*, translated by Charles Osborne, Gollancz, 1971,

pp. 70–73

Some Verdi premières were given at the Fenice in Venice, including the disastrous first performance of La traviata:

Rigoletto went into rehearsal towards the end of February 1851. One item from the opera, however, Verdi kept back until the last possible moment; this was the aria for the Duke in the last act — '*La donna è mobile*'. He was afraid that if he let the tenor have it too soon the tune would get around all over Venice and its initial impact on the first night would be lost. As it was, the tenor was sworn to silence once he had seen the number. The secret was well kept and on the opening night, 11 March 1851, like everything else in the opera it was a stupendous success with the Venetian audience . . .

On 6 March 1853, *La traviata* was performed and failed, a spectacular, catastrophic failure without parallel in the history of opera, for it was not even redeemed by its second performance like *Madam Butterfly* and *The Barber of Seville*.

It is recorded that Act I was received favourably enough, though the audience was plainly perturbed to see an opera staged in contemporary costume. The prima donna, Fanny Salvini-Donatelli, sang well and the act is reported to have had *successo*.

It was in Act II that the trouble began. Felice Varesi, playing Germont, alternately bawled and, considering his part unworthy, sulked and was generally uncooperative. The tenor Lodovico Graziani became so hoarse that he was hardly able to emit a sound.

Act III was the real disaster. No sooner did the Doctor on the stage remark that Violetta was dying of consumption and had only a few hours to live than the house was in an uproar of hilarity. Signora Salvini-Donatelli's figure was what the kinder Venetians euphemistically referred to as '*troppo prosperosa*'.

Spike Hughes, *Great Opera Houses*, Weidenfeld & Nicolson, 1956, pp. 82–3

The English music critic Henry Chorley, writing midway through Verdi's career, did not have a high opinion of the composer:

Signor Verdi has obviously shown earnest solicitude to vary, to enrich, and to temper his orchestral effects in his later operas. He has, also, in them – as in the quartet of *Rigoletto*, and one or two scenes from *Il trovatore* – been more happily and simply inspired than in his earlier works; but the style to which he has chosen to cling and abide, the style of a bad musical time, ill wrought out in Italy, has remained essentially the same in all – spasmodic, tawdry, untruthful, depending on musical effects of a lower order and coarser quality than those of any Italian predecessor . . .

The part of his buffoon's daughter, in the opera of *Rigoletto* . . . is cold, childish, puerile. The air sung by her when she retires to sleep on the evening of the outrage is but a lackadaisical yawn. Even in the quartet of the last act, happily combined, her share amounts to little more than a chain of disconnected sobs – tragedy as physical in its way as the cough of the Camellia lady [Violetta in *La traviata*]. These devices belong to low art. We have lived to see operas with a sneezing chorus (in time), with a chorus of dogs that bark, and other such prosaic compliments. Why not as well present the effects of a cold in the head? – to go no further in the category of maladies and sorrows accompanied by symptomatic noises . . .

Henry Chorley, *Thirty Years' Musical Recollections* (1862), Knopf, 1926, pp. 183–5

Verdi wrote to his publisher Giulio Ricordi on 10 July 1871 to exert his control over the forthcoming production of Aida *at La Scala in February 1872:*

Keep in mind, my dear Giulio, that if I come to Milan, it will not be out of vanity at having an opera of mine performed: it will be to obtain a really artistic performance. To achieve that, we must have all the necessary elements. So please answer me categorically whether, in addition to the company of singers,

1. the conductor has been chosen
2. the chorus has been engaged as I indicated
3. the orchestra will be composed also as I have indicated
4. the timpani and bass drum are being changed for bigger instruments than those of two years ago
4a. the standard pitch is being retained
5. the orchestra has adopted this pitch, in order to avoid the out-of-tune playing I have heard at times
6. the instruments of the orchestra will be arranged as indicated in a kind of sketch I made in Genoa last winter.

This arrangement of the orchestra is much more important than is usually believed, for the instrumental colouring, for the sonority, and for the effect. These small improvements will open the way to other innovations that will certainly come one day. One of them will be the removal of the spectators' boxes from the stage, thus enabling the curtain to come right up to the footlights. Another improvement would be to make the orchestra invisible. This idea is not mine, but Wagner's, and it's a very good one. It's incredible nowadays that we should tolerate seeing horrid white ties and tails, for example, between us and the costumes of Egyptians, Assyrians or Druids, etc., etc. and, in addition, see the whole of the orchestra, which should be part of a fictitious world, almost in the middle of the stalls among the crowd as it hisses or applauds. Add to all this the annoyance of seeing the tops of harps and contrabassoons as well as the flailing arms of the conductor waving about in the air.

Answer me, then, categorically and decisively, because if I cannot be given what I require, there is no point in continuing these negotiations.

Giuseppe Verdi, *Letters*, translated by Charles Osborne, Gollancz, 1971,

pp. 178–9

Aida *was immensely popular – except with Prospero Bertani who, after seeing the opera twice, wrote to the composer:*

On the second of this month, attracted by the sensation which your opera, *Aida*, was making, I went to Parma. Half an hour before the performance began I was already in my seat ... I admired the scenery, listened with great pleasure to the excellent singers, and took pains to let nothing escape me. After the performance was over, I asked myself whether I was satisfied. The answer was in the negative. I returned to Reggio, and on the way back in the railway carriage, I listened to the verdicts of my fellow travellers. Nearly all of them agreed that *Aida* was a work of the highest rank.

Thereupon I conceived a desire to hear it again, so on the 4th I returned to Parma. I made the most desperate efforts to obtain a reserved seat, but there was such a crowd that I had to spend five lire to see the performance in comfort.

I came to the following conclusion: the opera contains absolutely nothing thrilling or electrifying, and if it were not for the magnificent scenery, the audience would not sit through it to the end. It will fill the theatre a few more times and then gather dust in the archives. Now, my dear Signor Verdi, you can imagine my regret at having spent thirty-two lire for these two performances. Add to this the aggravating circumstance that I am dependent on my family, and you will understand that this money preys on my mind like a terrible spectre. Therefore I address myself frankly and openly to you, so that you may send me this sum. Here is the account:

Railway: one way	2.60 lire
Railway: return trip	3.30 lire
Theatre	8.00 lire
Disgustingly bad dinner at the station	2.00
Multiplied by 2	× 2
Total	31.80 lire

In the hope that you will extricate me from this dilemma, I am yours sincerely,

BERTANI

In reply Verdi wrote to his publisher that 'in order to save this scion of his family from the spectres that pursue him' he would be glad to pay the little bill. But he deducted four lire for the two dinners: 'He could perfectly well have eaten at home.' He also asked for a receipt and a promise that this young man would never again hear any of his new operas, 'so that he won't expose himself again to the danger of being pursued by spectres, and that he may spare me further travelling expenses!'

George R. Marek, *A Front Seat at the Opera*, Harrap, 1951, pp. 54-5

Verdi, in a letter of 14 July 1875 to his friend Opprandino Arrivabene, inveighs against his fellow composers' addiction to schools and groups:

Some want to be melodists like Bellini, some harmonists like Meyerbeer. I don't want to be one or the other, and I want the younger composers of today not to think about being melodists, harmonists, realists, idealists, futurists or any of these other devilish pedantries. Melody and harmony should only be tools for music-making in the hands of the artist; and, if ever the day comes in which people no longer talk of melody, harmony, German and Italian schools, the past, the future, etc., etc., then perhaps the kingdom of art will begin. Another evil of our time is that all the works of these young composers are born out of *fear*. No one writes by instinct. When these youngsters compose, the thought that predominates in their minds is how not to annoy the public, or how to get into the critics' good books.

You tell me that I owe my success to the fusion of the two schools. *I never thought about it.*

Giuseppe Verdi, *Letters*, translated by Charles Osborne, Gollancz, 1971,
pp. 196-7

In 1884 Giuseppe Giacosa published an account of a conversation with Verdi in the Gazzetta Musicale di Milano:

I remember how a few days after the first performance of *Otello*, certain of Verdi's words had filled my soul with a profound sadness – we were speaking, of course, of the opera and its triumph. At one point the Maestro, who had already grown pensive during the discussion, said: 'How painful to have finished it! I shall now suffer such loneliness. Till now I used to wake each morning and return to the love, anger, jealousy, deceit of my characters. And I would say to myself: today I have this scene to compose, and if it did not progress according to my wishes, I would arm myself for the struggle, confident of victory. And then, when the opera was finished, there were the rehearsals, the uncertainties, the task of explaining my thoughts clearly to the actors, to make them move on stage as I wished; and then the new ideas for the staging, that I was forever thinking up in the name of representational realism . . . and I would arrive home, still excited by the glorious life of the theatre, happy at the goals I had reached, thinking about those I intended reaching tomorrow, and I was not conscious of fatigue and I did not feel my age. But now? Since *Otello* now belongs to the public, it has ceased to be mine, it has become totally detached from me; and the place that it occupied within me was so great, that I now feel an enormous void, which I think I shall never be able to fill.'

Translated by Richard Stokes and reprinted in Marcello Conati, ed., *Interviews and Encounters with Verdi*, Gollancz, 1984, pp. 160–61

Pietro Mascagni, the composer of Cavalleria rusticana*, set down his memories of Verdi in a Milanese periodical,* La Lettura*, in January 1931:*

You must understand what it meant for a composer to be introduced to Verdi. As soon as he saw me, he shook my hand most warmly. He was not, as a rule, expansive, but rather a man of few words. His eyes made a profound impression. One did not see them immediately, they were so deeply set between his thick eyebrows, but you *felt* them at once: penetrating, bright, inquiring. They were the sort of eyes that read everything in our hearts, even those things we wished to keep secret. He spoke slowly, pensively, savouring his words. He never talked randomly or sententiously or over-excitedly . . .

One day he seemed even more confidential and affectionate, and wished to know which subjects I had in mind for future operas; without giving me time to reply, he told me that he knew I was considering *King Lear*. 'If that is true,' he continued, 'I can tell you that I possess a vast amount of material on that monumental subject, which I would be delighted to give you to make a heavy task lighter.'

I was seized with acute emotion, finding myself before that great man who was confiding to me such portentous things with sublime simplicity. The lump in my throat prevented me from speaking, but with a great effort and trembling voice I managed to stammer a question that came from my heart: 'Maestro, why have you not composed *King Lear*? . . .'

Verdi closed his eyes for several seconds, perhaps to remember, perhaps to forget. Softly and slowly he then replied: 'The scene when Lear is alone on the heath terrified me!' . . .

After the first performances of *Cavalleria rusticana*, a legend grew up which was believed both in Italy and abroad. It was said that Verdi, having read my opera, exclaimed, 'Now I can die content!' Verdi never uttered these words, which were certainly invented by the fertile imagination of some enthusiast, who was imperfectly acquainted with an affectionate episode. And to put the record straight, I wish to recall that episode, even at the cost of appearing immodest . . .

One evening at Sant'Agata [Verdi's home], Boito, Ricordi, Gallignani and Tebaldini were guests of Verdi. At a certain hour – which was always the same, for Verdi was orderly and precise in all he did – he rose to go to his room. He was going to bed . . . A little time had passed and Verdi should by now have retired to rest, when the guests suddenly heard some chords. Was the Maestro composing? . . . A few bars sufficed for them to understand that he was at the piano, reading the score of *Cavalleria rusticana*, which Giulio Ricordi had sent him at his own request.

'The next morning,' it is Giulio Ricordi speaking, 'I found the

Maestro sitting as usual in the grounds of his villa beneath the great trees in the silence of that verdure, which only for him possessed such divine and fruitful eloquence. We exchanged a few words; then, re-entering his bedroom and pointing to the score of *Cavalleria*, he said:

'"But it's not true that the tradition of Italian melody is dead!"'

This was the way Verdi praised my opera; and no praise, no homage could ever have been more dear to me.

Translated by Richard Stokes and reprinted in Marcello Conati, ed.,
Interviews and Encounters with Verdi, Gollancz, 1984, pp. 313–15

Verdi and his librettist Arrigo Boito corresponded in July 1889 about the as yet unwritten Falstaff:

Verdi: In outlining *Falstaff* did you never think of the enormous number of my years?

I know you will reply exaggerating the state of my health, which is good, excellent, robust . . . so be it, but in spite of that you must agree I could be accused of great foolhardiness in taking on so much! Supposing I couldn't stand the strain? And failed to finish it? You would then have wasted your time and trouble to no purpose! And I wouldn't wish that for all the gold in the world. The idea is intolerable to me, and all the more so if by writing *Falstaff* you had to, I won't say abandon, but distract your attention from *Nerone* or delay its production. I should be blamed for this delay and thunderbolts of ill will would fall about my head!

How are we to overcome these obstacles? Have you a sound argument to oppose to mine? I hope so, but I don't believe it . . . Still, let's think it over (and take care to do nothing that would harm your career), and if you can find me one, and I can find some way of casting off ten years or so . . . then what joy to be able to say to the public: 'Here we are again! Roll up!' . . .

Boito: The fact is that I never think of your age either when I'm talking to you or when I'm writing to you or when I'm working for you.

The fault is yours.

I know that *Otello* is little more than two years old, and that even as I am writing to you it is being appreciated as it should be by Shakespeare's compatriots. But there is a stronger argument than that of age, and it's this: it's been said of you after *Otello*: 'It's impossible to finish better.' This is a great truth and it enshrines a great and very rare tribute. It is the only weighty argument.

Weighty for the present generation, but not for history, which aims first and foremost to judge men by their essential merits. Nevertheless it is indeed rare to see a lifetime of artistic endeavour conclude with a world triumph. *Otello* is such a triumph. All the other arguments – age, strength, hard work for me, hard work for you, etc., etc. – are not valid and place no obstacle in the way of a new work. Since you oblige me to talk about myself I shall say that notwithstanding the commitment I should be taking on with *Falstaff* I shall be able to finish my work within the term promised. I'm sure of it.

I don't think that writing a comedy should tire you out. A tragedy causes its author *genuinely to suffer*; one's thoughts undergo a suggestion of sadness which renders the nerves morbidly sensitive. The jokes and laughter of comedy exhilarate mind and body . . .

All your life you've wanted a good subject for a comic opera, and that is a sign that the vein of an art that is both joyous and noble is virtually in existence in your brain; instinct is a wise counsellor. There's only one way to finish better than with *Otello* and that's to finish triumphantly with *Falstaff*.

After having sounded all the shrieks and groans of the human heart, to finish with a mighty burst of laughter – that is to astonish the world.

So you see, dear Maestro, it's worth thinking about the subject I've sketched; see whether you can feel in it the germ of the new masterpiece. If the germ is there, the miracle is accomplished. Meanwhile let us promise to maintain the most scrupulous secrecy. I've told nobody about it. If we can work in secret we can work in peace . . .

Verdi: Amen, so be it!

We'll write this *Falstaff* then. We won't think for the moment of obstacles or age or illness!

Quoted in Julian Budden, *The Operas of Verdi*, Cassell, 1981, pp. 422–4

The gossamer quality of Falstaff *stems from Boito's impeccable libretto as well as from Verdi's wonderfully deft music. Boito wrote:*

During the first few days I was in despair. To sketch the characters in a few strokes, to weave the plot, to extract all the juice from that enormous Shakespearian orange, without letting the useless pips slip into the little glass, to write with colour and clarity and brevity, to delineate the musical plan of the scene, so that there results an organic unity that is a *piece of music* and yet is not, to make the joyous comedy live from beginning to end, to make it live with a natural and communicative gaiety, is difficult, difficult, difficult; and yet must seem simple, simple, simple.

Quoted in Frank Walker, *The Man Verdi*, Dent, 1962, p. 497

The Irish composer Charles Villiers Stanford was invited by Boito to attend the 1893 première of Falstaff:

The Scala Theatre was a wonderful sight, crammed to the roof with an audience gathered from the four corners of the earth. The excitement was so tense that the least little point of danger set everyone on edge. So keen were the listeners for the success of the old hero, that they resented a single lapse from perfection. The performance had not started for two minutes before Maurel produced a high note in a way which displeased the stalls. In an instant they all shouted out '*Basta! Basta! Basta!*' in most angry tones. I thought the next thing would be a rapid descent of the curtain, but Maurel paid no attention and went ahead. A few bars farther on he sang the same note with the right effect. 'Ah! Ah! Ah!' said the stalls, equally loudly, with the unmistakable suggestion in their voices that he had better go on in the same style or it would be the worse for him. It was not ill nature, obviously; the interruption sprang from pure and simple eagerness that everyone should do his level best; and it was the first and last hostile outburst of the evening. The number of times which Verdi had to appear were impossible to count, but on each entry he preserved the same dignified demeanour; he might have been a king receiving his subjects at a levee. There was no suspicion of arrogance, no suggestion of false modesty. He knew that his audience understood him and he acknowledged their tribute with the grace and nobility of a born leader of men.

C.V. Stanford, *Pages from an Unwritten Diary*, Edward Arnold, 1914,
pp. 281–2

Walter Slezak gleefully tells about a performance of Otello *his father Leo gave in Houston:*

The programme not only told the story of the opera, but managed to sell space for advertising as well. This is the way it read:

'OTHELLO'
Opera In Four Acts

by Giuseppe Verdi

Act I

The people of Cypria, on their knees, are praying for the safety of Othello, whose ship is fighting the elements. The danger passes. Othello arrives and greets the people with the words:

USE CRISCO, THE BEST SHORTENING

'Rejoice! The Turk is vanquished and drowned in the sea.' The people hail Othello.

CRISCO IS UNSURPASSED

Iago, jealous of Cassio, who enjoys Othello's confidence, tries to render Cassio drunk. A drinking song

CRISCO HAS NO RIVAL

is heard and Cassio, by now quite drunk, attacks Montano. Othello rushes in and calls out:

CRISCO IS ECONOMICAL

'Down with your swords!' Cassio is being demoted. Desdemona, Othello's lovely bride appears in the doorway to the castle. Othello takes her hand and they sing a lovely duet

CRISCO USERS ARE SATISFIED

which belongs to the best Verdi wrote, and is considered one of the pearls of operatic music.

Thus ends the first act and thus Crisco seeps through all four acts until in the end:

After Othello has strangled Desdemona, he plunges his dagger into his breast and, dying, he sings the touching phrase:

ASK ONLY FOR CRISCO,
THE FAMOUS SHORTENING

'Kiss me, kiss me again!' He dies. End of the opera.

Walter Slezak, *What Time's the Next Swan?*, Doubleday, 1962, pp. 33–4

Claude Debussy writes with Gallic loftiness about a revival of La traviata *at the Opéra-Comique:*

Has anybody noticed their strange need to borrow French subjects that have already enjoyed a triumph? Take, for example, Verdi, who adapted *La Dame aux camélias*. And, closer to our own time, MM. Puccini and Leoncavallo are both composing operas based on *La Vie de Bohème*. It is not up to me to pass judgement on the literary merit of these two works, but they do represent a particular period of sentimentality in France, and could well benefit from being embellished with music. Verdi is at least straightforward, going from romances to cavatinas, an agreeable enough journey, in which one encounters, here and there, genuine passion. It never aspires to profundity; it's all just a facade, and despite the sadness of the plots, the sun always keeps shining. The aesthetics of such an art are certainly false, since you can't translate real life into songs; but Verdi is at least heroic in the attempt, depicting a life more beautiful than the 'realism' attempted by the younger Italian school. Puccini and Leoncavallo have pretensions to be students of character, and to a kind of crude psychology that in truth goes no deeper than simple storytelling.

Claude Debussy, article in *Gil Blas*, 16 February 1903, translated by
Stephen Brook

In a letter written on Easter Day 1901 to Camille Bellaigue, Arrigo Boito, Verdi's greatest librettist, paid tribute to the dead composer:

Verdi is dead; he has carried away with him an enormous measure of light and vital warmth. We had all basked in the sunshine of that Olympian old age.

He died magnificently, like a fighter, formidable and mute. The silence of death had fallen over him a week before he died . . .

His resistance was heroic. The breathing of his great chest sustained him for four days and three nights. On the fourth night the sound of his breathing still filled the room, but the fatigue . . . Poor Maestro, how brave and handsome he was, up to the last moment! No matter; the old reaper went off with his scythe well battered.

My dear friend, in the course of my life I have lost those I have idolized, and grief has outlasted resignation. But never have I experienced such a feeling of hatred against death, of contempt for that mysterious, blind, stupid, triumphant and craven power. It needed the death of this octogenarian to arouse those feelings in me.

He too hated it, for he was the most powerful expression of life that it is possible to imagine. He hated it as he hated laziness, enigmas and doubt.

Now all is over. He sleeps like a King of Spain in his Escorial, under a bronze slab that completely covers him.

Quoted in Frank Walker, *The Man Verdi*, Dent, 1962, p. 509

21: Puccini

Tosca, that shabby little shocker . . .

Joseph Kerman, *Opera as Drama*, p. 254

The Italian critic Carlo Bersezio reviewed the première of Puccini's La Bohème *in 1896:*

La Bohème, even as it leaves little impression on the minds of the audience, will leave no great trace upon the history of our lyric theatre, and it will be well if the composer will return to the straight road of art, persuading himself that this has been a brief deviation.

Quoted in G.M. Puccini, *Letters of Giacomo Puccini*, Harrap, 1931,
pp. 82–3

Madama Butterfly *received an even more dismal reception in 1904, as recalled by the director of La Scala:*

The cast was ideal. It had in the principal roles Rosina Storchio, Giovanni Zenatello and Giuseppe De Luca. Moreover, everyone else at the Scala, without exception, displayed an activity, zeal and enthusiasm that were out of the common. Therefore, the execution and the production in general were really excellent.

But certain extravagances desired by the authors and publishers, some truly without precedent, created an unfriendly atmosphere for *Madama Butterfly*. For example, the artists were obliged to study their roles only in the opera house, not being allowed to take home the score even once; no one was permitted to remain in the auditorium during rehearsal except the composer and the librettists, so that even I often abstained from attending, and when I did attend, I heard various rehearsals from a box; and finally, the press was not allowed to attend the dress rehearsal, whereas for other new operas it had been invited. These things, I say, did not help.

The opera, moreover, had long passages that were really long. It was in two acts, the second one being particularly lengthy, and not in three acts as it was later recast . . .

The first act was coldly received but with few open antagonisms. At the end there were two lean calls in which even poor Puccini participated. I can still see him leaning on a cane, because he was not quite recovered from a serious automobile accident, with a long and dolorous face, expressing, more than anything else, surprise at so unexpected a welcome.

In the second act there was warm applause for the duet between Butterfly and the Consul as well as for the duet of the flowers. But all the rest was a disaster. The public laughed, interrupted, shouted and catcalled, without the slightest consideration.

Campanini and the interpreters did not allow themselves to be disturbed by all this uproarious opposition. They defied it intrepidly to the very end, each one performing his own part perfectly. But the conclusion of the performance was even worse than the demonstration; an absolutely glacial silence! Not one iota of applause! . . .

Duke Visconti, after the first moment of painful stupor, called a meeting of the board, the direction, the authors and the publishers. The publishers declared in the name of the authors that they were withdrawing the opera immediately, and that they would refund on the next morning the fee that had been paid for the rights for the entire season . . .

The next morning the press was ferocious. I do not recall, in all my experience, having read anything to match it . . .

How sad and painful was the visit I paid Puccini the evening after the performance! Puccini lived in the immediate vicinity of the Scala, in one of the first houses of the Via Giuseppe Verdi. He was in his studio, the room being almost entirely dark. His hands

were running over the keyboard of a piano. Seeing me enter, he
greeted me with a wave of the hand. I saw that he was very upset,
that his eyes were full of tears. He sat there without saying a word
for some minutes, then, pulling himself together, he said to me:

'See here, Gatti, does it really seem to you that this poor
Butterfly was such an ugly thing and so ill conceived? We are old
friends. I am certain that I can call on your sincerity to tell me
what you think about it.'

'Look here, maestro,' I answered. 'The opera has some lengthy
passages. It ought not to be in two acts but in three. There are
some reminiscences of *La Bohème* that are too obvious. But I
absolutely do not believe that what happened last night will be the
final judgement. When you have made the changes I have mentioned the opera will certainly have the force to continue to live. I
believe in its future' . . .

As is known, the opera was divided into three acts, some cuts
were made, some additions and some changes, and a few months
later *Madama Butterfly* gained two contemporaneous successes. It
was directed by Campanini in Brescia and by Toscanini in Buenos
Aires. These were two full and unquestionable successes, and in
this manner began the triumphal march of the opera, which
extended through the entire world.

Giulio Gatti-Casazza, *Memories of the Opera*, Calder, 1977, pp. 132–7

*The première was further enlivened by the fact that Toscanini (who was
feuding at that time with La Scala) was having an affair with Rosina
Storchio:*

Shortly before the opening Puccini had told Toscanini that he
wanted his opinion of the score. They met at Storchio's and the
composer played a few carefully chosen excerpts at the piano.
Toscanini then asked to look at the score. He felt immediately that
the two-act format was a grave error: both acts were too long,
particularly the second. 'I thought at once, this length is impossible,' he said years later. 'For Wagner, yes! For Puccini, no!'

Knowing what effect his negative judgement could have on morale
at that late stage, he simply complimented what he felt were the
strong points of the score and gave Puccini his best wishes. As
much as he might have wanted to attend the première, he refused
to enter La Scala. He may have expected a lukewarm reception for
the opera; but he could not have anticipated the catastrophic fiasco
that in fact took place. One can only imagine his feelings on
learning that at one point, when a breeze on stage had made
Storchio's kimono billow out, someone in the audience had
shouted: '*È incinta!* [She's pregnant!] *Il bambino di Toscanini!*' By
the time the performance had ended to the accompaniment of
catcalls and whistles from the gallery, Puccini was crushed and
Storchio hysterical.

Harvey Sachs, *Toscanini*, Weidenfeld & Nicolson, 1978, p. 86

Puccini ambushed by a wily music critic:

Puccini tells of a performance in Milan, when he sat in the
audience next to a pretty girl. By this time *Tosca* was a complete
success. The audience was enthusiastic, the applause frantic. The
young lady became extremely annoyed because Puccini did not
clap or shout.

'Why don't you applaud this masterpiece?' she said.

'Masterpiece?' replied Puccini, and laughed sarcastically.

'Don't you like this music?' she asked in amazement.

'No,' said he, 'it is the work of an amateur.'

'You know nothing of music, or you wouldn't talk like that.'

'Yes, I do know music,' said Puccini, and proceeded to prove to
her according to the laws of harmony and counterpoint how poor
a work *Tosca* really was. He told her this aria suggested Verdi and
that chorus was stolen from Bizet. When he had finished the
young lady said, 'Is that your real opinion, your sincere
conviction?'

'Absolutely,' he said.

'Very well,' she said with a little laugh, and left him. At

breakfast the next morning, when Puccini picked up the newspaper, he saw a headline, 'Puccini on *Tosca*.' There he read word for word his remarks of the night before. The pretty young lady had been a music critic, had known all along with whom she was sitting in the theatre, and all the time Puccini had thought he was duping her, she had been fooling him.

George R. Marek, *A Front Seat at the Opera*, Harrap, 1951, pp. 86–7

Problems with the libretto and with his health hampered Puccini's work on Turandot. *In 1921 he wrote to Giuseppe Adami, one of the librettists:*

Turandot gives me no peace. I think of it continually, and I think that perhaps we are on the wrong track in Act II. I think that the duet is the kernel of the whole act. And the duet in its present form doesn't seem to me to be what is wanted. Therefore I should like to suggest a remedy. In the duet I think that we can work up to a high pitch of emotion. And to do so I think that Calaf must *kiss* Turandot and reveal to the icy Princess how great is his love. After he has kissed her, with a kiss of some – long – seconds, he must say, 'Nothing matters now. I am ready even to die,' and he whispers his name to her lips. Here you could have a scene which should be the pendant to the grisly opening of the act with its 'Let no one sleep in Pekin'. The masks and perhaps the officials and slaves who were lurking behind have heard the name and shout it out. The shout is repeated and passed on, and Turandot is compromised. Then in the third act when everything is ready, with executioner, etc., as in Act I, she says (to the surprise of everyone), 'His name I do not know.' In short, I think that this duet enriches the subject considerably and raises it to an emotional interest which we have not now attained. What do you think of it? . . .

My life is a torture because I fail to see in this opera all the throbbing life and power which are necessary in a work for the theatre if it is to endure and hold.

G.M. Puccini, *Letters of Giacomo Puccini*, Harrap, 1931, pp. 280–81

Joseph Kerman has nothing good to say about Puccini. Here he is on
Turandot:

Nobody would deny that dramatic potential can be found in this
tale. Puccini, however, did not find it; his music does nothing to
rationalize the legend or illuminate the characters; it is consistently,
throughout, of café-music banality. There is simply no insight into
any emotions that might possibly be imagined in any of the
situations, to say nothing of an imaginative binding conception.
Thus the action shows Calaf's lust for Turandot increase as she
grows more desperate; but his music is Puccini's eternal mawkish
serenade, and his vitality is exhausted in chinoiserie. Liù's soft
affection for Calaf, though prettily done, is altogether incommen-
surate with her gratuitous sacrifice. The three half-humorous coun-
cillors are gratuitous too, as is the Chinese chorus, for all its
unusually large part; the 'Hymn to the Moon' has as little to do
with the action as the '*Miserere*' in *Il trovatore*. Most damaging of
all, Turandot's surrender has no motivation, except the obvious
physical one, which Alfano dutifully wrote into the music, and
which decorous opera directors ignore. Considering the size of his
role, Timur (the father) is one of the weakest people in the whole
operatic repertory as far as musical definition is concerned. He is
of no real dramatic use, and we can hardly blame Calaf for
forgetting all about him at the end.

The inescapable central message of the piece, then, is that the
way to proceed with a frigid beauty is to get your hands on her.
Then she will shout 'love', in which sentiment you naturally share,
even though previously she has shown her hand by murderous
treachery towards you and by destroying the one half-appealing
character in the play. The outlines of the story, and even these
void characters, could have made a certain sense in the verismo
setting of *Il tabarro*. Then we might at least have been spared the
claim that the drama illustrates 'love'. But in China, as Puccini's
music portrays China, every gland has been torn from the tale.
There is no organic reason for the bogus orientalism lacquered
over every page of the score; the tremendous apparatus provides

exoticism for its own sake, but also, more deeply, a chance for the artist to wriggle out of his irresponsibility. Puccini must have been afraid of this story. But in the mysterious, exciting, cruel, inscrutable world of Chinese myth anything can be excused, and shades of meaning can drift aimlessly from one pentatonic tune to the next, and from one sentimental phrase to its almost inevitable repetition. Rarely has myth been so emptily employed as in this extravaganza. Genuine drama is entirely out of the question.

Joseph Kerman, *Opera as Drama*, Vintage, 1956, pp. 255–6

But Ernest Newman gave a more balanced assessment in 1918:

No artist, of course, ever achieves such popularity, and such enduring popularity, among art lovers of all kinds without there being excellent reasons for it. Puccini's genius is a very limited one, but he has always made the very most of it. His operas are to some extent a mere bundle of tricks: but no one else has ever performed the same tricks nearly so well.

The failure of *The Girl of the Golden West* is largely due to the fact that there he aimed at making the general tissue of the music more organic throughout, instead of relying upon his power to bluff us through the less vital portions of the work by means of those delightful irrelevant little orchestral garrulities that in *Manon* and *La Bohème* keep us too constantly and too agreeably interested for us to have either the time or the inclination to be critical. Puccini's music has none of the philosophical pity of *Parsifal* nor of the wistful pity of *Pelleas and Melisande*, but for blubbering, whimpering pity there is no music to compare with it. We weep with his little people because there is nothing so infectious as tears – even the tears of weak self-pity.

Ernest Newman, *Testament of Music*, Putnam, 1962, pp. 286–7

22: Richard Strauss

For Strauss, opera's destination was the museum.

Peter Conrad, A Song of Love and Death, p. 215

Sir Thomas Beecham recalls the British première of Elektra*:*

As all know who are acquainted with the work, there is a modest procession of sacrificial victims, a few sheep generally, to prelude the first entrance of Clytemnestra. But from the accounts in some journals one would have thought that half the inhabitants of the Zoo were being rehearsed to take their part in the show. One day I received a letter from a farmer living about one hundred miles from London whose imagination had been fired by reading of these marvels, and under the impression that I was seeking voluntary contributions to my production in the way of livestock, he had arranged for the transportation to London of a fine young bull, which he claimed to be mild in disposition and seemly in behaviour. As the animal had already started on his journey there was nothing to be done but wait for his arrival, have him photographed for the satisfaction of his former owner, and as we could not employ him in the service of art, put him to the next best purpose . . .

An audience of today would not find it easy to realize how strange and bewildering the score of *Elektra* sounded to the public of 1910. About the middle of the work there is a short scene where two men — messengers — rush excitedly on the stage and after singing a few phrases disappear. At one of our later performances this episode occurred in the usual way and the opera went on. About five minutes later the same performers entered again, and without regard to what was happening at the moment in a scene of totally different character went through their parts and vanished exactly as before. I pinched myself to make sure I was not dreaming and, bending down to Albert Sammons, who was leading, asked: 'Have those two fellows been on already?'

'Yes,' he replied.

'Are you certain?'

I put the same question to the leader of the second violins, and he was equally convinced that we had been treated to an unsolicited and highly original form of encore. At the close I went on the stage to discover the cause of this novel addition to the normal attractions of an operatic evening, and found the culprits in the company of the chorus master, all three of them looking very ill at ease.

'Am I right in assuming that you took upon yourselves to repeat your scene this evening?' I asked frigidly.

'I am afraid you are,' replied one of them.

'What is the explanation of this twice-nightly experiment?'

This question was answered by the chorus master, who explained that a part of his duty was to take the cue for the sending on of the two singers from a passage in the orchestra. On this occasion his attention had been distracted by the disagreeable task of forcibly expelling a rude and refractory chorister through the stage door into the street. This being successfully accomplished, he returned to his post aglow with victory, and presently there came along something that to his flushed ear resembled the familiar phrase which was his lighthouse in the polyphonic sea of whirling sound.

'Now you go on,' he called out to the singers.

'But we have been on,' they answered.

'Then it was at the wrong place – you must go on again'; and as they seemed unreasonably hesitant he literally pushed them on to the scene.

I was relieved to find that a more agreeable manifestation of human weakness than artistic vanity was at the bottom of the mystery, and I discharged the offenders with a caution and a reminder that there was quite enough rough and tumble going on

in the band without the actors joining in. As I never heard a
comment or received a protest from any member of the audience I
concluded that this curious variation from the orderly course of
performance had either passed unnoticed or had proved to their
liking.

Sir Thomas Beecham, *A Mingled Chime*, Hutchinson, 1944, pp. 90–92

The British première of Elektra *provoked controversy between two giants
of operatic criticism, G.B. Shaw and Ernest Newman:*

Newman [26 February]: The real complaint against the excited
music in *Elektra* is that it mostly does not excite you at all; you are
rather sorry, in fact, that the composer should take so much
trouble to be a failure. For he is so violent that, as a rule, you
cannot believe in the least in his violence. He has the besetting
Teutonic sin of overstatement, of being unable to see that the half
is often greater than the whole . . .

Nor do we need to wait for posterity to tell us that much of the
music is as abominably ugly as it is noisy. Here a good deal of the
talk about complexity is wide of the mark. The real term for it is
incoherence, discontinuity of thinking . . .

The result of it all is to give far more pain to Strauss's admirers
than it can possibly do to those who have always disliked him. In
spite of the pathetic way in which he wastes himself, playing now
the fool, now the swashbuckler, now the trickster, you cannot be
in doubt that you are listening to a man who is head and shoulders
above all other living composers. One still clings to the hope that
the future has in store for us a purified Strauss, clothed and in his
right mind, who will help us to forget the present Strauss – a
saddening mixture of genius, ranter, child, and charlatan. As it is,
one would hardly venture to prophesy more than a few short years
of life for *Elektra*, for the public will not long continue to spend
an hour and three-quarters in the theatre for about half an hour's
enjoyment.

*

Shaw [12 March]: May I, as an old critic of music, and as a
member of the public who has not yet heard *Elektra*, make an
appeal to Mr Ernest Newman to give us something about that
work a little less ridiculous and idiotic than his article in your last
issue? I am sorry to use such disparaging and apparently uncivil
epithets as 'ridiculous and idiotic'; but what else am I to call an
article which informs us, first, that Strauss does not know the
difference between music and 'abominable ugliness and noise';
and, second, that he is the greatest living musician of the greatest
school of music the world has produced? . . .

There is no reason why Mr Newman should not say with all
possible emphasis – if he is unlucky enough to be able to say truly
– that he finds Strauss's music disagreeable and cacophonous; that
he is unable to follow its harmonic syntax; that the composer's
mannerisms worry him; and that, for his taste, there is too much
restless detail, and that the music is over-scored (too many notes,
as the Emperor said to Mozart). He may, if he likes, go on to
denounce the attractiveness of Strauss's music as a public danger,
like the attraction of morphia; and to diagnose the cases of Strauss
and Hofmannsthal as psychopathic or neurasthenic, or whatever
the appropriate scientific slang may be, and descant generally on
the degeneracy of the age . . . Such diagnoses, when supported by
an appeal to the symptoms made with real critical power and
ingenuity, might be interesting and worth discussing. But this lazy
petulance which has disgraced English journalism in the forms
of anti-Wagnerism, anti-Ibsenism, and, long before that, anti-
Handelism . . .; this infatuated attempt of writers of modest local
standing to talk *de haut en bas* to men of European reputation, and
to dismiss them as intrusive lunatics, is an intolerable thing, an
exploded thing, a foolish thing, a parochial boorish thing, a thing
that should be dropped by all good critics and discouraged by all
good editors as bad form, bad manners, bad sense, bad journalism,
bad politics, and bad religion . . . I can stand almost anything from
Mr Newman except his posing as Strauss's governess.

Newman [12 March]: I shall be happy to discuss *Elektra* with Mr

Shaw when he knows something about it; and to discuss the general problem of aesthetic judgement with him when he shows some appreciation of the real difficulties of it. For a man who is always at such pains to inform the world that he is cleverer than most people, he really talks very foolishly – if I may be permitted to copy his own style of adverb. It is wrong for me to object to some of Strauss's music, even after careful study of it; but it is quite right of Mr Shaw to say I am wrong, while confessing that he himself has not heard *Elektra*! But Mr Shaw's logic was always peculiar.

G.B. Shaw, correspondence with Ernest Newman in *The Nation* from
February to April 1910, in *Shaw's Music*, Bodley Head, 1989, III,
pp. 597–605

In the same year Beecham wanted to mount Salome. *When the censors refused to license the performance, Beecham raised the matter with Asquith, the prime minister:*

I explained to him the nature of the *contretemps* over *Salome*. Strauss was the most famous and in common opinion the greatest of living composers, this was his most popular work; it was to be played for the first time to a few thousand enthusiasts who wanted to hear it; it did not concern, so far as I could see, those that did not want to hear it; being given in German, it would be comprehended by few; and lastly, I could not envisage the moral foundation of the Empire endangered by a handful of operatic performances. Would it not be more judicious to give the piece a chance? Otherwise we might run the risk of making ourselves slightly ridiculous in the eyes of the rest of the world by taking an exceptional attitude towards a celebrated work of art, as we had done so often in the past before the advent to power of the present enlightened government. The prime minister, more impressed, I think, by this last argument than the others, promised to speak to the lord chamberlain . . .

Some weeks after my conversation with the prime minister . . . I received an invitation to present myself at St James's Palace, where I was received by the lord chamberlain and his second in command, Sir Douglas Dawson. These gentlemen informed me that their refusal to grant a licence was due in no way to personal prejudice, but to the huge volume of letters they had received from every corner of the country protesting against the appearance on the stage of a sacred character, St John the Baptist. I at once pointed out that *Samson et Delilah* had been given now for many years in London although it laboured under a similar disadvantage; but the lord chamberlain, who had undoubtedly been waiting for this obvious rejoinder, caught me up quickly with, 'There is a difference – a very great difference; in one case it is the Old Testament and in the other the New.'

Here followed a lengthy dissertation on this important distinction, punctuated by a wealth of doctrinal example of which I, although severely brought up in the bosom of the Church of England, had hitherto been ignorant . . .

'But we think we have found a way out,' he interpolated. 'There is no doubt that there are many people who want to see this work, and it is the view of the prime minister that subject to the proper safeguards we should do everything we can to enable you to give it. Now if you will consent to certain modifications of the text likely to disarm the scruples of the devout it would help us to reconsider our decision' . . . We arranged for an early conference at which *Salome* would be trimmed so as to make it palatable to the taste of that large army of objectors who would never see it.

The first thing we did was to eliminate the name of John, who was to be called simply The Prophet; and having invested him with this desirable anonymity, we went on to deprive every passage between him and Salome of the slightest force or meaning. The mundane and commonplace passion of the precocious princess was refined into a desire on her part for spiritual guidance . . .

I handed over the strange document to my friend Alfred Kalisch, who was to make an equivalently innocuous German version and send it along to the singers for study. I was neither surprised nor disappointed when there poured in one by one the liveliest com-

munications from the unhappy creatures, who were asked to sing
to some of the most vivid and dramatic music ever written words
which not only had no discoverable association with it but were
utterly devoid of any dramatic significance, the chief complainant
being the leading lady, who did not see how it could be done at
all. But I fixed an adamantine front, and, resolutely declining to
discuss the matter with them for one moment, declared that
everything must go through exactly as prescribed. England was
not Germany, they should understand, but a country that took a
pride in doing things in its own particular way, especially where
the arts were involved . . .

In course of time the singers arrived, but rehearsals had hardly
begun when a mild bombshell was exploded among us by St
James's Palace, which had just remembered that the decapitated
head of John had to be handed to Salome on the stage, and that
she was to sing to it in full view of the audience for about twenty
minutes. This would never do . . . Some substitute must be found
for the offending member. We all went into close conclave, and it
was settled that Salome be given a blood-stained sword. But this
time it was the prima donna who put her foot down, objecting
that the gruesome weapon would ruin her beautiful gown and
flatly refusing to handle it at all. Despairingly I again made
representations to headquarters and once more the official mind
travailed and brought forth. The best and final concession we
could obtain was that Salome should have a large platter completely
covered with a cloth.

Sir Thomas Beecham, A Mingled Chime, Hutchinson, 1944,

pp. 97–9, 102–4

Elisabeth Söderström recalls some unusual performances of Der
Rosenkavalier:

In a recent production of *Rosenkavalier* in Stockholm, I was
singing the part of the Marschallin. During the first act, my
Octavian lost her voice completely. In the interval, the opera

management tried desperately but unsuccessfully to find our second Octavian. 'We'll have to send the audience home . . .' they said. I was shocked at the thought, for I knew how people had been queuing for tickets, and I also knew that if one act had been played, people did not get their money back. 'You can't do that to my audience. Get me a costume. I'll sing the second act, and please keep trying to find another Octavian.'

It was only when I was standing in the wings, the silver rose in my hand, that it flashed through my mind: 'God, it must be eleven years since I sang this part . . .' Then I walked on to the stage, automatically singing and acting, and when there was something in the part I had forgotten, I just turned upstage or kept my mouth shut! My colleagues helped me enormously and the enthusiasm of the audience, who loved what was happening, created an electric atmosphere. I enjoyed myself tremendously and did not for one second find it difficult.

When I came off after the second act, I was told that Kerstin Meyer had come to help us, in spite of the fact that she had not sung Octavian for three years. So in the third act, I returned to the part of the Marschallin. When the curtain came down that evening, it sounded just like the crowd in a sports stadium . . .

I remember with horror the first time I ever played Sophie in *Der Rosenkavalier*, at the Metropolitan Opera in New York . . . The dress I was to wear was of heavy silk, a splendid crinoline, which I am sure looked very romantic from the auditorium, but which weighed at least twenty pounds. As if in a dream, I heard the overture to the second act, the curtain went up to reveal for the first time Sophie-Elisabeth, who took a deep breath and tried to produce a teenage girl's trembling excitement in face of Rosenkavalier's arrival. It went quite well and my voice obeyed me.

You may think what you like about Strauss's music, but he is undeniably one of the very few composers who really can build up an entrance. The festive fanfare-like chords that bring Octavian on to the stage always send shivers of delight down my spine whenever I hear them. It was the same this time, too, as I, as Sophie for the time being, sank into a low curtsey.

My dress was of strong airtight material, and the crinoline acted just like a suction-cup. As I curtseyed, the air was pressed out and fifty beats later, when I tried to rise to my feet, the weight of the dress was unexpectedly great, my calf muscles locked themselves into cramp and I simply could not get up. My leg hurt, my head felt quite numbed, and somewhere in the distance I could hear music that I vaguely recognized, but my whole being was filled with one single thought: 'I must get up.' Every effort was in vain, and in the end, with my Octavian staring in confusion at this peculiar Sophie, who received the rose sitting on the floor, I hissed between my teeth: 'Help!', smelt the rose in my hand and repeated: 'Help!'

Not until the whole enchanting scene of the handing over of the rose and the duet that follows were over, did the others round me realize that there was something wrong with Sophie. Who knows ... Scandinavian singers have a style of their own in opera, haven't they, and as we had had no proper rehearsals, how could they know that this was not the way I had thought of playing the scene?

Octavian and Marianne helped me to my feet again, the cramp loosened and the rest of the opera continued normally. My first question when the curtain went down was of course: 'Did I sing?', and I was very relieved when they replied: 'Sure, your phrases came where they should, which was why we thought you wanted to sit on the floor.'

Elisabeth Söderström, *In My Own Key*, translated by Joan Tate, Hamish Hamilton, 1979, pp. 52–3, 67–9

ON STAGE

23: Opera Directors

It is the peculiar misfortune of the operatic composer that what he has to say in his work cannot be communicated to the world without the cooperation, often at great expense, and never without infinite trouble and anxiety on his part, of a small army of operatives of all sorts.

Ernest Newman, *The Life of Richard Wagner*, III, p. 73

The director of an opera house has a near impossible task, reconciling the wishes of singers, orchestral musicians, chorus members, stage-hands, shareholders, and the ever-demanding audience. In the eighteenth and nineteenth centuries the director was essentially an administrator and fixer. The opera producer, injecting interpretation into the staging, is a relatively recent phenomenon, and one that has encountered much resistance from that conservative creature, the opera singer. The impresario, nowadays a dying breed, had to combine the skills of entrepreneur, flatterer, rogue, and psychologist. The eighteenth-century impresario Aaron Hill had to find a way to dispose of a superannuated diva:

Margarita de l'Épine was the rage of the singing world in the early part of the eighteenth century. Her voice did not of course promise to last for ever, and when she and her singing began to decline, it became the duty of Aaron Hill   to communicate the unpleasant fact to her. He was sore pushed for a loophole through which he might introduce his harsh communication. Finding no more favourable opportunity, the ingenious impresario hit upon the following device. He knew that Mlle de l'Épine had a parrot – an exceedingly talkative one – which, when her ladyship was at home, she used to place at the open window of her lodgings in

Boswell Court, where it was constantly edifying the passers-by
with a line from Handel's *Julius Caesar*, and Hill, when he next
wrote to her, addressed his epistle 'Mlle de l'Épine, at the sign of
the Italian Parrot, Boswell Court'. Mademoiselle walked into this
trap in an exquisite manner. She wrote back to Hill saying that it
was a scandalous insult, and wound up by threatening to resign
her engagement. The impresario promptly replied to this in a most
insolent style, and informed de l'Épine that 'he could very well
spare her, in spite of her attractions, if she would but send her
feathered pupil'.

After this she sang little more for Mr Aaron Hill.

Frederick Crowest, *A Book of Musical Anecdotes*, Bentley, 1878, I,

pp. 302–3

*The most remarkable of the early-nineteenth-century impresarios was
Domenico Barbaia:*

He started life, it appears, as a bottle-washer or waiter, in which
capacity he presently acquired fame and, perhaps, merit by invent-
ing that mixture of whipped cream with coffee or chocolate which
remains to this day so popular in Vienna and Naples. Using the
little capital derived from this curious stroke of genius, he next
combined speculation in army contracts during the Napoleonic
wars with the exploitation of the gambling rooms at La Scala in
Milan. These activities made him so rich that he eventually became
impresario, first of La Scala itself, next of the San Carlo in Naples.

The most cruel things have been written about Barbaia by
imaginative biographers. He has been presented as a kind of super-
Falstaff, incredibly gross and fat, whose inability to read or write
was only matched by his inability to observe the most elementary
rules of decency and honesty. Every woman in all his theatres was
said to be a member of his harem; every librettist, conductor and
stage-hand was pictured as cowering in terror at his brutality and
coarseness. The only people in the world whom he was supposed
to treat with any respect were his leading lady and his cook –

especially the cook. To a great extent all this is mere libel. It is clear from Barbaia's portrait that his appearance was by no means gross. He seems to have ruled his theatres strictly but not unjustly. He certainly lived with his prima donna, Isabella Colbran; but that was expected of an impresario. His illiteracy, however, comparative or total, remains beyond question. He was one of those men whom nature had gifted with a shrewdness quite independent of any education. They are by no means extinct, even today. Far more extraordinary was his natural flair for artistic merit of every kind.

Francis Toye, *Rossini*, Heinemann, 1934, pp. 48–9

In 1817 when the San Carlo Opera in Naples reopened after a fire, Barbaia, as its director, exercised considerable power:

This greatest man in the kingdom, the director of its theatres and financier of its casinos, was the protector of his prima donna Mademoiselle Colbran, who made a fool of him all day long and led him by the nose. Colbran, who is now Rossini's wife, was from 1806 to 1815 one of the greatest singers in Europe. But in 1815 her voice began to tire, developing what, among second-rate singers, would be crudely called 'singing out of tune' . . .

We would wait for the first bars of Mademoiselle Colbran's aria. If we found her determined to sing off-key, we'd be equally firm, and would chat among ourselves or slip out to a coffee-house for an ice. After several months, the public, bored with these excursions, declared that poor Colbran had aged and awaited her dismissal. Since that didn't seem imminent, there was some grumbling, and at this point the fatal protection with which she'd been honoured appeared in its true colours, robbing the people both of its deepest pleasures and of the source of its pride and superiority over other nations. The public showed its annoyance in countless ways; nevertheless the limitless power of those in authority was exerted, and with an iron hand suppressed the indignation of the most excitable people on earth. This act of favouritism by the king towards Barbaia thrust him even further from the affections of the people than all the acts of despotism inflicted on a nation worthy of liberty.

In 1820, what would have brought real joy to the Neapolitans was not the bestowal of a Spanish constitution but the removal of Mademoiselle Colbran.

Rossini kept well out of Barbaia's machinations . . . but since he had been summoned to Naples by Barbaia and was known to be in love with Colbran, the Neapolitans couldn't resist occasionally holding him responsible for their irritation. Thus the Neapolitan audiences, who were regularly bowled over by the genius of Rossini, were equally likely to show their feelings by hissing his work.

Stendhal, *Life of Rossini*, chapters 11, 13, translated by Stephen Brook

Berlioz recalls the enthusiastic management style of Louis-Antoine Jullien:

[In 1847] I had been engaged by Jullien, the celebrated director of promenade concerts, to conduct the orchestra of the Grand English Opera, a company he had set up at the Drury Lane Theatre in a moment of wild ambition. Jullien, in his capacity of indisputable and undisputed lunatic, had assembled a splendid orchestra, a first-rate chorus and a tolerably good collection of singers. All he lacked was a repertory. *The Maid of Honour*, a new opera by Balfe which Jullien had commissioned, was to be the great panacea. Meanwhile, while Balfe's opera was being rehearsed, the season would open with an English version of that sparkling novelty, Donizetti's *Lucia di Lammermoor* – which novelty would have to take ten thousand francs a night in order to cover expenses.

The outcome was inexorable. The nightly receipts of *Lucia* fell short of the required ten thousand; Balfe's opera had a very moderate success; and within a short time Jullien was ruined . . .

Jullien, at the end of his resources, seeing that Balfe's opera was not making money, and more or less persuaded of the impossibility of putting on [Meyerbeer's] *Robert le Diable* in six days even if he rested on the seventh, summoned his committee of management to advise him what to do. This committee consisted of Sir Henry Bishop, Sir George Smart, Planché (the author of the libretto of Weber's *Oberon*), Gye (stage manager at Drury Lane), Marezzeck (the chief coach), and me. Jullien explained his difficulties and mentioned the names of various operas – all without translation or music – that he would like to put on. You should have heard the ideas and opinions expressed by these gentlemen as each master-piece came up for scrutiny! I was lost in admiration. At length we reached *Iphigénie en Tauride*, which the public had been promised by Jullien in his prospectus – as is the custom in London, where managers announce the opera every year but never give it. The other members of the committee, being quite ignorant of the work, were at a loss what to say. Jullien, impatient at my silence, turned abruptly to me and rapped out:

'Damn it all, say something. You must know it – you of all people.'

'Oh yes, I know it; but you haven't asked me anything. What do you want to know? Tell me, and I'll answer.'

'I want to know how many acts there are, what characters appear in the opera, what their voices are and, most important of all, what kind of scenery and costumes are wanted.'

'Very well, take a piece of paper and a pen, and write to my dictation: *Iphigénie en Tauride*, opera by Gluck (you know that, I presume) in four acts. There are three male roles: Orestes (bari-tone), Pylades (tenor) and Thoas (bass, going very high); one very important female role, Iphigénie (soprano), one small one, Diana (mezzo-soprano) and several for members of the chorus. The costumes, unfortunately, are not what you would consider very glamorous. King Thoas and his Scythians are a tribe of down-at-heel savages on the shores of the Black Sea. Orestes and Pylades appear dressed in the somewhat limited garb of shipwrecked Greeks. Only Pylades has more than one costume. He reappears in the fourth act, wearing a helmet and –'

'A helmet!' interrupted Jullien, excitedly. 'We're saved! I'll write to Paris for a gold helmet with a coronet of pearls and a plume

of ostrich feathers as long as my arm. We'll have forty
performances' . . .

I need hardly add that *Iphigénie* was not even put into rehearsal.
Jullien quitted London a few days after this learned conference,
leaving his company to fall to pieces.

Hector Berlioz, *Memoirs*, translated by David Cairns, Gollancz, 1969,
pp. 448–50

*The mid-nineteenth-century impresario Benjamin Lumley tells an anecdote
about the French impresario Severini, in order 'to illustrate the tyranny of
artists':*

Severini had occasion to be greatly displeased with Madame Malibran, and animadverted on her conduct in severe terms. The Diva,
conscious of her power over the subscribers and the public, and
believing that the theatre could not go on without her, observed –
'Sir, if you are dissatisfied with me, the remedy is easy. Let us
cancel our engagement.' '*Très bien, Madame*,' replied Severini, drily,
and, sending for his 'double' of the engagement, he requested the
astonished Diva to hand over her own duplicate, or counterpart
thereof, and having placed one within the other, he coolly and
leisurely tore them into pieces.

Rossini, whose direction of the music spread a lustre over the
establishment, observed to the manager – 'You have sacrificed
100,000 francs a year.' 'That may be so,' said Severini, 'but I prefer
to secure my peace of mind.'

Benjamin Lumley, *Reminiscences of the Opera*, Hurst & Blackett, 1864,
p. 10

The patient impresario J.H. Mapleson handles a difficult tenor:

One evening, when the opera of *Rigoletto* was being performed,
with Mongini as the Duke, feeling tired, as I had been working in
the theatre throughout the day, I went home just before the
termination of the third act. I had been at home about three

quarters of an hour when my servant hurried up in a cab to inform me that the curtain had not yet risen for the final act, and that a dreadful disturbance was going on in consequence of some question with Mongini, who was brandishing a drawn sword and going to kill everybody. I immediately slipped on my clothes and went down to the theatre.

At the stage door, without her bonnet, I met the tenor's charming wife, the only person, as a rule, who could control him in any way; and she entreated me not to go near him, or there would be bloodshed. I insisted, however, on going to his room without delay, as the curtain was still down and the public was getting tumultuous. I took the precaution of buttoning my overcoat across my chest, and in I went, my first words being –

'This time, Mongini, I hear you are right (*Questa volta sento che avete ragione*).'

With this preliminary we got into conversation, but he still remained walking up and down the room with nothing but his shirt on and a drawn sword in his hand. I saw that I had to proceed very slowly with him, and began talking on indifferent matters. At last I asked him the details of all the trouble. He thereupon explained to me that the master tailor, who had been requested by him in the morning to widen his overcoat by two inches, had misunderstood, and contracted it by two inches. I wished to have a look at the dress, which, however, was lying on the floor torn to pieces. I assured Mongini that the man should be cruelly punished, and he and his family put upon the street to starve early the next morning.

He then got calm, and I casually observed, 'By-the-bye, is the opera over yet, Mongini?' to which he replied, 'No, it is not.'

'Never mind that,' I continued; 'the public can wait. Everyone, by the way, is talking of the magnificent style in which you have been singing tonight.'

His eyes brightened, and he said he should like to go on with the opera.

'Not at all a bad idea!' I remarked.

'But I have no dress,' said Mongini, rather sadly; 'it is destroyed.'

I suggested that he should wear the dress of the second act,

putting on the breastplate and the steel gorget with the hat and
feathers, and he would then be all right, and '*La donna è mobile*'
would make amends for the delay. He dressed and followed me to
the stage, when I made the sign for the stage manager to ring up
the curtain, greatly to the astonishment of Mongini's wife, who
was fully expecting to hear that I had been run through the body.

The next day at twelve o'clock, as per appointment, Mongini
came to my office to be present at the punishment of the master
tailor. I had taken the precaution to inform the tailor, who was a
single man, that he had a wife and four children, and that he was
to be sure and recollect this. I called him into my room in the
presence of Mongini, and told him gravely that he with his wife
and children must now starve. There was no alternative after the
treatment Mongini had received the previous evening.

Mongini at once supplicated me not to let the children die in the
gutter, as it might injure him with the public, and he ended by
promising that if I would retain the tailor in my service he would
sing an extra night for nothing.

J.H. Mapleson, *The Mapleson Memoirs 1848–1888*, Remington, 1888, I,
pp. 95–8

Mapleson secured British performing rights to Gounod's Faust *in 1863:*

I then visited Gounod, who for £100 agreed to come over and
superintend the production of what he justly declared to be his
masterpiece . . .

Far from carrying out his agreement as to superintending the
production of the work, Gounod did not arrive in London until
nearly seven o'clock on the night of production; and all I heard
from him was that he wanted a good pit box in the centre of the
house. With this, for reasons which I will at once explain, I had no
difficulty whatever in providing him.

One afternoon, a few days before the day fixed for the production of the opera, I looked in upon Mr Nugent at the box office
and asked how the sale of places was going on.

'Very badly indeed,' he replied.

Only thirty pounds' worth of seats had been taken.

This presaged a dismal failure, and I had set my mind upon a brilliant success. I told Mr Nugent in the first place that I had decided to announce *Faust* for four nights in succession. He thought I must be mad, and assured me that one night's performance would be more than enough, and that to persist in offering to the public a work in which it took no interest was surely a deplorable mistake.

I told him that not only should the opera be played for four nights in succession, but that for the first three out of these four not one place was to be sold beyond those already disposed of. That there might be no mistake about the matter, I had all the remaining tickets for the three nights in question collected and put away in several carpet bags, which I took home with me that I might distribute them far and wide throughout the metropolis and the metropolitan suburbs. At last, after a prodigious outlay in envelopes, and above all postage stamps, nearly the whole mass of tickets for the three nights had been carefully given away.

I at the same time advertised in *The Times* that in consequence of a death in the family, two stalls secured for the first representation of *Faust* – the opera which was exciting so much interest that all places for the first three representations had been bought up – could be had at twenty-five shillings each, being but a small advance on the box-office prices . . .

Meanwhile demands had been made at the box office for places, and when the would-be purchasers were told that 'everything had gone', they went away and repeated it to their friends, who, in their turn, came to see whether it was quite impossible to obtain seats for the first performance of an opera which was now beginning to be seriously talked about. As the day of production approached the inquiries became more and more numerous . . .

The first representation took place on 11 June, and the work was received with applause, if not with enthusiasm . . . The paucity of measured tunes in the opera – which is melodious from beginning to end – caused many persons to say that it was wanting in melody.

The second night *Faust* was received more warmly than on the first, and at each succeeding representation it gained additional favour, until after the third performance the paying public, burning with desire to see a work from which they had hitherto been debarred, filled the theatre night after night. No further device was necessary for stimulating its curiosity; and the work was now to please and delight successive audiences by its own incontestable merit. It was given for ten nights in succession, and was constantly repeated until the termination of the season.

J.H. Mapleson, *The Mapleson Memoirs 1848–1888*, Remington, 1888, I, pp. 68–71

Mayhem at La Scala:

As the La Scala company in 1865 were rehearsing a new opera, with the composer in attendance, the impresario burst in, stopped the orchestra, and said he wanted to rehearse a different opera with a tenor who was making an emergency début the next day. The composer shouted, wept, and stamped his feet at the 'murder of Art'; the baritone shouted that he would not rehearse two operas in one evening; the impresario shouted back in dialect, 'I'm paying and I give the orders.' After an exchange of insults the impresario slapped the baritone; in the resulting scrum the conductor fell down, a drunken inspector from the supervisory board fell on top of him, the chorus intervened, and the baritone and the bass came to blows over the soprano, with the one grabbing the other in the 'reproductive region'. The impresario ran off.

John Rosselli, *Singers of Italian Opera*, Cambridge University Press, 1992, p. 155

Directorial arrogance is not a modern innovation, as Bruno Walter shows in his account of Hans Gregor:

Weingartner left the [Vienna] Opera in 1911, and Hans Gregor, who had been in charge of the Berlin Komische Oper, was appointed his successor . . . There are still in my mind a number of his utterances whose ludicrousness proved that his strangeness to art was bound decisively to lower the artistic level of the court opera in spite of his vigorous theatrical instinct. When, for instance, we were planning a new scenic production of *Das Rheingold*, he came out with the question whether a progressively minded stage direction ought not to put on the stage more than three Rhine-maidens. When I objected that Wagner had provided for only three voices, he replied: 'Well, why shouldn't there be three to sing, and another four to swim?' It was no easy matter to convince him that his arrangement would make the stage look like an aquarium. On another occasion, he found fault with me because of some scenic action in a Wagner performance. I explained to him that it was in accordance with Wagner's instructions, but he said: 'Wagner did not know much about the theatre. If he had submitted his *Flying Dutchman* to me, I should have told him: "What, two ships on the stage? Go home and change that, and then you may come back again."' I tried to make clear to him that I was at all times ready to bow reverently before the creative artist, but he protested: 'Let me be frank. You have entirely too much respect for the work of art. As for me, I consider that the composers relinquish their scores at the porter's desk.'

Bruno Walter, *Theme and Variations*, translated by James A. Galston, Hamish Hamilton, 1947, pp. 207 9

The American impresario Oscar Hammerstein adopted unusual methods of intimidating singers:

Hammerstein had engaged [the American soprano Lillian Nordica] for his second season (1907) at the Manhattan Opera House, and she opened it as the heroine of Ponchielli's *La gioconda*, giving a superb performance of a role that was new to her repertory. But after a few appearances in that opera and *Aida*, it became evident that Mr Hammerstein, for reasons of his own, was not particularly anxious for her to sing any more. Anyhow he tried to make things as unpleasant as he could for her.

Among the several devices he employed was one which she afterwards described as 'smoking me out'. Knowing her objection to tobacco fumes, and being himself never without a cigar in his mouth (even on the stage, where he sat puffing through every performance), Hammerstein arranged for a 'combined attack' during a matinée of *Aida*, and, with the assistance of his conductor (Cleofonte Campanini), his régisseur (Coini), and an army of stage carpenters, created an atmosphere so thick, so noxious to this prima donna, that she very nearly failed to get through the opera. The last entr'acte was extended to a smoky half hour, and an apology had to be made to the audience. That sufficed for Hammerstein's purpose. Mme Nordica was not called upon to sing again during the remainder of the season.

Herman Klein, *Great Woman-singers of My Time*, Routledge, 1931,
pp. 126–7

The composer Gustav Mahler was more celebrated in his lifetime as the brilliant director and conductor of the Vienna State Opera:

The singer, Mizzi Günther, came to him one day with an urgent and written recommendation from the Crown Prince, Franz Ferdinand. Mahler took the note and tore it up. 'Very well,' he said, 'and now – sing!'

The Emperor also demanded the re-engagement of the singer E. B.-F., with whom he had had a passing affair, but whose voice was no longer extant. 'Good,' Mahler said, 'but I will not let her come on.' To which Prince Montenuovo replied that it was the Emperor's express wish that she should, and a long-standing promise also, and in any case her salary would come out of his majesty's private purse. 'Then I suppose she'll have to,' Mahler replied. 'But

I shall have it printed on the programme "By Command of His Majesty the Emperor".' He heard no more of it. And it must be set down to the credit of the old regime that his audacity did him more good than harm.

Alma Mahler, *Gustav Mahler: Memories and Letters*, translated by Basil Creighton, Murray, 1946, pp. 93–4

In 1914 the conductor Otto Klemperer had a serious disagreement with Hans Pfitzner, the director of the Strasbourg opera:

My first opera was *Fidelio*. Pfitzner was accustomed to cut the whole beginning of the last scene up to the first words of the Minister, *'Des bestens Königs Wink und Wille'*. He found the opening chorus too foursquare. Ridiculous! Naturally, I restored the cut. Pfitzner made awful trouble. He told me that I was only his deputy, that I must do as he did. 'You have to give my version,' he said. I replied, 'I'm giving Beethoven's version.'

Peter Heyworth, *Conversations with Klemperer*, Gollancz, 1973, p. 45

The novelist E.F. Benson recalls Harry Higgins, managing director of Covent Garden and 'the wittiest man of our times'.

He was for some years on the board of the opera syndicate at Covent Garden. In this capacity he crossed the Atlantic to hear a tenor who had scored an immense success in New York in Wagnerian roles. This paragon was singing Tristan on the night of Harry Higgins's arrival, and an American friend had bidden him to her box. She talked to him so continuously throughout the performance, that he could give no serious attention to the stage. At the end she asked him to come to her box again three nights hence, when the star would be singing Lohengrin. 'Thanks very much,' he said. 'I shall be delighted. I've never heard you in *Lohengrin* . . .' On another occasion he had a business interview with a fine vocalist whose talent as an artist was a little overshadowed by her genius for friendship. There was an idea of getting her to sing at Covent

Garden, but when terms were discussed, she asked a price which seemed to him far in excess of her artistic merits. 'But, my dear lady,' he said. 'We only want you to sing.'

E.F. Benson, *Final Edition*, Longmans Green, 1940, pp. 211–12

Rudolf Bing found that a fiver worked wonders with a temperamental Italian bass:

[Salvatore] Baccaloni was unquestionably the hit of this [1936] and the succeeding seasons. Fat, jovial, and I think intelligent – I had no way to know: there was no language in which we could communicate – he brought to Glyndebourne the blessing of absolutely perfect comic timing, and a plummy voice of incomparable richness. He could be a trouble to directors, conductors, and general managers. For four seasons a regular feature of my life at Glyndebourne was the arrival of a furious Baccaloni in my office, sputtering streams of rapid Italian despite his knowledge that I did not understand a word of the language, furious about something that had just happened. I would listen until he seemed to have completed what he had to say, then reach into the desk and give him a five-pound note. That always seemed to be the right reply, and he would go away content.

Sir Rudolf Bing, *5000 Nights at the Opera*, Hamish Hamilton, 1972,

p. 59

Walter Felsenstein, director of the Komische Oper in Berlin, shows how opera production consists of more than stage design:

A few years ago I crossed paths with a young stage director who had been an assistant in my theatre, and whom I considered quite gifted. He told me proudly that he was in the process of staging *Lohengrin*. 'How are you going to do it?' I asked him, genuinely interested in learning his viewpoint. I expected to hear something about his conception – the behaviour of the chorus at the arrival of the swan, for example, or his ideas on the leading role.

'I am playing the work on a raked stage. Interesting, don't you think?' he said.

I proceeded to ask him about his family.

The Music Theatre of Walter Felsenstein, translated by Peter Paul Fuchs,
Quartet Books, 1991, p. 29

Bernard Levin recalls a momentous performance of Fidelio *in London:*

In February 1961 Dr Otto Klemperer made a surprisingly belated début at Covent Garden, conducting (and producing) *Fidelio*, with an international cast recruited specially for the occasion, including Sena Jurinac as Leonore, Jon Vickers as Florestan, Hans Hotter as Pizarro and Gottlob Frick as Rocco . . .

The very certainty of Beethoven's world lent a momentary, brittle strength to the fast-disappearing certainty of the world in which the production took place (the Cuba crisis, which may be said to have ended what little certainty the post-war world possessed, was twenty months away), and gave many in the audience the illusion that they were watching, indeed participating in, one of the climactic moments of a world in transition, and that the egg was cracking before their eyes, to emit what frightful bird? The production itself — otherwise careful, straightforward and unadventurous — contained two moments of symbolism, one obvious, one less so, that made this feeling most real. The first occurred in the opening scene of the opera, and was startling enough; the knocking at the door referred to by Jacquino is so explicitly present in the music that producers of the opera do not normally feel it necessary to have a stage-manager actually thump, in time to the knocking in the orchestra, on the outside of the door at the back of the stage, thus underlining what is already in italics.

Klemperer, however, had not only insisted that the knocking on the door be loudly and obtrusively present; he deliberately had it out of time with the rhythmic knocking in the music, thus producing a kind of aural-visual-psychological discord of shocking, and deeply disquieting, effect that upset all preconceived notions of

rhythm and order. Rhythm, after all, *is* order, and thus to shatter
the illusion that order reigns over all, and to do so, moreover, in
the warm, human, domestic setting of the first scene of *Fidelio*,
before either the heroine or the villain has made an appearance,
was a *coup de théâtre*, literally as well as metaphorically, which
announced that there was something abroad in the opera house
that night which had taken the measure of what was abroad in the
world outside.

The second example, as healing in its assertion of the triumph of
good as the first was destructive in its claim that the universe was
without form, occurred at the beginning of the final scene of
reconciliation and justice. To the rage of the purists, Klemperer
had reverted to the tradition of playing the *Leonora No. 3* Overture
between the dungeon scene in Act II and the apotheosis which
follows it. The curtain fell on the dungeon, and rose again,
therefore, after twenty minutes, on a setting that consisted, significantly, of a huge drawbridge – filling virtually the entire stage area
– which was, no less significantly, down. On this side, we were
given to understand, was the prison, so that the drawbridge was,
presumably, kept up against the intrusion of justice and liberation
from outside; on the other side was the world, stretching away
into the distance (though symbolically represented by a cyclorama),
from which justice and liberation were to come. Come they did, in
the person of Don Fernando and his forces, preceded by a
standard-bearer with a huge silk banner, and over the drawbridge
they marched to make all well. But before they did so, indeed
before they appeared from the back of the stage (which had been
raked away from the audience, so that the liberators had to climb
up to the drawbridge and thus emphasize the chiliastic nature of
the scene by being at first invisible), Klemperer played his second
card, which took on the nature of a Last Trump. As the curtain
rose, the eyes of the spectators were assailed by a burst of light
from the back of the stage, the direction from which the avenging
angel was to appear, so intense that it was for the moment as
unbearable as, we are told, looking upon the face of God will be,
and every head in the audience was simultaneously turned away in

an instinctive shrinking from the dangerous freedom that it her-
alded. So Beethoven's most important lessons, that evil has to be
conquered again and again, and that, since there is nothing but the
good in human beings to conquer it with, the human beings had
better nerve themselves for the battle, were driven home with
irresistible force.

Bernard Levin, *The Pendulum Years*, Cape, 1971, pp. 370–72

In 1965 Peter Hall directed Schoenberg's Moses and Aaron *at Covent
Garden:*

The production was certainly the largest I have ever done. Over
300 people thronged the stage: dancers, singers, a double chorus,
acrobats, actors. There was a menagerie of animals: goats, sheep,
horses, Highland cattle. At the dress rehearsal a camel teetered
down the precipitously raked stage, causing the whole of the
Royal Opera House orchestra to flee the pit in consternation. The
creature then shat copiously. He had to be cut.

I did ask myself, once or twice, where in all this was my belief
that less meant more? But we were, after all, presenting an opera
about excess and the danger of excess. It was essential to conjure
that up on stage. In one notorious scene, we had to create an
orgy of blood and lust around the Golden Calf which finally led
to the virtual insanity of the tribe. Large ornamental penises,
painted garishly and decked out with muffs of goat hair, were
designed to be strapped to the performers' middles. I kept ask
ing for these in rehearsal; they did not appear. In the end I
discovered the designs were under lock and key in, of all places,
the desk of the director of Covent Garden. David Webster,
ever an English gentleman, had hoped somehow that the penises
would go away. He asked me sadly whether I really wanted them.
I said I did. Reluctantly, but without argument, he unlocked his
desk.

I have always felt that nakedness in the theatre is a basic truth:
like earth, air, fire or water. It should therefore be used responsibly

and for a purpose. The ungoverned lust of the orgy round the
Golden Calf could be expressed only, it seemed to me, by some
degree of nudity. The Lord Chamberlain still functioned, so we
had to be careful.

Covent Garden allowed me to hire for the scene half a dozen
strippers from Soho who found it a highly diverting change from
their normal work. In those days, if you were naked on the stage
you had to stand still, the theory being, I suppose, that this
was less likely to inflame the audience. Our strippers, therefore,
were permitted to move only if they wore pads of false pubic
hair, and Elastoplast patches over their nipples. The effect was
to give the girls the most noticeable breasts in Old Testament
history.

Some of the staider members of the women's chorus were so
shocked that they refused to come on stage while this scene was
enacted, and insisted on contributing their atonal wails and cries of
lust while they knitted in the wings.

At the first dress rehearsal, Forbes Robinson as Moses and
Richard Lewis as Aaron found themselves singing their final
metaphysical debate over an altar on which lay a naked girl
covered in blood. Neither of them stopped nor made any observation about this additional prop . . .

Peter Hall, *Making an Exhibition of Myself*, Sinclair-Stevenson, 1993,

pp. 223–5

Purists would have shuddered at John Dexter's ideas for a production of
Un ballo in maschera *for the Hamburg Opera:*

I am quite interested in *Ballo*. However, as you have already
engaged a cast my ideas may not be possible as they depend a little
on having a coloured Ulrica and a coloured Oscar. Perhaps I
should explain. I would like to set the piece not in Boston in the
seventeenth century, but in the southern states of America, possibly
New Orleans, at the time of the Civil War. Jefferson, Lee, Grant,
and Lincoln up north, all move in an atmosphere of political

assassination. Ulrica would certainly work best as an old negro mamma on a plantation, and indeed all the scenes would respond to the atmosphere of heat and war.

Letter to Rolf Liebermann, 13 September 1971, in John Dexter,
The Honourable Beast, Nick Hern, 1993, p. 71

At the Metropolitan Opera in 1959, Birgit Nilsson triumphed in her début as Isolde. At one performance her Tristan, Ramon Vinay, felt ill. So did the understudy, Karl Liebl, and a third cover, Albert Da Costa. Bing had a problem on his hands:

I consulted with Miss Nilsson and then spoke with my three tenors again. None of them felt up to an entire *Tristan*; could each of them take an act? They agreed. When the house lights went down, before the music began, I came on to the stage, and was greeted by a great moan from all corners of the house – the general manager appears only to make the most important announcements, and everyone thought he knew that this announcement had to be: Miss Nilsson has cancelled.

So I began by saying, 'Ladies and gentlemen, Miss Nilsson is very well,' which brought a sigh of relief from almost four thousand people. Then I went on: 'However, we are less fortunate with our Tristan. The Metropolitan has three distinguished Tristans available, but all three are sick. In order not to disappoint you, these gallant gentlemen, against their doctors' orders, have agreed to do one act each.' There was laughter in the house. I added, 'Fortunately, the work has only three acts', and there was a roar of laughter. Never has *Tristan und Isolde* started so hilariously. But Miss Nilsson sang gloriously and to this day I am grateful to my three tenors for saving a terrible situation.

Sir Rudolf Bing, *5000 Nights at the Opera*, Hamish Hamilton, 1972,
p. 201

Igor Stravinsky did not have a high opinion of Rudolf Bing as director of the Metropolitan Opera:

What I find more difficult to explain is the installation of Mr Bing as a culture hero, not *how* it came about, of course – he has virtually no competition – but *why*. Why mythologize an artistic director who denies the possibility of new opera, as his commissions for the new house show; who supports the now generally discredited star system, which in effect contradicts the idea, at last gaining circulation elsewhere, that opera is a drama; and who keeps the tiniest inventory of operas of any company of its class in the world? Mr Bing disingenuously justifies his repertory as box-office taste, knowing full well that taste must be created, and, anyway, that a good salesman should be able to sell good merchandise as well as bad. With the advent of new interest in Wagner, wouldn't a new *Tristan* better have befitted the celebrations of the new house than the revival of a moth-eaten comedy like *La gioconda*? Or a progressive novelty, for example a double bill of *Curlew River* and *Suor Angelica*? But in spite of *Gioconda* and *Cleopatra* and *Adriana Lecouvreur* and *Cav* and *Pag*, Mr Bing is one of New York's top swingers. No doubt he will be made into a musical, which is a cultural achievement of a sort.

Igor Stravinsky, *Themes and Conclusions*, Faber, 1972, p. 104

Rudolf Bing justifies his reluctance to present contemporary opera at the Metropolitan Opera House:

Some day a new operatic genius will arise whose works draw the public, and when he does we shall all know about it. Failing such a genius, I was not wildly interested in presenting contemporary opera at the Metropolitan. My colleague in Hamburg does contemporary opera after contemporary opera and the press loves him, and he plays to empty houses, and the state pays. But in America the state does not pay. I dare say that if I had done three more world premières in my twenty-two years the Met would not have gone broke, but the finances would have been that much more difficult, and except for two or three reviewers nobody would have thanked me. The audience certainly would not have thanked me. I had only four new productions a year, and a necessity to give plums to singers; if I had taken more of those new productions for contemporary opera the singers would not have thanked me. You can't get a Tebaldi or a Callas (we tried Callas, for [Samuel Barber's] *Vanessa*) or a Nilsson or a Corelli or a Tucker to sing contemporary opera; you're lucky if you can get a [Evelyn] Lear. I am always being told that opera will die unless the new works are performed; it seems to me that these days a better case can be made for the proposition that opera will *never* die unless the new works are performed.

Sir Rudolf Bing, *5000 Nights at the Opera*, Hamish Hamilton, 1972,

p. 162

David Littlejohn explains the new spin that American director Peter Sellars gives to Mozart's masterpieces:

Don Giovanni, in Peter Sellars's 1989 version, is a feared and brutal young drug addict/rapist in a run-down New York neighbourhood, identified by some critics as Spanish Harlem. He and his greedy sidekick/dependent Leporello were played at Purchase in July–August 1989 by black twin brothers, Eugene and Herbert Perry. They dressed almost identically in jeans, black shirts, and dark leather jackets, which added a metaphysical, *doppelgänger* quality to their role switch in Act II. Whatever the precise locale, the population is racially mixed and not simply as a result of what is called 'open casting'.

 Giovanni is, of course, a notorious seducer, with (Sellars tells us) 'a preference for twelve- and thirteen-year-old girls.' Donna Anna, a white woman from a higher class and a better part of town, comes to his neighbourhood (the whole opera takes place on the same shabby street) for her heroin. She 'shoots up' on stage midway in '*Non mi dir*' (as does Giovanni during '*Finch'han del vino*'), and appals Don Ottavio by showing him the needle tracks on her arm. The *quattro doppie* that Giovanni offers Leporello at the start of Act II are lines of cocaine.

The opera begins with Giovanni's attempted on-stage rape of Donna Anna, from which she escapes into an abandoned four-storey apartment house that fills the rear of the stage. Her father, a distinguished-looking gentleman in evening dress, happens to arrive on the scene in search of his daughter at that very moment, which is where Giovanni shoots him dead. Anna, 'traumatized' by the attempted rape, forces her pathetically confused fiancé Ottavio (a local police officer) to a vow of revenge, repeatedly dipping their hands in her slain father's blood during the repeats of their duet. Ottavio radios for an ambulance, and a team of paramedics carries off the corpse. (Anna's later explanation to her fiancé of what took place is considerably at odds with what we have seen, but Sellars simply tells us that she is lying.)

Donna Elvira, one of Giovanni's 2065 former conquests, now arrives 'from the bus station', a tarty-looking woman in red tights, black boots, a striped miniskirt, and a gold-spangled black jacket. Masetto is a tall local black man given to violence; his new bride Zerlina, in the summer 1989 production, is a fickle young Chinese girl easily tempted by Giovanni. 'The palace' Giovanni invites the wedding company to is (we read, although we never see it) a nearby all-night disco. Giovanni's dominion over other members of the cast appears to derive from his reputation as a dangerous criminal entrepreneur, a kind of Mafia *padrone* offering *protezione* – two words of the Italian text that come close to fitting the action.

As there is no real palace (Sellars's Giovanni and Leporello appear to live on, and off, the streets), Giovanni gets Masetto drunk (we are told) at a local bar. Provisions for Giovanni's street party come from the looting of a neighbourhood grocery by a menacing gang of blacks, which may or may not be under his control. Masetto actually does beat Zerlina (we hear the blows coming from inside their flat) before she sings, '*Batti, batti*,' which makes her seem more a masochistic 'co-dependent' than a clever Mozartean flirt.

Anna, Ottavio, and Elvira emerge from the abandoned apartment house in jazzy party clothes (but unmasked) to join Giovanni's increasingly wild street dance, in the course of which their host strips down to his underwear ('*Viva la libertà!*'); some of his guests follow his example. After his second rape attempt in the opera (of Zerlina – inside, it would appear, the neon-crossed church where she was just married), he is surrounded by the three 'maskers', plus Masetto, who hold guns to his head and threaten to kill him, but do not.

Midway in Act II, a funeral procession comes on stage carrying the coffin of Anna's father, which is dumped in a gasworkers' hole in the road that has been there all along. Later, her dead father walks, red-eyed, on to a platform above the church facade at left – a platform that had earlier held a different, religious statue, until Don Ottavio yanked it down by a convenient rope.

After parleying with the new statue, Giovanni and Leporello share a final feast – milkshake, hamburger, french fries, chicken McNuggets – on the front steps of the apartment, while Leporello plays his master's musical requests on a giant 'boom box', or portable cassette player. Elvira, a suddenly born-again Christian, arrives bearing a Bible and haranguing Giovanni to repent. He throws his french fries at her. Anna's father's 'ghost' rises up, green-lit, inside the apartment lobby behind them. Once again Giovanni strips to his pale blue briefs and follows on his knees a pre-pubescent girl (a symbol of his vilest vice?) who leads him down a glowing manhole in the torn-up street. Suddenly the nude torsos of sixteen chorus members (souls in hell, perhaps) pop out of trapdoors in the floor like jack-in-the-boxes. Next, Giovanni's five adversaries, wearing shroud-like gowns, pop in and out of similar trapdoors to sing a reduced version of the finale, while Leporello, surrounded by four menacing black thugs, slouches on the darkened stage. The apartment house facade flies apart, red lights appear under the trapdoors, and an ashcan bursts into flames. End of opera.

David Littlejohn, *The Ultimate Art*, University of California Press, 1992, pp. 138–40

Lanfranco Rasponi takes exception to what he perceives as directorial excesses:

The liberties taken with scores and librettos are assuming scandalous proportions ... A mezzo pointed out to me that at La Scala, Georges Prêtre, one of France's leading conductors, had taken it upon himself to switch the role of Siebel in *Faust* from a mezzo to a tenor. 'I was shocked,' she said to me, 'not only because this is not respecting the score, but because it changes musically every scene in which the young man appears. If Gounod wrote it for a light mezzo, there was a musical reason. He wanted a particular sound for the part of the young man deeply in love with Marguerite. The enchanting aria *"Faites-lui mes aveux"* is intended to express the adoration of an almost sexless youth. If it is given to a tenor, the sensuous element comes in and the meaning is gone.'

There was much surprise when Zubin Mehta, for a new production of *Die Fledermaus* at Covent Garden, insisted on having a man sing Orlofsky. Strauss had wanted a woman to sing the part because the prince is only eighteen years old and he felt that not even a light tenor could handle the particular sound he had in mind. It was amusing to read Rodney Milnes in the *Spectator* commenting on this very fact: 'Mehta says he cannot stand female Orlofskys. Well, of course, composers will keep making these elementary mistakes, and how lucky we are with musicians like Mr Mehta who knows better and can tidy them up. I look forward to hearing a tenor Octavian and bass-baritone Cherubino when he gets around to giving us his *Rosenkavalier* and *Le nozze di Figaro*' ...

When La Scala in 1966 used a tenor Romeo instead of a coloratura mezzo in Bellini's *I Capuleti e i Montecchi*, purists were scandalized. Despite his good intentions, Giacomo Aragall could not sound like Marilyn Horne, Tatiana Troyanos, or Agnes Baltsa, who sing Romeo so admirably, much less like Giulietta Simionato, who was overwhelming in this part. The experiment was lamentable. Bellini had written Romeo and Giulietta for the Grisi sisters,

Giuditta and Giulia, but conductor Claudio Abbado ignored Bellini and made this foolish change, upsetting the entire balance of the score.

Lanfranco Rasponi, *The Last Prima Donnas*, Gollancz, 1984, pp. 596–9

Peter Hall on the difference between directing singers and actors:

Received opinion is that the diva goes her own way and will do nothing on the stage which she has not done before. I disagree. Singers are not hard to direct. They are indeed so used to doing what the man with the baton tells them, that they are equally obedient to the director. They will do precisely what he asks. The trouble is that they rarely do anything more – unless they are actors as well as musicians. The magic of working with a good actor is that he takes the suggestion of his director and transmutes it into something complex, subtle and human. The bad actor, or the average opera singer, does just what the director has said; nothing more and nothing less. The suggestion remains inert, simple and dead.

Great actors make a director's suggestions seem better than they are. Great opera stars such as Janet Baker and Maria Ewing can do the same – simply because they are superb actors as well as superb singers. Average singers are like circus performers – concerned with their physical selves rather than emotional truth. They want to sing and sing well; it doesn't need to mean anything.

. . . Actors depend entirely on each other. Singers need not. In opera, I discovered, it is all too possible to ignore everyone else on stage with you. As long as you are watching the conductor and keeping 'in' with the orchestra, you need never look at your colleagues. Eye contact, which is the very stuff of an actor's being, is something foreign to singers, for it tends to place them in a bad position so that the voice goes into the wings. It also takes their attention away from the conductor.

I insisted from my very first opera production that the singers, like actors, played off each other. Paradoxically, their singing

became better, the drama more alive and the communication with
the audience more eloquent.

It soon became plain to me that I loved working with singers. I
observed that a phrase of music could be made to convey almost
any emotion. You could play against it or with it; you could even
treat it ironically. The emotional support of the music meant that
singers could communicate the most complex things if only they
could be persuaded to do very little.

Peter Hall, *Making an Exhibition of Myself*, Sinclair-Stevenson, 1993,

pp. 219–20

Walter Felsenstein argues that the role of the stage director has nothing to
do with mere originality:

In this era of the ascendancy of the stage director we unfortunately
attach more importance to a director's interpretation of a work
than to the desire to have the work itself perfectly realized. We
must reject any interpretation whose primary aim is to produce an
interesting performance but which does not carefully explore the
intentions of the composer and the author and try to fulfil them as
closely as possible. Anyone who thinks he can reshape or modern-
ize a valuable work would do better to have a new work written
for him, rather than to misuse the existing one for his own
purposes.

A stage director must have a forceful personality, first of all to
be able to convey unmistakably the original substance of a work
by the means that are most likely to reach his audience. Beyond
that, he must be able, by his own methods, to help appropriately
cast singers, and also the conductor and designer, become profoundly familiar with the work, and to induce them to bring forth
a highly personal interpretation, but one that is completely faithful
to the work, according to the laws of the theatre. In no case may
the stage director confine himself to spatial and choreographic
arrangements, and in no case is he allowed to use the singers as
animated marionettes. Nor may he arrive at the staging without

the conductor's collaboration. He must see to it that the creative reshaping of a work by the singers in conjunction with the conductor is done according to the demands of the score, and will not be disturbed by inventive afterthoughts of the conductor . . .

When the stage director cares for nothing except originality — nothing except leaving the accustomed, traditional channels behind — with no concern about whether the audience understands him or not, he is so arrogant that he ought to be restrained from directing.

The Music Theatre of Walter Felsenstein, translated by Peter Paul Fuchs,
Quartet Books, 1991, pp. 121–2, 131, 133

24: Auditions

Singers and musicians to receive *only* their expenses, no *fees*.
Those who do not come for the honour and out of a sense of
enthusiasm may as well stay at home. Any singer – be they
male or female – who came to me only in return for one of
their insane *fees* would be a fat lot of good to me! How could
anyone like that satisfy my artistic demands?

Richard Wagner, letter of 12 April 1872 about his plans for the
Bayreuth Festival

*There is not a vast literature on the subject of auditions. They are chiefly of
interest when the singer makes a hash of things, and few singers want to
keep such memories fresh.*

*Jenny Lind was thoroughly humiliated, initially, by the renowned Manuel
Garcia:*

The maestro, slim and dark, with flashing eyes and a quick
vivacious manner, received her coolly but courteously. She sang a
few scales to enable him to assess the power and range of her
voice. Then he asked her to sing the aria, 'Perchè non ho', from
Lucia di Lammermoor. It was one of her most popular parts, she
had sung it thirty-nine times in the preceding year in Stockholm
and knew every note of it by heart. But the strain and her own
exhaustion were too much for her, and she broke down completely.
Garcia gave his verdict. 'It would be useless to teach you, *Mademoiselle. Vous n'avez plus de voix.*'

You have no longer a voice! It was a ruthless sentence to pass
on a twenty-year-old diva. She told Mendelssohn, years afterwards,
that the anguish of this moment exceeded anything she had ever
suffered before or since . . .

He found that Jenny had been trained in a faulty method of breathing. Consequently all the time she had been using her voice, she had been steadily damaging it. With the intensive use it had had recently, it was on the point of complete destruction, and she had gone to him only just in time. The upper notes were not so badly affected, but the middle register was veiled and there was an alarming degree of hoarseness.

He had to put her back to the beginning again. From the top of the ladder she had to go back to the first rung, unlearn everything she had ever learnt, and learn it all over again.

Joan Bulman, *Jenny Lind*, Barrie, 1956, pp. 38, 42

Sir Thomas Beecham clearly relished the auditions held at a boarding-house stuffed with budding sopranos:

In the 1920s and 1930s, the imposing house in Cromwell Road on the site of what is now the French Institute was occupied by Miss Nellie Rowe, quite a famous teacher of singing at that time, who boarded promising young singers in her house . . .

Beecham, who often went to Miss Rowe's saying that he wished to listen to her pupils, found the atmosphere created by a household of beautiful girls extremely pleasant, and few of the beginners there were capable of retaliation if his impish sense of humour got the better of him. Girls in their position rarely had the confidence of a young soprano auditioned by him at Covent Garden who found herself being accompanied by the great maestro through one of the many works he had not heard for fifteen years. 'I can't sing,' she protested plaintively after a few moments, 'if you don't play the right notes.' Every member of the Covent Garden staff who was there grew pale with terror, and Sir Thomas's entourage blenched, but the great man's suavity was unruffled, and no calamity occurred. Instead, the young lady was taken out to lunch!

However, things were not always so easy. I was telephoned one morning by Miss Rowe, who demanded my services because, as she put it, Sir Thomas wanted to hear some of her girls. One of

them, who had recently studied in Italy, sang an aria in Italian and
then unwisely went on to praise with exaggerated fervour the
maestro under whom she had worked in Milan. Before long,
Beecham was bristling so visibly that one could only wonder at the
young singer's insensitivity to the impression she was making. She
went on to sing another Italian aria.

'Thank you,' said Sir Thomas. 'Now can you please sing something in English?'

'I am sorry,' she said, 'but I don't sing anything in English.'

'Indeed, but that is strange, for I got the impression that you are
English,' Beecham remarked with increased suavity. 'And where
do you come from?'

'Bournemouth, Sir Thomas.'

'But surely they speak English in Bournemouth. Can you not
sing a simple folk-song? Or perhaps a nursery rhyme?' It was
obvious to everyone but the unfortunate girl herself that Beecham
would not let her go without punishment for her unrestrained
praise of her Italian teacher. 'No?' he continued with the most
courteous surprise. 'Will you then please sing for me one verse of
the National Anthem? We have here with us Mr Ivor Newton,
who is well known amongst singers for his ability to play the
National Anthem in any key, major or minor, which a singer may
desire. He will help you with the music, I myself will prompt you
with the words.'

This he did, mouthing each line deliberately as the poor girl
sang the one before.

> Ivor Newton, *At the Piano*, Hamish Hamilton, 1966, pp. 277–8

Rosa Ponselle, as recalled by the director of the Metropolitan Opera House:

One fine day, William Thorner met me and said, 'Mr Gatti, I have
a young woman, a pupil of mine, an Italian-American who really
has an admirable voice. She and her sister have been appearing in
the United States in vaudeville. But you must remember that this
is not the ordinary singer; this is a special case.'

We gave the girl, as well as her sister, an audition. She was nervous, upset, and somewhat ill. Nevertheless, I could see easily that this girl had a magnificent voice. We allowed her to come back a few days later and gave her another audition. This time she sang perfectly, with a beauty of voice and style that was truly amazing in a young and inexperienced singer.

I had already turned over in my mind the possibility of reviving *La forza del destino*. When I heard her the second time, I decided at once to go through with this revival. Caruso graciously agreed to sing the role of Don Alvaro and we went ahead with the preparations for the event.

I have been asked how I dared to give this inexperienced young artist so difficult a role to begin with. I will admit that it was a somewhat difficult problem, since the girl's only experience had been vaudeville. But I took a chance. I decided to run the risk, although I felt a certain amount of assurance since the young singer was extremely musical and very sure of herself.

We had a dress rehearsal to which we invited the press, and the response was immediately favourable. And at the performance she made a magnificent impression.

Giulio Gatti-Casazza, *Memories of the Opera*, Calder, 1977, pp. 201–2

Why Tito Gobbi's début at the Metropolitan Opera House was delayed:

One of the few auditions I remember vividly is that of Tito Gobbi, who had completed his Rome season a day or two before I arrived and was already too eminent an artist to participate in the day-long series of auditions held for me at the Teatro Argentina. But he graciously agreed that I should hear him before offering him an engagement, and he told me he had a large enough room at home. I went to his house and settled down on a couch to listen, and just as his pianist struck the first chord his pet lion came in through a swinging door and started straight for me. I am extremely fond of animals, and this was only a baby lion, but I must admit it was a distracting experience. Gobbi kept singing, and before the lion

reached me across the big room his little daughter came dashing
through the same door, grabbed the lion by the tail, and dragged
him back where he had come from. Eventually we did engage
Gobbi, but that audition did not speed the process.

Sir Rudolf Bing, *5000 Nights at the Opera*, Hamish Hamilton, 1972,

p. 122

The soprano Maria Carbone on vocal competitions in Italy:

'Agents are an absolute necessity. The youngsters go to sing at all
these vocal competitions where not one thing happens, for the
judges are chosen by the political parties and know nothing about
voices. After the stand I took at La Scala some time ago, I have
not been invited again to sit in on the jury, which now must
include representatives from the various unions of the male and
female choruses, the male and female comprimarios, and so forth.
Before one girl presented herself to sing, I was told she had to be
accepted because she was the member of a family very close to the
mayor. "Let us see what she can do" is all I answered, already
boiling with rage. Well, a dog would have sung infinitely better.
Everyone voted in her favour. I got up from my seat and said,
controlling myself, "Will someone kindly tell the mayor for me
that as I do not interfere in how he runs this city, I cannot accept
his interference in what has been my business for over fifty years."
To the amazement of those present, I walked out.'

Lanfranco Rasponi, *The Last Prima Donnas*, Gollancz, 1984, p. 361

Joan Sutherland's inauspicious audition at the Met:

Sutherland came in 1961–2. She had auditioned three years before,
on the recommendation of George London, who had been dazzled
by the Donna Anna she sang opposite his Don Giovanni in a
summer festival performance in Vancouver. To the astonishment
of [assistant director] John Gutman and [conductor Erich]
Leinsdorf, what she offered as her audition piece was *'Caro nome'* –

in English – and she was sent off, not unreasonably, to learn her trade. By the time Sutherland came back to New York for a concert performance of Bellini's *Beatrice di Tenda* at Town Hall, early in 1961, she was world-famous: nobody living had heard before such a combination of vocal power and flexibility.

Martin Mayer, *The Met: One Hundred Years of Grand Opera,*
Thames & Hudson, 1983, p. 282

25: Rehearsal

At the Komische Oper in East Berlin, Walter Felsenstein could afford to spend two years and 233 rehearsals to prepare his production of Offenbach's *Tales of Hoffmann*.

Joseph Wechsberg, 'Grand Price of Grand Opera', in *Opera Annual No. 8*, edited by Harold Rosenthal

Rehearsals, where everything is still in flux, can be unique sources of tension, creative at best, disastrous at worst. Rossini loathed them:

As for composing, there was nothing to it, Rossini used to say; it's rehearsals that are tiresome. That's the miserable moment when the poor maestro endures real torture hearing his finest inspirations, his most brilliant and supple cantilenas, distorted in every tone of which the human voice is capable . . .

Gathered around some clapped-out piano in the hovel known as the *ridotto* of the theatre in some small town such as Reggio or Velletri, I've seen eight or ten poor devils trying to rehearse against the background noise of the clatter of the kitchen and the groaning of the roasting-jack. I've seen them experience and express, in the most admirable way, the most fleeting and stirring nuances which music has to offer. It's in such circumstances that a northerner such as myself is astounded to watch these ignorant artists, who are incapable of picking out a waltz on a piano or telling one key from another, singing and accompanying – solely by instinct and with tremendous verve – the most remarkable and original music, which, moreover, the composer keeps revising and rearranging even as the rehearsals are taking place. The singers make no end of mistakes, but in music, all mistakes made through an excess of enthusiasm are easily forgiven, just as lovers overlook faults that arise from loving too ardently.

Stendhal, *Life of Rossini*, chapter 6, translated by Stephen Brook

John Ebers, the manager of the King's Theatre, had some harsh things to say about the rehearsal process:

The prima donna, whose part is settled, attends the rehearsal, and the seconda, being displeased with her own station in the piece, will not go on, and the first lady, indignant at being detained to no purpose, goes away, and the business is over for the day. If the manager is positive, the lady falls ill. Biagioli, being refused a part she wanted in *Elisa e Claudio*, took to her bed for two days, in consequence, as she said, of being so afflicted by my decision.

The refusal to proceed is the more effectual engine, because it puts all the rest of the company out of humour at their time being occupied needlessly: all complain, and a dialogue goes on, in which everybody talks at once; and probably three different languages, at least, being simultaneously employed by different speakers, the result may be conceivable, but not expressible. The *signori* protest, the *signore* exclaim, the choruses are wonderfully in concert in their lamentations, the director commands, entreats, stamps, and swears, with equal success, and, in the midst of the babel, the gentlemen of the orchestra, who wish all the singers at the devil, endeavour to get over the business of the day, by playing on without the vocal music. The leader of the orchestra, finding all ineffectual, puts on his hat, and walks away, followed by violins, basses, trombones, and kettle drums, *en masse*, and the scene at length concludes as it may, the manager, composer, and director being left to calculate together the progress of business.

The general wish before alluded to, on the part of performers, of strengthening their own parts by the introduction of extraneous matter, without regard to its effect on the general tone and character of the piece, is a principal cause of disunion between the

director and the singers, and seldom overcome without some
sacrifice.

To know how these jarring elements are to be composed into
harmony requires almost the experience of a life. The flatteries, the
compliances, the power of diplomacy requisite to effect this object
are infinite. Decision and address are indispensable; to be too
uncompromising is dangerous, but to be too accommodating is
worse.

John Ebers, Seven Years of the King's Theatre, Philadelphia, 1828,
pp. 220–22

*Maria Malibran found herself rehearsing in London in 1833 with the
unsophisticated Irish tenor John Templeton:*

In *La sonnambula* his character was to react passionately to hers;
Maria gave him definite thoughts and feelings to relate his acting
to. Failing this, she tried to get a reaction from Templeton himself.

'You are cold, inanimate! Are you a man? Do you have a wife?
And do you love that wife?' Templeton nodded in the affirmative.
'Then,' she continued, 'would you, if she were in such trouble,
stand so far from her and look at her with such indifference?
Come closer to me, and seem very sorry for my situation.'
Templeton moved closer. 'Come to me,' she urged. 'I won't bite
you!'

Templeton, annoyed at her constant needling, did the biting.
'Ah, Mr Templeton,' she told him one day, 'you are a very fine,
tall man, but you are a very bad lover. I would rather have Mr
Woodleg for my husband.' She indicated the prompter, Mr Wilmot,
who had a wooden leg, and the rehearsal was reduced to laughter
at Templeton's expense. As they continued he put so much passion,
or anger, into the love scene that he bit Maria on the neck and was
this time firmly admonished for his realistic acting. 'That's not
really necessary,' she told him sternly.

Maria treated Templeton as though she were a mischievous

older sister heckling her little brother. During one performance when his acting dissatisfied her, she pinched him sharply in the rump, causing him to jump suddenly and kick his leg. Annoyed at this disrespectful treatment on stage, he went to Mr Bunn [the impresario] for advice. Bunn suggested that he call on Malibran, let her know what was on his mind, and ask her what he had done to deserve 'such a total want of good breeding'. Templeton took his director's advice; the next morning he confronted her in Bunn's presence. Maria could barely keep from laughing, and she replied facetiously, 'I thought you wanted, sir, to kiss me.'

Bunn was stunned at the tenor's response. 'At this moment, when she was the idol of the people ... when peers would have given their coronets to press only the tips of her fingers, and the world at large was sighing at her feet, imagine the phlegmatic songster exclaiming: "Gude God, is that all? Mak your mind easy, I would na' kiss you for ony consideration", and shaking hands, he left the house.'

Howard Bushnell, *Maria Malibran*, Pennsylvania State University Press, 1979, pp. 158-9

The impresario J.H. Mapleson recalls how the great singers of his time avoided rehearsals if they could:

[The conductor Sir Michael] Costa would have been horrified at the way in which operatic enterprises are now too frequently conducted – especially, I mean, in a musical point of view; works hurriedly produced, and in some cases without a single complete rehearsal. Often, no doubt, the prima donna (if sufficiently distinguished to be allowed to give herself airs) is in fault for the insufficient rehearsals or for rehearsals being altogether dispensed with. When such singers as Mme Patti and Mme Nilsson stipulate that 'the utility of rehearsing' shall be left to their judgement – which means that they shall never be called to any sort of rehearsal – all idea of a perfect ensemble must, in their case, be abandoned. Sir Michael would, I am sure, have protested against the acceptance of such conditions. Nothing would satisfy him but to go on rehearsing a work until everything, and especially until the ensemble pieces, were perfect.

J.H. Mapleson, *The Mapleson Memoirs 1848–1888*, Remington, 1888, I,
pp. 224–5

Verdi in rehearsal in 1847:

Between piano and orchestral sessions, there were over one hundred rehearsals for *Macbeth*. The implacable Verdi spared no thought for his artists: he tired and tormented them with the same number for hours on end, and he never moved to a different scene until they had managed to perform the piece in a manner which fell least short of his ideal. He was not much loved by the multitude, for no word of encouragement, no 'bravo' of conviction ever passed his lips, not even when orchestral players and members of the chorus believed they had done everything possible to content him.

[*Jules Claretie gives an account of the composer in rehearsal twenty years later, this time for* Don Carlos:]

In a corner, in the glow of a little lamp, like confederates of some secret tribunal, the musicians – composers likewise – responsible for rehearsing the choruses, bend over the score or look questioningly at Verdi's eloquent gaze, read his thoughts from a single flash of his eyes or a single frown, take notes, attentive to the slightest gesture, the slightest word from the Maestro . . .

Verdi listens; his entire being, the whole might of his iron-like temperament strains towards a single goal. His sense of hearing is doubly, triply acute. He questions everything. In this thundering harmony he can hear the faintest of notes. He can hear everything at the same time: the chorus, the brass, the aria and all that happens on and off the stage. He gets up, leaps about, valiantly spurring on all these groups, shouting with that Italian accent which lends charm to his voice: '*Il y a un trou là! . . . Allons! . . . Vite! . . .*'

He gets up, beats time, snaps thumb against middle finger, and this strident, bright, terse note, this noise like the sound of castanets is heard above the orchestra and the chorus, goads them on, drives them forward like lashes from a whip. Then he claps his hands. He radiates harmony from head to foot, he measures himself against his ideal, he instils his artistic genius into these men and women, kindling them with his fire, himself devoured by fire, beating the floor with his heels, running to the back of the theatre, stopping the singers and rediscovering his original conception among the chaos from which an ordered world will emerge.

Eugenio Checchi, *Giuseppe Verdi*, 1926, and Jules Claretie, 'Une répétition de *Don Carlos* – Verdi', *Le Figaro*, 17 February 1867, translated by Richard Stokes and reprinted in Marcello Conati, ed., *Interviews and Encounters with Verdi*, Gollancz, 1984, pp. 25, 61–3

In 1893 Bruno Walter, aged seventeen, took up a post at the Cologne opera:

Soon after entering on my duties, for example, I had to rehearse the first act of *Die Meistersinger* with a number of soloists. Every time I corrected a false note or a rhythmical inexactitude, or called attention to one of Wagner's dynamic instructions, I could feel the singers' dissatisfaction and restlessness grow, until the Pogner said to me: 'Young man, you are dealing with mature artists. Don't give us any instructions, and keep your corrections to yourself' – or words to that effect. To my surprise I heard myself reply quietly and without shyness that it was my duty to correct musical mistakes; I would have to continue to do so, and I begged him not to make things difficult for me. Well, I had my way and kept up my energetic rehearsing. I was even buoyed up emotionally by the resistance I had experienced. At the end of the rehearsal, my former antagonist, a rather mediocre singer, threw his arms about me and assured me of his and his colleagues' utmost approbation. From that moment, I was on the best of terms with the artists . . . I had early adopted the habit of demonstrating by my own singing how the thing ought to be done. I never demanded of the singers what lay beyond their vocal possibilities, but I did demand everything that lay within their power and insisted that they do justice to their parts musically and dramatically.

Bruno Walter, *Theme and Variations*, translated by James A. Galston,
Hamish Hamilton, 1947, p. 73

Composer – Ethel Smyth – and conductor – Thomas Beecham – at war:

With her own experience, a considerable one, of continental theatres, Miss Smyth found his airy impracticality about rehearsals [of her opera *The Wreckers*] and such matters galling. He was rarely less than an hour late for rehearsals, a peculiarity for which he quickly became notorious among orchestral players. To the composer's metronome marks he paid little attention, imposing speeds of his own upon her music as the impulse or preference seized him. Rehearsals developed into a battle of wills. Miss Smyth made it clear that when it came to the handling of her music she had no intention of being complaisant ... At the last rehearsal she sat cross-legged on the stage, beating one tempo while Beecham in the pit beat another. Naturally, it was Beecham who won. But Miss Smyth's opposition was splendidly overt ...

Singers he tended to flail. At a *Wreckers* rehearsal, as he was approaching the final drowning catastrophe, John Coates, as Mark, the doomed hero, suddenly stopped singing. 'What's the matter, Mr Coates?' inquired Beecham, halting the orchestra. 'I was just wondering,' replied Coates – 'is this the place where I'm supposed to be drowned by the waves or by the orchestra?'

Charles Reid, *Thomas Beecham: An Independent Biography*, Gollancz, 1961,
pp. 84–5

Reflecting on the production of Borodin's Prince Igor *during the second season of the Russian Opera in 1914, Thomas Beecham observed:*

Quite as interesting as the performance of any opera by an all-Russian company is the rehearsal of it, and it still remains a mystery to me not only how we ever reached that first night, but how everything during it went with such accuracy and swing. The few final days beforehand Drury Lane was more like a railway station than a theatre, with scenery arriving from three or four different quarters, and, when unpacked, disclosing frequently the awful fact that the artist had gone no further than indicate the design on some cloth sixty feet long without adding a stroke of paint ... The orchestral parts were full of blunders with most of the cuts marked wrongly, so that it took hours to establish any kind of correspondence between band and stage. The proceedings were interrupted every five minutes by the agitated appearance of a small legion of dressmakers, wig-makers, and boot-makers, all of them insisting that if immediate attention were not given to their needs, the fruits of their labour would never be ready in time. The leading singers quarrelled, the temperamental Chaliapin had a fisticuff encounter with the baritone who sang the title role, and the chorus took sides with as much ardour as if they had been Capulets and Montagues. The actual day before the production the final rehearsal began in the early afternoon, went on throughout the evening well into the morning hours, and came to an end only then because the conductor had an attack of hysteria, had to be taken off his chair, carried into a dressing-room, and put to bed on a sofa. It now seemed humanly impossible that the work could be ready in time; and yet such is the calibre of this remarkable people that fifteen hours later everything fell into place like the diverse pieces of a jigsaw puzzle and yielded a performance as flawless as exhilarating. It is true that while the first act was being played some of the scenery for the last was still in the hands of painters, but it was all finished with a good half-hour to spare and, when hoisted into position, looked none the worse for its neck-to-neck race with the clock.

Sir Thomas Beecham, *A Mingled Chime*, Hutchinson, 1944, p. 127

The dramatic soprano Iva Pacetti was one of the few who stood up to Toscanini in rehearsal:

'He was determined to conduct Dukas's *Ariane et Barbe-Bleu* on a text by Maurice Maeterlinck – we were now in 1927 – an opera that has never encountered real success since its première in Paris in 1907. And the leading soprano part, terrifying in its length and vocal hurdles, was hard to cast. He listened to thirty-one sopranos (at least so I was told at the time) and then in despair asked for me . . .

'At the first stage rehearsal . . . when all of Bluebeard's wives are lined up, he screamed at me, "You are a sheep! For this role a lioness is needed!" The critics had always commented on my fiery temperament, and that day it blossomed in full. No one, not even the sublime Toscanini, had the right to insult me in front of everyone. With all eyes staring at me, I marched out of La Scala and began walking. "Pacetti, Pacetti!" I heard a voice cry out in back of me. It was the *metteur-en-scène* Gioacchino Forzano. "Are you insane? This can mean the end of your career." "Perhaps," I replied, "but no one is going to call me what he did!" And I walked away. By the time I had reached home on foot, Scandiani was already there. The question was very simple: either I continued or the production would have to be cancelled. So much pressure was put on me that I returned to the next rehearsal. Toscanini was icy but correct, and I sang the various performances. But to show his distaste, the great man never came out to take a bow with me, and that was that.'

Lanfranco Rasponi, *The Last Prima Donnas*, Gollancz, 1984,

pp. 200–201

After a twelve-year absence from Covent Garden, Sir Thomas Beecham returned to conduct there in 1951:

[He] was on his best behaviour during the first *Meistersinger* rehearsals and was full of praise for the orchestra and chorus; later, he had some trenchant things to say about the cast, even though he had been consulted about the singers. By the time of the first

full stage and orchestral rehearsals, everyone had been lulled into a
false sense of security. Beecham arrived late that morning, nearer
10.30 than 10, and announced, 'Gentlemen, we will reseat the
orchestra this morning'; at which a general post took place, and
after much noise and shuffling around, Tommy looked over his
half-glasses and turning to the double-bass player, Eugene Cruft,
asked 'Are you quite comfortable, Mr Cruft?' to which Cruft
replied, 'No, Sir Thomas, I cannot get my instrument into a comfortable position.' 'Oh, what is the matter then?' asked Beecham.
'It's this rostrum,' replied Cruft, pointing to a little platform
which, of course, had not been moved in the general post. 'Rostrum?' queried Tommy. 'Yes, Sir Thomas,' chimed in Thomas
Matthews, the leader of the orchestra. 'It was put in last autumn
when the Scala was here.' There followed a moment's pause while
Tommy stroked his little goatee, and then he roared, 'LA SCALA!
God in heaven! Since when has Great Britain and Covent Garden
in particular been a dependency of the Italian Empire? Remove it!!'
'I can't,' said Cruft, 'it's screwed down.' 'Well unscrew it,' stormed
Beecham. By now the chorus, who had crowded on stage for the beginning of the opening scene, were laughing aloud. 'It's all very well
for you to laugh, ladies and gentlemen,' said Tommy, 'but mark my
words, your turn will come.' And it did, with a vengeance.

Act II of *Die Meistersinger* opens with the enchanting but musically difficult scene for the apprentices and David; the chorus
could not get it right that morning, nor could Murray Dickie who
was singing David. Beecham's patience began to run out. 'What
do you think you're singing?' he shouted, and one foolish chorister
timidly murmured '*Meistersinger*, Sir Thomas.' 'Really,' he replied,
'I thought it was "Kiss Me up the Alley". Where's Mr Feasey?'
(Norman Feasey was head of music staff and had worked with
Beecham in the pre-war seasons.) Norman appeared, 'Yes, Sir
Thomas?' 'Take Mr Dickie away, and don't bring him back until
he knows his part.'

Harold Rosenthal, *My Mad World of Opera*, Weidenfeld & Nicolson,
1982, pp. 78–9

In the early 1970s Placido Domingo 'rehearsed' with Herbert von Karajan:

The soundtrack of the *Butterfly* film gave me my first chance to work with Herbert von Karajan. I had met him in Salzburg some time earlier, at an audition that had been arranged for me while I was singing in Vienna. He was supervising a lighting rehearsal for *Die Walküre* at the Grosse Festspielhaus, and I walked on to a completely dark stage. A mysterious voice called to me from the dark, in Italian, 'Good morning, what will you sing?'

'The Flower Song from *Carmen*,' I replied.

It was the only audition I ever had where I could not see the faces of the auditioners. In a way, it was like a performance.

When I arrived in Vienna for the *Butterfly* sessions, I met Karajan after dinner at the Imperial Hotel. He said simply, 'Tomorrow morning at 10 we will meet at the studio; we will rehearse; and then whenever we are ready – perhaps around 12 – we will record.' I arrived at 10 and took my place. All of a sudden I saw the red light next to him go on. He began to conduct, and in fifty-five minutes we had finished recording the first act.

'Maestro,' I said, 'I thought we were going to rehearse.'

'Among musicians,' he replied, 'rehearsal is not necessary.'

I can confirm that we were indeed together on every note. In the afternoon we recorded the third act, and that was that. Thus my first working experience with Karajan went by so quickly that it was almost as if it had not happened. Never before had I worked with a conductor of that calibre without having a piano rehearsal – without even exchanging a word about the role. I appreciated the great compliment he was paying me.

Placido Domingo, *My First Forty Years*, Weidenfeld & Nicolson, 1983,

pp. 108–9

Thomas Allen goes to Cologne to play Don Giovanni in a production by Michael Hampe:

I am familiar with the role of Don Giovanni, and I am now an experienced singer-actor, so I begin to reveal some, though not all, of my trademarks. Dr Hampe has other ideas. He's entitled; it's his production. But without a sense of sharing, of give-and-take between us, I'm anxious that I will feel too strait-jacketed to give of my best . . .

Dr Hampe is sticking rigidly to the production book of Salzburg five years ago. Robert Minder, his Austrian assistant, knows the production from the book and from their work together with Herbert von Karajan. He keeps the good doctor informed of who went where and when. I find myself raising the question: 'Are we going to follow action for action as written in the book or would it not be better to use the weeks of rehearsal to try to come up with some new ideas?' This elicits no immediate response and I sense that it could be the germ of trouble for me over the next few weeks.

The length of time allotted for rehearsals is becoming more and more of a talking-point wherever we go. A growing number of producers these days insist on a minimum of six weeks' rehearsal, and as I write this it has probably gone up to eight. Some producers certainly have the talent to hold one's interest for that length of time with their ideas, their anecdotes, their intellect or their personality. Others don't. In any case I believe it's too long. Frankly, I'm not prepared to give up six or eight weeks of my time to do something I've done more than a hundred times before.

Thomas Allen, *Foreign Parts*, Sinclair-Stevenson, 1993, pp. 59, 62

Janet Baker rehearses her final appearances at Covent Garden, in Gluck's Alceste in 1981:

26 October: Everyone met today. After a concentrated morning music session with producer, conductor, coach and tenor colleague, my Alceste is reduced to a wreck. She lies around my feet in shattered fragments. Everyone else has got hold of her and she is totally lost to me: the next weeks will be the process of putting her back together again. She is a muddle of beats in a bar and different

viewpoints and this is even before I have taken a single step. Tomorrow, when I use my body, things may seem a little better . . .

20 November: All hell let loose for the past two days! It's like some extraordinary circus; arguments in corridors, people wandering about half in costume, half out . . . Amid all the chaos something suddenly happens which looks and sounds indescribably beautiful. We are on the right track. When you think of the number of people involved in putting on a single opera it is a miracle . . .

25 November: During all these past weeks, packed so tightly with incident, the gathering of ideas, our searching, our works, our laughter, our fatigue, our enjoyment, we have all lived our days with a common purpose. Whatever the result of that purpose may be proved to be when the public sees it tomorrow, nothing and nobody can take away, mutilate, or destroy all that we have learned together and enjoyed during the rehearsal period. It is such a fruitful time in every possible way, and not surprising that I always find these weeks the most enjoyable part of operatic work. They are a microcosm of life, containing a beginning, when we painfully take everything apart, a middle, when we attempt to put it all together again, and an end, our final dress rehearsal, which is a death. A death, because the preparation is ended and something totally new begins; rehearsals are very far removed from the real performances. There is an enormous gulf between the two and no bridge . . .

26 November: The day I have been working towards for over a year . . . I feel calm and strong and full of joy to have such a role in such a house, and then walk out on to the stage. This first moment is unlike any of the rehearsal entrances. Now the final piece of the jigsaw puzzle is in place – the vital ingredient of all performances, the audience. With our weeks of work, our strivings and struggles towards some sort of perfection, we are helpless until the people are there to complete the circle; no magic, no communication, is possible until this moment, it is all self-indulgence until now. This living wall of human feeling reaches

out to me across the pit and locks into my heart; the performance can unfold. The first act goes by like a flash and I go back to my dressing-room knowing that I have sung that glorious music with my whole heart and soul.

Janet Baker, *Full Circle*, Macrae, 1982, pp. 10, 38, 41–4

26: Performances

Parsifal is the kind of opera that starts at six o'clock. After it has been going for three hours, you look at your watch and it says 6.20.

On 14 September 1716 Lady Mary Wortley Montagu described to Alexander Pope a performance of J.J. Fux's Angelica vincitrice di Alcina *in Vienna:*

I have so far wander'd from the Discipline of the Church of England to have been last Sunday at the Opera, which was perform'd in the Garden of the Favorita, and I was so much pleas'd with it, I have not yet repented my seeing it. Nothing of that kind ever was more Magnificent, and I can easily believe what I am told, that the Decorations and habits cost the Emperour £30,000 Sterling. The Stage was built over a very large Canal, and at the beginning of the 2nd Act divided into 2 parts, discovering the Water, on which there immediately came from different parts 2 fleets of little gilded vessels that gave the representation of a Naval fight. It is not easy to imagine the beauty of this Scene, which I took particular Notice of, but all the rest were perfectly fine in their kind. The story of the Opera ... gives Opportunity for a great variety of Machines and changing of the Scenes, which are perform'd with a surprizing swiftnesse ... The Ladys all siting in the open air exposes them to great Inconveniencys, for there is but one canopy for the Imperial Family, and the first night it was represented, a shower of rain happening, the Opera was broke off and the company crouded away in such confusion, I was allmost squeez'd to Death.

Mary Wortley Montagu, *Complete Letters*, Clarendon Press, 1965, I,
pp. 262–3

The première of Iphigenia *by Nicola Piccini (1728–1800) was enlivened by an inebriated singer:*

When the heroine appeared it was seen at once that Iphigenia, Mll
Laguerre, could not stand upright! She rolled about to al
compass points of the stage, hesitated, made faces at the or
– in short, she was drunk! Of course the opera was a fail
before she could be removed from the stage, a facetious
sung out: 'This is not *Iphigenia in Tauris*, this is
Champagne!'

For her misdemeanour 'her ladyship' was sent to F
where two days of imprisonment seems to have
beneficial effect upon her, for she came out and sang
first night of her release.

Frederick Crowest, *A Book of Musical Anecdotes*, Bentley, 18

Stendhal is awed by La Scala:

25 September [1816]. No time wasted: another visit to the fi
opera house in the world; another performance of *La testa di
bronzo*. I had time now to give full rein to my admiration. The
scene is set in Hungary; never was there a prince in that country
prouder or more imperious, more generous or more warlike
than Galli. He is one of the finest actors I have ever met with,
and he possesses the noblest bass voice that I have ever
heard . . .

And what a masterly handling of colour in the distribution of
costume! It was as though I beheld, constantly evolving before my
eyes, a series of most exquisite paintings by Paolo Veronese . . .
The whole stage of La Scala is afire with wealth and magnificence;
the crowd of singers and actors rarely numbers less than a hundred
at any given moment; and one and all are costumed with a
splendour which, in France, would be reserved most severely for
the star performers . . . La Scala is the focal point of the entire city;
it is the universal salon, the hub of society, which is here, and here
only.

26 September . . . It is quite customary to give and acknowledge greetings from box to box across the theatre; I have a footing now in seven or eight different boxes, in each of which there may be ▊ or six persons, and conversation firmly established, as in a ▊ The tone of society is utterly *natural*, gay without being ▊us, and ruthlessly stripped of *gravity* . . .

▊ber [1816] . . . In Milan, to all intents and purposes, ▊ng costs nothing. The price of a seat at La Scala, on a ▊cription, is precisely six-and-thirty centimes. For this ▊ the spectator may sit through the first act of an opera ▊ entertainment in itself: the whole performance is ▊ at half-past seven in winter; in summer, at half-past ▊d by a full-length serious ballet, lasting an hour and ▊ ballet comes the second act of the opera, say three-▊ an hour; and the evening finally closes with a short ▊t, usually exquisite, which is designed to see you off the ▊ in a gale of laughter towards half-past twelve or one ▊ in the morning. The purchase of an ordinary ticket (two ▊cs for occasional visitors, thirty-six centimes for regular subscribers) entitles you to a seat in the pit, which is equipped with benches comfortably upholstered and with a good back to lean against. The pit can seat about nine hundred persons. If you happen to enjoy the privilege of a box, it is normal to arrive there early so as to receive visitors . . .

Halfway through the evening, it is the normal duty of the escorting gallant to regale his mistress with ices, which are served in the box. There is invariably some wager afoot, and the stake is always the same: *sorbets*, or water-ices. These *sorbets* are divine; they may be of three kinds, *gelati*, *crèpe* and *pezzi duri*; and no one should fail to make so rewarding an acquaintance. I am still undecided which of the three species is the most exquisite; and so, every evening, I resort to experiment.

Stendhal, *Rome, Naples and Florence*, translated by Richard N. Coe,
Calder, 1959, pp. 6–7, 8, 24–5

Byron wrote from Venice to John Murray on 27 December 1816:

Went to the opera — at the Fenice theatre ... the finest by the
way I have ever seen — it beats *our* theatres hollow in beauty &
scenery — and those of Milan & Brescia bow before it. — The
Opera and its Syrens were much like all other operas & women —
but the subject of the said Opera was something edifying — it
turned — the plot & conduct thereof — upon a fact narrated by
Livy — of a hundred & fifty married ladies having poisoned a
hundred & fifty husbands in the good old times — the bachelors
of Rome believed this extraordinary mortality to be merely the
common effect of matrimony or a pestilence   but the surviving
Benedicts being all seized with the cholic examined into the
matter — and found that 'their possets had been drugged' the
consequence of which was much scandal and several suits at law.
— This is really & truly the subject of the Musical piece at the
Fenice — & you can't conceive what pretty things are sung &
recitativoed about the '*horrenda strage*'; the conclusion was a lady's
head about to be chopped off by a lictor — but (I am sorry to say)
he left it on — and she got up & sung a trio with the two Consuls
— the Senate in the background being chorus. — The ballet was
distinguished by nothing remarkable — except that the principal
she-dancer went into convulsions because she was applauded at
her first appearance — and the manager came forward to ask if
there was 'ever a physician in the theatre' — there was a Greek one
in my Box whom I wished very much to volunteer his services —
being sure that in this case these would have been the last
convulsions which would have troubled the Ballerina — but he
would not.

Lord Byron, *Letters and Journals*, Murray, 1976, V, pp. 151–2

Shaw sits through a performance of Les Huguenots *in April 1877:*

The announcement that the latest successor of Mario was to
appear as Raoul, in Meyerbeer's *Les Huguenots*, attracted to Covent
Garden Opera House a large audience desirous to judge of Signor

Gayarré's powers from a part which affords every possible opportunity to an artist . . .

We believe [Giuliano Gayarré] once had a voice – and a robust
voice, too – though not of remarkably fine quality, and to abuse
its wreck without taste or artistic skill constitutes his present
employment. His movements are awkward, and his few attitudes
are suggestive of nothing but a self-complacency the grounds for
which are wholly indiscernible. Why he should have been cast for
a character such as Scribe's ingenuous and rash hero, when M.
Capoul – who, though by no means immaculate, has, at any rate,
some pretensions as an artist – was available, we are unable to
guess. Signor Gayarré's Raoul was simply below criticism. After
the most exciting situation in lyric drama – the duet in the fourth
act of *Les Huguenots* – he was honoured with a single call. His C
sharp in the duel septet evoked some applause. Except at these
points, his performance seemed to produce no favourable
impression . . .

Signor Vianesi conducted, and under his direction the orchestra
quite surpassed themselves in rough and inartistic execution. The
choruses were quite worthy of the accompaniment, and the Rata-
plan in particular was received with a contempt which was richly
merited. The simple detail of the bells, which produce so striking
an effect by their interruption of the impassioned duet in the
fourth act, was neglected. The benediction scene gave the impression of a disorderly mob; and the finale of the last act, from the
entrance of the assassins, mutilated as it is, was not sung at all,
Mlle d'Angeri alone proving equal to the occasion by sustaining a
few random notes. Considering the performance as a whole, and
with special reference to the tenor, the orchestra, and the chorus,
we consider it to be the worst in our unhappy experience, even of
the operas of Meyerbeer.

George Bernard Shaw, article in *The Hornet*, 25 April 1877, reprinted in
Shaw's Music, Bodley Head, 1989, I, pp. 116–18

During a performance of Carmen *in 1886 a bizarre dispute arose between the two principal singers:*

It was in the middle of the third act, when Don José, the tenor (Ravelli), was about to introduce an effective high note which generally brought down the house, that Carmen rushed forward and embraced him – why I could never understand. Being interrupted at the moment of his effect, he was greatly enraged, and by his movements showed that he had resolved to throw Madame Hauk into the orchestra. But she held firmly on to his red waistcoat, he shouting all the time, '*Laissez-moi, laissez-moi!*' until all the buttons came off one by one, when she retired hastily to another part of the stage. Ravelli rushed forward and exclaimed, '*Regardez, elle a déchiré mon gilet!*' and with such rage that he brought down thunders of applause, the people believing this genuine expression of anger to be part of the play . . .

The details of the affair soon got known and were at once reproduced in all the papers . . . What could the public think of an opera company in which the tenor was always threatening to murder the prima donna, while the prima donna's husband found himself forced to take up a position at one of the wings bearing a revolver with which he proposed to shoot the tenor the moment he showed the slightest intention of approaching the personage for whom he is supposed to entertain an ungovernable passion? Don José was, according to the opera, madly in love with Carmen. But it was an understood thing between the singers impersonating these two characters that they were to keep at a respectful distance one from the other. Ravelli was afraid of Minnie Hauk's throttling him while engaged in the emission of a high B flat; and Minnie Hauk, on her side, dreaded the murderous knife with which Ravelli again and again had threatened her. Love-making looks, under such conditions, a little unreal.

J.H. Mapleson, *The Mapleson Memoirs 1848–1888*, Remington, 1888, II, pp. 175–6, 194

Shaw finds a performance of Carmen *slovenly but still manages to amuse the reader:*

On Saturday a rather slovenly performance of *Carmen* brought forward Mlle Zélie de Lussan, who looked the part well and sang it not at all badly . . . The Toreador is a role which Signor del Puente is supposed to have made peculiarly his own. We appeal to Mr Harris [the impresario] to make it peculiarly somebody else's who will at least take the trouble to sing it accurately and carefully. And we beg to assure Miss Macintyre that a less charming Micaela would have run some risk of being soundly hissed for the graceless interpolation with which she spoiled her part in the finale to the third act. Those who advise her to deface a composer's work by interlarding it with commonplaces by her singing master are no doubt quite ignorant enough to believe that Bizet's music needs improvement. Audiences nowadays know better, and they expect Miss Macintyre to know better too.

George Bernard Shaw, article in *The Star* of 9 July 1888, reprinted in
Shaw's Music, Bodley Head, 1989, I, pp. 518–19

Shaw wearily dismisses a performance of Ambroise Thomas's Hamlet:

If I take the trouble to criticize the Covent Garden performance of *Hamlet* . . . my object must be understood to be vindictive rather than artistic. Nobody wanted to hear the thing: many critics earnestly desired not to hear it. I suppose M. Lassalle wanted to sing it: if so, he might have done it privately, without dragging us to listen to him. I really never saw such a foolish opera . . . The title of the work ought to be changed. Since Ambroise Thomas has honestly done his very best not to remind us of Shakespeare, why should the subject be dragged in calling the people in the libretto Ophelia, Hamlet, Laertes, and so on? If this were altered, and the fifth and sixth acts cut out as the seventh has been, there would be time to have another ballet, and get the whole performance over by half-past eleven . . .

Madame Melba sings chromatic roulades very prettily, smiling

at the nobility and gentry in the pit and grand tiers, who applaud
her with that air of thorough connoisseurship in operatic execution
of the *haute école* which imposes on everyone who does not know
by practical experience how easy it is to take them in. Then she goes
to the water and drowns herself, in token whereof her 'double' presently appears supine on a sort of toboggan car, and shoots along
feet foremost through the bulrushes to the prompt side. It is all as
absurd as it can be; and I, dead beat at the end of the season, have
hardly energy enough to make fun of it even on this cheap scale.

George Bernard Shaw, article in *The World*, 20 July 1890, reprinted in
Shaw's Music, Bodley Head, 1989, II, pp. 132–4

Shaw takes apart a performance of Die Walküre*:*

There is another reform in the staging of these Nibelung dramas
upon which I must appeal to the leading artists. Why is it that
Brünnhilde always looks ridiculous and ugly, no matter how
attractive the artist impersonating her may be? And why, on the
night in question, did Fräulein Klafsky, in bounding up the
mountain staircase, trip, tumble, and have a narrow escape of
adding to the year's list of Alpine casualties? Simply because she
would go mountaineering, according to German etiquette, in a
trailing white skirt. Imagine a helmeted, breastplated, spear-armed
war-maiden dashing through battles and scaling crags in a skirt in
which no sensible woman would walk down Regent Street! I do
not suggest gaiters and a tailor-made skirt, nor yet bicycling
knickerbockers, though either would be better than the present
Valkyrie fashion; but I do urge the claims of a tunic.

The performance of *Die Walküre* improved as it went on. The
first act was bad – very bad. Sieglinde was a cipher. Alvary began
by singing out of the key. Later on he found the key, and merely
sang out of tune. He posed with remarkable grace and dramatic
eloquence: I can imagine no finer Siegmund from the point of
view of a deaf man; but he may take my word for it – the word of
a critic who has highly appreciated some of his performances –

that he will have to get much nearer the mark in point of pitch, and assimilate his vocal phrasing much more to his admirable pantomime in point of grace, if he intends to hold his own within two minutes' walk of Jean de Reszke.

George Bernard Shaw, article in *The World*, 27 June 1894,
in *Shaw's Music*, Bodley Head, 1989, III, pp. 252–4

How a death on stage won a round of applause:

For a season that began in dissension and proceeded with disaster, only the worst could suffice; and it occurred during a performance of *Marta* on 10 February [1897]. For the only time in a history of countless stage deaths at the Metropolitan, a performer expired in public view, and so ironically pertinent was his collapse that Armand Castlemary was loudly applauded as he gasped his last. The action at the end of Act II calls for Tristano to run about the stage and stumble. The exertion was too much for the sixty-three-year-old baritone, and he died in the arms of Jean de Reszke, who had been watching the performance from the wings.

Irving Kolodin, *The Story of the Metropolitan Opera*, New York, 1953,
p. 143

Animals on stage look adorable but sometimes come to a sticky end:

[In] Humperdinck's *Königskinder* geese are an essential part of the action. When *Königskinder* was given at the Metropolitan Farrar played the Goosegirl and caused a commotion at the première by appearing before the curtain carrying a live goose under her arm. The *Königskinder* was also given in Chicago when the Metropolitan was on tour. There the opera was so well liked that the management decided to schedule an extra performance. Then it was discovered that the geese were missing. Upon inquiry, the management was informed that the stage-hands, who believed that the geese had played their parts and were no longer needed, had eaten them.

George R. Marek, *A Front Seat at the Opera*, Harrap, 1951, p. 239

In his inimitable English, Caruso writes to his wife from Mexico City about a performance of Carmen *given in a bullring:*

[6 October 1919] . . . After I make all my preparatifs I went to the Plaza. This is the arena of bull fights, with now a stage in open air for the opera. There was a beautiful sunshine, but my voice was like midnight, dark very dark, and I was trembling. I dress quigly and put some things in my throat and ready for the performance. At half past three exactly we begin and I went out. An applause salut me but not enthusiasticaly. I beginning to sing and the voice wao very strong and eavy, but I quigly juge myself and tought that I go well to the end. Then come the duo with Michaela, poor, very poor, and at the end of the duo, being nervous, because the Michaela not go well, my voice dont sound well but pass, and the public applauded. From that time the weather beginning to change and big clouds beginning to gat up, in effect, before that the first act finished, beginning to reinning and I and Carmen were all wet. We supposed that the public goes away but nobody move. At the end of the act we have few calls. The second act beginning with eavy reinin and there were big spectale. Thousand of umbrellas was open and covered all the aera of the Plaza. We dont see any head and dont hear the orchestra. We hope allways to stop but the public was there. I begin to sing my romanza and at the midle I dont know if was effect of the rein on my condition, I think that was the reason, one note come out broken. Quigly I tought, 'Now come the revolution,' but nobody say enyting and I went to the end with more calor and entusiasm and the public make me a big ovation. But there the rein that come down strongly. We finished the act and had five callings. It was very funny to see one enorms bleek spot all around the Plaza with some color reed and bleu, there were all umbrellas.

The third act was worst and we went on just same, but at the end was insopportable. I ask, 'When we stop?' Somebody told me, 'When the public say stop.' But nobody told this word. I had a big ovation at the end of this act being in good condition as my voice warmed up. Somebody had the bed idea to say to the public that

the performance was finisched because the artists dont want sing
eny more on account of the weather. I was in my dressing room to
prepare myself for the last act and I heard a big noise. You most
know that our dressing room are under the stears of the Plaza and
precisely where the bulls are prepered. Then I heard this noise and
it seemed like a revolution. I sent out to see wath the matter and
they inform me wath happened. Quigly I sed to tell to the public
that the performance will continue. In effect, everybody whent at
place because they beginning to broke the stage. Then we finisch
the opera with a big pouring and half of the public which dont
hear enytinks because the noise of the wather was strong on the
umbrellas. We were all wetted and the succes was only for that
because artisticali we were all bed.

Dorothy Caruso, Enrico Caruso, Simon & Schuster, 1945, pp. 105–8

Leo Slezak's impish sense of humour sometimes found easy victims:

A performance of Gluck's *Armide* at the Met . . . was over and he
saw a dignified old gentleman with a long flowing white beard
standing around. With an iron grip he grabbed him and pulled
him out with him in front of the curtain to take a bow. There he
pointed to the bewildered old gent and bowed deeply. Two
reporters rushed backstage to Papa's dressing-room. 'That was Mr
Willibald Gluck, the composer!' Papa said reverently. 'He told me
that never in his life has he heard his opera sung so magnificently
as I have sung it tonight.' The following day two large metropolitan newspapers, who apparently weren't aware of the fact that
Christoph Willibald von Gluck had died in 1787, printed the story.
Papa was fined one hundred dollars by the Met. He put a black
veil over his head and went to the office of Otto H. Kahn, the
Maecenas of the opera. He got his hundred dollars back.

Walter Slezak, What Time's the Next Swan?, Doubleday, 1962, p. 211

Thomas Beecham was famed for his prodigious memory as an operatic conductor:

There was one prototype story which bred several variants. Returning from the Continent with hardly time enough to change into a white tie, he appeared in the pit at Covent Garden without a glance at his engagement book or the day-bills. Raising the baton, he turned to the leader and inquired, 'What are we playing tonight?'

'*Figaro*, Sir Thomas.'

'My dear fellow,' he returned, 'you amaze me!'

The performance from memory which followed (so runs the story) was pointed and polished in the ultimate Beecham manner; that is to say, in a manner without precursor or legatees. No man could have phrased Mozart with Beecham's wit and grace if his eye had been perpetually rooted in print. After one such scoreless, exquisite night, the Budapest-born conductor Fritz Reiner sought him out in his dressing-room. 'I wanted to thank you,' he said, 'for a wonderful night with Mozart and Beecham.' Beecham rotated his nose musingly. 'Why drag in Mozart?' he inquired.

Charles Reid, *Thomas Beecham: An Independent Biography*, Gollancz, 1961,

p. 192

Toscanini's hostility to Fascism was put to the test at the première of Turandot *on 25 April 1926 at La Scala which Mussolini was expected to attend:*

The rehearsals were many, long and difficult. Not long before the opening Toscanini informed the company that the very first performance would be given without Alfano's ending. And in fact, after the death of Liu in the third act Toscanini dropped his baton, turned partially towards the audience and said: 'The opera ends, left incomplete by the death of the Maestro.' With tears in his eyes, he left the podium and made his way out of the pit. No one dared applaud until finally someone shouted 'Viva Puccini!' which touched off an enormous ovation. There was an interesting report in the next day's *Corriere*: 'During the interval the audience awaited the previously announced arrival of Mussolini. But the prime minister did not want his presence to distract the public in any way: their attention had to be entirely devoted to Puccini.'

What had actually happened was rather more complicated. Mussolini had turned 12 April into a national holiday which he called Empire Day, and he ordered all places of public entertainment to play [the Fascist anthem] '*Giovinezza*' at their performances on that day. In 1925 Toscanini had made sure that a rehearsal, not a performance, was scheduled at La Scala that evening. Now, in 1926, he received word from highly placed persons that he was not to use the same trick again. He ignored the order and again scheduled a rehearsal. Mussolini, who arrived in Milan a day or two later, was furious, and sent for the theatre's directors. They were told that if they could not control Toscanini, they would either have to get rid of him or never expect to see Mussolini in the theatre. He wished to attend the *Turandot* première, but '*Giovinezza*' would have to be played.

The Scala directors found themselves in an unenviable position, caught between the wrath of Mussolini and the wrath of Toscanini. They told the conductor of the prime minister's order; Toscanini retorted that they could have '*Giovinezza*' played if they would get someone else to conduct both it and *Turandot*. At that point, of course, Toscanini was more essential than Mussolini to La Scala's well-being, so *Turandot* was performed with the Maestro and without the Duce.

Harvey Sachs, *Toscanini*, Weidenfeld & Nicolson, 1978, p. 179

In the 1920s Berlin was over-supplied with opera houses, which led to some unusual problems:

It soon became apparent that by arranging for simultaneous performances at the Opera unter den Linden and at Kroll's the general management had bitten off more than it could chew. The resulting chaotic condition might have been considered all right at

the Breslau Theatre, but, when mixed with strict Prussian bureaucratic methods, it represented a thoroughly indigestible and hellish
brew. One evening, when I was conducting *Das Rheingold* at the
Opera and had started the first measures of the Nibelheim scene, I
had to stop, for there was no sign of Alberich or Mime. A few
minutes passed before I was able to start again, this time *prestissimo*,
for the two dwarfs, confused and out of breath, sang their first
measures at a precipitate tempo. Lieban—Mime had been singing
the part of Alfred in the first act of *Die Fledermaus* at Kroll's. The
act over, he had been driven to the Opera and had hurriedly put
on his make-up and costume for *Das Rheingold*, intending to return
to the Kroll Theatre for the final act of *Fledermaus*. Too bad that
the timetable did not work properly.

Bruno Walter, *Theme and Variations*, translated by James A. Galston,

Hamish Hamilton, 1947, pp. 141–2

Few opera houses could match the extravagance of the performances
mounted at the Roman amphitheatre in Verona each summer. Gigli
describes the performances of 1932:

Two thousand performers took part in [Meyerbeer's] *L'africana*
alone, and fifteen assistant scenographers worked behind the scenes
to solve the difficult problems of stagecraft which the Verona
amphitheatre presents. Indeed, the attention devoted to sceno-
graphy was such that the singers, I felt, were reduced to mere
accessories.

This year, I learned, experimentation had been abandoned; the
effect aimed at was one hundred per cent realism. A rajah rode in
state on a fake elephant; torrential rain drummed on the luxuriant
vegetation of a tropical forest; but above all, there was the ship
and the shipwreck. This scene alone cost fifty thousand lire, a third
of the entire subsidy. Pericle Ansaldo, technical stage director of
the Rome Opera, had attempted an exact reproduction of a
fifteenth-century galleon, with its full complement of sails. The
stage proper formed the main part of the deck, but the poop was

constructed separately, and designed to roll, pitch and swerve. This movable part could hold about forty people. Behind it all was the 'ocean', with mechanical waves. The 'ship' navigated wildly, as if split in two, out of tune with both the wind and waves, not to mention the orchestra. The bulk of the crew squatted securely on the main deck, which was terra firma, while the principals and some of the chorus ducked and slid down the rocking cabin hatchways.

Were these extraneous contrivances really necessary to draw the crowd, I wondered. I was all for making opera popular; but I could not help feeling that this production of *L'africana* came perilously near to being a circus, with '*O Paradiso*' thrown in as an afterthought.

Beniamino Gigli, *Memoirs*, translated by Darina Silone, Cassell, 1957,

pp. 178–9

Toscanini attends a performance of Die Meistersinger – *and doesn't care for it:*

He was usually unaware of the sensation his appearance created. Once in Paris he saw in the morning paper that Furtwängler was conducting a gala performance of *Die Meistersinger* at the Opéra. 'Tonight we go,' he announced to [his wife] Carla. He, Carla, [their daughter] Wanda, and Horowitz, all dressed *à quatre épingles*, appeared at the theatre, whereupon a murmur of excitement flickered through the entire audience and all opera-glasses were trained on the four figures. Toscanini did not notice it. The overture began, it was ill-rehearsed and inexact, he started to curse to himself; the curtain rose, the chorus was singing the chorale in French and a quarter tone off-key. At this moment Toscanini rose and announced, 'We go.' The four of them groped their way out of the theatre. Wanda, recalling the incident, said it was the shortest performance of *Die Meistersinger* she had ever heard. The next morning Furtwängler phoned and said that he had come from Berlin and had not had sufficient time to prepare the performance.

George R. Marek, *Toscanini*, Vision Press, 1975, p. 100

Beecham in search of a Commendatore in Mexico City:

During the [1939 45] war, Beecham was booked for a season of opera in Mexico City, to which he was to take the company which he had just been conducting in Cincinnati. He was delighted to have John Brownlee, who had won great fame at Glyndebourne in the role, with him as Don Giovanni, and to hear that all the Cincinnati cast would be available except the bass who had sung the Commendatore. 'Well,' said Beecham on arrival in Mexico City, 'what are we to do? We simply have to find a singer here for the part.'

This, of course, was easier said than done in Mexico, for though the Commendatore's role is only a short one, it demands splendour and dignity of voice and bearing; the whole opera can be spoilt by a Commendatore who simply sings without suggesting that he is the instrument of divine vengeance. Nevertheless, before long Brownlee was able to report progress.

'I've found a Commendatore,' he said. 'But there's one great difficulty – he's out on parole,' and went on to explain that his discovery, who was not a professional singer, had gone home one night and found his wife in bed with a lover. In true Latin style, he had shot the lover dead and was released while awaiting trial.

Beecham was fascinated by the story 'We simply must have him,' he declared. 'If his voice is right, you must teach him the role and show him how to act the part.'

Brownlee liked the man's voice and found that he could learn music quickly; the only trouble was that he would not do what he was told. The details of the production did not meet with his approval, and he insisted that, at the end of the duel in the first scene, as soon as Don Giovanni had killed him, attendants should come on to the stage and carry him into the wings.

Once Sir Thomas heard the reason for this strange condition he agreed to it at once. 'The father of the man I killed,' the 'Commendatore' explained, 'has sworn to kill me. I cannot lie out there on the stage and make a sitting target for him.'

Ivor Newton, *At the Piano*, Hamish Hamilton, 1966, pp. 281–2

Lotte Lehmann returns to Vienna in 1955 for the reopening of the State Opera, which had been damaged by bombs in 1945. Vincent Sheean's account quotes liberally from her own account:

'It was an unforgettable moment when the iron curtain rose,' she says of the morning. 'Even now in memory, it chokes me. This wonderful old house which has served only beauty, which has given joy and uplift to thousands of music-loving people, had been mute for so long. Now it lives again. Now the old times will come back again; and I am sure of that. I don't belong to those people who always sigh for the past. Nobody is irreplaceable. Wherever some beauty dies, some new beauty is being born . . . [After some speeches] the wonderful Philharmonic Orchestra played the Prelude of the *Meistersinger*. It almost killed me. I was dissolved in tears. I sang at a kind of "trial performance", Eva, as a guest, coming from Hamburg. Standing on the stage behind the closed curtain I wanted to listen to the Prelude. But when the first bars sounded in all their splendour I had the sensational feeling that I had never heard it before. On the wings of this orchestra the music sounded almost unearthly beautiful to me. That was in the year 1914. And the same awesome shock gripped me again now forty-one years later when I listened to this orchestra again' . . .

Lehmann was so stormed by emotions of every kind that she seems to have been unable to give full attention to the performance of *Fidelio*, which, in any case, heard after these momentous eighteen years, must in itself have set her mind and heart wandering. I have been told by persons who saw all this that she was in tears most of the time, and I can well believe it. As she says, 'Beauty had awakened in ruins,' and 'the heart of Austria was beating again'. I have also heard that the singers and musicians themselves were so shaken by emotion on that night that they could not give the best account of themselves or of the music, which nevertheless sounded like the wonders of paradise to most of those who listened inside and outside (most of them outside) the house.

Vincent Sheean, *First and Last Love*, Gollancz, 1957, pp. 204–6

Placido Domingo tells of a performance of La traviata *in Mexico in 1961:*

Towards the end of the second act, after my lines 'Someone is in the garden. Who is there?' a messenger is supposed to enter, asking, 'Signor Germont?' 'It is I,' Alfredo replies. The messenger continues: 'A lady in a carriage, not far from here, gave me this note for you.' The messenger leaves, and Alfredo reads the shattering news that Violetta has left him.

Unfortunately, on that evening the messenger forgot to appear, and there was no answer to my 'Who is there?' I had to think quickly. I looked around and answered my own question by singing 'No one.' Then I walked over to the table where Violetta had written her note in the previous scene; luckily there were still some sheets of paper lying on it. I picked one of them up, sang 'From Violetta!' and proceeded with the scene, as if she had simply left the letter for me to find.

Placido Domingo, *My First Forty Years*, Weidenfeld & Nicolson,

1983, p. 1

On 15 December 1967 Robert Craft waspishly noted:

New York. To the Met's new *Carmen*, as the opera is billed, though both musically and visually it is unrelated to the traditional character of the piece. The set for the entire opera is a bullring of Colosseum proportions. In the first act it is an esplanade for strolling couples, fashion models apparently dressed in lavish Goya and Manet costumes. In apposition to this preposterously rich apparel, the children are gotten up like Cruikshank chimney-sweeps or the waifs in photographs advertising the plight of starving earthquake survivors.

The principal shortcomings of the musical reading are simply that the tempi are too fast, the orchestra is too loud, and the performance is innocent of all nuances, shadings, inflections. Singers and orchestra are seldom synchronized, moreover, despite Maestro Mehta's heroic strivings – between prizefighterly cues to cymbals and brass – to bring them together. Nor is Grace Bumblebee's [presumably Bumbry] beautiful voice enough equipment for the title role; she does not move like the sultry heroine, and is no temptress.

But no matter, either. The Met audience, corporation presidents and their blue-rinse spouses, applauds each ill-conceived and worse-executed stage trick as if the music did not exist.

Robert Craft, *Stravinsky: Chronicle of a Friendship 1948–1971*, Knopf,

1972, pp. 339–40

Placido Domingo performed in La gioconda *at the Metropolitan Opera in October 1982. The last performance proved problematic:*

He felt a cold coming, considered cancelling, and the people at the Met asked Carlo Bini, who was due to take over the role of Enzo a few days later, to make himself available. In the event, Domingo went on, began well despite his misgivings, technique seeming to carry him through, and Bini, relaxed and perhaps relieved, settled down in the audience to enjoy the performance. To Bini's consternation, word came in the first intermission that Domingo's cold was worse and he felt he would do himself harm if he continued to sing. He had three *Tosca*s the following week in Chicago and, reluctantly, felt he had to bow out of the rest of this performance. Domingo is not known as a canceller, but he is known to have the most scrupulous regard for the health of his own voice, and everybody appreciated his decision. Everybody, that is, except the luckless Bini who had hurriedly to change into an unfamiliar costume and step straight into Act II. Bini had had no proper stage rehearsal and was obviously unsure of his movements. Within minutes of the opening of Act II the tenor has the highlight of the whole opera, the ravishingly beautiful and cruelly exposed aria '*Cielo e mar*'. Bini had had no chance to vocalize, was obviously in no state to give a proper performance, and was received with a combination of mirth and disbelief. Things went from bad to worse. Mignon Dunn, trying to help Bini with his movements, held his hands tightly during their scene together, even to the point of moving his hands at one stage a little lower down her body. Sections of the audience could restrain themselves no longer. There was outright laughter, slow handclaps, and real fisticuffs from those in the audience who objected to the clapping and laughing. Eventually, conductor Giuseppe Patané turned round and begged the audience at least to have respect for Ponchielli. For a while things calmed down – and then, after the third act, it was announced that Maestro Patané was too ill and would have to withdraw from the rest of the performance. His blood pressure was apparently fluctuating dangerously, as whose would not under the circumstances. Further groans as staff conductor Eugene Kohn took on the unenviable task of guiding this ill-fated evening to its close.

Daniel Snowman, *The World of Placido Domingo*, Bodley Head, 1985,

pp. 143–4

Thomas Allen relates a story told him by producer John Copley about the time a replacement had to be found for the role of the Countess in Le nozze di Figaro:

The first Countess had a throat infection and cancelled forty-eight hours before the performance. Once again the international telephone exchanges were hot with calls from London to all corners of the globe . . . All without success. Finally, in desperation, a phone call was made to Dublin where the fine Irish soprano Veronica Dunne was found to be free and ready to fly in.

This she did. Copley made the introductions and Veronica began with her first aria, '*Porgi amor*'.

'That's very lovely,' said John. 'Now would you please go into the recitative – "*Vieni, cara Susanna*", etc.'

'Oh! I don't do the recitatives,' said Miss Dunne in her delightful Dublin brogue. 'I only do the *numbers*.'

'What *do* you mean?' asked John, the truth hardly yet dawning.

'I've only ever sung the numbers.'

A moment to let this news sink home.

Copley rushed from the stage, crossed Floral Street to Number 45, wherein was the seat of power at Covent Garden, Sir David Webster.

'Sir David is not available, Mr Copley,' intoned Miss Kerr, the long-serving secretary, barring his way to the great man.

'I must see him!'

John barged in on Webster, who was occupied with the organizing of various papers. Finally, when he was good and ready, he asked, 'Yes, what is it, Copley?'

'Veronica Dunne doesn't do the recitatives – only the numbers.'

'Oh dear! What do we do?' Sir David said, for once in his life at a loss.

Copley, never at a loss, replied: 'Well, I suggest *Swan Lake*.'

And so, I believe, it came to pass.

Thomas Allen, *Foreign Parts*, Sinclair-Stevenson, 1993, pp. 71–2

Stephen Brook attends the Budapest opera house in 1987:

The opera provides the Budapesters with an excuse to dress up, though for many the wardrobe must be severely depleted. The audience was overwhelmingly elderly. Venerable women, presumably widows hunting in pairs, tottered slowly on their heels along the corridors. Less well heeled, in every sense, than their grandchildren, they wore strange clothes probably kept in mothballs since the 1930s, or ill-fitting blouses cut by computers from rolls of Shimmerlene or Crumplex . . .

The opera house is blessed with an extraordinarily deep stage. During a production of Tchaikovsky's *Eugene Onegin* that was by far the best performance I saw in Budapest, Tatiana had at one point to sprint from backstage to front, where Onegin was waiting for her. Although this was no doubt intended as an expression of her ardour, it was also a physical necessity if she hoped to get to Onegin's side before the curtain fell. Not all the performances were up to this standard: *Rosenkavalier* was drab indeed, and the dutiful hamming from Baron Ochs elicited hardly a single twitter from the geriatric audience, some of whom probably went to school with the Marschallin.

Music critics mistakenly inform us that *Manon Lescaut* is one of Puccini's lesser operas. Since I hold a contrary view, I treated myself to a seat in a box. The curtain rose on a rooftop scene, smoke curling up lazily from a garret chimney. The set had a French feel to it, but seemed far removed from the courtyard of the inn where Act I of *Manon Lescaut* takes place. I soon realized that I was to be treated to a Puccini opera that I like a good deal less, *La Bohème* – or, in Hungarian, *Bohémélet*. During the interval I addressed the old ladies with whom I was sharing the box. One spoke rusty German. Why *Bohémélet*, when I had bought a ticket for a different opera?

'That is because the singer is ill.'

'What, all of them?'

'*Nein, nein*. The soprano is ill.'

'And for that they change the entire production? Why don't they find an understudy?'

At this point our German vocabulary failed us both, so I reconciled myself to sitting through this opera out of a masochistic desire to learn whether Rodolfo's singing could actually get any worse as the opera continued. It did. There was also something mesmerizing about hearing Puccini sung in Magyar, as are all operas performed at the Operaház. The language has an abundance of syllables, far more than Italian, and it was intriguing to follow the scramble as the singer crammed, say, '*uruggyel*' into the musical space reserved for '*si*'.

A week later I was back at the Operaház for *Così fan tutte*. The usherette, with whom I was by now on smiling terms, sold me a programme. As I moved away I glanced at the cover and stopped short. Mozart, to the best of my knowledge, never grew a bushy moustache, nor did he wear stripy neckties. A closer look confirmed my worst fears: the gentleman whose photograph gazed from the cover was Giacomo Puccini, and the opera I was about to hear was *Bohémélet*. I remonstrated with the usherette, explaining to her that this was the second time this had happened to me in two weeks, and didn't the opera company have any other work in its repertoire? A singer was ill, she told me.

'So? Why can't you find another Fiordiligi or Ferrando? This has to be less troublesome than mounting an entirely different production! And why must it always be *Bohémélet*? I actually *wanted* to see *Così*! If I'd wanted to see *Bohémélet* yet again I could have bought a ticket for it.'

She beamed. 'Puccini! *Schön!*' And with a kind of pirouette she began to prance about crooning an unidentifiable snatch of song from, I must assume, *La Bohème*. Then she wrinkled her nose. '*Così*,' she growled disdainfully, and began to mince before my eyes — 'Ti-ti-ti-ti-ti' — parodying, unknowingly, Don Basilio's capers in the final act of *Figaro*. In other words, I should be grateful for the change of programme. I decided to respond stoically and took my seat. The performance was gratifyingly bad. Gyözö Leblanc, the Singing Squirrel, was an abysmal Rodolfo. When Mimi returns to the garret in Act I, the stage lights failed, and Rodolfo had to grope for her tiny hand in near darkness. The lights came back on after a minute, followed by two backstage thumps so loud that even the cellists in the pit reeled with alarm. I left at the end of the act.

Stephen Brook, *The Double Eagle*, Hamish Hamilton, 1988, pp. 174–6

A high-minded explanation for such cancellations is given in a footnote by Peter Paul Fuchs to a collection of the opera director Felsenstein's writings:

One time, on the day of a *Traviata* performance at the Komische Oper [in Berlin], the singer who was to portray Annina became ill. Since there was no one in the ensemble who had rehearsed the role, Felsenstein cancelled the performance. He knew that any last-minute substitute from another theatre, no matter how well prepared, would have destroyed the dramatic unity and meaning of the production.

Introduction by Peter Paul Fuchs to *The Music Theatre of Walter Felsenstein*, Quartet Books, 1991, p. 2

27: *Audiences*

There is no audience at all for opera. As for an audience for a new work, to put on a new opera is like raising the most deadly danger signal. People at once avoid the district for weeks as though it were infected by the plague. A new work absolutely sends a shudder through people.

Thomas Beecham, quoted in Charles Reid, *Thomas Beecham*,

p. 109

William Beckford comments on the Italian hour of the theatre:

People are scarcely wide awake, till about dinner-time. But, a few hours after, the important business of the toilette puts them gently into motion; and, at length, the opera calls them completely into existence. But it must be understood, that the drama, or the music, do not form a principal object of theatrical amusement. Every lady's box is the scene, of tea, cards, cavaliers, servants, lap dogs, abbés, scandal, and assignations; attention to the action of the piece, to the scenes, or even to the actors, male, or female, is but a secondary affair. If there be some actor, or actress, whose merit, or good fortune, happens to demand the universal homage of fashion, there are pauses of silence, and the favourite airs may be heard. But without this cause, or the presence of the sovereign, all is noise, hubbub, and confusion in an Italian audience. The hour of the theatre, however, with all its mobbing and disturbance, is the happiest part of the day, to every Italian, of whatever station; and the least affluent will sacrifice some portion of his daily bread, rather than not enjoy it.

William Beckford, *Dreams, Waking Thoughts and Incidents*, 1783

Hector Berlioz recalls his youthful days attending the Opéra in Paris:

Once the overture had begun, all talking, humming or beating time was strictly against the rules. If any of our neighbours did so, we silenced him with the well-known mot invented by a music lover, which we had adopted for such occasions: 'Damn these musicians, they're preventing me from hearing what this fellow is saying.'

It was just as unwise for the performers to change anything in the score, for I knew every note and would have died rather than let the slightest tampering with the great masters pass unchallenged. I had no intention of waiting until I could protest coldly in print at this crime against genius. No, indeed! I denounced the offenders then and there, publicly and in a loud, clear voice; and I can vouch for it that there is no form of criticism so effective. One day – to give an example – *Iphigénie en Tauride* was on. I had noticed at the previous performance that cymbals had been added to the Scythians' first dance in B minor, which Gluck wrote for strings alone, and also that in Orestes' great recitative in the third act the trombones, which are so superbly appropriate to the dramatic situation, had been omitted. I decided that if the same errors were repeated, I should point them out. When the Scythian ballet began I waited for the cymbals. They came in precisely as they had before. Although seething with rage, I managed to contain myself until the end of the piece: then, in the short pause which ensued, I yelled out, 'There are no cymbals there. Who has dared to correct Gluck?'

There was a buzz of consternation. The public, who are very unclear about such artistic questions and do not care whether the composer's orchestration is altered or not, could not understand what this young lunatic in the pit was getting so angry about. But it was worse in the third act. The trombones in Orestes' monologue were suppressed as I had feared they would be, and the same voice rang through the theatre: 'Why aren't the trombones playing? This is intolerable.'

The astonishment of both orchestra and audience was only

equalled by the wrath – very natural, I admit – of Valentino, who was conducting that evening. It transpired that the trombones had only been obeying an express order not to play in that particular passage; the orchestral parts complied exactly with the score . . .

At subsequent performances everything was in order. The cymbals were silent, the trombones spoke. I contented myself with growling between my teeth, 'Ah, now that's better.'

Hector Berlioz, *Memoirs*, translated by David Cairns, Gollancz, 1969,

pp. 82–3

Maria Malibran confronts royal etiquette when she makes her Neapolitan début in 1832:

Maria learned that in Naples it was customary for singers to request the King's presence at their débuts. This meant nothing, but she was also told that audiences did not applaud in the presence of royalty unless the King set the example, a convention that greatly upset her since royalty and rulers of state were not known for displays of enthusiasm in the theatre. To complicate matters, [Giuseppina] Ronzi was rumoured to be King Ferdinand's mistress, and he might not want to offend her by applauding a rival. There was only one possible course of action, and Maria requested an audience: ushered into the royal chambers, she presented a strange appeal.

'Sire,' she said, 'I come to ask your majesty to please not come to the theatre tomorrow.'

The King, astonished, asked why this singer did not want him to visit his theatre: 'I would have thought that you would have asked me to come,' he responded.

Maria explained her fears, and Ferdinand, amazed at her daring, and liking her for it, promised to set the example for the audience. Not entirely sure of his word, however, she left nothing to chance and the next night stationed herself between the side scenes where he could see her from the royal box. Just before her entrance she caught his eye and mimed the action of clapping. He had not forgotten, and at her entry she received an enthusiastic welcome from the crowd. Unfortunately, the King would be less reliable in the future.

Howard Bushnell, *Maria Malibran*, Pennsylvania State University Press,
1979, p. 140

The Scottish soprano Mary Anne Paton and her husband Mr Wood got their own back on American hosts who exploited her in 1840:

A ludicrous incident marked their stay at Philadelphia. There was a shabby couple who desired to have the éclat of engaging the celebrated English prima donna to sing at one of their parties, and sent her an invitation. Being indisposed, Mrs Wood declined, but they so urgently pressed her that she consented to join the party. When the entertainments of the evening had fairly commenced, and several ladies among the visitors had sung, the hostess invited Mrs Wood to seat herself at the piano, as the company would be delighted to hear her beautiful voice; but Mrs Wood, with a very serious countenance, begged to be excused. At first the astonishment created by this refusal was evinced by a dead silence and a fixed stare; but at length the disappointed hostess burst out, saying, 'What! not sing, Mrs Wood! why, it was for this that I invited you to my party, and I told all my guests that you were coming.' 'That quite alters the case,' said Mrs Wood; 'I was not at all aware of this, or I should not have refused; but since you have invited me professionally, I shall of course sing immediately!' 'What a good creature,' rejoined the hostess; 'I thought you could not persist in refusing me.' So Mrs Wood sang the entire evening, giving every song she was asked for, and being encored several times. In the morning, to the utter consternation of the rich, parsimonious couple, a bill for 200 dollars was presented to them from Mr Wood for his wife's professional services.

Ellen Creathorne Clayton, *Queens of Song*, Smith, Elder, 1863, II,
pp. 64–5

How the British public vented its displeasure at the manipulations of the singers it had paid good money to hear:

On Saturday, 25 June [1842], Madame Persiani was announced to make her appearance in the *Puritani*. But at a late hour the favourite prima donna sent word to the theatre that she was too ill to be able to sing ... It was only a very few minutes before the opening of the doors that a genuine medical certificate could be posted at all the entrances, giving assurance of the inability of the lady to appear, together with an announcement of the necessity of changing the opera to *Beatrice di Tenda*, with Madame Frezzolini. The house was crowded, and at the very commencement of the evening the disappointed public began to give vent to its annoyance by hissing and hooting ...

For two long hours and more the hissing and yelling continued. In vain the opera was several times commenced; in vain Rubini appeared as a peace maker, offering to sing the favourite '*Vivi tu*'. In vain; after a futile attempt of M. Laurent, the stage-manager, to address the audience in French – a proceeding which only increased the fearful storm – I myself, as the manager, came forward, and offered the truth in the way of explanation. In vain I urged, as far as my voice could be heard in the din of tempest, that it was not fair that when I was tumultuously called to give an explanation the explanation was not to be heard – that 'health and sickness were not in my hands'. Nothing could calm the outraged public; the storm 'waxed fast and furious'. Many ladies left the house in terror. The Queen, who, it was stated, had intended to visit the opera, was informed by messenger of the tumult, and did not leave the palace. The greater part of the evening passed before I could make the audience understand that the money would be returned at the doors to those who felt themselves aggrieved. This announcement at last pacified the malcontents; but it was now too late to allow the performance to proceed. No opera was performed at all! ...

Such was one of the results of the long series of cabals and hindrances on the part of the artists, by which, during the season,

the management had been tampered with and tyrannized and the
public set at naught. Such was the final coup which led the
management to the resolution that . . . the fatal 'cold' and 'illness'
system should by any means be done away with, under the new
direction.

Benjamin Lumley, *Reminiscences of the Opera*, Hurst & Blackett, 1864,

pp. 54–6

The conductor Luigi Arditi encounters enthusiastic opera goers in Ireland:

Our Dublin season opened in September [1861] . . . with Tietjens
and Giuglini, Delle Sedie, Ciampi, and other big stars. Our reception was, as usual, a demonstrative and hearty one. 'The gods'
were as noisy as ever, and expressed their pleasure on seeing the
old familiar faces by vociferous shouts and whistling, which, from
the foreigner's point of view, is the very opposite to the correct
way of showing one's approval . . .

Tietjens liked the stormy exclamations of the pit and gallery that
were hurled at her . . . My appearance in the orchestra was also
greeted with robust shouting and applause, while such exclamations
as '*Viva Victor Emmanuel!*' 'Bravo, Arditi!' 'Where's your wig?'
and 'How's the Macaroni?' were to be heard emanating from all
parts of the house. They even cheered my wife when she entered
her box, and cries of 'Three cheers for Madame Arditi, and all the
little Arditis!' brought down the house.

The dwellers in Olympus were really a very queer lot in Dublin.
They thought nothing of singing songs and glees in the entr'actes.
I have heard many a solo correctly and tunefully played upon an
ordinary penny pipe.

Luigi Arditi, *My Reminiscences*, Skeffington, 1896, pp. 93–5

*The Italian authorities embarked on the hopeless task of controlling
audience behaviour in the nineteenth century:*

Regulations governing audience behaviour were largely uniform across the Italian states. It made little difference whether the government was republican or monarchical, Habsburg or Bourbon or Napoleonic, or was operating in the eighteenth century or the nineteenth. Their main points were: to forbid applause in the presence of the ruler (unless he gave the lead); to forbid curtain calls before the end of an act and encores at any time; to forbid whistling (hissing) and excessive noise, including excessive applause.

Since most Italian audiences wished to applaud wildly when they approved, to whistle unrestrainedly when they disapproved, and to have artists take curtain calls in mid-act and give encores, we need to ask what led governments to persist with regulations that went so clearly against the grain. There seem to be two main explanations. Governments had a not unjustified fear of riot in the theatre; this shifted somewhat from fear of rowdiness in the eighteenth century to fear of political trouble after the French Revolution. At the same time, however, the rules look like another manifestation of the parent–child relationship so many Italians saw as the model for dealings between ruler and subject . . .

This was shown by the way monarchs would deliberately refrain from applauding during a first performance – which was therefore heard in disconcerting silence – but would allow some applause at later performances: they displayed first their paternal power, then their indulgence.

As in many parent–child relationships, however, it was not always clear that prohibitions would stick. A Padua audience in 1794 got the representative of the Venetian Republic to allow an encore of the overture in spite of large placards forbidding such things; when he refused them an encore of a duet they booed and whistled for half an hour, the performance was suspended, and soldiers were brought in. It was not unknown for a Neapolitan audience to call out to the king in dialect 'if you don't applaud, we will,' and for a Milanese one to defeat an archduke's ban on applause or whistling by all coughing or blowing their noses at once . . .

John Rosselli, *The Opera Industry in Italy from Cimarosa to Verdi*,
Cambridge University Press, 1984, pp. 95–6

Shaw was savage about the way British opera was dependent on the munificence of the rich, most of whom couldn't care less about opera:

It must never be forgotten that the Royal Italian Opera, far from paying its way, depends on a subvention as much as any continental opera house. Unfortunately, this subvention is not yet forcibly levied on excessive West End incomes by the London County Council, and by them entrusted to Mr Harris [the impresario] for the purpose of maintaining a serious and progressive artistic institution for the performance of the best dramatic music. Instead, it has to be extracted by him from excessively rich people for the purpose of maintaining fashionable postprandial resort for them during the season.

The following are the steps by which these munificent patrons make their plutocratic power felt at Covent Garden. They delay the rise of the curtain until half-past eight, and then come late. They insist on intervals of twenty minutes between the acts for what is to them the real business of the evening: visiting and chatting. They waste invaluable space with their comfortless dens of boxes. The percentage of inconsiderate persons among them is so high that there are always at least three parties disturbing the audience by talking and laughing at full pitch during the performance. The prices which their riches enable them to bid for admission drive ordinary amateurs to swelter among the gods, whilst box after box is thrown away on inveterate deadheads whose mission in life is to pester impresarios for free admissions.

> George Bernard Shaw, in *The Star*, 26 July 1889, reprinted in
> *Shaw's Music*, Bodley Head, 1989, I, pp. 712–13

Social stratification among the Metropolitan Opera House audience in the 1890s was as complex as that of any aristocratic opera house in Europe:

Membership in the Opera and Real Estate Company was restricted to thirty-five – the number of the boxes in the single tier they planned to occupy as owners and social aristocracy . . . The requirement from each, in fresh capital, was $40,000. When the property was liquidated in 1940, each of those whose families retained the original 300 shares received \$43,200 in cash and bonds.

This was not at all an unreasonable recovery on an investment that permitted them to write into the bylaws of the company: 'No transfer of stock shall be made except to a person or persons previously approved by the directorate.' For nearly half a century the ownership company was a self-appointed, self-perpetuating judge and jury of what persons were socially acceptable in a city of mounting millions . . .

Of course, one could have 'a box at the opera' without being a stockholder – by payment of the charge of the moment. For this purpose, the new owners set aside the second-floor grand-tier boxes for whoever chose to lay out the necessary thousands of dollars. But the distinction was clear in the minds of those who made it, if not always realized by the general public . . .

If you 'owned', you were 'in'; if you merely 'rented', you were more than out – you were socially non-existent. Needless to say, those who 'rented' swallowed their unhappiness with this caste system, but extended it a bit farther by looking down on those who neither owned nor rented, but merely bought tickets. Some place in the house there was a dividing line between those who looked down on each other and those who looked at the stage, but I have not, in fifteen years of research, been able to determine just where it began.

Irving Kolodin, *The Story of the Metropolitan Opera*, New York, 1953,
pp. 57–8, 66–7

The social tone at the Met from 1892 onwards was set by Mrs Caroline Astor:

Few singers were as important to the success of the Metropolitan Opera in its first quarter-century as was one of the box-holders – Caroline Astor, the lady whose annual ball for her 400 defined the high society of the city. Mrs Astor decreed that appearance at the opera, at precisely nine o'clock each Monday in season, was the proper thing to do before supper. For the ticket buyers, it was definitely part of the show to watch the lavishly bejewelled Mrs Astor enter her box wearing the diamond stomacher that reputedly had belonged to Marie Antoinette, the variety and brilliance of her diamonds and emeralds giving her, as her friend Harry Lehr said, the appearance of a walking chandelier.

For two generations, both the box-holders themselves and the New York press placed great emphasis on the social aspect of the Metropolitan Opera. 'SOCIETY HEARS AND APPLAUDS TRISTAN,' was the headline of the front-page notice in the New York *Herald* of the incandescent performance by Olive Fremstad, Erik Schmedes, Louise Homer, and Fritz Feinhals that Gustav Mahler, its conductor, considered among the greatest of his life; and more than half the space in the review was given to detailing the occupants of the boxes and what they wore.

Martin Mayer, *The Met: One Hundred Years of Grand Opera*,
Thames & Hudson, 1983, pp. 23–4

Mrs Astor could dominate the audience, but Ludwig II of Bavaria was able to dispense with it altogether:

He had wandered into the Hof-Theater with Wagner during a rehearsal, and impressed by the stillness of the empty auditorium, had returned. The habit grew. And while he could not tolerate an unnecessary human face he remained absorbed in dramatic production, and after his solitude and his building it was all that he lived for. In the Hof and Residenz theatres performances were frequently commanded for him alone. In the beginning they were little more than dress rehearsals, and the King, watching every movement on the stage, would comment with crushing criticism. The first of these performances took place in 1871, and the last in 1885, a few months before his death. During that time there were two hundred and ten private representations including forty-five operas, the *Ring* being given four times in succession. *Parsifal* was another of his favourites. The productions changed in character and were done with increasing elaborateness, the scene-shifters wore felt slippers, the theatre was muffled in darkness, and at a signal announcing the King's arrival about midnight the uncanny perform-ance began. Ludwig could recline luxuriously in the royal box hung with red velvet. He was almost always unattended, and sometimes the eerie atmosphere would affect the actors and they would betray their nervousness.

Henry Channon, The Ludwigs of Bavaria, Methuen, 1933, p. 99

Ludwig III of Bavaria was a less enthusiastic opera goer, as Bruno Walter discovered when conducting in Munich:

Ludwig III, whose coronation I witnessed, and by whose grace the theatres at which I worked were maintained, fulfilled the duties of a Maecenas only from a sense of loyalty to the traditions of his house. The unpretentious and simple man was rather sober-minded, and unless some special occasion demanded his presence, he kept away from the theatre and from music. When, in 1913, thirty years after Wagner's death, we performed *Parsifal* at the Prince Regent Theatre, an opera which up to that time had been the prerogative of Bayreuth, the King felt obliged to be present at so momentous an event. After the long first act, Franckenstein and I called at his box to inquire how he had been impressed. The King replied with fine sincerity: 'Gentlemen, I thank you, but wild horses could not drag me here again.' After having thus voiced his impatience, he became quite affable and explained apologetically that he was quite fond of pictures but, he just couldn't help it, he didn't care for music.

Bruno Walter, Theme and Variations, translated by James A. Galston,
Hamish Hamilton, 1947, p. 226

Shaw on the dress code at Covent Garden:

On Saturday night I went to the opera. I wore the costume imposed on me by the regulations of the house. I fully recognize the advantage of those regulations. Evening dress is cheap, simple, durable, prevents rivalry and extravagance on the part of male leaders of fashion, annihilates class distinctions, and gives men who are poor and doubtful of their social position (that is, the great majority of men) a sense of security and satisfaction that no clothes of their own choosing could confer, besides saving a whole sex the trouble of considering what they should wear on state occasions. The objections to it are as dust in the balance in the eyes of the ordinary Briton. These objections are that it is colourless and characterless; that it involves a whitening process which makes the shirt troublesome, slightly uncomfortable, and seriously unclean; that it acts as a passport for undesirable persons; that it fails to guarantee sobriety, cleanliness, and order on the part of the wearer; and that it reduces to a formula a very vital human habit which should be the subject of constant experiment and active private enterprise. All such objections are thoroughly unEnglish . . .

But I submit that what is sauce for the goose is sauce for the gander. Every argument that applies to the regulation of the man's dress applies equally to the regulation of the woman's. Now let me describe what actually happened to me at the opera. Not only was I in evening dress by compulsion, but I voluntarily added many graces of conduct as to which the management made no stipulation whatsoever. I was in my seat for the first chord of the overture. I did not chatter during the music nor raise my voice when the opera was too loud for normal conversation. I did not get up and go out the moment the Statue music began. My language was fairly moderate considering the number and nature of the improvements on Mozart volunteered by Signor Caruso, and the respectful ignorance of the dramatic points of the score exhibited by the conductor and stage manager – if there is such a functionary at Covent Garden. In short, my behaviour was exemplary.

At nine o'clock (the opera began at eight) a lady came in and sat down very conspicuously in my line of sight. She remained there until the beginning of the last act. I do not complain of her coming late and going early; on the contrary, I wish she had come later and gone earlier. For this lady, who had very black hair, had stuck over her right ear the pitiable corpse of a large white bird, which looked exactly as if someone had killed it by stamping on its breast and then nailed it to the lady's temple, which was presumably of sufficient solidity to bear the operation. I am not, I hope, a morbidly squeamish person; but the spectacle sickened me. I presume that if I had presented myself at the doors with a dead snake round my neck, a collection of black beetles pinned to my shirt-front, and a grouse in my hair, I should have been refused admission. Why, then, is a woman to be allowed such a public outrage? . . .

I suggest to the Covent Garden authorities that, if they feel bound to protect their subscribers against the danger of my shocking them with a blue tie, they are at least equally bound to protect me against the danger of a woman shocking me with a dead bird.

George Bernard Shaw, letter to *The Times*, 1 July 1905

Walter Slezak unleashes a number of stories about good-humoured interventions from the audience:

At a performance of *I pagliacci* in Naples, the baritone sang the prologue. The audience didn't like him and yelled, stomped, and whistled. Suddenly, the poor devil, who was probably hungry, stepped down to the footlights and called out: '*Perche fischiate a me? – Aspettate il tenore.*' ('Why are you whistling at me? Just wait until the tenor comes.') In the second act, after Nedda had finished her aria – she had sung it badly and off pitch – there broke out wild applause from the gallery and calls of '*Bis*'. They wouldn't stop until she repeated the aria, and then they forced her to sing it a third time. When the customers in the orchestra protested, a voice from the gallery yelled: '*Deve cantarlo fina che lo conosce.*' ('She must sing it until she knows it.')

Walter Slezak, *What Time's the Next Swan?*, Doubleday, 1962, p. 36

The audience at the Teatro Regio in Parma was the most demanding in Italy:

'*Il loggione*' is the Italian equivalent in the opera house of the gallery . . . If the Parmesans are a people proud of their city and their musical tradition they are equally proud of their claim to be the toughest opera audience in Italy . . . It was not really such a bad Spanish tenor, for instance, who sang in *Rigoletto* not so many years ago at the Regio and found at the station when he left that none of the porters would carry his luggage for him. Anybody who sang as he did, they told him, could carry their luggage themselves.

The singer who appeared as Carmen, on the other hand, and getting the bird from the *loggione* threw her shawl defiantly at the audience not only had her luggage carried to the train but was escorted on to it by the police – not to protect her from the crowd's anger, but to make sure that she left the city.

Spike Hughes, *Great Opera Houses*, Weidenfeld & Nicolson, 1956,

p. 138

Chaliapin observes the La Scala audience as it demolishes a new opera:

I have also seen the indignation of the Italian public, and it could be terrifying. For some time there had been rumours of a new opera being produced in La Scala, with Tamagno, and I was surprised that the composer was rarely referred to. As a musician he was not discussed, but it was very much in the news that he was a handsome young man, that he sang songs and was his own accompanist, that a princess had fallen in love with him, had left her prince, and turned the poor musician into a rich man. This was the man who was now so rich that he was backing the opera himself, and had already engaged Tamagno, and a well-known French singer for the female lead . . .

The curtain rose, and on the stage I beheld something that smacked of ancient Rome. Somebody clad in a toga was drearily singing, accompanied by even more dreary music. It seemed to me that the public was paying no attention to the stage, indifferent to

it, singers, music, and all. They were far too busy talking to each
other . . .

Before I quite realized it the first act was over. There was no
public reaction. Not a sound, not a single clap. They rose and
went off into the foyer. Nobody appeared to have seen anything.
Perhaps the opera had not even begun.

In the second act the French singer was quite busy. A contralto,
she sang with a curious little wail in her voice, though it was
resonant enough. I could see and hear people wincing, and many
closed eyes. At that moment Tamagno appeared. The composer
had given him an effective entrance phrase, and this evoked an
immediate response . . .

The final act was original in the highest degree, since the entire
audience took part in it. I was sorry for the French contralto,
whom they mimicked, howled at, maiowing, mooing, barking,
imitating her singing. This was not all. In loud voices people in
the auditorium discussed the best place to have dinner. Malice was
quite undisguised when for the third time the composer of the
opera was led out by Tamagno. The public really broke out and I
watched the elegant, the noble, the splendidly accoutred officers
actually sticking out their tongues at the unfortunate man. In my
own box people were saying that the performance would never be
over. And the acid remark that killed – 'Perhaps it's the end that is
original.'

I wanted to laugh, to say to them as I waved my hand towards
the audience, 'But what can be more original than all this?'

I was answered immediately.

'It sometimes happens that several members of the public will pick
up the conductor, stand and all, and carry him out to the foyer . . .'

'Doesn't this hurt the conductor's feelings?'

'Not at all. Why? A friendly joke? It is then that the conductor
knows the opera cannot continue. So why should his feelings be
hurt?'

Feodor Chaliapin, *Chaliapin: An Autobiography as Told to Maxim Gorky*,
Macdonald, 1968, pp. 151–2

Hitler, it's reassuring to know, took a keen interest in opera, as Viorica Ursuleac reminds us:

'*Arabella* became the great favourite of Hitler, and he came to hear me sing it in Berlin ten times. He was Austrian, of course, and perhaps this eminently Viennese atmosphere made him somewhat nostalgic. I met him on several occasions, and cut down to life size, he was a strangely timid man in his contacts – at least with us artists. He never talked politics, but always asked questions about singing problems.'

Lanfranco Rasponi, *The Last Prima Donnas*, Gollancz, 1984, p. 135

Although the claque is usually associated with Italian opera houses, this is an apparent injustice – at least as far as nineteenth-century audiences were concerned:

It seems odd that Italy should have done without the claque, that well-known means of ensuring at least the appearance of success in the opera house. The most notorious of claques flourished in Paris, where it hired itself out on set terms. No such professional body existed in Italy: we have Verdi's word for it, and that of the tenor Adolphe Nourrit, with experience of both Paris and Naples; they should have known. The nearest thing we hear about is a group of 'fifteen or twenty hired people' at Modena in 1798, but not even that seems to have been a permanent institution.

For the rest, we have evidence of groups of students and the like organized by a singer to support him, but much more often of what might be called an anti-claque – a group organized to hiss and to bring about the failure of an opera, usually inspired by a rival impresario or singer or by their supporters in the town. The Italian opera house with its passionate clientele was subject to cabal and faction rather than to the straightforward commercial performance of the claque.

Still, even if it was not easy to lay on a commercially inspired ovation within the opera house, there are signs that so-called spontaneous demonstrations of enthusiasm could be rigged in advance by the impresario or by the friends of the composer or singer.

A refrain of Italian opera chronicles is the torchlight procession after the triumphal first performance, ending beneath the composer's windows, sometimes with a serenade by the theatre orchestra, all to tremendous cheers. On one occasion at least this torchlight procession had been planned in advance; we know this because the place was Rome in the troubled period just ahead of the 1848 revolutions and a friend of the composer who was to be honoured advised him to call it off for fear of getting mixed up with low-class radicals. How many more such demonstrations were similarly arranged? At least it can be said, once again, that partisanship rather than sheer commercial promotion was likely to be the motive.

John Rosselli, *The Opera Industry in Italy from Cimarosa to Verdi*,
Cambridge University Press, 1984, pp. 159–60

Yet baritone Thomas Allen found the claque flourishing in Milan:

These 'professional' cheerleaders emerge towards the end of the rehearsal period in the manner of so many farmers gone to market to prod with their sticks at the meat that is paraded before them. Searching for the tender, the vulnerable, spot, they seize on an innocent singer – young or old – and unnerve their victim to the point where it seems safest to play along with their game. For they are a protection racket. Other explanations of their worth and existence may be given, but as far as I can see they are there to take money from singers who feel it best to ensure that they've gone some way towards avoiding the cockpit booing and baying that has become such a feature of performances in some great theatres. The Milan claque actually gain access to backstage areas and dressing-rooms. Since La Scala have a strict security system, it's difficult not to think that they sanction this.

My first encounter with a claque was at the Teatro Communale in Florence many years ago. In the corridors of the dressing-room and backstage area I'd noticed for several days the presence of two benign-looking old men, one of whom was reminiscent of my own paternal grandfather. I felt a warmth of spirit and generosity towards them, as one does to a much older generation, passing each day with a friendly: '*Buon giorno*', to be met with an even friendlier: '*Oh buon giorno, maestro – come sta?*' A good way to start the day, I thought to myself ... Until, that is, the day that they entered my dressing-room and the following dialogue took place.

'Our compliments on your singing – it's very beautiful.'

'Thank you,' said I, 'that's kind of you. It's lovely to be in Italy, singing Mozart in Italian.'

'Very good,' said he. 'Do you like applause?'

'I can't deny we enjoy being appreciated,' I replied, modestly English to a fault.

'We lead the applause,' he explained, 'so the singer traditionally pays for us to have dinner or drinks.'

'Sorry?' said I, as if believing something had been lost in translation, though I'd been forewarned and was playing deliberately dumb.

They then produced from their jacket pockets wadges of official tickets which showed, quite clearly, that they were to have access to the private areas of the theatre because they led the claque in Florence.

'And for this clapping, you pay,' he explained, his grandfatherly smile now sickening. The other, I now noticed, had a sinister cast in his left eye.

Playing as naïve as I dared, I ventured: 'What a strange custom. When in England I can get people to clap for me for free. Thank you for coming. That was most interesting. *Arrivederci!*'

Thomas Allen, *Foreign Parts*, Sinclair-Stevenson, 1993, pp. 194–5

Record producer Fred Gaisberg defended the claque — not very convincingly — when he wrote: 'I do not frown at this institution like some purists, because I feel that for the Italian artist it is a sheer necessity that spurs him to excel himself, and at the same time acts as a cue to the public who need leadership for applause at the appropriate places.' Gigli also defended the claque, for the very good reason that he employed one:

I must confess that I myself had found it necessary to have a claque, at the Metropolitan, for the simple reason that everyone else had one. For established singers who had nothing to fear, it amounted to no more than a precaution that one's own legitimate, spontaneous applause would not be submerged by other people's claques. Normally speaking, the various claques cancelled each other out; they were composed of discerning music-lovers, and their applause was not indiscriminate. But an efficient claque could also help to consolidate the reputation of a young singer, or force into retirement a rival whose voice was beginning to decline.

Beniamino Gigli, *Memoirs*, translated by Darina Silone, Cassell, 1957,

p. 150

Andrew Porter observes audience behaviour at the Metropolitan Opera — and doesn't like what he sees and hears:

The Metropolitan Opera audience is generally deemed the most ill-mannered and ignorant to be found in any of the world's major houses, and often it lives up to its reputation. But it is also one of the world's most warm-hearted audiences: appreciative, enthusiastic, ready — all too ready! — with noisy acclaim for whoever or whatever pleases it. Its bad habits are rooted in generosity, not indifference. And so, although a musical person may feel fury when, say, the coda of Susanna's '*Deh vieni*', in *Le nozze di Figaro*, is blotted out by a volley of applause for the singer, that fury is tempered by pleasure in the fact that so many people are enjoying themselves.

Applause, like puffing, is of various sorts; the principal are, the applause preliminary, the applause automatic, the applause collusive, the applause interruptive, and, highest kind of all, the applause manifested by rapt silence, tribute to a spell that must not be shattered . . .

The applause preliminary greets the conductor as he advances to the rostrum . . . The applause automatic is that which breaks forth whenever the curtain rises in the theatre and a scene is revealed. It is always an exciting moment, but grown-ups should learn to control their excitement, to enjoy things inwardly and not make a noise – however striking the spectacle – if that noise is going to blot out several measures of a composer's music. It is a new phenomenon, this regular applause for the scenery, a bad new habit that must be stopped before it becomes an accepted part of audience behaviour . . .

Curtain-fall is another moment for the applause automatic; and modern audience practice in this country has made impossible an effect that many composers have valued – a slow curtain, and a soft instrumental coda after the scene has vanished from our eyes. The first acts of *La Bohème* and *Madama Butterfly* are not over once the soprano (along with the tenor, if he goes up, too) has sung the high C, but it is some years, I'll wager, since the final cadences of those acts have been audible in a New York theatre . . .

By the applause collusive, I signify that planned and paid for in advance. Claqueurs are still a pest in some Italian houses but, so far as I know, they are not active here. No need for them when vociferous volunteer enthusiasts abound. These enthusiasts are responsible for the applause interruptive, which occurs at three points: at the favoured one's entrance; improperly in the course of her aria; and, often properly, when that aria is done. Applause at entrance is plainly justified on very special occasions; when a Beverly Sills or a Magda Olivero makes her first-ever appearance on the Metropolitan stage, for example . . . But *regular* applause for the prima donna – or tenor or baritone – of the evening the moment she or he is glimpsed, regardless of what the music may be doing at that point, is a barbarism . . .

Mid-aria applause arises from enthusiasm coupled to ignorance . . . In *Rigoletto*, Gildas quite often find themselves interrupted

after the cadenza of '*Caro nome*' by people unaware that there are
further beautiful phrases to come . . .

Knowing when and when not to applaud after an aria needs
connoisseurship. Many arias call for applause – and require it
as soon as the singer has finished, even though the orchestra
may still be playing. The noisy tonic-and-dominant perorations
of Donizetti often serve best as accompaniment to cheers . . . In
La Bohème, a good Mimi and Rodolfo should be able to act and
inflect and time things so that '*Che gelida manina*', '*Mi chiamano
Mimi*', and '*O soave fanciulla*' are heard as an unbroken sequence
. . . But artists with both the wish and the ability to hold an
audience silent after a striking and familiar aria are rare. Maria
Callas is the only Tosca of my experience whose genius has
been able to keep listeners hushed and spellbound after '*Vissi
d'arte*'.

Andrew Porter, New Yorker article of 12 January 1976, in Music of
Three Seasons 1974–1977, Chatto & Windus, 1979, pp. 269–72

Etiquette expert Miss Manners lays down the law:

There shall be no talking, eating, rustling of papers, or prolonged
coughing during an opera. Those who feel obliged to perform one
of these actions must leave the auditorium.

However, one is permitted to enjoy the opera, particularly at
those prices. Enthusiastic clapping and laughter at appropriate
times is acceptable. At curtain calls, standing ovations are permitted, as are booing or shouting '*Bravo!*' provided one uses the
correct endings and does not shout '*Bravo!*' when one means
'*Brava!*' or '*Bravi!*'

There shall also be separate regulations for arriving at and
departing from the opera house. People who arrive late should not
attempt to sit until there is a break in the music. But it is perfectly
all right for anyone to leave when the programme has been
concluded, skipping encores and curtain calls; those who wish to
stay must simply let them pass.

Let us all understand this. Miss Manners remembers when many cities had no opera house, and does not wish to see them taken away because we don't know how to use them properly.

Judith Martin, *Miss Manners' Guide to Excruciatingly Correct Behaviour*,
Penguin, 1984, p. 622

28: Opera and Money

The most salient question about any large opera company always has been: who pays the deficit?

James Hinton, Jnr, 'The Opera Scene in America', in *Opera Annual 1954–1955*, edited by Harold Rosenthal, p. 102

Opera is expensive. Singers, orchestra, stage-hands, chorus must all be hired; sumptuous premises must be rented or otherwise paid for. Not surprisingly this has led to an often precarious balance of financial interest between impresario, artist, and public. In Italy, during the age of bel canto, the impresario was an entrepreneurial figure:

Opera management . . . was a concession, potentially a monopoly: even if the impresario did not himself enjoy an official monopoly the owners who granted him the concession often had the sole right to put on a particular type of opera in a particular season. But what was temporarily handed over to the impresario was not the opera house as a whole. It was not thought of as a single economic entity which he could exploit to greatest advantage. Just as the boxes were physically and socially distinct from the rest, so they – or some of them – might not figure in the theatre takings at all.

Italian opera-house takings were made up as follows. Anyone entering the theatre – except, sometimes, those who owned or rented boxes – paid admission to enter the building (*ingresso*); you could buy a season's subscription for this purpose. Since the opera house was the centre of social life you might pay *ingresso* merely to visit friends or gamble. In some eighteenth-century theatres, and occasionally in those of the nineteenth century, one therefore paid separately to enter the orchestra or stalls area, and again separately for one of a small number of fixed seats which an attendant unlocked.

In other theatres – at La Scala the arrangement dated from the return of the French in 1800 – the *ingresso* let you into the stalls as well. There you found in most theatres a good deal of standing room at the back as well as unnumbered bench seats, though you could still pay separately for a locked seat . . . The general movement during the nineteenth century was towards filling the stalls with fixed and numbered seats . . .

What happened about the boxes varied according to the ownership pattern and the management contract. Boxholder-proprietors were not ordinary customers. In many theatres they could sublet their boxes at a profit, thus in effect competing with the impresario for custom; this was something that impresarios at La Scala tried in vain to stop.

John Rosselli, *The Opera Industry in Italy from Cimarosa to Verdi*,
Cambridge University Press, 1984, pp. 47–8

For singers, 'benefit nights', which persisted well into the nineteenth century, were one way, not always reliable, to acquire a nest-egg:

Benefit nights were an important part of singers' earnings, particularly abroad. In Italy they were not insignificant, but the country was too poor to yield more than Fcs 1000–3000 per benefit even in leading theatres, whereas in Paris, London, or, later, in Buenos Aires they could bring in amounts far larger though seldom documented. Benefits enacted a personal relationship, ostensibly between the artist as humble servant and members of the public as appreciative and bountiful patrons. There was some financial risk where the singer agreed to pay the notional running costs of the theatre (as much as £130 at the King's Theatre in the Haymarket in 1717, nearly £50 more than the actual costs) while pocketing the night's takings; only the most famous singers could get a benefit clear of expenses. At other times the artist and the manager shared the profits, or staged a fake benefit with the manager collecting all the proceeds.

John Rosselli, *Singers of Italian Opera*, Cambridge University Press,
1992, pp. 142–3

For the innocent operatic composer in the nineteenth century, earning a living was a struggle in the face of unscrupulous impresarios and publishers:

Weber was the victim of a robbery so gross that it became a *locus classicus* in its epoch. He had neglected to engrave the score of *Der Freischütz* in Paris, but had sold copies of the German score there. This deprived him of all French rights in his own work. Castilblaze made a monstrous rehash of his own of the opera, that brought him a fortune: the French *Robin des Bois* was legally *his* work, and Weber could not collect a penny of the large fees it earned.

Ernest Newman, *The Life of Richard Wagner*, Knopf,
1933, I, p. 162

Composers in the nineteenth century had to contend with problems of piracy and manipulative impresarios:

The relative cost of the most basic component of opera – the music – seems to have changed little. Up to the 1840s the composer was paid a fee for writing a new opera, supervising rehearsals, and accompanying the first three performances at the keyboard. If the opera was not new, he, or, in the nineteenth century, his publisher had to fend off pirated scores that could be had cheap. Composers' fees went up, in absolute and probably in relative terms, from 1815, through the renewed enthusiasm for opera stirred by Rossini. By the 1830s Bellini could command a fee of 16,000 francs for a new opera in Italy; in the following decade Verdi received 20,000 francs . . .

In the first half of the nineteenth century the usual arrangement

was for the impresario either to buy the full score outright or to
divide the rights in it with the composer. Either way this meant an
iron watch on copyists and, if possible, on fellow impresarios to
whom the score was hired out. These safeguards generally failed
and the correspondence of the time is full of complaints about
pirated scores, often orchestrated by a hack composer from the
printed vocal score, but sometimes stolen.

Double standards prevailed. Impresarios complained bitterly
about others' piracy, but even Barbaia and Lanari were willing on
occasion to buy a pirated score cheap. Even Bellini, so indignant
on his own behalf, tried to make a secret deal for the Naples rights
in *I puritani* so as to cheat the Paris impresarios who had first
staged it of their legal share. A common negotiating ploy was for
one impresario to write to another that he could get a score locally
very cheap but that he would hire the other man's authentic
version if the price was reasonable. Occasionally a vigilant impresario managed to do good business out of secondary rights in scores,
as Lanari did out of some of 'his' Donizetti and Mercadante
operas, but this meant generally either putting on the works
himself in one city after another or else a straight exchange with an
impresario who had an equally valuable score to offer.

John Rosselli, *The Opera Industry in Italy from Cimarosa to Verdi*,
Cambridge University Press, 1984, pp. 56–8, 131

*Choruses in nineteenth-century opera companies could be mutinous and
troublesome:*

Italian chorus singers were notoriously cooks, street vendors,
minor artisans, and the like who sang part-time; few could read
music. Their inability to look like ladies and gentlemen was given
by the directors of La Fenice as the reason for putting *La traviata*
into the fashions of about 1700 – beneath which their low origins
'disappeared'. They were paid labourers' wages, were apt to smoke,
drink, and gamble in the dressing-rooms, and were altogether 'the
pariahs of art'.

Yet chorus strikes recurred throughout the nineteenth century, and so did strike-breaking by impresarios. Like orchestral players, many chorus members were mobile; it was not difficult to import them. Under the old governments entire choruses that had gone on strike were arrested at Lucca in 1836 and at Piacenza in 1844; a Parma chorus rioted in 1829 and its self-proclaimed leader was arrested by an officer who feared that any more trouble might lead the impresario to bring in 'foreigners'. Methods of discipline might be crude: Lanari's deputy, faced with an unruly chorus, slapped one member of it; he later threatened to have them all arrested and ostentatiously posted several policemen backstage.

John Rosselli, The Opera Industry in Italy from Cimarosa to Verdi,
Cambridge University Press, 1984, p. 118

The showman P.T. Barnum had the bright idea of bringing the 'Swedish Nightingale', Jenny Lind, to the United States:

It was in October 1849 that I conceived the idea of bringing Jenny Lind to this country. I had never heard her sing, inasmuch as she arrived in London a few weeks after I left that city with General Tom Thumb. Her reputation, however, was sufficient for me . . . The sum of all my instructions, public and private, to [John Hall] Wilton, amounted to this: he was to engage her on shares, if possible. I, however, authorized him to engage her at any rate, not exceeding one thousand dollars a night, for any number of nights up to one hundred and fifty, with all her expenses, including servants, carriages, secretary, etc., besides also engaging such musical assistants, not exceeding three in number, as she should select, let the terms be what they might. If necessary, I should place the entire amount of money named in the engagement, in the hands of London bankers before she sailed . . .

I had an interview with Wilton, and learned from him that, in accordance with the agreement, it would be requisite for me to place the entire amount stipulated, $187,500, in the hands of the

London bankers. I at once resolved to ratify the agreement, and immediately sent the necessary documents to Miss Lind . . .

[After she arrived in New York] presents of all sorts were showered upon her. Milliners, mantua makers, and shopkeepers vied with each other in calling attention to their wares, of which they sent her many valuable specimens, delighted if, in return, they could receive her autograph acknowledgement. Songs, quadrilles and polkas were dedicated to her, and poets sang in her praise. We had Jenny Lind gloves, Jenny Lind bonnets, Jenny Lind riding hats, Jenny Lind shawls, mantillas, robes, chairs, sofas, pianos – in fact, everything was Jenny Lind. Her movements were constantly watched, and the moment her carriage appeared at the door, it was surrounded by multitudes, eager to catch a glimpse of the Swedish Nightingale . . .

Jenny Lind's first concert was fixed to come off at Castle Garden, on Wednesday evening, 11 September, and most of the tickets were sold at auction on the Saturday and Monday previous to the concert . . . One thousand tickets were sold at auction on the first morning for an aggregate sum of $10,141 . . .

The reception of Jenny Lind on her first appearance, in point of enthusiasm, was probably never before equalled. As Mr Benedict [the conductor] led her towards the footlights, the entire audience rose to their feet and welcomed her with three cheers, accompanied by the waving of thousands of hats and handkerchiefs. This was perhaps the largest audience to which Jenny Lind had ever sung. She was evidently much agitated, but the orchestra commenced, and before she had sung a dozen notes of '*Casta diva*', she began to recover her self-possession, and long before the *scena* was concluded, she was as calm as if she was in her own drawing-room. Towards the last portion of the cavatina, the audience were so completely carried away by their feelings that the remainder of the air was drowned in a perfect tempest of acclamation. Enthusiasm had been wrought to its highest pitch, but the musical powers of Jenny Lind exceeded all the brilliant anticipations which had been formed, and her triumph was complete. At the conclusion of the concert Jenny Lind was loudly called for, and was obliged to appear three times before the audience could be satisfied. Then they called vociferously for 'Barnum', and I reluctantly responded to their demand . . .

The Rubicon was passed. The successful issue of the Jenny Lind enterprise was established. I think there were a hundred men in New York, the day after her first concert, who would have willingly paid me $200,000 for my contract. I received repeated offers for an eighth, a tenth, or a sixteenth, equivalent to that price. But mine had been the risk, and I was determined mine should be the triumph.

P.T. Barnum, *Struggles and Triumphs*, Courier, 1889,
pp. 100—101

Wagner, making a career as an operatic conductor, pleaded poverty and frustration in a somewhat paranoid letter to his friend Düringer in August 1850:

'I confess to you, what I have not done yet to anyone else, that as the result of these last fatal years, my many changes of residence, the many times I have been out of an engagement, and, above all, the three years during which I have drawn nothing for an opera, I am so poor that Germany ought to blush for shame, if it had any shame in it. God and my family know I have always worked; but in the last three years I have had bad luck with three new operas – that is to say, none of them has failed, but they have not done as well as people expected, and the intendants, directors, stage-managers and other vermin, unless they smell out a success like that of *Der Freischütz* or *Czar und Zimmermann*, leave the German composer in the lurch – just because he is a German. How they angle for French operas! What fees Bote and Bock have paid for Halévy's *Val d'Andorra* – a work that has not done well anywhere. Oh, if only there could be a revolution in the theatre! Like the murderers of Latour and Lamberg I would lay a hand to the work and help to string up the gentleman I have named . . . My small savings have gone, my bits of silver and jewellery were long ago pawned; and on top of it all I owe some hundreds of thalers in Leipzig. My tiny salary of 600 thalers (without a benefit) of course hardly buys us any food, and I have even to ask for part payment in advance, which will have to be repaid in instalments by deduction from my salary. I assure you that often I am in need of the veriest necessities, for I have nothing more to pawn.'

Ernest Newman, *The Life of Richard Wagner*, Knopf,

1933, I, p. 159

Verdi struggles with his publisher Tito Ricordi in a letter of 24 October 1855:

Why, since I have rights in the sale of my score to foreign countries, do you no longer sell the score, but a copy? In this way you deprive me of all benefit. You may answer that the foreign publishers only want the copy, but they used to buy the entire score of my first operas, and the last could have been handled the same way if you wanted it. Another thing (though I am not sure if it is true): I am told that when you sign contracts you often add an amount for printing charges or something. For instance, last carnival season, in the contract for *Il trovatore* at La Scala, there was a sum of ——, and then you added another small sum in order to recompense yourself for printing costs. If that is true, permit me to say that it is behaviour unworthy of a great business man. The same thing happened another time with *Luisa Miller*. This is nothing better than evasive quibbling. I know that you can say 'I have the right to do this. The law allows it.' I know, I know. But I hoped that you would not behave like this to me. Many and many a time I have done things for you that I was not obliged to. I, after all, am the main source of your colossal fortune. Don't deny it. Examine your books, and observe the profits you have gained from my operas.

I wish to lodge a bitter complaint about the editions of my latest operas which have been produced in a slovenly manner, and with countless misprints. Above all, I must protest that you have not yet withdrawn the first edition of *La traviata*. This is an unpardonable negligence. If I had not by chance visited Escudier on business, this edition would be circulating in France. Who knows whether or not it is circulating in Germany, Spain, and other countries? You know this edition should have been withdrawn two years ago!! It was on condition that this was done (a condition in the contract – I asked no money for it), that I made an agreement with [the baritone] Coletti. But who cares about the reputation of a composer? I can't help reflecting and feeling heartily discouraged. Throughout my long career I have always found impresarios and publishers hard, inflexible, always inexorable, and ready to invoke the law on their side when necessary. Always fine words and very bad deeds. I have never been treated as anything but an object, a tool to be used as long as it brings profits. This is sad but true.

Giuseppe Verdi, *Letters*, translated by Charles Osborne, Gollancz,

1971, p. 102

In the nineteenth century it was not always easy for singers to get paid by wily impresarios such as J.H. Mapleson:

Novara arrived at the theatre in time to dress, and when he asked Levelly, Mapleson's agent, for his salary, Levelly said Mapleson was dining out, and had 'forgotten to sign a cheque for him'.

Novara, however, was determined not to sing unless he were paid, and so he told Levelly that Mapleson must be searched for until found.

'I don't know where he is,' said Levelly, in despair. 'Here, take my watch as a guarantee, Novara, and, for God's sake, get into your clothes.'

'I don't require your watch, man,' answered the obdurate baritone, 'I want my money, and unless I get it before the curtain rises I shall take off this d—d wig, and the stage carpenter can sing the role of Rocco.'

Levelly was rushing about like a madman by this time, and

Novara, with his hand on his wig, calmly awaited eventualities in his dressing-room.

It will be remembered that when the curtain rises on the first act of *Fidelio*, Rocco is heard singing behind the scenes, and I was filled with consternation at the strange voice that greeted my ears. Of course, I knew nothing at that time of the contretemps between Levelly and Novara, and it was only on making inquiries that I learned that Novara had refused to sing Rocco's opening bars, and that Parry, the stage manager, had been obliged to sing them instead, and had, to the best of his ability, imitated Novara's deep bass notes.

Levelly, seeing that Novara meant what he said, had taken a cab and gone, Heaven knows where, in search of the truant impresario. Whether he found Mapleson or not I never knew, but he obtained Novara's salary, and reached the theatre, dripping with perspiration, and thrust the cash into Rocco's hand, who, stuffing it in his pocket, rushed on to the stage just in the nick of time to save the performance.

Luigi Arditi, My Reminiscences, Skeffington, 1896, pp. 264–6

Mapleson's wiles and cool nerves were often put to the test by singers such as Adelina Patti, who was well aware of her commercial worth:

About two o'clock, Patti's agent called upon me to receive the 5000 dollars for her services that evening. I was at low water just then, and inquiring at the booking-office found that I was £200 short. All I could offer Signor Franchi was the trifle of £800 as a payment on account.

The agent declined the money, and formally announced to me that my contract with Mme Patti was at an end. I accepted the inevitable, consoling myself with the reflection that, besides other good artists in my company, I had now £800 to go on with.

Two hours afterwards Signor Franchi reappeared.

'I cannot understand,' he said, 'how it is you get on so well with prima donnas, and especially with Mme Patti. You are a marvellous man, and a fortunate one, too, I may add. Mme Patti does not wish to break her engagement with you, as she certainly would have done with anyone else under the circumstances. Give me the £800 and she will make every preparation for going on to the stage. She empowers me to tell you that she will be at the theatre in good time for the beginning of the opera, and that she will be ready dressed in the costume of Violetta, with the exception only of the shoes. You can let her have the balance when the doors open and the money comes in from the outside public; and directly she receives it she will put her shoes on and at the proper moment make her appearance on the stage.' I thereupon handed him the £800 I had already in hand as the result of subscriptions in advance . . .

After the opening of the doors I had another visit from Signor Franchi. By this time an extra sum of £160 had come in. I handed it to my benevolent friend, and begged him to carry it without delay to the obliging prima donna, who, having received £960, might, I thought, be induced to complete her toilette pending the arrival of the £40 balance.

Nor was I altogether wrong in my hopeful anticipations. With a beaming face Signor Franchi came back and communicated to me the joyful intelligence that Mme Patti had got one shoe on. 'Send her the £40,' he added, 'and she will put on the other.'

Ultimately the other shoe was got on; but not, of course, until the last £40 had been paid. Then Mme Patti, her face radiant with benignant smiles, went on to the stage; and the opera already begun was continued brilliantly until the end.

Mme Adelina Patti is beyond doubt the most successful singer who ever lived. Vocalists as gifted, as accomplished as she might be named, but no one ever approached her in the art of obtaining from a manager the greatest possible sum he could by any possibility contrive to pay.

J.H. Mapleson, *The Mapleson Memoirs 1848–1888*, Remington, 1888, II, pp. 23–5

In his old age Wagner was tempted by an offer to live and work in the United States. He discussed terms in a letter to the American dentist Newell Sill Jenkins on 8 February 1880, but nothing came of the negotiations:

It is not impossible that I may yet decide to emigrate to America with the whole of my family, and take my latest work with me. Since I am no longer young, I should need a very substantial concession from the other side of the ocean. An association would have to be formed that would place a lump sum of one million dollars at my disposal, thus enabling me to settle there and repaying me for all the trouble involved, half of the sum being used to pay for my settlement in some climatically beneficial state of the Union, the other half being deposited in a state bank as a capital investment at 5 per cent. In doing this, America would secure my services for all time. In addition the association would have to raise the funds necessary to enable an annual festival to be held at which I should present all my works by easy stages in model performances: we would make an immediate start with the *first* performance of my latest work, *Parsifal*, which I would not allow to be performed elsewhere until that time. Whatever I do in the future, whether as performance manager or as a creative artist, would belong to the American nation, free of charge and for all time, on the basis of the sum that had already been transferred to me.

Richard Wagner, *Selected Letters*, translated by Stewart Spencer and
Barry Millington, Dent, 1987, p. 899

Performers used to be far more militant than they are today:

Mention must be made of a distressing 'season' promoted by M. Carillon at Her Majesty's [in London] in March 1886 ... The climax and finale was reached when *Faust* was announced, and was started in the presence of a small audience. It is correct to say that it started, but it never finished. It proceeded, between long intervals, until the garden scene was due to open, when the interval seemed endless and the audience grew boisterous.

The trouble, it was explained, was that the chorus were threatening to walk out unless they received their money in advance. Evidently it had leaked out that there was not sufficient cash in the box office till to ensure satisfaction to all. 'Noises off' found a ready response in the audience; they were inclined to sympathize with the unfortunate stranded Italians, who eventually took matters into their own hands, and pushing their way to the front of the curtain, loudly begged for alms, in pathetic attitudes of appeal. Coins were thrown on to the stage, and were avidly gathered up. Waving their thanks, the poor supers withdrew, only to find that the manager had fled. The audience then vented their feelings by tearing up and destroying everything breakable or tearable, leaving the theatre as though a typhoon had passed through it. There was much righteous indignation in the press next day, and solemn sermons were preached on the iniquity of allowing speculating managements to use London theatres for their operations.

P.G. Hurst, *The Age of Jean de Reszke*, Christopher Johnson, 1958,

pp. 101–2

Sir Thomas Beecham sank much of his personal fortune into subsidizing his operatic ventures, but was quite keen to have this financial burden removed from his shoulders:

'To make an opera a success in England is the simplest thing in the world,' he would say. 'All you have to do is interest about a dozen very rich people who would be willing to spend for the next five or seven years not less than £50,000 a year. It has been done in America. Why not here?'

The very rich did not respond.

Charles Reid, *Thomas Beecham: An Independent Biography*, Gollancz,

1961, p. 183

*The development of gramophone recordings in the early twentieth century
exploited the popularity of opera. But these early recordings, especially on
the prestigious Victor Red Seal label, were very expensive:*

There was, aesthetic satisfaction aside, a redolent snob appeal
attached to Red Seal Records. They were expensive, and expensive
in an autocratically stratified way. Red Seal artists were ranked,
monetarily speaking, according to their eminence. Thus, 'The Last
Rose of Summer' could be heard on four twelve-inch Red Seal
discs, single-sided of course, priced variously from $5.00 to $1.50,
depending on whether it was Patti, Tetrazzini, Sembrich, or Alice
Nielsen who sang. Quantity as well as quality entered into the
calculations. Caruso's twelve-inch solo records sold for $3.00; but
when he sang duets with other Red Seal artists, the price went up
to $4.00 (excepting only his one duet with Melba, 'O soave fanciulla'
from *La Bohème*, which sold for $5.00). When Victor brought out
its first recording of the quartet from *Rigoletto* in March 1907 (with
Caruso, Scotti, Bessie Abbott, and Louise Homer), it charged
$6.00 for four singers – and four minutes of music. A year later,
when the *Lucia* sextet was added to the catalogue, the buyer had to
part with $7.00 for the warblings *en masse* of Sembrich, Caruso,
Scotti, Journet, Severina, and Daddi. Since a dollar bill, *circa* 1910,
would buy a seven-course dinner at a first-class restaurant, it can
be appreciated that the *Lucia* sextet at $7.00 represented consider-
ably more than a casual purchase made by the head of the family
on his way home to dinner.

Roland Gelatt, *The Fabulous Phonograph 1877–1977*, Cassell, 1977,
pp. 148–9

The fees paid for single performances by the Metropolitan Opera House:

1905–6: Melba was promised $2000 but never appeared; in 1907
Oscar Hammerstein at the rival Manhattan Opera paid her $3000;
Nordica, $1250; Eames, $1500; Fremstad, $1382 for ten perform-
ances a month. An average family's annual income in New York
was estimated at *c.* $850.

1907–8: Caruso, $2000; Farrar, $800; Fremstad, $750; Chaliapin, $1344.

1908–9: Fremstad and Farrar level-pegged for one season at $1000; Mahler earned slightly less at $5050 a month for six performances, while Toscanini got only $4800 for twelve performances a month.

1909–10: Destinn, $900; Farrar, $1200 (making a total of forty appearances, and singing at least twice a fortnight); while Fremstad stayed at $1000 (also for forty appearances); Nordica kept to her 1905–6 fee of $1250. Hammerstein at the Manhattan paid Tetrazzini $1500 and Mary Garden $1400.

1911–12: Destinn, $1200; Farrar, $1250; Fremstad, $1000. Toscanini was still down at $7000 a month, averaging twelve performances in that period. Seats at the Met were priced, as they had been for some years, at between one and five dollars.

1926–7: Galli-Curci on tour commanded $3500 in New York, $2250, with Jeritza a whisker ahead at $2300; Schumann-Heink's return cost $500 ... Martinelli took $1700, the baritone Ruffo $1500; Gigli, $16,000 per month for approximately eight performances. In the mid-twenties a motor car cost *c.* $1000, a gramophone record $1, and a round-the-world cruise *c.* $2000. A seat at the Met could cost up to $8.25 in 1929.

1930–31: the Depression had begun, but had not yet bitten into the upper end of the earnings scale. The charming and stalwart lyric soprano Lucrezia Bori, $1400; Jeritza, $2500; Ponselle (after her Covent Garden triumph) $1700; Rethberg, $1200.

1935–6: the Depression had hit. Flagstad and Lotte Lehmann, $750; Grace Moore, Ponselle, Bori, $1000; Melchior, $1000; Rethberg, $900; Martinelli, $800 – less than half what he earned in 1926–7. Average earnings in 1929, $1300; in 1935, $850.

1956–7: in the intervening twenty years, fees had not increased either in real or inflated terms. Tebaldi, Milanov, and Callas all earned the $1000 top.

Rupert Christiansen, *Prima Donna*, Bodley Head, 1984, pp. 208–9

Gigli defends his failure to participate in the cost-cutting to save the
Metropolitan Opera House during the Depression:

At the beginning of April 1932, Paul Cravath, president of the
Metropolitan Opera Company since the previous October, had
made an official announcement. 'Reduced receipts due to the
prevailing financial depression,' he said, had 'practically wiped out
the company's capital of $550,000 and most of its reserve, leaving
it with insufficient funds to assure another season.' An 'earnest
effort', he continued, would be made to work out a plan of
reduced expense 'and other measures', so that in spite of everything there might still be opera in New York the following
winter.

At the same time it was learned that all employees of the
Metropolitan Opera House, from soloists to ushers, would be
asked to take a 'voluntary' salary cut of 25 per cent if the 1932–3
season should be decided on. This was the chief economy measure
proposed to avert closing down. An earlier 'voluntary cut' of 10
per cent had already been proposed the previous December. There
was, of course, nothing voluntary about these cuts, they were
decided by the management and all concerned had no option but
to give their consent.

These proposals were the rock on which I split with the
Metropolitan. My behaviour in doing so was widely criticized, a
fact I resented at the time; but now I have enough detachment to
realize that my critics were to some extent justified. I did act
unwisely – above all, tactlessly. People cannot be expected to see
behind appearances, and appearances were against me. It looked as
though, after a happy and fruitful association that had lasted
twelve years, I were leaving the Metropolitan in the hour of its
distress, over a question of money.

That, however, was not the way I saw it ... I acted, quite
frankly, in a fit of pique. I am ready now to admit that it was
unwarranted.

I would like to stress the fact that I fully shared the general
anguish about the survival of the Metropolitan. Had I been asked

to help, in my own way and at my own discretion, I would gladly
have given, not a quarter but half my salary to an emergency fund.
I would equally gladly have given extra performances for nothing.
I found it intolerable, however, that my contribution should be
demanded as a right, decided for me in advance, stopped out of
my salary. I found it intolerable that my hard-earned contract,
which had still three years to run, should be – to all intents and
purposes – scrapped. I felt angry at this high-handed approach. I
suddenly felt that I wanted to revolt against the almighty Gatti-
Casazza.

Beniamino Gigli, *Memoirs*, translated by Darina Silone, Cassell, 1957,
pp. 174–6

*Raoul Gunsbourg remained as director of the Monte Carlo Opera from
1892 to 1951. Late in 1950, at the age of ninety and losing his grip, he
retired, writing pitifully to Prince Rainier:*

'Serene Highness. From the bottom of my heart, and with all my
soul, I pray God that He will accord your highness happiness,
health and a long life, and all that your highness could wish for.
Live a long time, Monseigneur, for yourself, for your country, and
for all those who surround you. If, at the time when your highness
thought of reducing the number of opera performances by eight, I
had been able to take the train to Monaco, I should have been able
to explain to your highness my system of directing by apportioning
to the eighteen performances all the costs of the entire season.
Your serene highness, with his legendary perceptiveness, would
not have failed to realize that the cancellation of eight performances
made the amortization of these high costs no longer possible, and
would have resulted in a loss of three to four million [francs], a
sum I did not, and do not, have; nor would you have allowed it,
that I – who have kept my word and honoured my obligations –
should find myself in so embarrassing a situation; all would have
been worked out in one way or another. My great age hindered me
from making this lightning journey, and so it is a sad old stricken

man who offers his excuses. But, if with the arrival of the New Year, your highness will condescend to pardon me, I will be greatly rewarded, having during more than half a century contributed to the glory of the opera of your serene highness, and having loyally served three great princes' . . .

On 10 April 1950, Prince Rainier appointed Gunsbourg a Grand Officer of the Order of St Charles, and on his retirement a year later, conferred on him the decoration of Commander of the Ordre de Mérite Culturel. The SBM [the powerful Société des Bains de Mer, which controlled the Casino and other facilities] though was not so rewarding, and his application for a pension on retirement was finally refused on 11 February 1954. Having been appointed to the post on 2 June 1892, he had spent almost sixty years in their service, and at his great age, financially it could have been little more than a gesture of respect. He died at Monaco on 30 May 1955.

T. J. Walsh, *Monte Carlo Opera 1910–1951*, Kilkenny, Boethius Press,
1986, pp. 239–40

The Metropolitan is faced with great temptation:

The financial plight of the Metropolitan, and of opera producers generally, is no laughing matter. However, it was brought to public notice this year by an affair that was not entirely lacking in comic relief. A year ago last spring, a well-to-do Philadelphia man died. His name was McNair Ilgenfritz. He loved opera. For years he had been a box-holder at the Metropolitan. He also liked to compose a bit. Ten years before, he had submitted two opera scores to Edward Johnson – a one-acter called *Le Passant* and a three-acter based on *Phèdre*. The Metropolitan took no action; Mr Ilgenfritz brought no pressure; the scores rested on a shelf. But in his will, Mr Ilgenfritz bequeathed a part of his estate – the rounded figure given out was $150,000 – to the Metropolitan, *provided* the company produced one of his operas. Rudolf Bing had the scores taken down and dusted. They turned out to be piano scores only, but completely factured, post-Debussy in style.

Problem: to produce or not to produce. Everyone argued the pros and cons. The Metropolitan certainly could use $150,000, and if *Le Passant* were to be produced (nobody seemed to even mention producing *Phèdre*) only a small part of the bequest would be used up – orchestration, a setting, rehearsals, and all. Reactions ranged from white-hot indignation at the very idea of anyone (even a deceased putative composer) attempting to suborn the World's Greatest Opera Company to cheerful assent that so much money would be cheap at the price of a couple of performances of an Ilgenfritz opera. At first, it was understood that the company was willing to meet the terms, then that it was not, then that the problem was being reconsidered, then that the answer was definitely 'No'. The period within which the Metropolitan must decide is two years, then it must implement an affirmative decision within another two. At that point, other first-class houses get in on the act. As matters stand, it seems wildly improbable that *Le Passant* will ever be heard at the Metropolitan. In fact, there is no record of anyone having expressed a desire to *hear* it anywhere. But $150,000 are $150,000, and these particular Ilgenfritz dollars are waiting to be spent. A nice problem in artistic morality. Really, the nut of the question is this: what if Mr Ilgenfritz had left, say, a million?

James Hinton, Jnr, 'The Opera Scene in America', in *Opera Annual*
1954–1955, edited by Harold Rosenthal, Calder, 1954, pp. 104–5

Negotiating with Callas:

Backstage in the opera house, at the last night of her Chicago season [of 1955], Miss Callas had been served with a summons by Richard Bagarozy, who claimed that during her stay in New York in the 1940s (when she took lessons from Bagarozy's wife Louise Caselotti) Miss Callas had signed an exclusive management contract with him pledging him 10 per cent of all her earnings as a singer for ten years. This had mounted up (eventually Bagarozy would claim no less than $300,000), and he wanted to be paid. Miss Callas

exploded with rage, and accused Kelly and Miss Fox [the managers
of the Chicago Lyric Opera] of failing to protect her. It was
understood that in New York the Metropolitan would have to
protect her.

The best our lawyers could work out, after consultation with
the lawyers in Chicago who were handling the case with Miss
Callas, was an agreement to deposit the money for her appearances
in a Swiss bank, which meant that she would have no salary in
America for the Bagarozys to attach. We perfected the arrangement
in great detail, but [Callas's husband] Meneghini rejected it. In
fact, Meneghini rejected all arrangements that did not involve
payment to him *in cash*, before the curtain rose, of his wife's fee for
each performance. Towards the end, I had him paid in five-dollar
bills, to make a wad uncomfortably large for him to carry.

Sir Rudolf Bing, *5000 Nights at the Opera*, Hamish Hamilton, 1972,

pp. 182–3

The soprano Gilda dalla Rizza laments the modern mercenary age:

'I went to a dress rehearsal not long ago, and while the unfortunate
mezzo-soprano was in the middle of an aria the conductor stopped
and the orchestra walked out. "What is happening?" I asked, not
believing my eyes. "Every hour they have the right to a twenty-
minute break," they answered me. Is that art, I ask you? When
Toscanini conducted at Bayreuth he refused to accept payment,
because he declared it would desecrate the memory of Wagner.
And when he was music director at La Scala he insisted that they
subtract from his salary the equivalent of the days he spent away
from Milan. Now that is dedication to art, as I knew it and
practised it myself. We never spoke of singers, only of artists.
Today there are only singers, no more artists. They all have villas
in Switzerland and Swiss bank accounts. They will sing anywhere
and anything for a good fee. You will not find the great names of
today in thirty years' time at the Casa Verdi [a home for impoverished singers], where I and many distinguished colleagues live

quietly, for we cannot afford anything else. These people sell their voices the way a salesman sells shirts or ties.

'In my day,' she continued, 'we gave everything of ourselves for art's sake, because we believed in what we were doing. Puccini could ask me to go anywhere to sing for him at a low fee, and I would accept. There are great voices today, to be sure – some just as great as, perhaps even greater than in my own time. But they give nothing of themselves.'

Lanfranco Rasponi, *The Last Prima Donnas*, Gollancz, 1984, pp. 121–3

No tickee, no washee:

On 17 June 1979 the Teatro Municipal in Rio de Janeiro was giving its last performance of *Tosca*. As the curtain rose on Scarpia's study in the Palazzo Farnese, Orianna Santunione and Nunzio Todisco, the Tosca and Cavaradossi, to the astonishment of the audience advanced towards the footlights, gestured to the conductor to stop the orchestra, and announced that they would not finish the performance since they had not been paid in full. Then they calmly walked out. One minute later a spokesman for the opera house came on-stage and begged the public to be patient; the performance would continue with two Brazilian singers. The contracts with both Santunione and Todisco were for $4500 a performance, it was reported, but the artists did not want to have the money deposited in Italy; they wanted it immediately so that they could change the dollars on the black market. Both singers were then sued for breach of contract.

Lanfranco Rasponi, *The Last Prima Donnas*, Gollancz, 1984, p. 605

The baritone Thomas Allen explains how an opera singer earns a living:

I have an agent in London who serves several purposes in my life. He acts as a poste restante, so people can find out where I am in the world, what I'm doing and when. Theatres, opera companies, orchestras will telephone him to inquire after my services. He informs those people and others of my availability for any particular season. Other agents based in Paris, Vienna, New York, representing my interests in these various countries, will also be in touch, with similar inquiries. All agents have to be paid, and usually in the form of various percentages from my earnings.

Let us suppose I am engaged by a German opera house for a new production of *Figaro*. Their management will make an offer of a fee, which my agent and I discuss, and eventually agree upon. This sum then appears in a subsequent contract. The opera house will provide me with funds to get to the first rehearsal and to leave after the last performance. Managements in Europe offer a normal economy fare. In America most theatres also offer economy or coach, but because of the distance involved, particularly to the West Coast of America, I argue for a business-class fare – not first class, as I've no wish to cripple the economy of the Arts and I'm not greedy. This is everything I receive by way of payment.

I have to find somewhere to live for what may be a period of two months or more. It should be warm, so that I don't run the risk of colds and ill health. It should be near my workplace. Opera houses have a habit of being in the centre of a city, the area around which everything revolves, and prices tend to reflect this. Consequently a flat or room in such a situation can cost quite a lot of money. I have to provide every meal I eat when I'm away from home. Absolutely all outgoings have to be paid out of the money already negotiated.

Even more strenuous are the demands on some of the women. The strain on marriages is always very great, as a singer's life is not unlike a politician's. Many of my female colleagues have young families. It does not take much imagination to guess how little is left in their purses at the end of a month in, say, Geneva, with normal living costs doubled or tripled by the added burden of nanny and charges in tow. My admiration for them in pursuing their careers in the circumstances knows no bounds . . .

Too well-paid? Too high the fees? Never.

Thomas Allen, *Foreign Parts*, Sinclair-Stevenson, 1993, pp. 146–7

ISSUES IN OPERA

29: The Nature of Opera

Opera is more musical novel than musical drama.

Peter Conrad, *Romantic Opera and Literary Form*, p. 1

John Dryden offered the following definition of opera:

An opera is a poetical tale, or fiction, represented by vocal and instrumental music, adorned with scenes, machines, and dancing. The supposed persons of this musical drama are generally supernatural, as gods, and goddesses, and heroes, which at least are descended from them, and are in due time to be adopted into their number ... Human impossibilities are to be received as they are in faith; because, where gods are introduced, a supreme power is to be understood, and second causes are out of doors. Yet propriety is to be observed even here ... The recitative part of the opera requires a more masculine beauty of expression and sound; the other, which, for want of a proper English word, I must call the *songish part*, must abound in the softness and variety of numbers; its principal intention being to please the hearing rather than to gratify the understanding.

John Dryden, Preface to *Albion and Albanius*, 1685

Bernard Mandeville admired opera for its decorum:

At the Opera every thing charms and concurs to make Happiness compleat. The Sweetness of Voice in the first place, and the solemn Composure of the Action, serve to mitigate and allay every Passion; it is the Gentleness of them, and the calm Serenity of the

Mind, that make us amiable, and bring us the nearest to the
Perfection of Angels; whereas the Violence of the Passions, in
which the Corruption of the Heart chiefly consists, dethrones our
Reason, and renders us most like unto Savages. It is incredible,
how prone we are to Imitation, and how strangely, unknown to
ourselves, we are shaped and fashioned after the Models and
Examples that are often set before us. No Anger nor Jealousy are
ever to be seen at an Opera that distort the Features, no Flames
that are noxious, nor is any Love represented in them, that is not
pure and next to Zeraphick; and it is impossible for the Remembrance to carry any thing away from them, that can sully the
Imagination. *Secondly*, The Company is of another sort: the Place it
self is a Security to Peace, as well as every ones Honour, and it is
impossible to name another, where blooming Innocence and irresistible Beauty stand in so little need of Guardians. Here we are sure
never to meet with Petulancy or ill Manners, and to be free from
immodest Ribaldry, Libertine Wit, and detestable Satyr. If you will
mind, on the one hand, the Richness and Splendour of Dress, and
the Quality of the Persons that appear in them, the Variety of
Colours, and the Lustre of the Fair in a spacious Theatre, well
illuminated and adorn'd; and on the other, the grave Deportment
of the Assembly, and the Consciousness, that appears in every
Countenance, of the Respect they owe to each other, you will be
forced to confess, that upon Earth there can not be a Pastime more
agreeable: Believe me, Madam, there is no Place, where both Sexes
have such Opportunities of imbibing exalted Sentiments, and
raising themselves above the Vulgar, as they have at the Opera;
and there is no other sort of Diversion or Assembly from the
frequenting of which young Persons of Quality can have equal
hopes of forming their Manners, and contracting a strong and
lasting Habit of Virtue.

Bernard Mandeville, *Fable of the Bees* (1714), First Dialogue, II,
pp. 39–40

Gluck was keen to introduce reform into the bloated stagings that passed for opera in the baroque period:

When I undertook to write the music for *Alceste*, I decided to rid it altogether of those abuses which, introduced either by the inappropriate vanity of the singers or an exaggerated complaisance on the part of the composers, have long disgraced the Italian opera, and which have transformed the most stately and most beautiful of all spectacles into the most foolish and boring one. I sought to restrict music to its true function, namely to serve the poetry by means of the expression – and the situations which make up the plot – without interrupting the action or diminishing its interest by useless and superfluous ornament . . . Accordingly, I did not wish to stop an actor in the greatest heat of dialogue in order to let him wait for a full *ritournelle*; nor did I want to interrupt a word on a suitable vowel to let him display, in an extended passage, the agility of his fine voice; or let him wait for the orchestra to indicate, by a cadence, the resumption of the melody. I refused to let the singers glide rapidly over the second part of an aria, which may be the most passionate and important one, to have them repeat four times the words of the first part; or to end an aria when its full meaning has perhaps not yet been conveyed, in order to give the singer a chance to show how capriciously he can vary a passage in diverse manners. In short: I have done my best to banish all those abuses against which common sense and reason have vainly protested for such a long time.

C.W. Gluck, Dedication of *Alceste*, 1769, translated by Ulrich Weisstein, in Ulrich Weisstein, ed., *The Essence of Opera*, Collier Macmillan, 1964, p. 106

Weber was less concerned with the formal structure of opera than with its overall effect. His was an essentially Romantic conception:

The nature and essence of opera, consisting, as it does, of wholes within a whole, causes this enormous difficulty, which only the masters have managed to overcome. Each musical number, on account of the structure that is peculiar to it, appears to be a self-contained, organic unit. Yet as part of a larger unit it is supposed to vanish as we contemplate the latter. Nevertheless, the operatic ensemble, revealing several external aspects at one and the same time, can and should be a Janus head to be taken in at one single glance.

This is the inmost secret of music, which can be felt but cannot be explicitly stated: the undulation and the contrasting natures of wrath and love, of blissful pain, in which salamander and sylph embrace and merge, are here united. In other words: what love is to man, music is to man as well as to the arts; for it is love itself, the purest, most ethereal language of the passions, containing their innumerable and constantly changing colours, yet expressing only one truth that is immediately understood by a thousand people endowed with the most widely divergent feelings.

Carl Maria von Weber, 'On the Opera *Undine*' (1817), translated by Ulrich Weisstein, reprinted in Ulrich Weisstein, ed., *The Essence of Opera*, Collier Macmillan, 1964

Thomas de Quincey found a kind of sublimation in the opera house:

Tuesday and Saturday were for many years the regular nights of performance at the King's Theatre (or Opera House); and there it was in those times that Grassini sang; and her voice (the richest of contraltos) was delightful to me beyond all that I had ever heard. Yes; or have since heard; or ever shall hear. I know not what may be the state of the opera house now, having never been within its walls for seven or eight years; but at that time it was by much the most pleasant place of resort in London for passing an evening. Half a guinea admitted you to the pit, under the troublesome condition, however, of being *en grande tenue*. But to the gallery five shillings admitted you; and that gallery was subject to far less annoyance than the pit of most theatres. The orchestra was distinguished by its sweet and melodious grandeur from all English orchestras ... When Grassini appeared in some interlude, as she often did, and poured forth her passionate soul as Andromache at the tomb of Hector, etc., I question whether any Turk, of all that ever entered the paradise of opium eaters, can have had half the pleasure I had. But, indeed, I honour the barbarians too much by supposing them capable of any pleasures approaching to the intellectual ones of an Englishman. For music is an intellectual or a sensual pleasure, according to the temperament of him who hears it ... The mistake of most people is, to suppose that it is by the ear they communicate with music, and therefore that they are purely passive as to its effects. But this is not so; it is by the reaction of the mind upon the notices of the ear (the *matter* coming by the senses, the *form* from the mind) that the pleasure is constructed; and therefore it is that people of equally good ear differ so much in this point from one another ...

It is sufficient to say that a chorus, etc., of elaborate harmony displayed before me, as in a piece of arras-work, the whole of my past life – not as if recalled by an act of memory, but as if present and incarnated in the music; no longer painful to dwell upon, but the detail of its incidents removed, or blended in some hazy abstraction, and its passions exalted, spiritualized, and sublimed. All this was to be had for five shillings – that being the price of admission to the gallery; or, if a man preferred the high-bred society of the pit, even this might be had for half a guinea; or, in fact, for half-a-crown less, by purchasing beforehand a ticket at the music shops. And over and above the music of the stage and the orchestra, I had all around me, in the intervals of the performance, the music of the Italian language talked by Italian women – for the gallery was usually crowded with Italians – and I listened with a pleasure such as that with which Weld, the traveller, lay and listened, in Canada, to the sweet laughter of Indian women; for the less you understand of a language, the more sensible you are to the melody or harshness of its sounds.

Thomas de Quincey, *Confessions of an English Opium-eater*, 1821

For Weber it was a question of truth; for Robert Louis Stevenson, writing
to his mother in 1872, a matter of reality:

An opera is far more *real* than real life to me. It seems as if stage
illusion, and particularly this hardest to swallow and most conventional illusion of them all – an opera – would never stale upon me.
I wish that life was an opera. I should like to *live* in one; but
I don't know in what quarter of the globe I shall find society
so constituted. Besides, it would soon pall: imagine asking for
three-kreuzer cigars in recitative, or giving the washerwoman
the inventory of your dirty clothes in a sustained and *flourishing*
aria.

Robert Louis Stevenson, Letters, Methuen, 1899, I, p. 38

For many opera lovers, the medium is one of musical drama, with an
emphasis on the dramatic qualities of the work. Eric Bentley, as a theatre
critic, looks at opera from an unusual perspective:

Singers would sing had opera never been invented. The question
of opera is the question of musical drama.

I am not referring to Musik-Drama in the narrow sense, but to a
conception that includes Mozart as well as Wagner, Gluck as well
as Mozart. Though the composer might be imagined to be the foe
of dramatist and librettist, it will be found that, in fact, the great
operatic composers have all conceived opera dramatically. It is
only necessary to add that they have also conceived dramas which
it takes music to create. Those who think Mozart's *Figaro* better
than the play of Beaumarchais should grant that Mozart, for
example, fills in the Countess's character by musical means. Music
has been called 'the imagination of love in sound'. Be that as it
may, music can communicate the feeling of romantic love with a
sudden power and glory not possible even to Shakespeare in
Romeo. Some of Beaumarchais's people say they love; Mozart's
people give off love in sound . . .

According to a convention which serves no purpose but to
stultify the operatic stage, operas consist of silly stories and lovely

arias. Actually, some satisfactory operas consist of only adequate song and rather good narrative. An example from the current Met repertoire is [Puccini's] *The Girl of the Golden West*. Others disclose their musical value when you have granted the melodramatic premise: *Il trovatore* is a mad, splendid opera, founded on a mad, splendid story . . .

Some people will tell you the dramatic problem has been solved by the hiring of regular stage directors like Tyrone Guthrie and Margaret Webster. But they make no difference. Or rather, they make a difference that is not the needed one. These directors come into a few rehearsals and have everyone stand somewhere other than where they have been standing these fifty years. This is merely putting a good face on a bad body. Singing becomes operatic performance, not when the singer is moved to stage left or is forbidden to face front when embracing her lover, but when every moment in the opera is acted out as meticulously as every moment in a play is acted out. Naturally, operatic acting is going to be different, since gestures and moves have to be found for situations that never happen except in opera, especially for one situation that never happens except in opera, that the actor is singing.

In a brief exchange of letters with Mr Leopold Stokowski, Mr Rudolf Bing has recently declared that the Met does rehearse its operas enough. If the singers were not together with the orchestras, he went on, it was *not* for lack of rehearsal . . . But enough rehearsal for what? When I was at the Met this winter, the singers and the orchestra were together quite often, and it really didn't help much.

Eric Bentley, article in *Theatre Arts*, 1962, reprinted in *What is Theatre?*,
Methuen, 1969, pp. 388–90

Debussy believed in the dramatic centrality of opera, but tried to find a musical language as far removed as possible from the grandiloquence of aria:

Having been an impassioned pilgrim to Bayreuth for several years,

I began to cast doubt on the Wagnerian formula; or rather: it seemed to me that it fitted only the peculiar genius of that composer . . . It was necessary, then, to go beyond Wagner rather than follow in his path.

The drama *Pelléas*, which in spite of its dream-like atmosphere is more human than the so-called documents after life, seemed to be admirably suited to my purpose. Its evocative language expresses a sensibility which can be extended by the music and through the orchestral embellishment. I also endeavoured to adhere to a law of beauty that is singularly forgotten in relation to dramatic music. The characters in this drama try to sing like normal human beings, and not in an arbitrary language based on outdated traditions. It is on that account that I am reproached with having used monotonous declamation without the slightest token of melody . . . But the feelings of a person cannot constantly be expressed in melodic fashion, and the dramatic melody ought to be clearly distinguished from melody in general.

Claude Debussy, letter to the secretary general of the Opéra Comique, 1984, translated by Ulrich Weisstein, printed in Ulrich Weisstein, ed., *The Essence of Opera*, Collier Macmillan, 1964

Alban Berg too had to fashion a new musical language when composing the music for the poetic drama Wozzeck:

I have never entertained the idea of reforming the structure of opera through *Wozzeck*. Neither when I started nor when I completed the work did I consider it a model for further efforts by any other composer. I never assumed or expected that *Wozzeck* should become the basis of a school.

I simply wanted to compose good music; to develop musically the contents of Georg Büchner's immortal drama; to translate his poetic language into music. Other than that, when I decided to write an opera, my only intention, as related to the technique of composition, was to give the theatre what belongs to the theatre. The music was to be so formed that at each moment it would fulfil its duty of serving the action. Even more, the music should be prepared to furnish whatever the action needed for transformation into reality on the stage . . .

It was first necessary to make a selection from Büchner's twenty-five loosely constructed, partly fragmentary scenes for the libretto. Repetitions not lending themselves to musical variation were avoided. Finally, the scenes were brought together, arranged and grouped in acts. The problem therefore became more musical than literary, and had to be solved by the laws of musical structure rather than by the rules of dramaturgy.

It was impossible to shape the fifteen scenes I selected in different manners so that each would retain its musical coherence and individuality and at the same time follow the customary method of development appropriate to the literary content. No matter how rich structurally, no matter how aptly one might fit the dramatic events, after a number of scenes so composed the music would inevitably create monotony. The effect would become boring with a series of a dozen or more formally composed entr'actes which offered nothing but this type of illustrative music, and boredom, of course, is the last thing one should experience in the theatre.

I obeyed the necessity of giving each scene and each accompanying piece of entr'acte music – prelude, postlude, connecting link or interlude – an unmistakable aspect, a rounded off and finished character. It was imperative to use everything essential for the creation of individualizing characteristics on the one hand, and coherence on the other . . .

What I do consider my particular accomplishment is this. No one in the audience, no matter how aware he may be of the musical forms contained in the framework of the opera, of the precision and logic with which it has been worked out, no one from the moment the curtain parts until it closes for the last time, pays any attention to the various figures, inventions, suites, sonata movements, variations and passacaglias about which so much has been written. No one gives heed to anything but the vast social

implications of the work which by far transcend the personal
destiny of Wozzeck.

Alban Berg, 'A Word about *Wozzeck*,' (1927), translated by
Willi Reich, *Musical Quarterly*, 1952

*For Brigid Brophy operatic music transmits emotions in 'a texture of
delight':*

The convention in which Mozart sets his operatic world is the
utmost development of the operatic – indeed, of the artistic –
convention itself, and in developing it he accomplished the deepest
exploitation of opera's potentialities; for opera of all arts offers the
opportunity of the most direct expression of emotions by the least
naturalistic method. Nature does not endow bereaved fathers with
blank verse like King Lear's or permit bereaved daughters, like
Donna Anna, to burst into soprano flames at a touch to the blue
paper. The sounds which issue from the lips of King Lear and
Donna Anna would, if they were sounds alone, without context,
provoke us to an ecstasy of pleasure. Yet both Shakespeare and
Mozart are psychologists of such expertise that we cannot doubt
that King Lear and Donna Anna are 'real' characters feeling
genuine grief. At the same time their authors are artists so versed
and masterly that they can introduce into their pleasing texture
recognizable hieroglyphs of the sounds people really do make in
grief, so that at the end we are almost gulled into thinking we
have truly listened to a naturalistic transcription of their sorrow
and yet remain aware that the texture of delight has never in
fact been flawed. This is, of course, the height and the very
definition of dramatic art. Mozart practises it through the ravishment of his music, Shakespeare through the ravishment of his
poetry, for which no one has ever found any synonym except
music . . .

Opera . . . may occasionally drown out the sense, but never the
emotion. It is anything but mute. At an absolute court, as Saint-
Simon shows us, only the king may have emotions freely; other

people must have them in relation to his. Protocol – that is, primitive taboo – governs other people's behaviour; the king alone may twitch according to his whims, and acquires thereby a puppet's semblance of the personal and independent psychology which in reality he is not free to develop in his artificial vacuum. Puppet-psychology, together with a measure of allegory (usually through classical prototypes), which foreordained the characteristics of the dramatis personae as predictably as protocol foreordained the behaviour of courtiers, survived from the masque into the early, rhetorical days of opera. But since an emancipated public existed, opera quickly threw off the masque and fairly soon the classical masks as well, and developed into the world's most unconstrained vehicle for personal emotions.

As a form, opera is ill-adapted to depicting the massy and seemingly impersonal forces of taboo. Even its dignity, that quality most necessary to absolute monarchy, totters. Its crowd scenes are its most dangerous moments. On the stage, the chorus moves as well as sings in consort; and its drilledness, which impresses us in a church or a concert hall, easily gives us the giggles in the opera house. For reinforcing its choruses or characters with the weight of centuries of numinous awe, opera possesses no acceptable metaphor: hence the unhistorical, fancy-dress-ball air of nineteenth-century opera's costume dramas; and hence, at another remove, the cheapness of effect when Puccini pierces his own admirably blown bubble of operatic convention by introducing touches of Christian liturgy. Opera can no more portray the mass psychology of taboo than it can tracts of landscape or lapses of historical time. (Or, at least, it could not portray those until Wagner made splendid effects of mass and time by the literal method of deploying masses of singers and instrumentalists and keeping the audience in the theatre for great lengths of time.) What opera excels in creating, by its nature (Wagner, though magnificently, was working against its nature), is, as Mozart was to show, precisely what the enlightenment had created: not a society but a nexus of characters on whom external social forces impose nothing more constraining than good manners and who reflect society at large only in the freedom it has given them to form and express their personal inter-relationships.

Brigid Brophy, *Mozart the Dramatist*, Faber, 1964, pp. 32-3, 53-4

There is a sense in which even suffering depicted on the operatic stage can become a source of pleasure for the audience:

The paradox implicit in all drama, namely, that emotions and situations which in real life would be sad or painful are on the stage a source of pleasure becomes, in opera, quite explicit. The singer may be playing the role of a deserted bride who is about to kill herself, but we feel quite certain as we listen that not only we, but also she, is having a wonderful time. In a sense, there can be no tragic opera because whatever errors the characters make and whatever they suffer, they are doing exactly what they wish. Hence the feeling that opera seria should not employ a contemporary subject, but confine itself to mythical situations, that is, situations which, as human beings, we are all of us necessarily in and must, therefore, accept, however tragic they may be.

W.H. Auden, 'Notes on Music and Opera', in *The Dyer's Hand*,
Vintage Books, 1968, p. 468

Bellini was quite explicit about his wish to extract above all an emotional response from the audience, as he made clear in a garrulous letter to the librettist Carlo Pepoli in 1834:

Don't forget to bring with you the libretto [for *I puritani*] so that we can finish discussing the first act, which, if you will arm yourself with a good dose of monastic patience, will be interesting, magnificent, and proper poetry for music in spite of you and all your absurd rules, which are good subjects for chatter, but never will convince a living soul initiated into the difficult art that *must bring tears through singing*. If my music turns out to be beautiful and the opera pleases, you can write a million letters against composers' abuse of poetry, etc., which will have proved nothing. Deeds, not tittle-tattle that deludes because of a certain polished eloquence; in the face of that fact, everything else becomes *very watery soup*. You can call my reasons all the names you like, but that won't prove a thing. Carve in your head in adamantine letters: '*The opera must draw tears, terrify people, make them die through singing*.' It's a defect to want all the pieces to be equally accomplished, but a necessity that they all be moulded in such a way as to render the music intelligible by the clarity with which they are expressed, as concise as it is *striking*. Musical contrivances murder the effect of the situations, more so the poetic contrivances in a *dramma per musica*; to make their effect, poetry and music demand naturalness, and nothing else; anyone who turns off that road is lost, and in the end will bring to light a ponderous and stupid opera that will please only the sphere of the pedants, never the heart . . . and do you know why I told you that a good libretto is the one that does not make good sense? because I know what a ferocious and intractable beast the man of letters is, and how absurd he is, with his general rules of good sense.

Quoted in Herbert Weinstock, *Vincenzo Bellini*, Knopf, 1971, pp. 170–71

The power of opera is that its scale of emotion is larger than life; its nature is excess:

Opera has the power to warn you that you have wasted your life. You haven't acted on your desires. You've suffered a stunted, vicarious existence. You've silenced your passions. The volume, height, depth, lushness, and excess of operatic utterance reveal, by contrast, how small your gestures have been until now, how impoverished your physicality; you have only used a fraction of your bodily endowment, and your throat is closed.

Wayne Koestenbaum, *The Queen's Throat: Opera and Homosexuality and the Mystery of Desire*, Gay Men's Press, 1993, p. 44

30: Opera and Ideology

Only when the operatic stage can share the freedom of the dramatic stage can the medium exist in the twentieth century and maybe help us understand the world and ourselves, instead of remaining the morphine of the over-privileged.

John Dexter, *The Honourable Beast*, p. 87

Arguing that the modern theatre is epic theatre, in 1930 Berthold Brecht, having written the libretto of Mahagonny *for Kurt Weill, wanted opera to be modernized in a similar fashion:*

Mahagonny pays conscious tribute to the senselessness of the operatic form. The irrationality of opera lies in the fact that rational elements are employed, solid reality is aimed at, but at the same time it is all washed out by the music. A dying man is real. If at the same time he sings we are translated to the sphere of the irrational. (If the audience sang at the sight of him the case would be different.) The more unreal and unclear the music can make the reality – though there is of course a third, highly complex and in itself quite real element which can have quite real effects but is utterly remote from the reality of which it treats – the more pleasurable the whole process becomes: the pleasure grows in proportion to the degree of unreality . . .

When the epic theatre's methods begin to penetrate the opera the first result is a radical *separation of the elements*. The great struggle for supremacy between words, music and production – which always brings up the question 'which is the pretext for what?': is the music the pretext for the events on the stage, or are these the pretext for the music? etc. – can simply be bypassed by radically separating the elements. So long as the expression '*Gesamt-kunstwerk*' (or 'integrated work of art') means that the integration is a muddle, so long as the arts are supposed to be 'fused' together, the various elements will all be equally degraded, and each will act as a mere 'feed' to the rest. The process of fusion extends to the spectator, who gets thrown into the melting-pot too and becomes a passive (suffering) part of the total work of art. Witchcraft of this sort must of course be fought against. Whatever is intended to produce hypnosis, is likely to induce sordid intoxication, or creates fog, has got to be given up.

Berthold Brecht, 'Notes on the Opera', translated by John Willett, in
Brecht on Theatre, Methuen, 1964, pp. 35–8

Kurt Weill was convinced he had found a new kind of musical language which would break down the exclusivity of the current operatic idiom:

With the *Dreigroschenoper* [Threepenny Opera] we reach a public which either did not know us at all or thought us incapable of captivating listeners whose number far exceeds the size of concert-hall and operatic audiences.

Seen from this point of view, the *Dreigroschenoper* is part of a movement which affects almost all of our young musicians. The renunciation of the *l'art pour l'art* principle, the rejection of individualism in matters artistic, the present concern with music for the cinema, the newly established connection with the movement sponsoring music for young people, and the simplification of the musical means of expression which results from all this, are all steps in one direction.

Opera alone persists in its splendid isolation. The operatic audience still constitutes a coherent group of people who seem to exist apart from the average theatre fans. *Opera* and *theatre* are still regarded as two completely different phenomena. Dramaturgically as well as in the use of language and choice of subject matter, modern opera remains totally anachronistic . . . Opera was founded as an aristocratic form of art, and all operatic conventions serve to emphasize the sociological nature of the genre. But no other such genre is now in existence; and the theatre in particular is bent on reshaping society. If the framework of opera is unable to withstand the impact of the age, then this framework must be destroyed . . .

In the *Dreigroschenoper*, reconstruction was possible insofar as here we had a chance of starting from scratch. We wanted, most of all, to restore the primitive form of opera. Every new work for the music stage raises the question: how is it possible that music and, especially, song can be used in the theatre? We solved the problem in the most primitive manner possible. I was faced with a realistic action and had to use music in opposition to it, since I do not think that music can achieve realistic effects. Thus we either interrupted the action in order to introduce music or deliberately led it to a point where singing became necessary . . .

This return to a primitive form of opera entailed a drastic simplification of the musical language. I had to write music that could be sung by actors, i.e. laymen. But what originally seemed to be a limitation, soon turned out to be a real blessing. For the creation of a new type of musical theatre, such as we have in the *Dreigroschenoper*, became possible only through the use of easily grasped and identifiable melodies.

Kurt Weill, 'On the Composition of the *Dreigroschenoper*' (1929),
translated by Ulrich Weisstein, in Ulrich Weisstein, ed., *The Essence of Opera*, Collier Macmillan, 1964, pp. 331–2

Hans Werner Henze, the German composer, takes a Marxist view of opera:

The notion that opera is 'bourgeois' and an obsolete art form is itself one of the most outdated, tedious and musty notions. There are, to be sure, outmoded styles, outdated and tedious productions, and slipshod routine that make it difficult for many theatre-lovers and young comrades to grasp the content of the works being performed . . . But this art form contains riches that are among the most beautiful inventions of the human spirit. They belong to all people; they were not written for the ruling class, but in a spirit of human brotherhood. Anyone who has seen, for example, how young workers and peasants in Havana have made symphonic music and opera their own, and how they fill the opera house, *their* opera house, to listen to *their* composers, Mozart, Verdi, Caturia, Beethoven, and Brouwer, will no longer be able to retain any doubts about which direction progressive cultural work must take; certainly not that of doing away with one of the fundamental factors of our culture.

It is not opera that is reactionary. What is bourgeois is an (undialectical) belief in linear progress, titillated by fashionable notions, frustrated and élitist, which calls for different forms of music and music-making as if to escape reality, to bypass it: forms that could not exist at all, because they would have no basis (in the political and philosophical sense). Progress in art (and in artistic life) is conceivable only in connection with social progress. One must start at the foundations.

> Hans Werner Henze, 'Opera Belongs to All', in *Music and Politics*,
> translated by Peter Labanyi, Faber, 1982, pp. 217–18

In the Tuscan town of Montepulciano, Henze and others put such ideas into practice by establishing the Cantiere Internazionale d'Arte or International Construction Site for the Arts:

Henze explained in a programme note, 'The form, content, and character of this little didactic festival are the result of numerous meetings with the citizens and of public debates. Each event has been prepared with the intention of creatively involving the public. Young people collaborate in the shows, artisans have offered their aid ... schoolchildren have designed costumes and scenery and worked as librettists, children have composed a song about Don Quixote, the town band has studied the Paisiello numbers transcribed for it' ... The artists, he declared in his programme note, 'are fighting to help this city in its struggle against reaction, against civil death, in its struggle for a happy future and an improvement in social conditions' ...

The Cantiere came to a confused close. The Teatro Poliziano

was filled by an audience awaiting the second performance of *Il turco* [*in Italia*, by Rossini]. The mimes came before the curtain and, finding lively tongue as well as eloquent gesture, declared that they would not go on unless their travel expenses to and from Montepulciano were paid. There was perhaps an hour of noisy public argument. The mayor attempted placatory speeches; the mimes were implacable. The well-known music critic Fedele D'Amico mounted the stage to propose that the audience should pay the fares, but only on condition that the mayor should resign. Singers wandered on from the wings; a performance without mimes nearly took place. At length, Henze himself appeared, but only to announce that the orchestra would strike in solidarity with the mimes. The Cantiere was over – until next year.

Andrew Porter, article in *New Yorker* of 11 October 1976, in Andrew
Porter, *Music of Three Seasons 1974–77*, Cape, 1979, pp. 405–7

Henze gave his own account of the above incident:

[Sandro Sequi and Riccardo Chailly] staged a wonderful *Turco in Italia* in the first year. We assembled a cast of young volunteer singers from various countries . . . We sang from a box while the action was executed on stage by a Milanese mime group that had unexpectedly turned up. The production (in original nineteenth-century sets) was brilliant, and made a favourable impression on the *poliziani* . . .

A sit-in was staged, by the Milan mimes and Mr Perlini [a Roman producer], in front of the curtain in the theatre, on the last evening of the 'Festival'. The mime group refused to go on stage in the second and last performance of *Turco* unless the mayor paid them their travel expenses, which he had refused to do for some trivial bureaucratic reason and because Aglioti, the designer, had bought fresh pizza for 200,000 lire without permission from the administration, telling the baker the Cantiere would pay, and had rather foolishly paved a classroom with it in the *Tradimenti* show.

A vociferous argument now took place in the theatre, during which Perlini called the mayor a *buffone* and an eminent Rome music critic, Dr Fedele D'Amico, stood up and suggested that the travel money for the mimes be collected among the audience, on condition that the mayor sacked himself on the spot. There were more insults and shouting. I had no idea how to break that deadlock, until the leader came to me saying that the orchestra wouldn't play unless the mimes were given their money. So that was that, I explained the situation to the audience, and everyone went home.

Hans Werner Henze, 'The Montepulciano Cantieri, 1976–80', in *Music and Politics*, translated by Peter Labanyi, Faber, 1982, pp. 264–6

Catherine Clément notes the obsession of opera with death, and in particular with the deaths of women:

Three women in opera die three deaths: by Japanese dagger, by Spanish knife, and by love. Three women: three foreigners, Isolde from Ireland, a foreigner on Breton soil; Carmen, a foreigner on Spanish soil, who has come from all over the world via Africa and Egypt; Butterfly, a foreigner to the Occident, but who makes herself a foreigner in her own country by marrying a man whose name – not of her land – she openly claims. Butterfly, whose Japanese name is masked in Italian by the English signifier for an insect, regains her country at the same time as she dies a Japanese death. Carmen the Gypsy rediscovers her origins by accepting the destiny fixed for her by cards and by fate. Isolde, the Irish woman, finds her proper identity with great difficulty, through the song that finishes her and that finally belongs to her and to her alone; but it is a song of death.

You will see: opera heroines will often be foreigners. That is what catches them in a social system that is unable to tolerate their presence for fear of repudiating itself. This is how opera reveals its peculiar function: to seduce like possums, by means of aesthetic pleasure, and to show, by means of music's seduction (making one forget the essential), how women die – without anyone thinking, as long as the marvellous voice is singing, to wonder why. You will see; their foreignness is not always geographical; it appears in a detail, a profession, an age no longer said to be womanly. But always, by some means or other, they cross over a rigorous, invisible line, the line that makes them unbearable; so they will have to be punished. They struggle for a long time, for several hours of music, an infinitely long time, in the labyrinths of plots, stories, myths, leading them, although it is already late, to the supreme outcome where everyone knew they would have to end up.

> Catherine Clément, *Opera, or the Undoing of Women*, translated by
> Betsy Wing, Virago, 1989, pp. 58–9

The composer Susan McClary gives us a glimpse of the ideological future:

In keeping with a post-modern aesthetic, many artists are re-engaging with icons of the past. But rather than transmitting them as sacred objects, they are deconstructing them – laying bare their long-hidden ideological premises – and yet re-enacting them, so that one experiences a shared heritage and its critique simultaneously. The sounds of whiplash, the masochistic rap, and the controlling phallic pulse that bombard '*Un bel dì*' in [Malcolm] McLaren's *Madame Butterfly* tell us a good deal more about what is at stake in that opera than any traditional production. In Richard Schechner's contemporary production of *Don Giovanni*, the action was repeatedly ruptured by discussions that forced the audience to focus on the patriarchal violence perpetrated by that beautiful musical text. In my recent music-theatre piece *Susanna Does the Elders*, a musicologist is seduced by and entrapped in her own presentation of a seventeenth-century oratorio by Alessandro Stradella and is obliged to come to terms with the politics of sexual representation.

> Susan McClary, foreword to Catherine Clément, *Opera, or the Undoing*
> *of Women*, Virago, 1989, p. xvii

31: Words v. Music

Words and music are united by antagonism. Opera is the continuation of their warfare by other means.

Peter Conrad, *Romantic Opera and Literary Form*, p. 178

Richard Strauss managed to write an entire opera, Capriccio, *ostensibly about whether words or music have the primary role in opera. Stendhal was in no doubt about the matter:*

The variety of inflections of which the voice is capable, indeed the very impossibility for any voice to express itself in a dispassionate way, these factors in my view prevail over the voice's other function of conveying language.

For a start, the dreadful verses in which Italian arias are written are never heard as poetic, because the words are so often repeated. What reaches the ears of the listeners is prose. Thus it's not the most forceful and dramatic phrases – such as 'I loathe you deeply' or 'I love you madly' – which give beauty to these verses; rather, it is the nuances, the subtle ordering of words, which demonstrate the authenticity of the feelings and which awake our sympathies. But there is no place for such nuances in the fifty or sixty words which form an Italian aria. There the language can never be more than a bare canvas, and it is the function of music to apply brilliant colour to animate that canvas.

Do you need any further proof that language fills a thoroughly secondary role in music, and functions as a kind of label to which emotion is attached? . . . That explains why one can derive genuine pleasure from a well-sung opera even when the words are in a language that is unknown to us, as long as someone in your box is prepared to give you a hint as to what the principal arias are about.

Stendhal, *Life of Rossini* (1824), chapter 34, translated by Stephen Brook

Words in opera seria could often be reduced to gibberish:

Just after being condemned to death, rejected by your lover, or betrayed by your best friend – all good motives for a passionate exit-aria explosion – you must sing four lines (sometimes five or three; even two, in Handel) expressing your plight; sing them again, modulating to the dominant or the relative minor; and then sing them a third time, back to the tonic. Then sing a second stanza, in a related rhythm or key, perhaps taking back, qualifying, or reflecting on your original four lines. And then assert (da capo) your original outburst more passionately than ever, over and over (singing your poor heart out) and over again. In this way, eight short lines can be made to fill up five to ten minutes of vocalizing on stage – which is what people came to hear.

In one of Cleopatra's best-known arias in Handel's *Giulio Cesare*, what she is saying in her first two-line stanza is 'Unless you show me pity, just heaven, I will die.' What she *sings* is '*Se pietà di me non senta, giusto ciel, io morirò, giusto ciel io morirò io morirò giusto ciel, giusto ciel io morirò, se pietà di me non senta, giusto ciel io morirò, giusto ciel io morirò, giusto ciel io morirò, se pietà di me non senta, giusto ciel, giusto ciel io morirò, giusto ciel, giusto ciel io morirò, giusto ciel io morirò.*' After a short break for two other lines and ritornellos, she sings these same words again.

David Littlejohn, *The Ultimate Art*, University of California Press,

1992, p. 98

Arrigo Boito, a librettist as well as a composer, wrote to Verdi on 18 October 1880:

An opera is not a play; our art lives by elements unknown to spoken tragedy. An atmosphere that has been destroyed can be

created all over again. Eight bars are enough to restore a sentiment
to life; a rhythm can re-establish a character; music is the most
omnipotent of all the arts; it has a logic all its own – both freer and
more rapid than the logic of spoken thought, and much more
eloquent.

Quoted in Julian Budden, *The Operas of Verdi*, Cassell, 1981, p. 309

*W.H. Auden takes a debatable view of the psychological simplicity of
operatic characters:*

The quality common to all the great operatic roles, e.g. Don
Giovanni, Norma, Lucia, Tristan, Isolde, Brünnhilde, is that each
of them is a passionate and wilful state of being. In real life they
would all be bores, even Don Giovanni.

In recompense for this lack of psychological complexity, however, music can do what words cannot, present the immediate and
simultaneous relation of these states to each other. The crowning
glory of opera is the big ensemble.

The chorus can play two roles in opera and two only, that of the
mob and that of the faithful, sorrowing or rejoicing community. A
little of this goes a long way. Opera is not oratorio.

W.H. Auden, 'Notes on Music and Opera', in *The Dyer's Hand*,
Vintage Books, 1968, pp. 470–71

*Music's primacy derives, says Auden, from its ability to transcend the
intrinsic absurdity of plots that we would not find acceptable in the
theatre:*

No opera plot can be sensible, for in sensible situations people do
not sing; an opera plot must be, in both senses of the word, a
melodrama. When sensible, or unemotional moments occur in the
story, and it is very difficult to eliminate them entirely, then the
characters must either speak or employ a musical convention, like
recitative secco . . .

In a spoken play, for example, I think we should laugh if we were told that a woman had been careless enough to throw her own baby into the fire instead of the child of her enemy, but when this happens in *Il trovatore* we have little difficulty in swallowing it. Again, the emotional persuasiveness of music is so much greater than that of words, that a character in opera can switch from one state of feeling to another with an abruptness which in a spoken drama would be incredible.

W.H. Auden, *Secondary Worlds*, Random House, 1968, p. 96

Catherine Clément proclaims the primacy of music:

A double, inseparable scene: the words give rise to the music and the music develops the language, gives it dialect, envelops it, thwarts or reinforces it. Conscious and unconscious: the words are aligned with the legible, rational side of a conscious discourse, and the music is the unconscious of the text, that which gives it depth of field and relief, that which attributes past to the text, a memory, one perceptible not to the listener's consciousness but to his enchanted unconsciousnesses. A word seeps through, an aria. This is the beginning of the opera. You are not on your guard. The story advances. But at the moment of denouement, at the crucial moment when, in a flash, the conflict is played out in all its violence, the tune comes back without its words. You are caught up in a musical memory. And, even if you are not paying attention, you will have 'gotten it into your head', as they say, you will have the barely formulated idea of this ephemeral word that is now returning in your unconscious. At the beginning of [Verdi's and Boito's] *Otello*, the Moor embraces his blond, white wife and asks for a kiss, and the music is all passion, everything light and pure, a wedding night. But when he has killed her, the same music returns to complete the words that he, stifled by death, is already no longer able to speak. That is how music works on words.

The words are forgotten. An extraordinary paradox: in a world where the unconscious takes up so little room, where so much is made of spoken words, as if they meant what they said, with no past and no roots, we have the opera, where the conscious part, the part played by words, is forgotten. No doubt it is because opera is the place for unformulated dreams and secret passions, a place Brecht saw as the link between pleasure and unreality. Consequently, the less one hears the words, the greater the pleasure.

Catherine Clément, *Opera, or the Undoing of Women*, translated by
Betsy Wing, Virago, 1989, p. 21

The theatre critic Eric Bentley finds no correlation between the literary quality of the libretto and the opera for which it provides the text:

What the librettist needs is a command, not of great poetry, but of operatic dramaturgy ... Great poetry set to music is not an ideal recipe for opera, in fact there is no great dramatic poetry written that operatic music would not ruin.

Eric Bentley, *The Dramatic Event*, Dobson, 1954, pp. 235–6

For Peter Conrad, words and music are antagonists, and opera is the resolution of their conflict:

The equivalence between music and words which Wagner's theory of opera as drama assumes is a false compact. Actually the two are more like enemies. Music liquefies words, subduing them into notes; song infects language with an inspired unreason. Few words can be heard distinctly, and even those many opera goers prefer not to acknowledge, defending their right to listen to works performed in languages foreign to them because they know that incomprehension exalts and mystifies ...

As music is often the enemy of words, drowning their sense in lyrical sound, so it is liable to act against the interests of drama, slowing down action while rendering it sentimentally internal. Opera is inefficient as drama simply because it takes so much longer to sing a phrase than to say it. But, novelistically, this may be its justification, for in extending the phrase it allows its characters time to reflect on and absorb the implications of what they are uttering. Ambiguously accompanied by music, the multiple repetitions of one another's names by Tristan and Isolde have a constantly varying significance which they could never have in drama . . .

[Opera's] genius lies in the potentiality for an enriching contradiction between its elements. Rather than a sedate marriage between text and music, it proposes a relationship of unremitting, invigorating tension . . . Opera combines text and music in the way that the dissimilar features and qualities of parents are merged in their child.

Peter Conrad, *Romantic Opera and Literary Form*, California University
Press, 1977, pp. 4–5, 113, 177

32: Anti-Opera

Some people, sir, from a very fashionable absurdity have affected to be in raptures at a beauty they did not understand.

James Ralph, *The Fashionable Lady*, 1730

The French critic Saint-Évremond couldn't stomach the 'unnatural' aspects of opera:

I begin by frankly stating that I am not especially fond of the comedies in music now in vogue. I admit that I enjoy the magnifi-cence of the spectacle, that the machines provide a modicum of surprise, that the music occasionally affects me, and that the whole seems marvellous. But I must also confess that the marvels soon grow boresome; for where the mind has so little to say the senses needs begin to languish . . .

There is another thing in opera that is so unnatural that it stuns my imagination. It is the fact that the whole piece is sung from beginning to end, as if the characters on stage had conspired to present musically the most trivial as well as the most important aspects of their lives. Can one imagine that a master sings when calling his servant or when giving him an order? That a friend confides a secret to another musically? That deliberations in a council of state are sung? That commands are chanted, and that people are killed melodiously in battle? To arrange things in this way means to violate the spirit of drama, which takes precedence over that of music, which latter ought to be used solely as accompaniment . . .

If you want to know what an opera is, I tell you that it is a bizarre mixture of poetry and music where the writer and the composer, equally embarrassed by each other, go to a lot of trouble to create an execrable work.

Seigneur de Saint-Évremond, letter to the Duke of Buckingham (1678),
in *Letters of Saint-Évremond*, ed. John Hayward, Routledge, 1930

Rousseau deplores the blandness that afflicted contemporary opera:

At the birth of opera, its creators, wishing to avoid what might seem unnatural in the union of music and language in the imitation of human life, decided to transplant the scene to heaven or hell. And since they did not know how to make human beings speak, they made gods and devils rather than heroes and shepherds sing. Soon magic and the marvellous became the props of the lyrical stage; and, content with having a new genre, nobody thought of inquiring whether it was the one that ought to have been invented . . . That famous nation, of whose ancient virtues only the artistic ones remain, squandered its taste and wit to endow the new spectacle with all the pomp it needed. All over Italy theatres, equal in size to royal palaces and in elegance to the ancient monuments which abound in that country, were erected. To decorate them they perfected the arts of perspective and scenery. The artists of each genre let their talents shine. The most ingenious machines, daring flights, storms, thunder and lightning were employed to stun the eyes, while a multitude of instruments and voices astounded the ears.

In spite of all this, the action remained always cold, and the situations lacked interest. Since there was no intrigue that could not be solved easily by the intervention of some god, the spectator, aware of the poet's power, wholly relied on him for rescuing his heroes from the most dangerous situations. Thus the machinery was immense without producing much effect, since the imitation was always imperfect and crude, the action unnatural and without human interest, and the senses ill disposed towards illusion which did not involve the heart. All told, it would have been difficult to bore an audience at a greater expense.

Jean-Jacques Rousseau, *Dictionary of Music* (1764), translated by
Ulrich Weisstein, reprinted in Ulrich Weisstein, ed., *The Essence
of Opera*, Collier-Macmillan, 1964, pp. 85–6

*Paul Claudel takes a dim view of the medium, though he makes allowances
for a few transcendent examples:*

I go to the opera as rarely as possible, and I have had little experience on this side. So far as I can see, a regular opera is composed of a series of musical numbers, connected by some sort of action: say, solos, choruses, duets, ballets, overtures, trios, septets, and so on, affording an opportunity for the musician to exercise his talent. In short, it is a concert in fancy dress, the intervals and transitions of which are more or less filled up by some vague noise. Only, in a concert, the singers can stand motionless if they choose, while in an opera they feel bound to indulge in conventional, ridiculous gestures of absolutely no use for their essential purpose, such as the long-drawn elaboration of some dizzy F. I shall not speak of the costumes, the scenery, and staging, which are generally wretched and which will before long become insufferable to the most patient audience . . .

Of course, there is no form of art, however mediocre and absurd, that will not yield to genius or to that mysterious force, often so oddly applied, which we call 'conviction'. And genius and conviction sometimes manage to do something even with the opera. Of this strange outcome I can give a few examples, such as Gluck's *Orpheus*, Beethoven's *Fidelio*, Berlioz's *Trojans*, Wagner's *Tannhäuser*, Verdi's *Rigoletto*

Paul Claudel, 'Modern Drama and Music', *Yale Review*, 1930

Lord Chesterfield despised opera:

As for operas, they are essentially too absurd and extravagant to mention; I look upon them as a magic scene, contrived to please the eyes and the ears, at the expense of the understanding; and I consider singing, rhyming, and chiming heroes, and princesses, and philosophers, as I do the hills, the trees, the birds, and the beasts, who amicably joined in one common country dance, to the irresistible turn of Orpheus's lyre. Whenever I go to an opera, I leave my sense and reason at the door with my half guinea, and deliver myself up to my eyes and my ears.

Lord Chesterfield, *Letters to His Son*, letter clvii, 1774

The critic Queenie Leavis graciously explains that any culture in which opera has an elevated place cannot be a serious one:

Opera appeared first in Italy, and though aristocratic in content and origins (like the French novel) became popular with all classes, not only with the wealthy as in other countries ... Now opera, like film, is a much simpler thing, as regards characterization and action, than a major novel, even when the opera is based on a novel or poetic tragedy (for example, *Lucia di Lammermoor*, compared with the original novel ... or even Verdi's *Otello* with Shakespeare's); the opera libretto is *necessarily* a crude reduction of Shakespeare's tragedy and with simplified type-characters. One concludes the frequentation of opera as a national entertainment is inimical to the effort of grappling with and possessing a serious novel.

Q.D. Leavis, 'The Italian Novel', in *Collected Essays*,
Cambridge University Press, 1985, II, pp. 258–9

Claude Debussy seemed to think along the same lines. In February 1893 he wrote to Prince Poniatowski giving a rapid survey of the French operatic scene:

We've just had a *Werther* by Massenet, displaying an extraordinary talent for satisfying all that is poetically empty and lyrically cheap in the dilettante mind! Everything in it contributes to providing

mediocrity and it's all part, too, of this appalling habit of taking
something which is perfectly good in itself and then committing
treason against its spirit with light, easy sentimentalities: *Faust*
eviscerated by Gounod, or *Hamlet* more honoured in the breach
than the observance by Monsieur Ambroise Thomas. Those who
put their energies into forging banknotes are prosecuted, but
nothing happens to these other forgers whose aim, equally, is to be
rich. I should have every sympathy with an author who printed a
notice on his works saying, 'It is forbidden to park your music
anywhere on this book.'

Claude Debussy, *Letters*, translated by Roger Nichols, Faber, 1987,
p. 41

33: Libretti and Translations

> Composers and librettists are almost always forced to reduce a large fresco into a miniature form while somehow – through the amplifying power of music – retaining the original's expressive magnitude.
>
> Gary Schmidgall, *Literature as Opera*

Benedetto Marcello, in 1720, offers tongue-in-cheek advice to would-be librettists:

A writer of operatic librettos, if he wants to be modern, must never have read the Greek and Latin classic authors, nor should he do so in the future. After all, the old Greeks and Romans never read the modern writers . . .

He should write the whole opera without any preconceived plan but rather proceed verse by verse. For if the audience never understands the plot their attentiveness to the very end of the opera will be insured. One thing any able modern librettist must strive for is frequently to have all characters of the piece on the stage at the same time, though nobody knows why. They then may leave the stage, one by one, singing the usual canzonetta.

The librettist should not worry about the ability of the performers, but much more about whether the impresario has at his disposal a good bear or lion, an able nightingale, genuine-looking bolts of lightning, earthquakes, storms, etc . . .

Real life is imparted to the opera by the use of prisons, daggers, poison, the writing of letters on stage, bear and wild-bull hunts, earthquakes, storms, sacrifices, the settling of accounts, and mad scenes. The audience will be deeply moved by unexpected events of that kind . . .

If the plot should require husband and wife to be put into prison together, and if one of them should have to die, it is absolutely necessary to have the other one stay alive so that he or she can sing an aria of a merry character. This will cheer up everyone in the audience as it will make them realize that, after all, it is all only make-believe . . .

Librettists who do not enjoy great fame or credit will make a living during the rest of the year, when the opera season is over, by taking care of legal matters, administrative affairs, by supervising other people's business, by copying parts and proof-reading, and by trying to ruin each other's reputations.

Benedetto Marcello, *Il teatro alla moda*, quoted in R.G. Pauly, 'Benedetto Marcello's Satire on Early 18th-century Opera', *Musical Quarterly*, 1948

Lorenzo Da Ponte, the great librettist, wrote in 1819 about his craft:

If the words of a dramatic poet are nothing *but a vehicle to the notes, and an opportunity to the action,* what is the reason that a composer of music does not take at once a doctor's recipes, a bookseller's catalogue, or even a spelling book, instead of the verses of a poet, and make them a vehicle to his notes, just as an ass is that of a bag of corn? . . . Mozart knew very well that the success of an opera depends, FIRST OF ALL, ON THE POET: that without a good poem an *entertainment cannot be perfectly dramatic,* just as a picture cannot be good without possessing the merit of invention, design, and a just proportion of the parts: that a composer, who is, in regard to a drama, what a painter is in regard to the colours, can never do that with effect, unless excited and animated by the words of a poet, whose province is to choose a subject susceptible of variety, incident, movement, and action; to prepare, to suspend, to bring about the catastrophe; to exhibit characters interesting, comic, well supported, and calculated for stage effect; to write his *recitativo* short, but substantial, his airs various, new, and well situated; in fine, his verses easy, harmonious, and almost singing of themselves, without all which requisites, the notes of the most sublime and scientific composer will not be felt by the heart, the passions remaining tranquil and unmoved, their effect will be transient, and the best of his airs, after a short time, will be heard with no more attention or pleasure than a trio or a sonata . . .

I think that poetry is the door to music, which can be very handsome, and much admired for its exterior, but nobody can see its internal beauties, if the door is wanting.

> Quoted in Sheila Hodges, *Lorenzo Da Ponte*, Granada, 1985, p. 63

W.H. Auden finds that the librettist invariably draws the short straw:

A librettist is always at a disadvantage because operas are reviewed, not by literary or dramatic critics, but by music critics, whose taste and understanding of poetry may be very limited. What is worse, a music critic who wishes to attack the music but is afraid to do so directly, can always attack it indirectly by condemning the libretto. A librettist is at a further disadvantage because music is an international language and poetry a local one. Wherever an opera is performed, audiences hear the same music but, outside the country of its origin, either they hear alien words which are meaningless to them or a translation which, however good – and most translations are very bad – are not what the librettist wrote.

> W.H. Auden, review of *The Correspondence between Richard Strauss and Hugo von Hofmannsthal*, reprinted in Auden, *Forewords and Afterwords*,
> Faber, 1973, p. 349

A parody libretto from Weber:

Weber wrote a most affecting tragedy called *Agnes Bernauerin*, 'a romantic-patriotic play with music . . . The action takes place in the heart of Germany – with as many persons as necessary' . . . The imposing first-act finale is set in a mountainous forest land-scape. 'In the background to the left a castle; to the right a vineyard; in the foreground a hermit's hut, a cave, and an arbour, and in the centre two hollow trees plus a subterranean passage.' At one and the same time the hermit sings a prayer; Agnes sings an aria in the castle, accompanied by a chorus of vintners; on the other side of the stage Albrecht, sleeping in the arbour, emits some disjointed tones in his dream; Caspar, in the tree-trunk, is so frightened that he sings a polonaise; a band of robbers hiding in the cave shout a wild chorus; and several genii float protectively above Albrecht. The noise of war is heard behind the scenes. A march is played far off. (Of course, everything happens simultaneously.) Then two bolts of lightning crash on the stage from opposite sides and strike a few assorted objects. All sing 'Ha!' and the curtain falls.

George R. Marek, *A Front Seat at the Opera*, Harrap, 1951, p. 220

ORIGINAL LANGUAGE V. TRANSLATION

Opera in English is, in the main, just about as sensible as baseball in Italian.

H.L. Mencken

The debate about whether opera should be performed in its original language, in which the composer's setting of a specific libretto is respected, or whether it should be translated into the language understood by the audience is not a recent argument. The issue was alive in early eighteenth-century England, as Joseph Addison made clear:

There is no question but our great-grandchildren will be very curious to know the reason why their forefathers used to sit together like an audience of foreigners in their own country, and to hear whole plays acted before them, in a tongue which they did not understand. *Arsinoe* was the first opera that gave us a taste of Italian music ... We immediately fell to translating the Italian operas; and as there was no great danger of hurting the sense of those extraordinary pieces, our authors would often make words of their own which were entirely foreign to the meaning of the passages they pretended to translate; their chief care being to make the numbers of the English verse answer to those of the Italian, that both of them might go to the same tune.

Joseph Addison, *The Spectator*, 21 March 1710

British opera producer David Pountney takes a strong line in favour of translated opera and against the compromise solution of surtitles that offer simple translations while the opera is being performed in the original language:

A composer chooses to set words, rather than to write pure music, because the one thing that words have which music does not is 'meaning'. Words also have sound and rhythm, and these elements may be compromised in translation, but so long as meaning is preserved, the fundamental reason for adding words to music is intact. Anyone who now breathes the word 'surtitles' should be made to learn this book by heart, because it is absolutely clear that the vivid, spontaneous re-creation of music and drama for which Felsenstein was striving leaves no time for the audience to glance up and read the instructions. The sense arrives, like a glowing hot coal, straight from the mouth of the singer, and strikes instantly at the head and heart of the listener. The surtitle is a catastrophic gooseberry in this vital act of theatrical intercourse. It is a device for a tourist, who looks but does not participate . . .

Far too few people consider the expressive range that is lost to the singer by not performing in his own language to his own people. With the exception of the very talented few, it is rare for a performer to be able to generate the same sense of immediacy and force in a foreign language: the instinctive engagement of all his modes of perception is set in motion so much faster and more directly in his own language, and the fact that an audience returns the communication rapidly, as in a tennis rally, serves to heighten the intensity of the relationship between singer and audience.

Introduction by David Pountney to *The Music Theatre of Walter Felsenstein*, Quartet Books, 1991

Two defences of opera in the original language:

Translations, which move the words out of place, away from the melody related to them, always seem to me like a family group photograph in which the heads have been cut off and replaced on the wrong necks and shoulders. The plea that this makes the whole thing more understandable to the general public is paltry and verges on impertinence. Better surely to have some explanation in the programme and a truer and more faithful performance from the interpreters.

Tito Gobbi, *Tito Gobbi on His World of Italian Opera*, Hamish Hamilton,

1984, p. 31

It is precisely because I believe that, in listening to song (as distinct from chant), we hear, not words, but syllables, that I am not generally in favour of the performances of operas in translation. Wagner or Strauss in English sounds intolerable, and would still sound so if the poetic merits of the translation were greater than those of the original, because the new syllables have no apt relation to the pitch and tempo of the notes with which they are associated. The poetic value of the words may provoke a composer's imagination, but it is their syllabic values which determine the kind of vocal line he writes. In song, poetry is expendable, syllables are not.

W.H. Auden, 'Notes on Music and Opera' in *The Dyer's Hand*,

Vintage Books, 1968, p. 473

Rudolf Bing on how the Metropolitan opera abandoned its occasional attempts to produce opera in English:

It seemed to me arriving in New York that our best hope for building a bigger and younger audience was to give opera in the language the whole audience could understand. *Fledermaus* and *Così* encouraged that belief; both were excellent translations, of comedies. Flagstad sang *Alcestis* for us in English. In 1952–3, however, the translator of *Fledermaus* returned to attempt *La*

Bohème, and the results were disastrous, doggerel verse totally unsuitable for the tragic play and by no means perfectly fitted to Puccini's phrasing . . . The Metropolitan had long done *The Magic Flute* and *Gianni Schicchi* in English; as time passed, we added to the English-translation list *Boris Godunov*, *Arabella*, *Eugene Onegin*, *Queen of Spades*, *Martha*, and operettas which we hoped, in vain, would duplicate the success of *Fledermaus* – Offenbach's *Périchole* and Strauss's *Gypsy Baron*.

What made opera in English translation so difficult for us was, of course, the international casts; one can get away with mispronunciations of a language not that of the audience (Glyndebourne did, for years), but when the whole audience knows that the word is being mispronounced the damage to dramatic viability is great, even in comedy. Too often, moreover, because the prosody has been applied after the music, the words may be incomprehensible however well pronounced. In every translation, too, something of the original phrasing is necessarily lost. A decade or so after my arrival at the Metropolitan, I had a questionnaire distributed, asking the audience at a performance of a *Marriage of Figaro* whether they would rather have the opera presented in English or in Italian. The preference for Italian was overwhelming, and we gradually returned works like *Zauberflöte*, *Così*, and *Schicchi* to their original languages.

Sir Rudolf Bing, *5000 Nights at the Opera*, Hamish Hamilton, 1972,
pp. 158–9

OPERA IN FICTION

34: Opera in Fiction

I used to dream about marriage: towering wedding cakes, and
Jordan almonds wrapped in fake lace, favours for the guests.
Now I dream about opera.

Wayne Koestenbaum, *The Queen's Throat*, p. 197

Jos and Amelia Sedley, travelling through Germany, attend the opera:

They went to the opera often of evenings – to those snug,
unassuming, dear old operas in the German towns, where the
noblesse sits and cries and knits stockings on the one side, over
against the bourgeoisie on the other; and His Transparency the
Duke and his Transparent family, all very fat and good-natured,
come and occupy the great box in the middle; and the pit is full of
the most elegant slim-waisted officers with straw-coloured mus-
tachios, and twopence a day on full pay. Here it was that Emmy
found her delight, and was introduced for the first time to the
wonders of Mozart and Cimarosa. The Major's musical taste has
been before alluded to, and his performances on the flute com-
mended. But perhaps the chief pleasure he had in these operas was
in watching Emmy's rapture while listening to them. A new world
of love and beauty broke upon her when she was introduced to
those divine compositions: this lady had the keenest and finest
sensibility, and how could she be indifferent when she heard
Mozart? The tender parts of *Don Juan* awakened in her raptures so
exquisite that she would ask herself, when she went to say her
prayers of a night, whether it was not wicked to feel so much
delight as that with which '*Vedrai carino*' and '*Batti, batti*' filled her
gentle little bosom?

W.M. Thackeray, *Vanity Fair*, 1848, chapter 62

Emma Bovary pays a visit to the opera to see Lucia di Lammermoor:

The musicians filed in one after the other, and there began a
prolonged din of rumbling double-basses, creaking violins, barking
cornets, and chirruping flutes and flageolets. From the stage came
the sound of three knocks to signal the performance was about to
begin. The drums began to roll, the brass instruments blared out
their chords, and the curtain, as it rose, revealed a rural
landscape . . .

Emma's mind wandered back to the books she had perused in
her youth, immersed in Walter Scott. She seemed to hear, through
the mist and across the heather, the persistent sound of bagpipes.
Moreover, her recollections of the novel helped her to understand
the libretto, so she was able to follow each turn of the plot, while
fleeting thoughts came back to her, only to fade beneath the squall
of the music. She allowed herself to be lulled by the melodies and
felt all her being vibrating as though the violin bows were being
drawn across her very nerves. She hadn't eyes enough to take in
the costumes, the scenery, the characters, the painted trees that
shook when anyone crossed the stage, the velvet caps, the cloaks
and swords, this whole world of the imagination that shimmered
in harmony so as to create an other-worldly atmosphere. A young
woman stepped forth and threw a purse to an equerry in green.
She remained alone, and then came the sound of a flute murmuring
like a fountain or like the warbling of a bird. Lucia solemnly began
her cavatina in E major, expressing her love and yearning for
wings to bear her away. Emma too longed to flee from life and be
carried away in the embrace of passion. All of a sudden, Edgar
Lagardy appeared on the scene . . .

From the moment he stepped on to the stage the audience went
wild. He flung his arms around Lucia, then left her only to return
again in a frenzy of desperation. He had explosions of anger, then
elegiac reflections of infinite tenderness, the sound, filled with sobs
and kisses, escaping from his bare throat. Emma leaned forward to
see him better, digging into the velvet of the box with her nails.
Her heart swelled up with these plangent lamentations drawn out

to the accompaniment of the double-basses, like the cries of the
shipwrecked in the tumult of a storm. She recognized all the
ecstasies and anguish of which she had almost died. The singer's
voice seemed like nothing else but the echo of her own consciousness, and this intoxicating illusion seemed at one with her own life.
Surely no one on earth had ever loved her with such passion . . .

Lucia came forward, half supported by her women, a wreath of
orange blossom trailing through her hair, her face paler than the
white satin of her dress. Emma recalled her wedding day, and saw
herself again among the fields of corn, treading the small path that
led to the church. Why hadn't she, like the heroine on stage,
resisted, entreated? Instead she had been merry, unaware of the
chasm into which she was about to fall . . . If only, in the freshness
of her beauty, before the defilement of marriage and the disillusion-
ment of adultery, she could have joined her life with some great-
hearted man, then virtue and affection, sensuality and duty, would
have joined together so that she would never have wanted to let
go of such a perfect happiness. But such joy, it was plain, was a
fiction designed to render all desire pointless. Now she knew how
petty were the emotions that art magnified. Trying to dispel such
thoughts from her mind, Emma resolved to see nothing more in
this presentation of anguish than a visual fantasy, suitable to divert
the eyes of the audience. She was even enjoying a surreptitious
smile of disdain when she saw, emerging from the velvet hangings
at the back of the stage, a man in a black cloak.

The gesture he made as he stepped out dislodged his large
Spanish hat. A moment later the instrument and the singers on
stage launched into the sextet. The voice of Edgar, blazing with
fury, soared above the others. Ashton, in sombre tones, threatened
him with death. Lucia sang with a piercing wail; Arthur's voice
filled the middle range and the deep bass of the minister rumbled
like an organ, while the exquisite voices of the women repeated his
lines in chorus. The singers had moved forward so that their
movements were in harmony. Anger and vengeance, jealousy and
terror, pity and dismay poured from their open mouths. The
indignant lover brandished his sword; his lace collar rose jerkily

up his neck as his chest swelled out when he strode from side to side, while his silvery spurs on his soft open-ankled boots clanked against the floor. He must, thought Emma, feel an inexhaustible love to let such floods of emotion deluge the audience. All her impulses to denigrate the spectacle vanished under the poetic spell of the performance, and drawn to the man by the power of his acting, she tried to imagine his actual life, so thrilling and extraordinary and splendid – indeed, the kind of life she herself might have led had the fates willed it. They might have met each other, and fallen in love! She would have travelled by his side to all the kingdoms of Europe, from capital to capital, sharing with him his weariness and his glory, gathering up the flowers that were flung at him, and embroidering his costumes with her own hands. Every evening, hidden within her box, behind a grille with gilt trellis-work, she would have opened herself to the outpourings of the noble soul that sang as though for her alone; and from the stage, even as he was performing, he would have directed his gaze at her. Then a wild notion seized her: surely he was looking at her now! She felt a longing to rush into his arms to take refuge there in his strength as though it were the very incarnation of love, and to cry out: 'Take me away, lead me away from here, let us fly! I'm yours, I'm yours! To you alone I offer all my passion and all my dreams!'

The curtain fell.

> Gustave Flaubert, *Madame Bovary*, Part II, chapter 15, translated by
> Stephen Brook

Emma Bovary is overwhelmed by the opera, finding it a deep source of passionate expression. Natasha Rostov, unhappily apart from her fiancé Prince Andrew, attends the opera in Moscow and has the opposite experience:

The floor of the stage consisted of smooth boards, at the sides was some painted cardboard representing trees, and at the back was a cloth stretched over boards. In the centre of the stage sat some girls in red bodices and white skirts. One very fat girl in a white silk dress sat apart on a low bench, to the back of which a piece of green cardboard was glued. They all sang something. When they had finished their song the girl in white went up to the prompter's box, and a man with tight silk trousers over his stout legs, and holding a plume and a dagger, went up to her and began singing, waving his arms about.

First the man in the tight trousers sang alone, then she sang, then they both paused while the orchestra played and the man fingered the hand of the girl in white, obviously awaiting the beat to start singing with her. They sang together and every one in the theatre began clapping and shouting, while the man and woman on the stage – who represented lovers – began smiling, spreading out their arms, and bowing.

After her life in the country, and in her present serious mood, all this seemed grotesque and amazing to Natasha. She could not follow the opera nor even listen to the music, she saw only the painted cardboard and the queerly dressed men and women who moved, spoke, and sang so strangely in that brilliant light. She knew what it was all meant to represent, but it was so pretentiously false and unnatural that she first felt ashamed for the actors and then amused at them. She looked at the faces of the audience, seeking in them the same sense of ridicule and perplexity she herself experienced, but they all seemed attentive to what was happening on the stage, and expressed delight which to Natasha seemed feigned. 'I suppose it has to be like this!' she thought.

Leo Tolstoy, *War and Peace*, translated by Louise and Aylmer Maude,
Oxford University Press, Book VIII, chapter 9

Philip, his sister Harriet, and Miss Abbott decide to go to a performance of Lucia di Lammermoor *in Monteriano. The women find Italian exuberance hard to take:*

[Philip] had been to this theatre many years before, on the occasion of a performance of *La zia di Carlo*. Since then it had been thoroughly done up, in the tints of the beetroot and the tomato,

and was in many other ways a credit to the little town . . . There is
something majestic in the bad taste of Italy; it is not the bad taste
of a country which knows no better; it has not the nervous
vulgarity of England, or the blinded vulgarity of Germany. It
observes beauty, and chooses to pass it by. But it attains to
beauty's confidence. This tiny theatre of Monteriano spraddled and
swaggered with the best of them . . .

Lucia began to sing, and there was a moment's silence. She was
stout and ugly; but her voice was still beautiful, and as she sang
the theatre murmured like a hive of happy bees. All through the
coloratura she was accompanied by sighs, and its top note was
drowned in a shout of universal joy.

So the opera proceeded. The singers drew inspiration from the
audience, and the two great sextets were rendered not unworthily.
Miss Abbott fell into the spirit of the thing. She, too, chatted and
laughed and applauded and encored, and rejoiced in the existence
of beauty. As for Philip, he forgot himself as well as his mission.
He was not even an enthusiastic visitor. For he had been in this
place always. It was his home.

Harriet, like M. Bovary on a more famous occasion, was trying
to follow the plot. Occasionally she nudged her companions, and
asked them what had become of Walter Scott. She looked round
grimly. The audience sounded drunk, and even Caroline, who
never took a drop, was swaying oddly. Violent waves of excitement, all arising from very little, went sweeping round the theatre.
The climax was reached in the mad scene. Lucia clad in white, as
befitted her malady, suddenly gathered up her streaming hair and
bowed her acknowledgements to the audience. Then from the
back of the stage – she feigned not to see it – there advanced a
kind of bamboo clothes-horse, stuck all over with bouquets. It was
very ugly, and most of the flowers in it were false. Lucia knew
this, and so did the audience; and they all knew that the clothes-
horse was a piece of stage property, brought in to make the
performance go year after year. None the less did it unloose the
great deeps. With a scream of amazement and joy she embraced
the animal, pulled out one or two practicable blossoms, pressed

them to her lips, and flung them into her admirers. They flung them back, with loud melodious cries, and a little boy in one of the stage-boxes snatched up his sister's carnations and offered them. '*Che carino!*' exclaimed the singer. She darted at the little boy and kissed him. Now the noise became tremendous. 'Silence! Silence!' shouted many old gentlemen behind. 'Let the divine creature continue!' But the young men in the adjacent box were imploring Lucia to extend her civility to them. She refused, with a humorous expressive gesture. One of them hurled a bouquet at her. She spurned it with her foot. Then, encouraged by the roars of the audience, she picked it up and tossed it to them. Harriet was always unfortunate. The bouquet struck her full in the chest . . .

'Call this classical?' she cried, rising from her seat. 'It's not even respectable! Philip! take me out at once.'

E.M. Forster, *Where Angels Fear to Tread*, chapter 6

The protagonist of Gertrude Atherton's novel Tower of Ivory *is a Wagnerian soprano, Margarethe Styr. Her admirer, John Ordham, attends a performance of* Tristan und Isolde *at Bayreuth, and Atherton's description aspires to a Wagnerian rapture of its own:*

The last bell rang, darkness descended upon the house, the overture began . . .

Never had been and never will be so full an expression of unsatisfied longing. Surge upon surge from the opening phrase, presaging a yearning that is not all bliss and a torment that is not all pain, so long as mortals may die; surge upon surge of aching passion, sweet oblivion, mortal disappointment, infinite desire, a love that only the immortals could satisfy and only death can quench. The imagination reels along with this appalling betrayal of mortal love. The curse and the boon of imagination, the indomitable pursuit of happiness, even while the mind holds its sides like a chuckling monk, the inevitable awaking, the cry for death, annihilation, nirvana – all and far more are in this mighty tonal

dirge of the human heart to lift Wagner's masterpiece to the apex
of all the masterpieces the world has preserved . . .

When Isolde raised herself slowly from the cushion of the couch
in the pavilion of the ship which was bearing her to the old king
of Cornwall she had consented to marry, abandoning something of
her first attitude of utter despair, and lifting her head toward the
joyous singing of the sailors, her eyes in one long look expressed
everything. The dullest could not entertain the delusion that here
was merely an unhappy young princess of 'Irenland', speeding
against her will to fulfil a detestable marriage, but a woman of
the maturest passions, who had already drunk deep of the cup
of love, scornful of every law that might exist for princess or
peasant, and who had watched and waited, and accepted the fact
of betrayal.

And the audience felt itself, not in the presence merely of a
woman eaten with hatred, fury, desire for vengeance, but of a
primeval force, passion incarnate, such as Earth unlooses in convulsions that have annihilated millions and buried continents. No
other Isolde has ever been as great as Styr, for no other has been
able to suggest this ferocious approach of a devastating force, this
hurricane sweeping across the mind's invisible plain, tearing at the
very foundations of life. And all this she expressed before singing
a note, with her staring moving eyes, her eloquent body, still and
concealed as it was, a gesture of the hand. It was a concentration
of the mental faculties, such as gives weak women superhuman
physical strength in moments of terror or anger; in her own case
they were whipped up like a whirlwind by the released horrors in
her soul, and used with a supreme exercise of art that made her the
risen Isolde.

[*And so it continues for many pages, demonstrating yet again how baleful
could be the influence of the great composer.*]

Gertrude Atherton, *Tower of Ivory*, John Murray, 1910, pp. 166–70

In Willa Cather's study of an opera singer, Thea Kronborg (a portrait partly modelled on Olive Fremstad) reflects on her career:

'There's so much that I want to tell you,' she said at last, 'and it's hard to explain. My life is full of jealousies and disappointments, you know. You get to hating people who do contemptible work and still get on just as well as you do. There are many disappointments in my profession, and bitter, bitter contempts!' Her face hardened, and looked much older. 'If you love the good thing vitally, enough to give up for it all that one must give up, then you must hate the cheap thing just as hard. I tell you, there is such a thing as creative hate! A contempt that drives you through fire, makes you risk everything and lose everything, makes you a long sight better than you ever knew you could be . . .

'You see,' she went on more calmly, 'voices are accidental things. You find plenty of good voices in common women, with common minds and common hearts. Look at that woman who sang *Ortrud* with me last week. She's new here and the people are wild about her. "Such a beautiful volume of tone!" they say. I give you my word she's as stupid as an owl and as coarse as a pig, and anyone who knows anything about singing would see that in an instant. Yet she's quite as popular as Necker, who's a great artist. How can I get much satisfaction out of the enthusiasm of a house that likes her atrociously bad performance at the same time it pretends to like mine? If they like her, then they ought to hiss me off the stage. We stand for things that are irreconcilable, absolutely. You can't try to do things right and not despise the people who do them wrong. How can I be indifferent? If that doesn't matter, then nothing matters . . . What one really strives for in art is not the sort of thing you are likely to find when you drop in for a performance at the opera. What one strives for is so far away, so beautiful' – she lifted her shoulders with a long breath, folded her hands in her lap and sat looking at him with a resignation which made her face noble – 'that there's nothing one can say about it.'

Willa Cather, *The Song of the Lark*, 1915, Part VI, chapter 9

Martin Amis's unsavoury hero John Self goes to the Met:

Opera certainly takes its time, doesn't it. Opera really lasts, or at least *Otello* does. I gathered that a second half would follow this one, and this one was travelling awful slowly through its span. The other striking thing about *Otello* is – it's not in English. I kept expecting them to pull themselves together and start singing properly, but no: Spanish or Italian or Greek was evidently the deal. Maybe, I thought, maybe it's some kind of guinea fest or beaner evening, a rally for the Hispanics or the Ricans. But the audience seemed stolidly non-ethnic. I mean, those guys in buffalo beards and busby haircuts, those six-foot chicks with tomahawk profiles and Venusian suntans – I mean, they're just Americans. Uneasily I craned my neck in search of a fellow tuxedo. The ladies had turned it on a bit, true, but the prongs were all in office gear. Yeah, I should have dressed down a bit . . .

Luckily I must have seen the film or the TV spin-off of *Othello*, for despite its dropped aitch the musical version stuck pretty faithfully to a plot I knew well. The language problem remained a problem but the action I could follow without that much effort. The flash spade general arrives to take up a position on some island, in the olden days there, bringing with him the Lady-Di figure as his bride. Then she starts diddling one of his lieutenants, a fun-loving kind of guy whom I took to immediately. Same old story. Now she tries one of these double-subtle numbers on her husband – you know, always rooting for the boyfriend and singing his praises. But Otello's sidekick is on to them, and hoping to do himself some good, tells all to the guvnor. This big spade, though, he can't or won't believe it. A classic situation. Well, love is blind, I thought, and shifted in my seat.

To be honest, all this was far from centre-stage in my own mind. A jungly night in young New York, and the outer heat was proving far too much for the theatre's thrashed cooling systems. I began to notice that an impressively candid odour was seeping from my hired jacket, not one smell but a deadly anthology of fatso emanations, the trail of the thousand soaks and sweats who

had used it before me and would use it again when I was done.
The people behind, were they getting wind of me? Martina herself
now frowned and sniffed. Each time I squirmed in my seat the
jacket selected another noxious parallel from its quiver. Either it
was paranoia of the nostril or I was getting the lot here: ashtrays,
soup-kitchen explosions, used stalls in porno emporiums, magazine
wax, booze bubbles. No question, this bit of shmutter had done
time on some very fat, hot and unhealthy guys. I scratched my
nose. *Pew*. There came another wicked fart from my right armpit.
Martina sniffed and writhed. Gently does it, I thought, and
searched for a state of fixity and trance.

Fate had given me another good reason for staying put. My
need to take a leak – intense enough an hour ago, when in the cab
downtown I was obsessively rehearsing a grateful and copious
session in Martina's john – was now evolving into a new era of
detailed distress. I felt I was sitting with a white-hot cannonball on
my lap. I considered barging off to the can, of course, but it clearly
wasn't done around here. You're not in the flicks now, you know.
People who go to the opera, they don't go to the toilet, not even
at home. And if I stood up in this gear I'd bring the house down
anyway. I winced and twisted and tried to loosen the bladder-
throttling cummerbund. Smells shimmered. Otello howled for his
lost handkerchief. Martina sniffed and stirred. Maybe she thought
Otello was having a bad time. She didn't know what *Otello* was
putting *me* through, the excruciation, the supersuffering endured
by the big boiler at her side.

Martin Amis, Money, Cape, 1984, pp. 280–82

*Malcolm Bradbury provides helpful programme notes by Dr F. Plitplov for
a famous Slakan opera:*

VEDONTAKAL VROP
('The Secret Unmasked')

Vedontakal Vrop is one of the highest treasures of the great Slakan music tradition, an oper bouffe created from authentical folk sources by national writer-hero Z. Leblat. Performed first before the ears of many listening bishops at the Cast'ullu Vlam in 1770, for two hundred years score and liber were unhappily lost. Yet in modern times fortune laughed and the work was rediscovered with revolutionary enterprise in 1970, missing only Acta 3. Triumphantly restorated, in 1984 the work was reperformed for the first time since 1770 at the Oper Prole'tannuu Slakam, in a repertoire with *Frollin Schmutterlunki* (Frollin Schmutterlunki po Panhilda Pic, Upratti Linkerton po Peti Lavo), *Katya Kabana* dan Janocekim, *Katti* dan A.L. Webberim, *Sondo Musikam* dan J. Andrewsim, and *I Placebo* dan L. Spirin, beneath the expert dirigation of Leo Fenycx (geb. Praha, 1958), our leading operturge.

What constructs the undoubted greatfulness of *Vedontakal Vrop*? Many have asked this question. Yet, primitive and sophistical all at once, this tale of disguises and mistook identities offered new futures to operatic history. At the one hand a simple folk-oper, at the other it is the origin of oper in the modern world of today. Criticals everywhere have rightly seen it as the true prefigure of all other great oper works, and it is clear that Mozart himself could not have been conceived without the assistance of Leblat. Thus the Mozartian *Figaro Weds* and *The Hareem-Slaves*, and *The Seville Haircutting Man* of Rossini, owe everything to this opera, for so long sadly losted and mislooked.

The plot of *Vedontakal Vrop* is so laughable that no one can fail to take a delight in its immense confusions. When ups the curtain, unfolds a brilliant scene. We are at a clear in the midst of a forest where the apothetic magician Zenu keeps his cave, where he likes to close himself with the pretty fun-servant Yukka and make strange experimentations. Smokings arise in the air to manufest his strange activities. Then in the glade appears a young student imitting an old man with a grey beard. A bear has near wolfed him, and only for food are some throstles. His woe are many. His crude father no more loves him, and tells him he must not marriage but make travel to the big city and take his examen to become famous bureaucrat. But because he likes to stay near to his loved one he does not travel and puts on beard instead. Heartily he tells how he loves that girl, the daughter of the apothetic magician who despicates them both. Yet no sooner has he sung his woe than who does appear in the forest but no als than his beloved love, disguised as a soldier with an arm. She likes to go to the city to find her lover, but is lost in her ways. Yet so good do they make their maskings that these fond lovers do not recognize, and she thinks he is old and he believe her of a very strange sex. But now appears in sedan a great king from Turk. He sings us that he is really the uncle of the girl who love the mutter of the boy and comes in an impressive disguise to woodle her and make his wedding. Of course this is not so possible because she is married still the apothetic magico. With him als is his servant Boco, who has annoyed the magico in the forest and is turned to a bear. When he encounts the pretty servant Yucca, naturalistically he falls als in love with the soldier boy who is a girl. So does a famous cavalry officer and many more. Of course soon appears in the centrum of the forest the father and the mutter of the boy, the mutter of the girl, the apothetic magician, the servants of the shah, and many villagers who like to celebrate a natural festival with a cake, some policemans, some sailors and a big host.

Herewith, in only Acta first, are the beginning of many confusions which can but delight and amuse. Good drink is available at the interspersum, and our oper house is one of the architectonic glories of Europe. Join then our music-loving workers in this great revivification of the oper to end all opers . . .

Malcolm Bradbury, *Why Come to Slaka?*, Secker & Warburg, 1986, pp. 70–71

In Bradbury's Rates of Exchange*, the Bradford academic Dr Petworth, visiting Slaka, is taken to see this celebrated opera by his guide Miss Lubijova:*

'Let us in any case enjoy our evening. It ought to be our nice time. You do not mind to sit for five hours for an oper in another

language?' 'Aren't all operas in another language?' asks Petworth.
'Yes, well, tonight you have interpreter,' says Lubijova, slipping
her arm in his . . .

The taxi has stopped; the high, well-lit dome of the opera house
is above them, and bright lights illuminate the great windows.
Outside, on the gaunt pavement, a great crowd mills, as fine-
looking couples descend in large numbers from orange taxis or big
black Volgas and cross from the kerb towards the great marbled
entrance . . .

'Well, do you impress?' asks Lubijova, as they stand in the great
plush foyer. 'Splendid,' says Petworth, standing in his old clothes,
as the ladies in front of him expose black dresses and décolletage,
and the men stand neat as penguins in their dinner jackets and
evening dress. 'Yes, you surprise,' says Lubijova, laughing. 'Of
course we are a music-loving nation, and since socialism the loving
has much increased. The tickets are sent to the factories for the
best workers and they come with a great pleasure, as you see . . .'
'These are workers?' asks Petworth. 'Yes, you see our people like
to make good display,' says Lubijova . . .

[Lubijova explains:] 'Now here inside is explained it is oper
bouffe of two hundred years. You know bouffe? It means is very
funny. Here is explained it is played in a typical style, but with
some modernizations. The technic is influenced by China oper of
Sichuan province, but also by Bolshoi. The play has always been
lost but now is found, except part of acta three. But with brilliant
improvisations this small difficulty is triumphantly overcome. The
story is from the folk, but Leblat, who makes the liber, has
changed all things round to make them more unusual, so it is not
the same any more' . . .

'Our seats are in stall,' says Lubijova, as they are led to the
second row from the front . . . In a cloud of dust, the great curtain
in front of them ascends. A three-dimensional painted landscape of
very bosky aspect is disclosed, with barrel-shaped tree-trunks
rising up to branches that shake paper leaves. Centre stage is a
papier-mâché cave; from the cave comes a young man dressed as
an old man and wearing a long grey beard. He sings lustily at the

audience: 'Tells he is a very old man with a long grey beard,' whispers Lubijova to Petworth. In the orchestra pit a flute-bird twitters; from stage left comes, tripping lightly, a young girl dressed as a boy. 'Tells she is a young girl dressed as a boy,' whispers Plitplov from the row behind, after a moment. 'Of course the old man does not know she is really girl,' murmurs Lubijova, 'because now she is telling him she is soldier.' 'Also she does not know he is really her uncle,' whispers Plitplov, 'because he tells her he is really the king of another country.' But now, backstage, a singing boy, wrapped in a very large cloak, has appeared, slinking through the cardboard trees, and singing. 'Oh, what a silly boy!' cries Lubijova, laughing. 'He tells he is a young man in love with a girl who is lost.' 'That is this girl,' whispers Plitplov. 'But he cannot marry her because all the fathers forbid, so he hides in the forest dressed like robber,' says Lubijova. 'He tells he likes to take from the rich to give to the poor.' 'To spend on his bets,' says Plitplov. 'To give to the poor,' says Lubijova, firmly. 'Now he sees the old man and thinks he will steal his purse, so everyone will know he is robber.' 'Look, he steals it,' whispers Plitplov. 'But the girl wants to show now she has the honour of a man,' says Lubijova. 'She tells that boy she fights him to a duel. Doesn't she know he is her best lover?' 'No,' says Plitplov. 'Look, they both pull out their arms,' says Lubijova. 'Oh, what a pity. He shoots her and she falls. She sings she dies of a plum in her breast.' 'A plum?' asks Petworth. 'The plum he has shooted from his arm,' says Lubijova.

  'Bullet,' whispers Plitplov. 'Plum is a make of fruit.' 'I am right, plum,' says Lubijova. 'Now he sings he is sorry. He thinks he will bend to loosen her blouses. Perhaps he will find there a very nice surprise, don't you think so?' 'No,' says Plitplov, 'because now is coming a man who tells a wizard has turned him into a bear.' 'It is funny,' says Lubijova, laughing . . .

Malcolm Bradbury, *Rates of Exchange*, Secker & Warburg, 1983, pp. 228–37

Index

Abbado, Claudio, 365
Addison, Joseph, 491–2
Albanese, Licia, 155
Albani, Emma, xxiii, 98–100
Alda, Frances, 129
Allen, Thomas, 224, 254, 384–5, 407–8, 427–8, 453–4
Amis, Martin, 506–7
Arditi, Luigi, 106–7, 108
Arrivabene, Opprandino, 18, 313
Astor, Caroline, 419–20
Atherton, Gertrude, 503–4
Auber, Daniel
 Fra Diavolo, 264
Auden, W. H., 247, 264, 468, 479–80, 490, 493
Austral, Florence, 281

Baccaloni, Salvatore, 354
Baker, Janet, xxi, 202–3, 365, 385–7
Balfe, Michael William
 The Bohemian Girl, 36
 Maid of Artois, 69, 83
 The Maid of Honour, 344
Barbaia, Domenico, 342–4, 436
Barber, Samuel, xvi
 Vanessa, 361
Barnum, P. T., xxii, 437–9
Beckford, William, 411
Beecham, Sir Thomas, 1, 35–6, 116–17, 137–8, 150, 168, 278–9, 329–31, 333–5, 369–70, 380–81, 382–3, 399, 403, 411, 445
Beethoven, Ludwig van, 233
 Fidelio, xviii, xix, 78–9, 94, 159, 233, 353, 355–7, 404, 441–2, 485
Bellini, Vincenzo, 10, 67–8, 79, 214, 236–7, 313, 435–6, 468–9

Beatrice di Tenda, 373, 415
I Capuleti e i Montecchi, 364–5
Norma, 17, 71, 91, 94, 105, 176–7, 192, 219, 236–7, 438
Il pirata, 178–9, 236
Il puritani, 213, 214, 415, 436, 468
La sonnambula, 67–8, 83, 90, 106, 174, 214, 220, 236, 376
La straniera, 79–80, 236
Bemberg, Herman 112, 113
Benedict, Julius
 The Lily of Killarney, 36
Berg, Alban, 296–7
 Wozzeck, 464–6
Berger, Roland, 283
Berlin, Sir Isaiah, 136–7
Berlioz, Hector, xiv, 12–13, 29, 40–41, 234, 344–6, 412–13
 Benvenuto Cellini, 238–9
 The Damnation of Faust, 20
 Les Troyens, xxi, 485
Bianchi, Bianca, 98–9
Bianci, Francesco, 58
Bing, Sir Rudolf, 37–8, 155–6, 158, 175, 198, 354, 359–61, 371–2, 450, 463, 493–4
Bini, Carlo, 406–7
Bishop, Anna, 82–4
Bizet, Georges
 Carmen, 23, 31, 35, 97, 102–4, 156–8, 161, 162, 188–9, 384, 393–4, 397–8, 405–6, 424, 475
Björling, Jussi, xx, 154–5
Blessington, Countess of, 11–12
Boito, Arrigo, 315, 316–18, 321, 478–9, 480
 Mefistofele, 139–42, 145, 152
Bonynge, Richard, 200, 212

Bordoni, Faustina, 55
Borodin, Alexander
    Prince Igor, 380–81
Boult, Sir Adrian, 279–80
Bradbury, Malcolm, 507 11
Brahms, Johannes, 99–100, 246
Brecht, Berthold, 470–71, 481
Britten, Benjamin
    A Midsummer Night's Dream,
    247
Brophy, Brigid, xv, 466–8
Brownlee, John, 403
Bumbry, Grace, 405–6
Burnacini, Ludovico, 44
Burney, Dr Charles, 4–5, 10, 51–2
Busch, Fritz, 37 8
Butt, Clara, 117–18
Byron, Lord, 259, 391

Caballé, Montserrat, xvii, 201–2
Callas, Maria, xx, 171–85, 201, 361,
    431, 447, 451–2
Calvé, Emma, 102–4, 209
Caniglia, Maria, 151 2
Cappelli, Elena Bianchini, 122
Cappuccilli, Piero, 222–3
Carbone, Maria, 372
Carestini, Giovanni, 52
Carreras, José, 21, 22
Caruso, Enrico, 85, 111, 117, 120–34,
    140, 148, 151, 152, 161 2, 186,
    189, 197, 213, 214, 215, 222, 245,
    371, 391–8, 422, 446, 447
Castilblaze, François
    Robin des Bois, 435
Castlemary, Armand, 396
castrati, 5–8
Catalani, Angelica, 72 5
Cather, Willa, 505
Catherine II, Empress of Russia, 57,
    242, 243
Cavalieri, Lina, 186–7
censorship, 15–17
Cesti, Antonio
    Il pomo d'oro, 44

Chaliapin, Feodor, 135–47, 152, 197,
    246, 381, 424–5, 447
Cherubini, Maria Luigi Carlo, 29, 234
    Ali Baba, 234
Chesterfield, Lord, 485–6
Chopin, Frederick, 91, 208
Christie, John, 38
Cigna, Gina, 209
Cilea, Francesco
    Adriana Lecouvreur, 186, 360
Cimarosa, Domenico
    Il matrimonio segreto, 80
claques, 20, 125–6, 141–2, 235, 426–9,
    430
Colbran, Isabella, 343–4
Copley, John, 180–81, 407–8
Corradetti, Iris Adami, 211–12, 219–
    20
Corelli, Franco, 156–8, 222,
    361
Costa, Sir Michael, 377–8
Cresci, Gian Paolo, 22, 23
Cruvelli, Sophia, 85–7
Cuzzoni, Francesca, 55 6

Dal Monte, Toti, 220
Da Ponte, Lorenzo, xxii–xxiii, 250,
    252, 253, 489–90
Debussy, Claude, xv, 29–30, 36–7, 112,
    244–6, 277–9, 320–21, 463–4,
    486–7
    Pelléas et Mélisande, 245, 328, 464
Delacroix, Eugène, 70–71
Delibes, Léo, 112
    Lakmé, 220
Del Monaco, Mario, 156–7
De Luca, Giuseppe, 322
Destinn, Emmy, 148, 447
Dexter, John, 358–9, 470
Dickie, Murray, 383
d'Indy, Vincent
    Fervaal, 276–7
Di Stefano, Giuseppe, 154, 156
Domingo, Placido, xx, 384, 405,
    406–7

Donizetti, Gaetano, 10, 79, 83, 214,
    256, 436
  Anna Bolena, 62–3, 201
  Don Pasquale, 109
  L'elisir d'amore, 12, 83, 122–3, 125,
    126, 130–31
  La favorita, 89
  La Fille du régiment, 90, 91
  Lucia di Lammermoor, 16, 18, 72, 77,
    96, 109, 111, 113, 118, 119, 175,
    183, 199–200, 216, 220, 344, 368,
    446, 486, 498–500, 501–3
  Lucrezia Borgia, 95
  Maria Stuarda, 70, 237–8
Donzelli, Domenico, 33
Dryden, John, 457
Dukas, Paul
  Ariane et Barbe-Bleu, 382
Duma, Marie, 36
Dunn, Mignon, 406–7
Dunne, Veronica, 407–8
Duprez, Gilbert, 76–7, 225,
    239

Eames, Emma, 111, 197, 446
Endler, Franz, 47-8
Épine, Margarita de l', 341–2
Ewing, Maria, 365

Falcon, Cornélie, 76–7
Falcon, Ruth, 201
Farinelli (Carlo Broschi), 8, 51–3
Farrar, Geraldine, xxiii, 111, 186, 187–
    90, 197, 396, 447
Fauré, Jean-Báptiste, 18
Felsenstein, Walter, 220–21, 354–5,
    366–7, 374, 410, 492
Fétis, François, 65
Flagstad, Kirsten, 51, 194–7, 301, 447,
    493
Flaubert, Gustave, 498–500
Flotow, Friedrich von
  Martha, 89, 107, 396, 494
Fodor, Josephine, 259–60
Forster, E. M., 501–3

Franchetti, Alberto
  Germania, 124
Frederick the Great, of Prussia, 39–40
Fremstad, Olive, 420, 446, 447, 505
Freni, Mirella, 219
Freschi, Domenico
  Berenice, 4–5
Frick, Gottlob, 355
Furtwängler, Wilhelm, 402
Fux, Johann Joseph, 388

Gabriella, Caterina, 56–7
Galli-Curci, Amelita, 210–11, 447
Garcia, Manuel, 64, 70–71, 90, 207,
    368–9
Garden, Mary, 143, 447
Gatti-Casazza, Giulio, 122–4, 132, 134,
    138–9, 151, 188–9, 192, 194, 195,
    245, 322–4, 370–71, 449
Gayarre, Julian, 123, 214, 392
Gerster, Etelka, 107–8
Ghiringhelli, Antonio, 174, 178–9
Gigli, Beniamino, 151–4, 190–92, 220,
    226, 401–2, 429, 447, 488–9
Giordano, Umberto, xviii
  Andrea Chénier, 153
  Fedora, 190–92
Giuglini, Antonio, 88–9, 416
Glinka, Michael, 237
Gluck, Christoph Willibald von, xix,
    263, 459
  Alceste, 385–7, 459, 493
  Armide, 398
  Iphigénie en Tauride, 23, 345–6, 412–
    13
  Orfeo, 202, 232, 485
Gobbi, Tito, xix, 152, 180–81, 371–2,
    493
Goethe, Johann Wolfgang von, 74–5
Goldoni, Carlo, 26–7
Goossens, Eugene, 117
Göring, Hermann, 163–5
Gounod, Charles, 112, 348
  Faust, 85, 115, 117, 156, 183, 188,
    348–50, 364, 444–5, 487

Grassini, Josephina, 460–61
Graun, Carl Heinrich
   Cesare e Cleopatra, 39–40
Grieg, Edvard, 288
Grisi, Giulia, 80–81, 91, 364–5
Gunsbourg, Raoul, 190, 246, 449 50
   Ivan the Terrible, 246

Hahn, Reynaldo, 112
Halévy, Jacques
   La Juive, 76
   Le Val d'Andorre, 439
Hall, Peter, 284, 357–8, 365–6
Hammerstein, Oscar, 351–2, 446, 447
Hampe, Michael, 384–5
Handel, George Frederick, xii, 51, 53–5
   Giulio Cesare, 342, 478
   Ottone, 54
   Rinaldo, 231–2
Hanslick, Eduard, 48, 236, 292–4
Harwood, Elizabeth, 202–3
Hauk, Minnie, 393
Henze, Hans Werner, xvi, 472–5
Hérold, Ferdinand
   Zampa, 264
Higgins, Harry, 118–19, 353–4
Hitler, Adolf, 300–301, 426
Hofmann, Ludwig, 196
Hofmannsthal, Hugo von, 51, 332
Hotter, Hans, 355
Humperdinck, Engelbert, 271
   Königskinder, 396

Jeritza, Maria, 162–3, 166, 190–99, 447
Jullien, Louis-Antoïne, 344–6
Jurinac, Sena, 355

Karajan, Herbert von, 47, 198, 219,
   384, 385
Kelly, Michael, xxii–xxiii, 250–52
Kittel, Hermine, 163
Klemperer, Otto, xix, 41–3, 160–61,
   302, 353, 355–6
Knappertsbusch, Hans, 198
Kollo, René, 225

Konetzni, Hilde, 168–9
Kraus, Alfredo, 216–17
Krauss, Clemens, 149, 167
Kurz, Selma, 111

Lablache, Luigi, 81, 90
Lalande, Henriette, 67, 79–80
Laui-Volpi, Giacomo, 21
Lavenu, Louis
   Loretta, 83
Lehmann, Lilli, 197, 286, 296
Lehmann, Lotte, 91, 160–70, 193, 404,
   447
Leider, Frida, 194, 204, 206 7, 281,
   301
Lemnitz, Tiana, 168
Leoncavallo, Ruggiero, xviii, 320–21
   I pagliacci, 35, 112, 130, 148–9, 423
   Zaza, 187
Leopold I, Emperor of Austria, 43–4
Lind, Jenny, xxii, 85, 90–92, 207–8,
   368–9, 437–9
Liszt, Franz, 270
Ludwig II of Bavaria, king, xiv, 267–
   9, 420–21
Ludwig III of Bavaria, king, 421
Lully, Jean Baptiste
   Armide, 231

Maazel, Lorin, 47–8
Mahler, Gustav, xv, 47 8, 197, 244,
   274–5, 352–3, 420, 447
Malibran, Maria, 32–3, 39, 64–71, 79
   80, 207, 218, 346, 376–7, 413–14
Manelli, Francesco
   L'Andromeda, 2–3
Manelli, Maddalena, 2
Mapleson, J. H., 88 90, 92 4, 96–8,
   107–9, 272, 346–50, 377–8, 393,
   441–3
Marchesi, Luigi, 7, 9, 57–8, 111
Mariani, Maddalena, 19
Mario (Giovanni de Candia), 81, 84,
   85, 123, 391
Martinelli, Giovanni, 190, 447

Mascagni, Pietro, 314–16
  Cavalleria rusticana, 213, 314, 315–16
  Iris, 153
  Lodoletta, 220
Massenet, Jules, 112
  Werther, 486–7
Maurel, Victor, 101–2, 197, 318
Mayr, Richard, 193
Mehta, Zubin, 364, 405
Melba, Nellie, xxiii, 51, 105, 111–18,
  124, 128–30, 394–5, 446
Melchior, Lauritz, 196, 447
Mendelssohn, Felix, 32–3, 90, 235, 368
Mercadante, Saverio, 436
Méric-Lalande, Henriette. *See* Lalande,
  Henriette
Messager, André, 37
Metastasio, Pietro, 9
Meyer, Kerstin, 336
Meyerbeer, Giacomo, 111, 235–6, 261,
  313
  L'Africaine, 118, 401–2
  Les Huguenots, 45, 76–7, 85, 86, 87,
    107, 219, 265–6, 391–2
  Robert le Diable, 84, 90, 235, 344
Milanov, Zinka, 209–10, 447
Milnes, Sherrill, 221–2
Mödl, Martha, 302
Mongini, Pietro, 346–8
Montagu, Lady Mary Wortley, 388
Monteverdi, Claudio, 1
Monti, Vincenzo, 16
Mozart, W. A., xxii, 35, 248–57, 263,
  332, 422, 466–7
  La clemenza di Tito, 255
  Così fan tutte, xiii, xvii–xviii, 248,
    409–10, 493, 494
  Don Giovanni, xiii, 183, 197, 252–4,
    255, 361–3, 372, 384–5, 403, 476,
    497
  Die Entführung aus dem Serail, 248–9
  Idomeneo, xix
  Le nozze di Figaro, xiii, xviii, xix,
    42–3, 98–9, 166, 250–52, 399,
    407–8, 410, 429, 462, 494

  Die Zauberflöte, 38, 254–5, 494
Murska, Ilma di, 89–90
Mussolini, Benito, 399–400
Mussorgsky, Modest, 239–41
  Boris Godunov, 135–8, 143, 152, 223–4,
    239–41, 494
  Khovanshchina, 240

Napoleon, 73–4
Neumann, Angelo, 272–3
Newman, Ernest, 99–100, 282, 328,
  331–3, 341
Nicolini, Ernest, 52, 95–6
Niemann, Albert, 267
Nilsson, Birgit, xx, 158, 186, 198–9,
  359, 361, 377
Nordica, Lillian, 351–2, 446, 447

Obraztsova, Elena, 201–2
Offenbach, Jacques
  Périchole, 494
  Tales of Hoffmann, 374
Olczewska, Maria, 163, 193–4, 196
opera houses
  Bayreuth, 30, 101, 195, 275, 284,
    285–303, 368, 421, 452, 463,
    503–4
  Berlin, 18, 38–41, 115, 148, 163–5,
    166–7, 354, 374, 400–401, 410
  Berlin (Kroll), 41–3, 400–401
  Bologna, 14
  Brooklyn, 130–31
  Budapest, 408–10
  Buenos Aires (Colon), 154, 193
  Chicago, 113, 175, 396, 451–2
  Cologne, 379–80, 384–5
  Dresden, xiv, 38–9, 265–6
  Dublin, 88, 416
  Florence, 14, 57–8, 216, 427–8
  Genoa, 11–12
  Glyndebourne, xv, xvi, xix, 37–8,
    48, 197, 202–3, 354, 403, 494
  Hamburg, 160–62, 274–5, 358–9
  Houston, 319–20
  Leipzig, 272

London, xiv, 31–2, 34–5, 55–6, 67, 79, 90–91, 344–6, 346–50
London (Coliseum), 203
London (Covent Garden), xv, xvii, xix, xx, xxi, 20, 36–7, 51, 91, 109, 111, 116–17, 118, 124, 125, 128, 159, 162, 168–70, 179–81, 193, 198–200, 203, 214, 224, 232, 353, 355–7, 357–8, 364, 369, 382–3, 385–7, 391–2, 394, 399, 418, 421–3, 447
London (Her/His Majesty's), xv, 54, 62–3, 93, 95, 97, 272–3, 444–5
London (King's Theatre), 3–4, 373, 434, 460–61
Mexico City, 403, 405
Milan (La Scala), xv, 10, 13–14, 16–17, 19–20, 102, 122, 123, 124, 125, 126, 134, 138–42, 174, 175, 178–9, 193, 201–2, 236–7, 304–5, 310–11, 318–19, 322–5, 342, 350, 364–5, 372, 382, 383, 389–90, 391, 399–400, 417, 424–5, 427, 434, 440, 452
Monte Carlo, 190, 246, 449–50
Munich, 279–80, 421
Naples, 14, 17, 83, 93–4, 413–14, 423, 426
Naples (San Carlo), 20–21, 125–7, 238, 257–8, 342–4
New York (Manhattan Opera), 132, 143–5, 351–2, 446, 447
New York (Metropolitan), xix, 103, 114, 129, 131, 132, 134, 145–6, 151, 155–6, 158, 162, 175, 186–9, 190–92, 194–6, 197, 198, 226–7, 245, 273–4, 336–7, 359–61, 370–73, 396, 398, 405–7, 418–20, 429, 446–9, 450–52, 463, 493–4
Padua, 4–5, 14, 417
Paris, xiv, 26–8, 64–7, 75–6, 259–60, 267, 426, 435, 436
Paris (Opéra), xiv, 18, 24–5, 28–30, 73, 85–7, 147, 190, 234, 238–9, 254–5, 262, 402, 412–13

Paris (Opéra-Comique), 30–31, 320–21
Parma, 16, 119, 173–4, 312, 424, 437
Prague, 45–6
Rio de Janeiro, 171–3, 453
Rome, 14, 21–3, 52–3, 151–2, 176–8
St Petersburg, 240, 241–3
Salzburg, 166, 169
Stockholm, 335–6
Strasbourg, 353
Sydney, 114–15
Turin, 10, 232
Venice, 1–3, 14, 258, 309
Venice (La Fenice), 11, 14, 16, 118, 258, 309, 391, 436
Verona, 401–2
Vienna, xiv, xv, 18–19, 43–5, 46–8, 91, 148, 149, 162–3, 164–5, 167, 233, 244, 250–52, 351, 352–3, 388, 404

Pacchiarotti, Gasparo, 9, 206
Pacetti, Iva, 382
Pacini, Giovanni, 10, 16
Paer, Ferdinando, 207
Pandolfini (a baritone), 19 .
Pasta, Giuditta, 33, 59–65, 70–71, 91, 204
Patané, Giuseppe, 201–2, 407
Paton, Mary Ann, 414
Patti, Adelina, 17, 105–10, 377, 442–3, 446
Pavarotti, Luciano, xix, 22, 148, 215–16
Peri, Jacopo, 1
Persiani, Fanny, 415
Pfitzner, Hans, 353
Philidor, François, 232
Piccini, Nicola
  Iphigenia, 389
Plank, Fritz, 100–101
Plishka, Paul, 202
Ponchielli, Amilcare
  La gioconda, 351–2, 360, 406–7
  I lituani, 20

Ponselle, Rosa, 184, 192, 204, 205, 370–71, 447
Porporino (Antonio Uberti), 40
Pountney, David, 492
Prêtre, Georges, 364
Puccini, Giacomo, 320–21, 322–8, 467
  La Bohème, 112, 113, 124, 127, 128–9, 152, 211, 215, 220, 322, 324, 328, 409–10, 430, 431, 446, 453, 493–4
  Gianni Schicchi, 153, 494
  The Girl of the Golden West, 188, 328, 463
  Madama Butterfly, 188, 211, 224, 309, 322–5, 384, 430, 475, 476
  Manon Lescaut, 122, 153, 155, 186, 328, 409
  Suor Angelico, 360
  Il tabarro, 327
  Tosca, 151–2, 171, 180–81, 195, 215, 322, 325–6, 406, 431, 453
  Turandot, xiii, 47, 158, 326–8, 399–400

Quincey, Thomas de, 460–61

Raimondi, Ruggiero, 223–4
Ravelli, 96–8, 393
recordings, 104, 110, 124–5, 127, 183, 280–81, 384, 446
Reiner, Fritz, 399
Reszke, Jean de, 133, 396
Ricciarelli, Katia, 219
Richter, Hans, 37
Ricordi, Giulio, 310, 315–16
Ricordi, Tito, 440
Rimsky-Korsakov, Nicholas, 239–41
  Christmas Eve, 241–3
  The Invisible City of Kitesh, 193
  The Maid of Pskov, 135, 136
  Mozart and Salieri, 146
Rizza, Gilda della, 452–3
Rossini, Gioacchino, xiii, 10, 16–17, 111, 206, 213, 214, 256–63, 343, 344, 346, 374–5, 435

Il barbiere di Siviglia, 81, 143, 156, 220, 256, 309
La Cenerentola, 34
Edoardo e Cristina, 258
Moses in Egypt, 257–8
Otello, 32–3, 60, 64–5, 259
Semiramide, 258, 259–60, 261
Sigismondo, 258
Tancredi, 66
Il turco in Italia, 34, 474
William Tell, 13, 16–17, 225, 263
Rousseau, Jean-Jacques, 25, 484–5
Rubinelli, Giovanni Battista, 9
Rubini, Giovanni Battista, 9, 77–8, 84, 213, 225, 415

Sacconi, Rosalinda, 119
Saint-Saëns, Camille, 112
Saint-Simon, Duc de, 24–5
Salieri, Antonio, 250
Santunione, Orianna, 453
Sarti, Giuseppe
  Giulio Sabino, 9
Scheff, Fritzi, 113
Schipa, Tito, 132, 151, 215
Schoenberg, Arnold
  Moses and Aaron, 357–8
Schorr, Friedrich, 196, 226, 281
Schroeder-Devrient, Wilhelmine, 78–9, 94, 302
Schumann, Elisabeth, 193
Schwarzkopf, Elisabeth, 173–4
Scotti, Antonio, 446
Scotto, Renata, 219
Segurola, Andrés de, 127
Sellars, Peter, 361–3
Senesino (Francesco Bernardi), 52, 53
Serafin, Tullio, 183, 184
Shaw, George Bernard, xv, 24, 34–5, 95–6, 100–101, 102–3, 109, 214, 290–92 295–6, 331–3, 391–2, 394–6, 418, 421–3
Simionato, Giulietta, 201–2, 364
Sitwell, Osbert, 129–30, 146
Slezak, Leo, 148–50, 319, 398

Slezak, Walter, 208–9, 319–20, 423
Slobodskaya, Oda, 193
Smart, Sir George, 28, 69–70, 345
Smetana, Bedřich, 45–6
    The Bartered Bride, 150
Smyth, Dame Ethel, 279–80, 380
    The Wreckers, 380
Snazelle, G.H., 36
Söderström, Elisabeth, 335–7
Solti, Georg, 282, 284
Sontag, Henriette, 60
Spinach, Marietta, 72
Spontini, Gasparo
    La vestale, 13, 86
Stanford, Charles Villiers, 107, 289–91,
    318–19
Stendhal, 14 15, 60–61, 206, 256, 260–
    61, 343–4, 374–5, 389–90, 477–8
Stevenson, Robert Louis, 462
Stokowski, Leopold, 158, 463
Storace, Nancy, 57–8
Storchio, Rosina, 322, 324–5
Strakusch, Maurice, 105, 106
Strauss, Johann
    Die Fledermaus, 364, 401, 493, 494
    The Gypsy Baron, 494
Strauss, Richard, 148, 166, 329–37
    Die Aegyptische Helena, 162
    Arabella, 166, 167, 426, 494
    Ariadne auf Naxos, 162
    Capriccio, xvii, 477
    Elektra, 166, 168, 169, 329–33
    Die Frau ohne Schatten, xv, 162
    Der Rosenkavalier, 166, 168–70, 193,
        202–3, 335–7, 408–9
    Salome, 198, 333–5
Stravinsky, Igor, 231, 247, 297–8, 360
    The Rake's Progress, 247
Supervia, Conchita, 91
Sutherland, Joan, xix, 199–201, 212,
    372–3
Szell, George, 195

Tacchinardi, Nicholas, 75–6
Tamagno, Francesco, 126, 214, 424–5

Tauber, Richard, 150
Tchaikovsky, Peter Ilyich, 288–9
    Eugene Onegin, 241, 408, 494
    Queen of Spades, 494
Tebaldi, Renata, 171, 175, 361, 447
Tedeschi, Arnaldo, 18
Templeton, John, 376–7
Testori, Angelo, 8
Tetrazzini, Luisa, 105, 118–19, 446,
    447
Thackeray, W. M., 90, 497
Thomas, Ambroise, 112
    Hamlet, 394–5, 487
Tippett, Michael, xvi
Tietjens, Theresa, 89, 94 5, 416
Todisco, Nunzio, 453
Tolstoy, Leo, 500–501
Toscanini, Arturo, xv, 19–20, 122–4,
    140–41, 184, 188–9, 211, 245,
    298–300, 301, 324–5, 382, 399–
    400, 402, 447, 452
Tucker, Richard, 361
Twain, Mark, 141, 293–5

Uberti, Antonio (Porporino), 40
Ursuleac, Viorica, 166–7, 426

Varnay, Astrid, 302
Veasey, Josephine, xxi
Verdi, Giuseppe, xiii, 18–19, 83, 101,
    125, 210, 275, 276, 285, 299, 304–
    21, 378–9, 426, 435, 440, 440–41,
    478
    Aida, xvii, 125, 175, 197, 219, 241,
        310–12, 352
    Un ballo in maschera, 15, 19–20, 358–9
    Don Carlos, 378–9
    I due Foscari, 16, 05
    Falstaff, 304, 316–19
    La forza del destino, 175, 371
    King Lear (unwritten), 305–8, 315
    Luisa Miller, 20, 440
    Macbeth, 216, 378
    I masnadieri, 90
    Nabucco, 304–5

Verdi, Giuseppe – *contd*
  Otello, 112, 156, 214, 313–14, 317,
    319–20, 480, 486, 506–7
  Rigoletto, xv, 15, 18, 21, 125, 190,
    220, 309, 310, 346–8, 424, 430–31,
    446, 485
  Simon Boccanegra, 17
  La traviata, 114, 118, 173–4, 179–80,
    184, 187, 220, 304, 309, 310, 320–
    21, 405, 410, 436, 440–41, 443
  Il trovatore, 18, 36, 304, 310, 327,
    440, 463, 480
  I vespri siciliani, 86–7
Viardot, Pauline, 62, 64, 216, 235, 302
Vickers, Jon, xvii, 159, 355

Wagner, Cosima, 269–71, 275, 286–7,
    297, 301
Wagner, Richard, xiv, xviii, 35, 196,
    236, 245, 261–3, 264–303, 304,
    311, 360, 368, 420, 439–40, 444,
    452, 464, 467, 481
  Der fliegende Holländer, 42, 289–90,
    351
  Götterdämmerung, xvii, xx, 194, 195,
    198–9, 270, 272, 281, 288, 289, 293
  Das Liebesverbot, 264–5
  Lohengrin, 148, 160–61, 197, 302, 354
  Die Meistersinger von Nürnberg, 275,
    301, 379, 382–3, 402, 404
  Parsifal, xvii, 20, 101, 196, 270, 271,
    273–4, 277–9, 290, 293–5, 296–8,
    301, 328, 388, 420–21, 444
  Das Rheingold, 37, 273, 281, 282–3,
    285–6, 287, 289, 293, 351, 401
  Rienzi, 265–6
  Ring cycle, 30, 198, 272–3, 278–9,
    281, 282, 284, 288–9, 290–92,
    302–3, 420–21

Siegfried, 198, 269, 270, 274–5, 283,
    287, 295–6
Tannhäuser, 159, 193, 226, 262, 267,
    485
Tristan und Isolde, xvii, xxi, 159, 195,
    196–7, 226, 266–7, 270, 276, 294–5,
    299, 300, 359–60, 420, 475, 482,
    503–4
Die Walküre, 24, 37, 162, 163, 167,
    195, 196, 226–7, 264, 280–81, 286,
    292–4, 295, 384, 395–6
Wagner, Siegfried, 271, 275, 296, 297,
    299
Wagner, Wieland, 301–2
Wallace, Vincent
  Maritana, 36
Walpole, Horace, 54, 55
Walska, Ganna, 190
Walter, Bruno, 46–7, 274–5, 280, 351,
    379–80, 400–401, 421
Warlock, Peter
  Curlew River, 360
Weber, Carl Maria von, 263, 459–60,
    462, 490–91
  Der Freischütz, 435, 439
  Oberon, 345
Webster, Sir David, 199, 357, 408
Weikl, Bernd, 226
Weill, Kurt, 470–72
  Dreigroschenoper, 471–2
  Mahagonny, 470
Wharton, Edith, 88
Wilhelm II, Kaiser, 115
Windgassen, Wolfgang, 198
Wolf, Hugo, 244
  Corregidor, 244

Zenatello, Giovanni, 19–20, 322
Zingarelli, Nicola, 10